REINHARD HEYDRICH

REINHARD HEYDRICH

A BIOGRAPHY

Günther Deschner

STEIN AND DAY/*Publishers*/New York

The author would like to take the opportunity of thanking all those individuals and institutions without whose assistance this book could never have come into being. His thanks are due, above all, to Frau Lina Heydrich (Todendorf, Fehmarn), Reinhard Heydrich's widow, and to Dr. W. Sommer, Heydrich's schoolfriend. The author is also indebted to Herr Heinz Höhne (Hamburg) and to Dr. Robert M. W. Kempner (Frankfurt) who helped him with their advice and interest, the staffs of the Wiener Library and the British Museum Library and Reading Room (all in London) who for many months assisted him in his research, and all those, including Heydrich's former colleagues, contemporary eyewitnesses, writers and historians, who on numerous occasions supplied information. Particular mention must be made of Mr. David Irving (London), Dr. Paul Schmidt-Carell (Hamburg), Dr. Otto-Ernst Schüddekopf (Braunschweig), Herr Bruno Streckenbach (Hamburg) and Herr Walter Wannenmacher (Darmsadt). All have enriched this book with interviews, references and advice.

The author is also grateful to the following for supplying photographs:
Archiv Ustavu Marxismu-Leninismu, Prague, 8
Bundesarchiv, Koblenz, 1, 3, and 6
Janus Piekalkiewicz, 4, 7, and 9
Süddeutscher Verlag, 2 and 5
Photograph 10 came from the author's collection.

First published in German as *Reinhard Heydrich:*
Statthalter der Totalen Macht by Bechtle Verlag, 1977
Translated by Sandra Bance, Brenda Woods and David Ball

First published in the United States of America in 1981
Copyright © 1977 by Bechtle Verlag,
Esslingen am Neckar
English language copyright ©1981 by Orbis Publishing, Ltd.
Printed in the United States of America
STEIN AND DAY/Publishers
Scarborough House
Briarcliff Manor, N.Y. 10510

Deschner, Günther, 1941–
    Reinhard Heydrich, a biography.

    Translation of: Reinhard Heydrich, Statthalter d. totalen Macht.
    Bibliography: p.
    Includes index.
    1. Heydrich, Reinhard, 1904–1942. 2. National socialism—
Biography. I. Title.
DD247.H42D4713   943.086'092'4   [B]   80-6263
ISBN 0-8128-2809-7   AACR2

CONTENTS

(Photos between pages 176 and 177)

Chapter 1

THE ENIGMA

Of all the prominent figures in the Third Reich none was more enigmatic nor more controversial than Reinhard Tristan Eugen Heydrich. Some saw him as the driving force behind the destruction of the Jews, while others claimed that his own grandmother was Jewish. When he played the violin his audience was moved to tears: yet his signature condemned thousands to the concentration camps. He was an outstanding competitive athlete, excelling in the decathlon and fencing, whose voice never lost its adolescent timbre.

At the peak of his success Heydrich had power over life and death throughout the German Reich and in all territories occupied by German military forces. There were no checks to the meteoric rise of his career. By the age of twenty-seven he was head of the Security Service of the SS and at thirty-two he commanded the Secret State Police, as well as the entire German Criminal Police. When war broke out, the Reich's security HQ in Berlin, the largest security organization in Europe, was set up expressly for him.

Among his other duties Heydrich was entrusted with the 'solution' of the 'Jewish problem', which he organized from migration to extermination. The high point of his career coincided with the zenith of the Third Reich. At thirty-eight he was at his peak; unprecedented power lay at his sole disposal. By 1941 he was Hitler's deputy in Prague where, after a few months, his use of carrot and stick politics successfully transformed the rape of the Czechs into a seduction and converted that turbulent Protectorate into a smooth-running German arms factory. It was this last achievement that led to his murder in 1942 by two parachutists flown in from London by the Czech government-in-exile. His death was a serious setback for the security of the Nazi Reich, and a considerable victory for the Allies. It was to result in that blind escalation of hatred of which the destruction of the Czech village, Lidice, was the first stage. No one else was to embody the SS state so completely. A number of contradictory myths and legends grew up about Heydrich after his death, in which praise and curses, blind hatred and objective scrutiny were irreconcilably mixed. The effect was of a fantastic firework display bathing the erstwhile Deputy of the Greater German Reich in a brilliant but distorting light, a distortion from which he has yet to emerge.

At once the Saint-Just and the Fouché of the Nazi state, this tall, slim, blond Saxon from Halle an der Saale was both the designer and the driving force behind the total security of the Reich. He was the founder of a ruthless police network which, armed with lists, set about tracking down and mercilessly destroying opponents of the regime, the so-called 'enemies of the people'. Yet, at the same time, he was the model of the successful careerist, a moral, upstanding German, and a loving husband and father. In addition he was a discerning and enthusiastic amateur musician, an ambitious athlete, and a courageous fighter pilot, who relaxed by going on combat missions during his holidays. It is hardly surprising that such an outstanding personality should have aroused conflicting responses of attraction and repugnance, both among his contemporaries and historians, taking into account the limitless power he wielded, the range of his activities, his dynamism and his inner conflicts of brutality and sentimentality.

Even during his own lifetime rumour hung heavy about him. The discrepancy between this cloud of rumours and the verifiable details of his life poses the most fascinating questions about the real man. He had a certain stature at a time when trust was placed in the untrustworthy and the mediocre, a time when nothing was what it seemed. His contemporaries betrayed their uncertainty in their reluctance to have any close dealings with the man. The words they used about him tend to describe the dark side of his nature as unpredictable, avoiding a fuller analysis with the excuse that he was unfathomable.

The truth about Heydrich's complex, 'twilight' personality has never been fully understood. Many essays, chapters, commentaries and foot- notes have chipped away at this historical giant, scattering pieces over countless monographs on the SS and the Gestapo, the German Secret Service, twentieth-century espionage and the persecution of European Jewry. The one attempted biography of Heydrich, completed in 1962, was a total failure, due partly to the obvious inadequacy of the available source material but also to the unhistorical aims of the author.[1]

The fantastic tale-spinning which the figure of Heydrich has provoked is, again, hardly surprising, though its inclusion in studies of the period calls into question the reliability of a number of authors. Some renowned historians accept at face value rumours spread by several Nazi leaders alleging Heydrich to be of Jewish origin; the 'split' personality is automatically produced as the motive for his obsession with power; the 'stigma of Jewish origins' is called in to explain Heydrich's compliance with Hitler and Himmler and provide the motivation for his excessive zeal in the planned extermination of the Jews. Thus Heydrich himself is made a victim of the racial theories of the Third Reich. Many writers are given to shoddy attempts at psychoanalysis coupled with exaggerations on the level of the tabloid press, a wholly unsuitable approach to the subject.[2]

There is no disputing the controversy which surrounded Heydrich: the Allied press and the Czech Resistance movement called him the 'butcher of Prague', whereas the Czech press under the Prague Protectorate government hailed him as the 'darling of the Czech workers'. In praising him for being the 'man with the iron heart', Hitler expressed the same opinion as the Allies. The English author, Edward Crankshaw, heaped abuse on 'the typical blond mongrel, commonly found in German night clubs', while Himmler cited him as an example of a 'flawless character of unusual purity'. The historian Michael Freund called him a 'born criminal', and 'in the mould of the devil'. And SS-General 'Sepp' Dietrich, Commander of the 'Leibstandarte Adolf Hitler', greeted the news of Heydrich's death with the following startling sentence: 'Is the swine dead at last?'[3]

This conflict of opinions makes any attempt to reconstruct the life of Heydrich look like an unpromising task. More than just an historical enigma, he was a mystery in his own lifetime to anyone who knew him or had dealings with him. He remained anonymous even to those victims of his security machine who were directly subjected to his will. He covered all his traces – even from his prey.

But, in the final analysis, who was it that the opponents of the regime grew to fear most? Who made the decisions that led to freedom, or to the concentration camps and death? Whose men were standing there when the door-bell was rung in the early hours of the morning, and not by the milkman? The knowledge that these were Heydrich's men was restricted to the elite circle of those who were at home in the jungle of the Third Reich's power structure. Outside this circle it was generally believed that Himmler was responsible.

Many of his contemporaries, whether directly or indirectly connected to Heydrich's organization, heard his name for the first time when he was assassinated in Prague in 1942. Is it true then that Heydrich's power depended on orders from above? Did his position carry no authority in its own right? Was he merely a zealous, ingenious and unusually energetic administrator, with no warrant to wield power on his own behalf, or at his own discretion?

How does such an interpretation square with the possibility that the SS might have been Adolf Hitler's sole heir, had he retired in victory, and only because Reinhard Heydrich played a leading role in its ranks? Admittedly several other commanding officers ranked equally with Heydrich. Yet he had something more than high rank: he was in a position to make history. It is an opinion shared by many that it was Heydrich who made SS-*Reichsführer* Himmler, pushing the phlegmatic *Reichsführer* before him like a battering ram, to remove all obstacles from his path. There may well be some justification for the view that in an understanding of Heydrich lies the key to comprehension of the SS.[4]

The contrast between the historic power of the SS, its tremendous development not only to a state within a state but to a state in overall control, and the prosaic, colourless character that was SS-Chief Himmler is scarcely credible; the exploits of the SS are unhesitatingly ascribed to Heydrich. For many he was Siegfried incarnate, the ideal Nazi, the only man who could possibly have planned the deeds and atrocities of the SS.

It is likely that only his early death prevented him from overthrowing the man he habitually pushed ahead of himself. Göring was heard to declare that Himmler's brain was called Heydrich. The real creator of the entire SS undertaking, still to be equalled in world history, would then have risen to be its master: this man was undoubtedly Reinhard Heydrich.[5]

There has been a recent development in historical research which interprets the relationship of this Castor and Pollux pair quite differently, and offers a new answer to the question of who was pushing whom. The colourless Himmler, generally regarded as the typical bureaucrat, has been credited with more extensive talents by recent research. It is now contended that he was 'in the front rank of those who have mastered the exploitation and manipulation of people'.[6]

Consequently, the suggestion was advanced that Himmler had been under-rated while Heydrich's role had been overplayed – was he not just a cog in the SS machine, even if a crucial one, and not the motor of it? A particularly interesting contribution to this debate has recently been made by an Israeli historian, Shlomo Aronson, whose monograph about the early days of the Gestapo and the SD (the Security Service built up and run by Heydrich to serve the SS) covers the period up to 1935. He deals with Heydrich's biography up to this date and with his role in the development of the organization. He has unhesitatingly declared Heydrich's role during this period to have been greatly overestimated.[7]

But this is a bizarre claim. Heydrich, we are to believe, became the executioner of countless thousands not out of hatred or personal conviction but purely as a consequence of his sense of discipline, out of indifference, cowardice, even impotence. Is there any evidence in the ensuing period of his life to support this refutation of the Heydrich myth? After all, Heydrich's real career began only in 1936, when he was appointed chief of the German Security Police, a post which gave him control of the Criminal Police and the State Secret Police, in addition to the SD. Only three years later, in 1939, the Reich's security HQ was set up under Heydrich, with outposts throughout the German Reich and occupied Europe, and by 1941 he had been appointed Deputy Reich Protector in Bohemia and Moravia.

Heydrich has been called 'Hitler's most evil henchman', and not without justification. Were one to restrict oneself to the 'how it was then' school of history, excluding present day comparisons, this would be an adequate enough conclusion. His biography could be written on the basis of such a formula, leaving the principle which he embodied unexplored, historically 'defused', by the gloss of 'henchman Heydrich'.

Yet set against the background of material newly available on the Third Reich, revealing its pitiful lack of basic ideology, Heydrich stands out as far more than a 'leader' in the style of Göring, Himmler or Rosenberg. He was, as any close investigation of his life demonstrates, a technocrat *par excellence*. A role common in our own day was developed by him to an unusual degree of perfection; he personified the competitive spirit. In all he did it was his aim to be the first, the biggest, the best, above all the most powerful. Peak efficiency was to the fore in all his enterprises: in the extermination of entire populations, in military Intelligence intrigues, in fencing, in the decathlon, in musical evenings (where he had a reputation as a talented violinist), in courageous forays into enemy territory as a fighter pilot, and, finally, in his self-motivated campaign of destruction against the 'enemies of the state', which included Catholics, the conservative aristocracy, communists and the criminal classes.

The Third Reich would undoubtedly have collapsed much earlier had not a handful of technocrats held it together. In the realm of security it was Heydrich who played this vital role. He had nothing but scorn for the dogmas and fantasies of the despised chicken-farmer, Himmler. The craniometric proportions of the different races, the care of a 'deteriorating homeland' or the Teutonic excavation of the 'ancestral heritage' on the Crimea were of no concern to him. His interests lay purely in power and in perfection. Those duties within the Third Reich which appealed to the technical side of his nature, grouped under the heading of security, were most likely to guarantee him the acquisition of power. He dedicated himself to his task with the same remarkable talent for organization, the same devotion, attention to detail and impartiality as did his colleague Albert Speer to his.

Seen in this light, Heydrich emerges as one of those technocratic geniuses whose appraisal depends on the nature of their task. They themselves do not care whether it is good or bad, and it is this attitude which is the seed of their guilt.

Chapter 2

A CHILD OF MUSIC

Reinhard Tristan Eugen Heydrich was a child of his time. He was born on 7 March 1904 in Halle an der Saale, and christened four days later in the Catholic church in Mauerstrasse, St Elisabeth's.[1] His mother called him Reinhard, 'wise in counsel', after a heroic figure in one of her husband's operas of which she was particularly fond. His father called him Tristan after the opera by Richard Wagner: this was homage both to the Wagnerian spirit of the age and to the actual works of the Bayreuth master, in which Heydrich's father found his source of creative inspiration. His third and final name was Eugen, the high-born, after his maternal grandfather, who as professor, Royal Saxon Councillor and founder of the world-famous Dresden Conservatoire, had brought to the Heydrich family the highest level of social standing it could ever desire.

Reinhard's father, Richard Bruno Heydrich, had also achieved the status of a founder and director of a conservatoire, opened in Halle in 1899 as a private school of music and dramatic arts.[2] Born in 1863 in lowly circumstances in the Saxon town of Leuben, Bruno Heydrich had secured acceptance in the high society of the then Prussian provincial town in Saxony by means of hard work, musical talent and a 'good' marriage.

The eldest in a one-parent family of seven, six of whom were girls, Bruno Heydrich was obliged at many stages in his musical career to earn a living through 'not strictly legitimate music', and to be dependent on scholarships.[3] At the age of twelve he began studying in Meissen, first the violin and the tenor horn, then the double bass and the tuba. At the Dresden Conservatoire he held a double bass scholarship for three years, terminating this with honour in 1882. He then played the double bass in the Meiningen and the Dresden court orchestras, studying composition and conducting at the same time. After this he was given a singing scholarship and he made his debut in 1887 in Sondershausen, speedily following this with engagements as a lyric and heroic tenor. His vocal career as 'Lohengrin', 'Faust', 'Tannhauser', 'Stolzing' and 'Tristan' took him to Weimar, Stettin, Aachen, Cologne, Magdeburg and Braunschweig. Heydrich's success was considerable, yet he was never to gain entry into the elite of his era. He was always second- or even third-rate. The longed-for consummation of his singing career, an appearance at Bayreuth, never materialized; his fate was the limited glory of a few weeks' study under Cosima Wagner in the summer of 1890.

The more recognition as a singer was denied him, the more Bruno Heydrich busied himself with displaying another aspect of his astonishingly wide musical talent, that of composition. In his student days at Meissen he had already begun to compose; some of his rich repertoire of pastoral songs are performed to this day. His opera *Amen* was premiered in Cologne in 1895, to great critical acclaim. *Peace* was performed in 1907 in Mainz, and in 1914 the opera *Chance* in Halle. Although *The Lyre Child* and *The Eternal Light* were never performed, *Amen* had numerous performances in Cologne and was also put on in Leipzig. A contemporary critic from Saxony wrote that *Amen* displayed 'outstanding use of Wagnerian musical principles and method'.

A self-made man, Heydrich needed recognition by society. He wanted his *magnum opus* to be staged at the Berlin Court Opera: it would have been his breakthrough as a composer and musician. But success was to elude him. Nevertheless his extensive range of compositions, including, apart from opera and *lieder,* numerous choral works, orchestral and chamber music, trios and duets, has assured him a place in the history of music, beyond local and contemporary acclaim.[4]

Although he dedicated many of his compositions to members of the German court circles, publicizing his quest for recognition by the 'establishment', Heydrich in fact acquired his entrance into high society by marriage to Elisabeth Krantz. In December 1897, when he was almost thirty-five, he married the daughter of a former teacher, professor and *Hofrat* (a civil honour), Eugen Krantz, director and founder of the Royal Conservatoire in Dresden.

Unlike her husband Bruno, Elisabeth Anna Amalia Krantz, born in

Dresden in 1871, came from a secure and prestigious family.[5] By dint of extreme discipline and economy her father had worked his way up to distinction as a music teacher, achieving royal support for his conservatoire. Her mother, Maria Antonie (*née* Mautsch), herself the daughter of a comfortable business family in Bautzen, had brought Elisabeth up fully cognizant of such hard-won social status.

After a strict Catholic childhood, Elisabeth's education was completed in a convent in Lugano. Given musical instruction at her father's conservatoire, she grew into a typical upper-middle-class German lady: her bearing was strict and well-disciplined; her interests lay in music and the arts, but she set great store by order, decency, cleanliness and efficiency. Those traces of arrogance she possessed were held in check by the moral rectitude and strength of character which she cultivated.

Bruno Heydrich was the complete opposite. Artistic by nature, in him talent and a somewhat distasteful pushiness combined to form a mixture of bohemian and bourgeois, connoisseur and sharp dealer. The traits of the *nouveau riche* were always to blur the contours of middle-class respectability.

The heroic tenor was a jocular man, given to boasting about his success, showing no reticence in his attempt to muscle into good society. His nature was more that of an actor than of a musician; in the course of normal conversation he would imitate comic figures, amongst these the Jews. He would repeatedly slip into the tones of an 'Isidor' as the Jews were then known in the local Halle dialogue. As a result of his excellent mimicry and his black hair he was often taken for a Jew.[6]

Politics were of little interest to Bruno Heydrich. He was content with the customary concessions to prevailing opinion. Loyal to the Kaiser, Wagnerian in outlook, half liberal, half conservative, he had no time for the socialists. In any case one of the unwritten laws of his occupation was not to be politically conspicuous. His position as owner and director of a private school of music and drama made him dependent on the good will of both the Halle and the Prussian cultural administrations; but more important, if his school was to develop into a conservatoire, was the confidence of the bourgeoisie of Halle and the surrounding neighbourhood, who paid him handsomely for the musical education of their sons and daughters.

The idea of his own music academy had been prompted by two factors. When he married, it became clear to Bruno Heydrich that he would never achieve the desired breakthrough as a singer and that he would therefore have to turn his talents in other directions. Admittedly he continued to sing *Heldentenor* in Halle for some years. But Heydrich was fully aware that this would be his final engagement; it would never lead to social recognition and a secure way of life.

In addition, the idea of a school of his own seems to have been encouraged by his father-in-law and his wife. In a prospectus for his school Heydrich himself wrote: 'After marriage into a pedagogic family, in December 1897 (his wife is the daughter of his former teacher, Professor Krantz), Heydrich also became a teacher, through the encouragement and instruction of the latter.'[7]

Heydrich and his wife both hoped that on the death of Frau Heydrich's mother, they would inherit the Dresden Conservatoire. But Elisabeth Krantz's brothers saw to it that the very profitable conservatoire remained in their own hands until after the war. Although incapable of directing the Dresden school themselves, they gave their sister in Halle no more than a third of the annual proceeds.

So, although they regarded Halle as a stop-gap, and its little conservatoire as a practice-ground, the Heydrichs were confined to the provinces before they had a chance to settle in the 'more elegant' city of Dresden; they had to content themselves with remaining on the Saale. Elisabeth Heydrich considered this a loss of social standing; it was a lifelong disappointment for her. However, she devoted her energies to making the most of this second-best situation.

It was she who was the financial and administrative head of the undertaking, holding together what would perhaps have soon disintegrated had it been left in the hands of the devil-may-care Bruno Heydrich. As she had been trained as a pianist by her father, she filled the role of piano teacher in her husband's conservatoire. Two years later, in 1901, the school of singing, with a register of only twenty pupils, had been transformed into a fully fledged conservatoire. It was the first establishment of its kind in Halle. Progress was swift in the following years. The citizens of a rich and fast-growing university and industrial town were well able to afford to send their children to the conservatoire. Besides, in his prospectus, Heydrich had addressed himself to all 'lovers of music', presenting his courses as a vital part of their education. His gamble paid off: a musical education was highly prized at that time, and, in addition, a conservatoire was a fashionable novelty for the somewhat provincial town of Halle.[8]

With his wife's assistance, Heydrich succeeded in making his first contacts with society, with the Mayor, and the journalists of the local newspaper. His appearances at the local theatre were also an attraction, so that by 1902 they had 116 pupils. At this point there were ten teachers of music and song in the school. Apart from Heydrich, who taught double-bass, violin, mime and elocution, among other things, and Heydrich's wife who gave piano lessons, there were five permanent music teachers and three assistants. Several times a year Heydrich's pupils staged public concerts which soon became a considerable factor in Halle's cultural life.[9]

In 1903 Bruno Heydrich requested recognition from the State Governor in Merseburg. It was his aim to reinforce his as yet insecure existence by means of a state charter. But the mills of the administration ground slowly. The desired concession was granted only in 1906. First Merseburg had enquired of the Halle schools committee 'whether there is any opposition to the proposed application of Herr Heydrich'.[10] The committee verified that Herr Heydrich had 'achieved good results' with his conservatoire. The Mayor, two privy councillors, an inspector and several rectors who sat on the schools committee testified that the applicant was well-known to many experts, his reputation in the community was good and that they could recommend him 'in every respect'.[11]

The social life on which Elisabeth Heydrich laid such importance was also developing. Bruno Heydrich was one of the founders of the 'Schlaraffia' lodge, later to be suspected by Reinhard Heydrich's SD of freemasonry; he was also made honorary member of several of the town's musical societies.

There were some social setbacks, but these weighed only lightly in the balance of his success. After the recognition of the school by the state, Bruno Heydrich set his heart on acquiring the title of professor. He himself employed professors as teachers and considered his own work as a teacher and composer to be outstanding: he therefore thought of the nomination as a certainty. It was, however, denied him. 'For this, Bruno Heydrich was not quite of the right standing' infers an Israeli historian.[12]

Yet despite such minor disappointments there could be no doubt about it: little Reinhard Tristan Eugen Heydrich was born, in March 1904, into a family which, if not possessing quite the status and wealth of the leading families of the town, did have a considerable role to play in the community. In spite of Bruno Heydrich's humble origins his family was accepted by the upper classes and was practically unacquainted with material need.

Following his sister Maria, three years his senior, Reinhard was the second child in the family; then, eighteen months later, another boy was born, christened Heinz Siegfried. The children's upbringing lay almost exclusively in the hands of their Silesian nurse. Both parents were too busy in the conservatoire to be able to pay any particular attention to the children. However, the mother was a strict supervisor, occasionally even meting out punishment herself. In the free time which the conservatoire afforded him, the father was occupied with numerous social duties and never cultivated any close relationship with his children. Countless social events took up his time: choral societies, the '*Schlaraffia*' or his role as honorary fencing instructor to the German imperial fencing school. He was also a member of the Masonic Lodge 'The Three Daggers', although, as a Catholic, this incurred the risk of excommunication. During the carnival season he was an ideal master-of-ceremonies.

Since she was a convinced, even fanatical Catholic, the mother supervised most closely the religious aspect of the children's upbringing. She led the children in their evening prayers and on Sundays the whole family attended mass. The musical education of the children was likewise under her control. Before starting school little Reinhard or 'Reini', as he was known in the family circle, had learnt musical notation, could play Czerny's piano *études* perfectly and had begun violin lessons. At six he started primary school, where he was found to be hard-working, gifted and intelligent, if a little introverted.[13] Thus was Reinhard Heydrich born into a world difficult to reconcile with his later career – the world of music. In the summer of 1904 the family had moved to No. 21 Poststrasse, a four-storey house in the centre of town, which provided accommodation for the school and its director; so the cries of the new-born infant mingled with the music of the instruments from the classrooms below, Bruno Heydrich's choirs and the vocal exercises of the public-speaking classes.

Unlike his elder sister and younger brother, who resembled their father both in character and appearance, Reinhard took after the Krantz side of the family; he was quiet, introverted, always abstracted; generally he was considered to be a difficult child. According to other members of the family, his mother tried to bring him into the limelight. However, outsiders had the opposite impression. A boyhood friend remembers: 'I always had the feeling that the sister was given preferential treatment.' His impression was that Reinhard Heydrich was isolated and ignored, withdrawn into a world of his own which he sheltered from outside influence through his growing sense of arrogance.[14]

In 1914 he moved to the *Reform-Realgymnasium* (high school). The 'Reform', as it was popularly known, had grown out of a pet theory of Kaiser Wilhelm II's: he wanted to reconcile the characteristics of the classical *gymnasium,* and its claims to elitism, with the science and technology of the age. As with the majority of the Technical Universities in the German Reich, the *Reform-Realgymnasium* had its origins in the reforming zeal and enthusiasm for technology professed by the Kaiser.

Reinhard Heydrich's character and interests were decisively determined by the years he spent at this school prior to sitting his matriculation examinations. In addition to the main scientific subjects of the time, particularly chemistry, physics and mathematics, emphasis was laid on two other key areas: modern languages and combined instruction in German and history. French was taught from the first form onwards; from the lower-fourth up to eight periods a week were spent on Latin; in the lower-fifth English was introduced. Therefore, to claim, as is occasionally done, that 'he was unfamiliar with foreign languages' is unjustifiable. [15]

Reinhard Heydrich's fellow pupils declared his scholastic achievements to be 'very good'. One of these was the writing of German essays resembling philosophical treatises. 'He was first-class.' [16] His results in chemistry were outstanding: in his early teens he experimented with chemical substances at home, in strict seclusion. At that time his determined ambition was to be a chemist.

The protective shield of arrogance was thrown off during this period of scholastic success: a markedly excessive competitive spirit took its place. Reinhard wanted to surpass all others. This struggle for achievement led to the development of an early but considerable cynicism. Receiving yet another hiding from a mother convinced of the educational value of the stick, he would make no protest, presenting himself instead, with icy politeness, for a second dose.

Once, when he received the mark 'good' instead of the expected 'very good' for a test paper in chemistry, Reinhard complained to the class teacher. He was punished for his attitude, but he persisted in his claim that he deserved 'very good'. The higher mark did not materialize.

He was in the process of developing the outlines of a lifelong code of honour, based principally on toughness and achievement. On the way to school from his elegant home at 20 Gutchenstrasse, whither the family had moved in 1906, it was his habit to walk along the pavement in a way which compelled those coming from the opposite direction to step aside, to avoid bumping into him. One lunch hour he climbed to the very top of the school building, purely to show off his courage.

The reasons behind the inferiority complex for which Heydrich compensated in this way were not hard to find. According to his boyhood friend Erich Schultze, he acquired it 'at school, somehow or other'. Originally a weakling, he was often beaten by the bigger and stronger boys. His classmates made fun of his high falsetto voice and he was nicknamed *'die Hebbe'* (the goat). It was a long time before he lost this falsetto voice; much later, in a naval newspaper, he was mocked as 'the white billy-goat'.[17] However, the second nickname given to him by some boys at school was even more hurtful than *'die Hebbe'*.

In accordance with the rumours current in Halle that the director of the conservatoire, Bruno Heydrich, so clever at imitating Jews, was in fact a Jew himself, his classmates would run after the tall, lanky blond with jeers of *'Isi, Isi'*. The Heydrich family was to deny all such insinuations, even in a jubilee brochure published by the conservatoire.[18] However, it appears that the cry of *'Isi'* at school was brought to an end only when the younger brother, Heinz Siegfried, resorted to threats with a knife.

However, the intentions behind this catcalling were certainly worse than the effects. The Heydrichs laid a great deal of importance on denying the rumour, yet their own relations with the Jewish citizens of Halle were quite normal. Jews sent their sons and daughters to Heydrich's conservatoire; they belonged to the social acquaintance of the Heydrichs and were frequent visitors at their home.

At that time Halle already had more than one hundred thousand inhabitants; out of these barely a thousand were registered as Jews, thus forming less than one per cent of the population. Nine-four per cent of the population were Evangelical; the Catholics, numbering approximately five thousand, therefore constituted the second minority.[19] Reinhard Heydrich belonged to this minority from birth. Two conversions had turned the Heydrichs from the Evangelical to the Catholic Church. On his marriage to the Catholic Maria Antonie Mautsch Reinhard's maternal grandfather, *Hofrat* Professor Krantz, had changed his faith. In the subsequent generation the Evangelical Bruno Heydrich gave in to the wishes, indeed demands, of Reinhard's mother, Elisabeth Krantz, and was converted to Catholicism. Young Reinhard was thus brought up in an atmosphere of consciously maintained Catholicism. His very father was instrumental in making him an outsider.[20]

A loner even within his own family, he created a private world, into which it was hard to gain entrance. In many respects even the family was singularly ignorant about him. For example, after the war, his sister Maria claimed to have rarely seen her brother Reinhard reading, and then only adventure novels and travel books. But a friend was better informed. During the war years Reinhard had spent a part of his holidays in a forester's house in Wollnau, on the Dueben heath; his first visit was during the autumn of 1914 and the last in the summer of 1918. This house belonged to the Schultze family; Reinhard had struck up a friendship with the son Erich, four years his senior. In these surroundings Heydrich made visible progress and his behaviour was quite different from the kind being developed by his externally musical and pious home background. He was unselfconscious, eager to help with work on the land and 'visibly more self-confident'.[21]

But most important of all for the younger boy was the spiritual and intellectual nature of the friendship. In order to converse with the Russian prisoners of war working on the farm, the boys drove a cart to Eilenburg and with their pocket-money bought the only two Russian phrase-books in stock. They set to work; after two weeks they had mastered the Cyrillic alphabet and were ready to try out their first sentences on the Russian foresters. Schultze, already in the upper-sixth in 1918, brought Heydrich up to his level. For preference they read history and civilization and Schultze claims that they worked their way through the original French of Charles Seignobos' *Histoire de la civilisation*, then an accepted standard work, and further that they discussed the text in French, or at least attempted to do so.[22]

During this period Heydrich worked systematically. His scholastic achievements gave him confidence in his own abilities. He intended to overcome his physical weakness by means of vigorous sports training. 'I'll show them' became his motto. As his arrogance diminished, his self-confidence increased.

But the events of November 1918, the fall of Wilhelm II's Reich, and its consequences, resulted in particular hardship for the Heydrich family. Heydrich learnt for the first time, when barely fifteen years old, how politics could alter one's fate.

Soon Halle was affected by the unrest in central Germany, the activities of the KPD (the Communist Party), the bands of anarchists led by Max Hölz and by the volunteer corps, and the recriminatory measures they took on behalf of the new democratic government in Berlin. The Heydrich family was brought to the verge of nervous collapse and into the greatest financial difficulties by the unrest and, worse still, by the ensuing inflation. In a begging letter to the Mayor of Halle the proud director of the conservatoire was obliged to write that 'as a result of rising prices, a drop in income, the attrition of private property' the family was 'at the end of its tether' and the Institute 'was frankly about to go under'.[23]

The proud, elegant world of Elisabeth Krantz was swallowed up by the 1918 revolution, and the effects of the catastrophe on his family made a strong impression on the young Reinhard. Previously indifferent to politics, Bruno Heydrich became a member of the German Nationalist Party *(Deutschnationale Volkspartei)*. Admittedly the situation of the conservatoire was to improve in the twenties, but the old sparkle had gone and the Heydrichs held the revolution responsible.

The revolution also brought Reinhard Heydrich face to face with the two powers which were to shape his life: the Army and politics. The wave of civil war which swept over Germany in the early months of 1919 reached Halle in March. In the course of several bloody struggles a 'Spartacus' uprising, which aimed to set up a Soviet Republic in Saxony, was thwarted by volunteer corps. The volunteer land army led by General Maerker, known as the *Freikorps Maerker*, which had originally been formed to protect the Weimar Parliament against communist uprisings, came to the defence of the Weimar Coalition.[24] Heydrich was later to claim, in a *curriculum vitae*, that he had served as a dispatch rider in Maerker's Volunteers: he was then only a few days from his fifteenth birthday. However, this *curriculum vitae* was written at a time when Heydrich would have done anything to be taken on in Himmler's *Schutzstaffel* (SS). Was there a better recommendation than early military service with such famous troops as those of General Maerker?[25]

Another statement in Heydrich's doctored *curriculum vitae* was, however, the truth. He did actually belong to Halle's volunteer corps. These troops were formed as a civil defence wing under the responsibility of General Maerker; in its one year of existence it escaped any military conflict. Almost all the able-bodied youths in the local population joined this civilian wing without consideration for any political implications. Included was the entire upper school of the *Reform-Realgymnasium*, including, of course, Heydrich. At the age of sixteen he wore a steel helmet for the first time, though it was only for Saturday afternoon training.

Chapter 3

THE WOULD-BE ADMIRAL

The instructors opened their eyes wide in amazement, while the recruits grinned and nudged each other. It seemed that a mistake had been made in the manning policy of this first, post-war German Navy. Who was this youth, over six feet tall, narrow in the hips and with a bony figure which gave the impression of being all arms and legs? If the body of the young recruit seemed out of proportion, this impression was further reinforced by the bony skull under the white-blond hair. The most distinguishing feature was a protruding, outsize nose, which gave his face an unusual construction, impossible to forget. Above the nose his glassy, ice-blue eyes were set slightly too close together; finally this nose had the effect of making his chin, although prominent in itself, appear to recede.[1]

All things considered, naval cadet Reinhard Heydrich presented a strange figure on first taking up service in Kiel-Holtenau and during the early weeks of his training. Moreover, when he joined up, on 30 March 1922, shortly before Easter and a few weeks after his eighteenth birthday, he was carrying what was, in naval circles, a very unusual piece of luggage: a black case containing his beloved violin, a farewell present to his son from Heydrich, the director of the conservatoire.[2]

Initially the Heydrich family had shaken their heads at the eighteen-year-old Reinhard's decision to become a naval officer once he had passed his matriculation exams. The conservatoire director had hoped to find in his son a successor to direct and develop the school of music. Reinhard's musical development had been excellent: his violin playing was brilliant and he had been successful in his mastery of the piano, the cello and musical

23

composition. His matriculation results at the Catholic *Reform-Realgym-nasium* were well above average. If he were to choose not to remain loyal to the world of music in which he had grown up, the family expected him, at the very least, to study one of the sciences at a German university. For years he himself had professed a desire to be a chemist.

Yet Heydrich's decision not to study music or the sciences, preferring to serve in the Navy left to Germany under the Versailles Treaty, had arisen from his personal inclinations and the ideals then acceptable to him. As a schoolboy, on summer holiday with his family at the Baltic Sea resort of Swinemünde, he had seen the 'proud' units of the Reich's Navy on manoeuvres and had been very impressed by them. The famous 'Sea Devil', Admiral Luckner, a frequent visitor at the Heydrich family home, had doubtless fired the youth with the enthusiasm for the Navy which was rife in the Wilhelmine period. Young Reinhard, a restless and compulsive over-achiever, may well have dreamed of travelling round the world and of an adventurous life as a naval officer, similar to the one so often described by Admiral Luckner.

In the words of his school friend Sommer,

Reinhard Heydrich joined the Navy primarily as a result of the inspiring lectures which Admiral Luckner delivered to us boys, in halls filled to capacity, and because of his book *Seeteufel* [The Sea Devil]. His complex about his alleged Jewish origins must also be taken into account. He always wanted to be more 'nordic' than anyone else. Hence his attraction to the 'nordic' Navy and later to the 'nordic' Lina, from Fehmarn.[3]

So much of his time in his parental home had been taken up with music that he had no desire to continue with it as a career. In the turmoil of the post-war years and the economic difficulties which it brought to the Heydrich family, the pursuit of science seemed to impose too great a financial burden, especially since one son, Reinhard's younger brother Heinz, was already at Technical University.

For these reasons Reinhard's father agreed to his son's choice of career. Even his status-conscious mother approved. The events of November 1918 had admittedly somewhat damaged the Navy's reputation in conservative bourgeois circles. But there had never been an officer in the family, and it was generally felt that a career as an officer meant prestige and security:

after ten years' service one was guaranteed a pension.[4]

Heydrich began his career in Crew 22 of the Reich's Navy. The first six months of his service, the training period in Kiel, was a difficult time for the young recruit. He was not assigned to the first squad, under an 'elite-trainer', but to the second. Here, ordinary seamen and aspiring officers were trained together. In the early months his fellow crew members found the recruit Heydrich 'too soft'. He never found it easy 'to submit to the harsh physical demands made of him'.[5]

His odd physical appearance and restrained life-style brought him another problem: he was made to realize that a potential sailor who brought his violin on service with him, who neither smoked nor drank, was not considered 'a proper man'.[6] His thin, high-pitched voice, which at school in Halle had already earned him the nickname of 'goat', now led to mockery by the 'more manly' members of the crew, who called him 'billy-goat'. Because he often used to seek consolation by playing his violin in his free time, a musical variation on the name grew up: 'heavenly goat'. His nordic appearance gave rise to 'blond Siegfried'; the rumour about his Jewish background, also current in naval circles, resulted in 'blond Moses', 'White Moses' and finally 'Moses Handel'.[7]

As a result of his colleagues' jeering, and of the physical hardship, which he overcame only by sheer force of will, Reinhard grew more and more withdrawn. He took the jibes of his comrades in deadly earnest and sought refuge in increasing isolation. In company he was curt and tight-lipped, showing his superior officers only reserved correctness. He was to slacken the iron band of isolation only on his promotion to Midshipman and then to Lieutenant.

He made no friends within the ranks of the trainees of the second squad, which he always thought second-rate. Years later he would still get upset at the memory of a certain Polish instructor from west Prussia. 'He was a small, fat man, stocky in build, with a head like a football', who 'took pleasure in bullying' the recruits, in particular the unusually tall and somewhat sensitive Heydrich. 'His favourite sport was the so-called test of courage. The idea was to kneel, arms folded behind one's back and then to let oneself fall straight forward. The sailor enjoyed demonstrating this, but he always fell on his stomach, whereas the skinny recruits fell flat on their faces; it was particularly painful for the bony Heydrich.' Even out of service hours, the Polish sailor had a particular way of amusing himself at Heydrich's expense. After a good drink in the mess, he always felt an urge for the 'higher things in life'. He had Heydrich called out of bed, ordering the 'heavenly goat' to appear before him and play something on his violin. 'Make it something sentimental!' He was particularly fond of the Toselli Serenade. Practically every night the young naval cadet had to play for his detested instructor until the latter was content to dismiss his virtuous recruit, with the ironical comment of 'Heydrich, you may go. You have given me peace.'

Neither the Toselli Serenade nor the Polish instructor allowed him to forget in later years what he saw as the degrading treatment he had received in the second squadron. During the war the Serenade was often played during the radio programme, 'Request concert of the German people': Heydrich's immediate reaction was to switch it off. And for the rest of his life Heydrich took 'an informed interest' in the 'little, fat, roundheaded racial types of the east'.[8]

By the end of the basic training period, and after a further half year on board the old-fashioned liner the *Braunschweig,* there had been no change in Heydrich's position in the crew. He still remained a loner. At this time too he ran into his first difficulties with the Navy's particular code of honour. One of Heydrich's fellow crewmen reported the following story to an Israeli historian, of which the outcome was apparently Heydrich's even greater isolation from his colleagues. When he was on leave in Halle a student made fun of Heydrich by referring to his supposed Jewish origins with the words, 'Just look at the little yid "Süss" in his naval uniform.' To his comrade's question about how he had chosen to retaliate, Heydrich is said to have replied helplessly, 'What should I have done?' At this point his comrade is said to have officially dissociated himself from Heydrich on the grounds that 'he had forfeited his honour'. The other comrades in room seventeen of Mürwick naval school are said to have followed his example and 'exchanged no further words' with Heydrich, 'man without honour'.[9] But in the interim Heydrich had created another world for himself. During service hours he remained isolated, but after hours he opened up another circle in which he felt more at home. In 1923, after three months of exercises on the training ship *Niobe,* he was ordered to complete his cadetship on the cruiser *Berlin* from 1 July 1923 to the end of March 1924.[10]

He bought a motorbike, enabling him to make regular, lengthy, cross-country journeys. He also travelled to Hamburg, where he developed his sporting talents in a private fencing club. As the Baltic Sea, ideal for sailing, was so close, the young cadet spent his spare time on the water.

However, the most important event of the time he spent on the *Berlin* was his meeting with someone whose path he was destined to cross at almost magically frequent intervals. On 1 July 1923 Commander Wilhelm Canaris was appointed First Officer aboard the cruiser. Among his charges was the young recruit Reinhard Heydrich.[11] The thirty-seven-year-old Commander soon became aware of a special talent possessed by this solitary recruit. Until that point in his naval career, his violin had turned him into a mere figure of fun: now, for the first time, it brought him into social contact with his superior officers, and with a world until then unfamiliar to him in naval circles. Canaris' wife was in the habit of entertaining a string quartet in their house, and just at that time the position of second violin was vacant. Canaris invited the recruit to his home and his wife was soon enthusing over Heydrich's talented and passionate playing. He was now to spend many weekends at the Canaris' home in Kiel – a precedent accorded to this youth, barely twenty years of age, and followed by scarcely any of his year.[12]

There is no doubt that Commander Canaris spoke to his young guest about his adventurous commands during the First World War. When war had broken out, in 1914, Canaris had been serving on the cruiser *Dresden* in the south Atlantic. In the following year the *Dresden*, sole survivor of the battle in the Falklands, was blockaded in the Magellan Straits by the British ship *Glasgow*, whereupon it was scuttled. Lieutenant Canaris passed himself off successfully as a Chilean and managed to get back to Europe on board a Dutch ship. He then became involved in Intelligence work in neutral Madrid. If Canaris did indeed talk to Heydrich of his experiences, this might well have encouraged him to return to his dream of an adventurous future career as a naval officer, and to help him recover from the misery which had until then been his lot in the Navy.[13]

Music provided Heydrich with an entry into other officer families in Kiel and later in Wilhelmshaven. Apparently at these musical evenings he often gave a first impression of being an 'insignificant sailor'. This impression vanished whenever he played or talked about music.[14] In small gatherings he was always charming and correct, displaying good humour and a cultivated mind, and he always made a good impression on the ladies in the company. Older women were charmed by his good manners, but the younger ones were even more under his spell.[15] One of his closest colleagues in later life testified that he was 'a conqueror in this field too'[16]: he combined his sailing trips with innumerable conquests of blonde beauties, mostly from high society in Schleswig-Holstein. One of his fellow crewmen surmised that a 'need for acceptance at any price' lay behind these compulsive conquests.

Heydrich was not, however, irresistible, as is demonstrated by reports of a gathering of the German colony in Barcelona, at which the Senior Midshipman Heydrich was present. He had quickly made the acquaintance of a young lady 'from the highest echelons of society' and they had gone for a walk together. 'As he obviously believed himself to be an object of general admiration, he felt he could turn this to his advantage and had behaved in such a manner that the lady slapped him.' Since the lady then made a formal complaint to the Commander, the event was not without consequence and the whole matter was settled only when Heydrich had made an official apology.[17]

Yet he remained convinced of his success in society. This social recognition, coupled with promotion first to Midshipman, then to Senior Midshipman, helped him to cope far better with the outside world than he had as a recruit. In fact, during his period of study at the Mürwick naval school, which followed his service on the *Berlin,* and training in the use of arms in 1925, his self-confidence increased sufficiently to encourage the growth of a more relaxed relationship with his fellow trainees and superior officers.

The time he spent as Midshipman and Senior Midshipman on the liner *Braunschweig* and on the flagship *Schleswig-Holstein* was so successful in smoothing his rough edges that the German Navy began to see in him the promise of a future officer.

And yet, despite his recognition in small social gatherings, and on his home ground of the world of music, there were still many traces of insecurity in the personal development of the future officer. It was particularly evident when he had to prove himself at ease in the 'elegant' world of more formal social occasions, hidebound by convention. His desire to do everything perfectly, the mannered way in which he tried to conceal his lack of ease in a crowd, often made him appear clumsy and awkward; not quite 'elegant' enough. The following event is reported to have taken place at the exclusive Reyd's Hotel, in Funchal on Madeira, during the course of a 1926 summer expedition to Spain and Portugal undertaken by Crew 22 on board the *Schleswig-Holstein.* A member of the crew had received an invitation to a social gathering from a member of a private English society, consisting of British naval officers and their wives, and had been requested to bring a few young officers from the *Schleswig-Holstein* with him.

Heydrich was among those he invited; after the war his colleague gave the following account of the event:

> The British gave us a warm welcome and then took no further notice of us. The band was playing dance music but there was no-one on the floor. Heydrich could not understand English reserve and was outraged by their behaviour, taking it as an affront. Paying no heed to our warnings, he walked up to one of the English tables and, without any formal introduction, asked a lady to dance. As was to be expected, his request was denied and he was obliged to return, red-faced, to my table, across the empty dance floor, whereupon he demanded that we should all ostentatiously leave the company. This we refused to do and Heydrich had to accept the snub. With the customary aplomb the English show in such situations, one of the officers known to me personally immediately appeared at our table and apologized on behalf of the lady. She herself then appeared and invited Heydrich to dance. With the exception of Heydrich, we all felt rather foolish because of his behaviour.[18].

Neither during his period of naval service nor later as a General in the SS was Heydrich to feel at home in the world of strict social convention. When he was head of the Reich security network and later as Protector in Prague, he would always try to avoid social duties which involved more than a small circle: he sent a representative in his place. In his Berlin days he willingly left everything to Himmler. '*Reichsführer*, you must be seen to be present' was a phrase he often used to Himmler. It was always with relief that he said to his wife, 'Himmler's going. He's nowhere near as good a representative as Göring but he's twice as good as I am.'[19]

On 1 October 1926, after a training period of four and a half years, Heydrich was at last appointed Lieutenant and then trained as a wireless officer. In this capacity he once again served on the Admiral's flagship, using the greater freedom now available to him to work on his physical fitness. He aimed for the highest achievements in sport, especially in fencing, swimming and sailing. Any trace of physical weakness or lack of coordination was to be eradicated. He used up thousands of bullets in target practice. He took up riding and trained for cross-country events. He soon became a member of the Navy pentathlon team, but despite his good results he was not chosen for the Reich Services Championships in 1927.

His first appearance for the Navy, in competition with the Army, took place in the following year, where, much to his disappointment, two Army officers were placed above him in the pentathlon. One of his fellow crew members made the following judgment on his sporting ambition: the young officer had to prove to all and sundry that his capabilities were far higher than was generally believed. 'He did everything with astonishing energy, combined with reckless over-estimation of his constitution and capabilities.'[20] One of his sports instructors at the naval school in Flensburg-Mürwick where fencing was part of the syllabus also commented on this tendency in Heydrich. He described his pupil as a 'very good and enthusiastic fencer'. In 1927 Heydrich, his instructor and two other naval officers took part in the Second German Officers' Fencing Tournament held in Dresden.

> The other competitors were only reserve officers, but many were expert fencers. Heydrich was eliminated in the preliminary rounds. In his disappointment, spurred on by ambition and a lack of self-control, he behaved in a manner which seemed abominable to those of his comrades still in the tournament. In front of everyone he flung his rapier angrily on the floor after his final defeat.[21]

He strove for perfection in other subjects too, improving, for example, his schoolboy knowledge of foreign languages. Particular attention was paid to the Russian language which he had learned on his own initiative during his youth. He did well in naval oral examinations in English, French and Russian.[22] Although his results in many other subjects remained average, his performance as wireless officer was not. This technical subject tied in well with those interests he had developed as a schoolboy.

In 1928 he was promoted to First Lieutenant and took up a posting in the Admiral's division of the naval station in the Baltic as a trainee wireless officer.[23] Nothing stood in the way of further progress in his dreamed-of career as an officer. Reports written on him by superior officers were favourable, though it was noted that, 'convinced of his own abilities, he has always been ambitious and anxious to put forward his own views'. Yet according to one of his former superiors it was this very tendency which convinced many of his ability. Heydrich had no failures to report, right across the board. 'His talents, knowledge and ability have placed him well above average.' This report was written as early as the mid-twenties by his instructor in the naval wireless college, later to become Vice-Admiral Kleikamp. 'Without doubt this will be endorsed by many later superior officers.'[24]

His boyhood friend Schultze, with whom he kept in contact during his years in the Navy, recalls:

We were all certain that he would go far in the Navy because of his ambition and his ability. He was never content with what he had achieved. His impulse was always for more; to go one better; to go higher. As a Lieutenant he was already dreaming of becoming an Admiral.[25]

Chapter 4

TRAPPED

It is of complete indifference to me what an officer in the German Navy can or cannot do.

Reinhard Heydrich, 1930

The dream of certain progress towards an Admiral's career was soon shattered. On 6 December 1930 First Lieutenant Reinhard Heydrich, along with many of his fellow officers from the garrison, went to a ball held by the Schleswig-Holstein Rowing Club in Kiel; there he made the acquaintance of a blonde beauty, eighteen-year-old Lina von Osten. His attraction to her was immediate and the wedding took place a year later. She was the daughter of a village schoolmaster from the Baltic island of Fehmarn. The family belonged to the bureaucratic nobility of Danish society, which went into decline when the island passed from Danish to German hands.[1]

At the time of this encounter Lina von Osten was shortly to take her matriculation exams. Her classmates were also at the ball, but Heydrich had eyes for Lina alone, danced almost exclusively with her and at the end of the evening took her home. The young lovers made a date to meet in a café a mere two days later, on 8 December, whereupon Heydrich produced theatre tickets for the following evening. After the performance he invited his young lady to Wicks Weinkeller, a local wine bar.

Although proceeding at a faster rate than was normal in such matters, Heydrich nonetheless confined himself to strict bourgeois convention in his courtship, following the standard pattern of ball, café, theatre and wine bar. It was not without some surprise, therefore, that on only the fourth day of their acquaintanceship, the schoolgirl Lina von Osten received a proposal of marriage. 'At that stage all he knew was my name, my address and that I went to school in Kiel. And he asked me straight out, "Fräulein von Osten, will you marry me?"'

The girl was speechless. 'You know absolutely nothing about me. You know even less about my family. You don't even know who or what my father is.' The schoolmaster's daughter explained to him that for all he knew her father might be a shoe-shiner and that a First Lieutenant in the German Navy could hardly marry a shoe-shiner's daughter. Heydrich's reply to this was: 'It is of complete indifference to me what an officer in the German Navy can or cannot do.' And he repeated his proposal.[2]

It was love at first sight. Lina von Osten was impressed by Heydrich's good looks, his manners, military bearing and short, precise way of expressing himself, by his blend of charm and austerity, in her own phrase, 'bitter-sweet'. On 18 December the couple became secretly engaged and First Lieutenant Heydrich wrote to the village schoolmaster, von Osten, in Fehmarn, asking him for his daughter's hand.

At Christmas Heydrich was invited to the von Osten family home to introduce himself. He arrived with his violin case under his arm and played his instrument in courtship of the Fehmarn schoolmaster's daughter.

Even Lina, already secretly engaged, was once again captivated by Heydrich's 'restrained, gentle' playing of the violin. More than forty years after the event, she still says, 'I doubt if I would ever have married him had he not played the violin so beautifully.'

But even without his violin a First Lieutenant in the German Navy would have been an acceptable son-in-law to the von Osten parents. The Navy was still considered thoroughly Wilhelminian and German nationalist, and the von Osten family were committed German nationalists. In both his daughter Lina and her brother Jürgen the father had inculcated strong nationalist principles, along with a specifically Schleswig-Holstein patriotism. For years the von Osten family had even been familiar with what was then, in north Germany, the relatively under-developed NSDAP (National Socialist Party) and saw in Hitler 'the hope of Germany'.

During this Christmas holiday period Heydrich, for the first time in his life, came into direct contact with National Socialism. His future brother-in-law Jürgen von Osten had been so impressed by Hitler in 1928, when he had heard him in Eckenförde delivering one of his earliest speeches in north Germany, that he had joined the party and the SA. He spoke enthusiastically to his sister Lina of this 'outstanding orator, who alone can save Germany'. In 1929 when still a schoolgirl in Kiel she was herself attracted by a big Party rally and became Party member number 1,201,380, later joining the National Socialist women's group. Heydrich, on the other hand, did not share the von Osten family's admiration for Hitler. According to his widow, Heydrich was 'indifferent' and:

> . . . at this stage politically clueless. As a naval officer he found party politics beneath contempt, despising the party machine. The NSDAP, which he knew only from hearsay, caused him to turn up his nose, as did its leader, Corporal Hitler, and its crippled star orator, Goebbels. His career in the Navy was the most important thing in his life then.[3]

The couple became officially engaged on Boxing Day. Amongst those to whom Heydrich sent the announcement of his engagement was a girl he had courted before meeting Lina von Osten, a former pupil of the *Kolonialfrauenschule*, a boarding school in Rendsburg. Now living with her parents in Potsdam, she was the daughter of a dockyard superintendent who had influence in Berlin and was on familiar terms with Admiral Raeder.[4] From the beginning of their relationship in the summer of 1930, Heydrich and this girl of good family had gone out together in both Potsdam and Kiel. Very much taken by the naval officer, she had already imagined herself as his wife. She was so shocked at the announcement of his engagement, sent without any further explanation, that she suffered a nervous breakdown.

Her father considered Heydrich's behaviour disgraceful and after he himself had failed to make the stubborn First Lieutenant see reason, lodged an official complaint with Admiral Raeder, casting doubt on the escapee son-in-law's honour.

Heydrich was obliged to defend himself before a naval Court of Honour and was suspended from duty for the duration of the proceedings. The then twenty-six-year-old First Lieutenant found the whole affair ridiculous and was convinced that the court would decide in his favour. Certainly he did not reckon with punishment or as much as dismissal from the

Navy. In the event the relationship had not transgressed beyond the bounds of what was then normal in the world of dockyard superintendents and post-Wilhelminian officers; indeed even more censorious times would have found it harmless. There is no evidence for the popular tale that the girl was pregnant and that Heydrich had left her in the lurch.[5] The actual court proceedings were secret, but the reason for the complaint against Heydrich, made by the offended father on behalf of his slighted daughter, was common knowledge. The superintendent backed up his complaint with the charge that if Heydrich were 'a man of honour', he would prove it by marrying the girl.

Heydrich's fellow crew member, later naval Captain Beucke, read the transcript of the trial; after the war he reported that one incident in particular had been advanced as the major reason for Heydrich's being 'honour bound to marry'. In the early stages Heydrich had made all the running and had invited the young lady to Kiel. 'He had airily dismissed her expressed desire to book a hotel room. On her arrival in Kiel, he informed her she could spend the night in his lodgings, which would be much cheaper. Out of necessity she complied, but managed to withstand Heydrich's advances.'[6] Freiwald and Puttkamer, both later to become Admirals, also confirm this version.[7]

The affair was harmless enough in itself and not really sufficient to justify expulsion from the Navy. However, Heydrich was so irritated by the behaviour of the superintendent and his daughter who, exploiting their good relations with the Berlin naval command, were determined to teach him a lesson, that his conduct during the trial fell far short of the standard his judges expected of him. In his opinion he had not behaved in a dishonourable fashion and he attempted to gloss over his actions in order to bring what was to him a trivial matter to an end. His judges took a dim view of what they considered to be his deceit. According to Admiral Puttkamer 'A Court of Honour is not to be compared to any ordinary court, where it is self-evident that the accused may lie.'[8]

Four naval officers sat on the Court of Honour. The chairman was the then commander of the Baltic naval station Admiral Gottfried Hansen, and also present was Lieutenant-Captain, later Vice-Admiral, Gustav Kleikamp. Kleikamp criticized 'Heydrich's unpleasant behaviour towards a young, innocent student from the Rendsburg *Kolonialfrauenschule*', calling it 'unforgivable'. Furthermore Heydrich's 'patently obvious insincerity' resulted in the court's feeling obliged, in its final summing-up, 'with respect to the public nature of the decision, to call into question the possibility of such an officer remaining in the Navy'.[9] It was as much Heydrich's general behaviour in front of the court as the 'unfortunate story of the girl' which led to the final negative judgment.[10] There is no doubt that Heydrich's indifference to the accepted code of honour, discernible throughout the trial and from the very incident which gave rise to it, had annoyed his judges more than the actual misdemeanour. Were he to have repeated here his phrase that it was to him a matter of 'indifference, what an officer of the German Navy can or cannot do', then it would have been all over for him at the end of these proceedings.

The Court of Honour delivered its judgment to the naval commander in Berlin, Admiral Raeder; at this stage the question of Heydrich's remaining in the Navy was merely under scrutiny. Without further ado Raeder pronounced against the insubordinate officer. In April 1931 First Lieutenant Heydrich was given a 'straightforward dishonourable discharge'. This was made known to the entire naval command. There was no chance of Heydrich becoming a reserve officer, since these were forbidden under the Versailles treaty. Acting First Lieutenant became retired First Lieutenant. For two years he would receive a monthly payment of 200 Reichsmarks. He had been cashiered from the Navy one year before attaining pension rights. The dream of becoming an Admiral was over. His world totally collapsed.

His next move was to return to his parents in Halle, where he wept for days on end.[11] But the atmosphere in his parents' house only added to his depression. His mother, Elisabeth Heydrich, who had laid such importance on her son's elevated social status and secure income, was completely at a loss. His father, Bruno Heydrich, now almost seventy, had no time to spare, since he devoted himself entirely to keeping his conservatoire and the associated seminary for music teachers out of financial trouble; it had been going steadily downhill for some years.

As for Reinhard's brother Heinz, after breaking off his studies at the Dresden Technical University, he had been obliged to make ends meet as a casual labourer, but was now also unemployed. And it was at this stage that the elder brother Reinhard, once so dynamic and successful, so often held up as an example, returned home, out of work, a broken man. For months catastrophe held the entire Heydrich family in its thrall. Reinhard could find no comfort in this atmosphere of total gloom and was obliged to seek it from his friends. More than anyone else, his schoolfriend Erich Schultze, who had originally fired him with enthusiasm for the Navy, was the person who, with his parents' assistance, attempted to set Heydrich back on his feet again.

Once he had told the tale of his dismissal from the Navy, or at least given his version of it, and revealed he was now out of work, good advice was hard to come by. In a time of high unemployment few were in a position to make an attractive offer to a young man who had learnt nothing other than how to be an officer and who had been given a 'straightforward dishonourable discharge' from the Navy under circumstances hardly inspiring confidence.

His first lifeline was a boyhood friend of Schultze's, also known to Heydrich, the lawyer Dr Günter Gericke, who lived on his small estate in Pressel, not far from Halle. At that time Gericke was a member of the *Reichstag* (German Parliament) for the *Bauernpartei* (Farmer's Party), President of the German *Landgemeindeverband* (Rural District Council) and a German nationalist by descent. In 1932, in his capacity as president of the German presidential election committee, he was instrumental in Hindenburg's victory. With the precept 'nothing is as bad as it seems', Gericke offered Heydrich an advisory position in the *Landgemeindeverband*, endowed with what was then a relatively good monthly salary of 350 Reichsmarks.[12] But Heydrich could not make up his mind and sought other offers. A frequent victor in Baltic sailing regattas, he was offered a job as a sailing instructor in either Ratzeburg or Kiel.

The Hanseatic Yachting School in Neustadt, in Holstein, offered him a post as instructor, with a salary of 300 Reichsmarks. Another possibility was joining the Merchant Navy.[13] Heydrich entered into various negotiations, but without any serious intent. Not one of the posts offered him could replace the lost call to arms, the uniform, the dream of a military career. In letters and on visits to Hamburg, he explained to his fiancée that a military career was his only option. His widow is of the opinion that 'discharge from the Navy was the heaviest blow of his life. It had a far more oppressive effect on him than the injury he suffered at the hands of his assassin. It was not the lost earning power which weighed on him, but the fact that with every fibre of his being he had clung to his career as an officer.'[14]

Heydrich's next move was to Hamburg, both out of a hope that based there he would find a post earlier and out of a desire to be nearer to Kiel, Fehmarn and his fiancée. The couple wanted to marry as soon as possible, although in the interim both sets of parents had taken to opposing the match. Lina von Osten's parents soon learned that Heydrich had had to leave the Navy 'because of a girl' and they were now urging their daughter 'to give the man up. He's got women everywhere!' However, in this matter Lina von Osten was as little influenced by her parents as by an Admiral's decree or by the naval code of honour. The fact that, in spite of the village gossip quickly spreading through petty bourgeois and narrow-minded Fehmarn, she now stood by Heydrich, naturally strengthened the union later.

For her part Heydrich's mother was not impressed by her future daughter-in-law. She had hoped for a better match; more musical and better-off. Admittedly Lina von Osten had a noble name, but she was still too rough and peasant-like, and her father was 'only' a village school-master.

It was this very concern with social status felt by Elisabeth Heydrich which helped to provide the 'saving idea'. Reinhard Heydrich's godmother and longstanding friend of the family, Frau von Eberstein, was made aware of the situation and her advice was requested. She turned to her son Karl, known in the Heydrich household as 'Karlchen'. Baron Karl von Eberstein,[15] later SS-General, was one of the earliest National Socialists. At this point, in May 1931, he held the rank of SA-Brigadier and was under the direction of the SA High Command, in command of the SA in Munich and Upper Bavaria. He was on familiar terms with both the influential SA-leader Röhm, and the then almost unknown SS-*Reichsführer*, Heinrich Himmler. Thus it came about that Heydrich's mother enquired whether 'Karlchen' might be able to find her son Reinhard a good post which would provide a uniform and a military atmosphere.

As far as Elisabeth Heydrich was concerned, a post in the NSDAP would have been 'absolutely socially acceptable'. After all, even Baron von Eberstein was in it. 'The main thing is that he should not lose his social status.'

On the other hand, as far as Heydrich himself was concerned, the prospect of an SA uniform was insufficient compensation for the loss of a naval uniform. His fiancée was in agreement with him over this, fervent National Socialist though she was. To this day his widow claims that the SA units were mere rabble. Quite another matter, however, was the SS, then still in its infancy, which she had first encountered at a Party rally in Kiel; it 'was really the elite, the military cream'.[16] However, she succeeded in persuading him to accept von Eberstein's intercession, but to continue pressing for a superior position, preferably in the ranks of the SS.

Only after von Eberstein had held out the prospect of such a position was Heydrich ready to join the Party: 'but only to get a foot in the door'. His membership number was 544,916. On 1 June 1931, in Hamburg, he signed his application form.[17]

Now he was in a position to apply for a 'command position' from the Party leaders of the NSDAP in Munich, but he chose to let his application pass through von Eberstein. Its first resting-place was the desk of the SA-Chief, former Army Captain, Ernst Röhm, who had not the slightest inkling of what to do with a cashiered naval First Lieutenant. So he sent this application, together with von Eberstein's recommendation, through the official channels. Its first destination was the office of SS-*Reichsführer* Heinrich Himmler.

Founded in 1925 as a security force for Hitler's personal safety, the SS was intended to be an elite corps, completely devoted to Hitler. When, in January 1929, Heinrich Himmler was appointed SS-*Reichsführer* by Hitler himself, he was in command of no more than 280 men throughout Germany. But by the summer of 1931, two and a half years later, membership of the black-shirts had become almost fashionable. No longer were members of the SS only part-time workers, drivers, men out of work or students, combining their fanatical National Socialist convictions with discipline and physical strength, but also an increasing number of academics, intellectuals and aristocrats. In 1931 ten per cent of the sectional and storm troop leaders were of noble birth: Himmler's chief of staff was a nephew of the Dutch queen, the Crown Prince Josias of Waldeck and Pyrmont. That same year the number of SS-men exceeded ten thousand.

Himmler himself was always eager to embrace any ideas which would promote the further development of the SS. In a speech made to the SS leadership in Berlin in the summer of 1931 he expounded his theory that the *Schutzstaffel* (security force, i.e. SS) should develop from 'body-guards' into 'national guards', into 'the cream of outstandingly talented men'. Military disputes and wars should be conducted by the mass of the people, the present political struggle by the ranks of the SA. They were the 'rank and file'. The role the SS would fulfil was that of: 'an organization which can be brought into play at crucial moments and later withdrawn, in its role as the Führer's final reserve'. This principle of the SS constituting a Brigade of Guards should be realized above all by the 'selection of men of the greatest racial purity' chosen according to physical proportions and 'nordic blood'. For this reason any prospective candidate for the SS had to attach a passport photograph to his application.[18] Such was the case with Heydrich's application. Himmler was immediately impressed by the 'nordic appearance' and looked favourably on the application. His interest was particularly aroused by the fact that Heydrich had served as a wireless officer *(Nachrichtenoffizier)* in the Navy. Only a few weeks previously he had received a commission from Hitler to establish his own Intelligence Service running on parallel lines to that of the SA. The latter had revealed the existence of too many leaks in the Bavarian Ministry of the Interior and the political division of the Munich police force.[19] So his receipt of Heydrich's application coincided with Himmler's quest for a tailor-made Intelligence man. After discussing the matter with von Eberstein, he decided to have a closer look at the *'Nachrichtenmann'* (Intelligence man) and gave the intermediary an interview date to transmit.

Apparently Himmler was unaware of the distinction between *Nachrichtenoffizier* (wireless officer) and *Nachrichtendienst-Offizier* (Intelligence officer); at all events it was not clear to him that Heydrich was by no means an expert in espionage and military Intelligence, but rather in naval radio communications.

After hearing of the favourable reaction to his application, Heydrich, still based in Hamburg, waited impatiently for his appointment with Himmler, which had been arranged for 16 June 1931. However, on the afternoon of the fifteenth, when he was packing his case for the trip to Munich, he received a telegram from von Eberstein, informing him that the appointment would have to be delayed. It appeared that Himmler was ill and could not receive Heydrich. The truth of the matter was that Himmler had used a genuine cold as a welcome pretext in order to avoid reaching a quick decision: Heydrich had acquired a rival, a former police captain called Horninger, and Himmler was now unable to decide to which of the two candidates he should give preference.

In a state of disillusionment and total apathy, Heydrich was inclined to take the telegram at face value and continue waiting. But this was to reckon without his fiancée. She completely ignored the cancellation of the appointment and telegraphed Baron von Eberstein, informing him that her fiancé would arrive in Munich the next day. Heydrich was put on the night train from Hamburg to Munich and duly arrived in Munich on the following morning. The old family friend von Eberstein was somewhat annoyed by this turn of events and when he met Heydrich at the station, he repeated his telegraph message, 'Himmler cannot see you. He is ill and not available for duty.'

But Heydrich, unwilling to have made the long journey in vain and inspired by his fiancée's pugnacity, convinced von Eberstein that he should at least telephone Himmler to inform him of his arrival.

After some hesitation, Himmler agreed to the suggestion that Heydrich should visit him at his home in Waldtrudering, a Munich suburb, where Himmler had bought himself a house with a small patch of land. Here he ran a chicken farm (he had a diploma in agriculture) and cultivated rare medicinal herbs.

When Heydrich arrived, Himmler, quite untypically, came straight to the point, with the intention of displaying his authority to a possible future subordinate. He explained to Heydrich his need for a *'Nachrichtenmann'* and enquired whether the discharged First Lieutenant understood what this would involve. Heydrich replied in the affirmative. Himmler continued as follows, 'I want to establish an Intelligence Service for the SS and am looking for a suitable man to take charge. If you are confident of being able to undertake the task, take twenty minutes and write down how you would organize the exercise.'

Now, for the first time, the *'Nachrichtenoffizier'* (wireless officer) realized that Himmler was actually looking for a *'Nachrichtendienst-Offizier'* (Intelligence officer). He chose, however, not to explain the misunderstanding, but rather to grasp immediately the opportunity it offered him. He cobbled together what he could remember from naval seminars on Intelligence with the theories he had evolved for himself while reading countless adventure stories about the world of the British Secret Service during long months at sea, topped this with the catchphrase 'Work in relation to life's possibilities', putting it all on paper in the correct military terminology. He added a sketch of a suitable organizational structure and, with a pounding heart, presented the result to the *Reichsführer*.

However little actual knowledge of the business Heydrich had put into his outline, it was apparently greater than that possessed by Himmler, who was highly impressed as much by the applicant's 'understanding of the matter' as by his manner and nordic appearance. His decision was quickly reached. Heydrich was taken on and was to take up his duties in Munich in August.

The former police captain, Horninger, was eliminated from the contest – fortunately for Himmler. For it had been Horninger's task, as a spy for the political division of the Munich police force, to infiltrate Himmler's entourage. After seizure of power by the NSDAP he hanged himself, in February 1933.[20]

For his part, Heydrich returned to Hamburg, where he made preparations for his move to Munich. He turned down the offer of a job with the Hanseatic Yachting School. Even Dr Günter Gericke, who was once again urging him to accept the advisory position in the *Landgemeindeverband,* received a refusal. Although Himmler could only offer him a monthly salary of 180 Reichsmarks, only slightly more than half the money attached to these other positions, Heydrich stuck by his decision to set up the SS-Intelligence Service. After the war Heydrich's closest boyhood friend gave his opinion that 'it offered him the chance of wearing uniform: military matters were still close to his heart. And this task for Himmler was to him a military matter. He believed that it would provide him with far greater opportunities for development than anything he might find in civilian life.'[21]

On 14 July, four weeks after his Munich introduction, Heydrich entered the Hamburg SS, where he took up duty as SS-Lance-Corporal. In a memorial speech Himmler himself described how he had:

called him into the SS in the July of that year [1931]. Heydrich, a former First Lieutenant, now joined the Hamburg SS as an ordinary member of the SS ranks and served his time in the company of all those stout-hearted boys, mostly from the unemployed, who were there from the start. He participated in the early struggles and in the propaganda campaigns in the numerous red districts of the city. Not long afterwards I summoned him to Munich, where I entrusted him with his new duties in the SS-Supreme Command, still a small affair at the time.[22]

The once apolitical officer was now becoming increasingly enmeshed in the world of National Socialism. Thus were the foundations laid for the career which, a decade later, was to horrify the world; by a dubious code of honour, a revenge-seeking official, an obstinate Admiral, Heydrich's own desire for a uniformed career and, most influential of all, by a fiancée whose seductive beauty was matched by her political fanaticism. Lina von

Osten, Heydrich's *femme fatale*, now made preparations for the wedding. The scruples of the future parents-in-law were laid to rest, since Heydrich had been offered an 'elevated position with some social standing', and the wedding date was fixed for Christmas 1931. By this time Heydrich had his first months in Munich behind him. A complete transformation had taken place. Heydrich's widow reports the atmosphere at the wedding:

> On Boxing Day we were married in the Evangelical faith in the little village church of Grossenbrode. My bridegroom was practically unknown then, but I had some standing in the Party. This was true also of my brother, known as one of the 'first hundred thousand', after Hitler's speech in Eckenförde. Our wedding guests were the NS women's group from Heilingenhafen and the SA from Grossenbrode and the surrounding villages. At that time the SA and the SS were proscribed. But the police could hardly move in on the graveyard surrounding the church. In their white shirts and black trousers the SA and the SS formed a cordon reaching the exit from the graveyard.
>
> Even the pastor was in the movement. The church interior was entirely decked out in green. A swastika made of green fir, provided by the women's group, took the place of the dove. For a wedding text the Pastor gave us the Lutheran 'And were the world full of devils, we would yet reach our goal.' Reinhard's father, Bruno Heydrich, had composed a *Pater noster*. As we left the church, the organist played the Horst-Wessel song. As soon as the wedding party had left the graveyard, a number of those who had been in the cordon were arrested; the pastor was later disciplined and sent to another parish.[23]

It appeared that, after the collapse of his bourgeois naval career, Reinhard Heydrich had found himself a new world. And yet, as long as the NSDAP and its SS had not achieved power in the German Reich, he felt that any hope of a career in the black uniform was highly uncertain, like a cheque to be cashed only on some unspecified date. Only the future could tell whether he would ever rediscover those elements of his earlier career which he now sought in the SS. Nostalgia for the Navy remained with him over the years; the fate which had befallen him, unjustly in his opinion, was like a thorn in his flesh. Lina Heydrich reports that 'whenever a naval uniform came into view, he had to look away'.[24] Even after years spent building up a career in his new position, he still could not recover from the stigma of the 'straightforward dishonourable discharge'. In 1936, by this time bearing the rank of SS-Major-General, he was invited to a routine naval reception, along with Himmler. He sat amongst the guests of honour; nearby were Admiral Hansen, who had been in charge of the proceedings during Heydrich's trial, and who had been pensioned off in the interim, Admiral Raeder, who had signed his discharge, and the 'Sea Devil', Graf Luckner. 'That was his moment of triumph! When he walked in, in the dress uniform of SS-Major-General, and Raeder and Hansen, as hosts of the evening, had no option but to welcome him officially – how he relished it!'[25]

On another occasion, in January 1939, at a conference held by the inspectors of the Security Police and the SD, he entered the hall at the same time as Admiral Canaris of German Counter-Intelligence. He began his speech of welcome as follows: 'You see before you, gentlemen, a formerly insignificant First Lieutenant in the Navy now entering this room in the company of Admiral Canaris . . .'[26]

He never in his entire life forgot his dishonourable discharge. After 1933 he adopted a distinctly dismissive attitude to the Navy and more particularly to Raeder, who had been promoted first to the rank of *General-admiral*, then to that of Admiral-in-Chief. An abortive attempt was made in 1934 by his former fellow cadets to give Heydrich comparable status. And yet even when he had risen to the position of one of the most powerful individuals in the Third Reich, he never attempted any action against the former members of the Court of Honour, as Gustav Kleikamp was to testify after Heydrich's death.[27]

Chapter 5

IN THE SECRET INTELLIGENCE SERVICE

The SD of the SS was founded before we took power, at a time when the Party did not have any executive opportunities but, on the contrary, endured the opposition of the executive.

Reinhard Heydrich

'The Secret State Police, the Criminal Police and the Security Service of the SS (called the SD) are still surrounded by the whispering and murmuring secrecy of a political detective novel. Abroad they like to attribute to the men who do this work brutality, inhumanity, and heartlessness bordering on the sadistic. This arises from a mixture of fear and horror; yet beneath the surface there is a certain feeling of security on account of their existence.' But at home there was understanding and respect for their activities: 'Here there is nothing, not even the most insignificant egoistic desire but people think the Secret State Police must have the answer for it.' These were the very words with which the future SS-General Reinhard Heydrich described the organizations which had evolved from the SD of the 'era of struggle' on German Police Day in 1941.[1]

When, a decade before, on 10 August 1931, he began his duties as Himmler's 'Intelligence man' with great expectations and a minute salary, even he could not have dreamt of all the possible developments that might ensue from these first steps. He had reckoned on 'a prominent position' in which to continue his career as an officer. He admitted to friends that he found what was waiting for him in Munich to be 'indescribable'.[2] His first office and the HQ of the Intelligence Service was in a room of the 'brown house', which Heydrich had to share with Richard Hildebrandt, Chief-of-Staff for Sepp Dietrich of the SS-Group, South. The young SS-Lieutenant Heydrich was soon friends with SS-Major Hildebrandt, who was seven years older, had studied history and art history, political economy and languages, and had spent many years abroad.[3] In their shared office Heydrich was given an old kitchen table and a chair, and allowed to borrow Hildebrandt's typewriter on an hourly basis. Heinrich Himmler himself remained director of the Secret Intelligence Service, contrary to Heydrich's expectations. In the 'higher command' of the SS to which the ex-naval officer now belonged, the newly created department was described as the 'Ic'-Service, following the model of the old German general staff in which section 'Ic' meant enemy reconnaissance. If the *Reichsführer* did not transfer the leadership of 'Ic' to Heydrich alone, it was not so with the work. He handed over a pile of files which contained the first rudiments of a reconnaissance outline of friends and foes. The files originated from the time when Himmler had been secretary to Gregor Strasser, a Party worker, and had collected press-cuttings and recorded his own observations on prominent National Socialists and their opponents. At first Heydrich was not given any additional assistance. The newly appointed head of the private Secret Service of the SS wielded scissors and paste himself, as well as catalogue cards, files and the borrowed typewriter.

Those weeks at the end of the summer of 1931 saw the real birth of the SD. For what Himmler had assembled more or less by chance, Heydrich soon organized into a survey of the 'investigation of hostile elements'. The Intelligence material yielded by the observation of rival organizations provided Heydrich with the pieces which fitted together to form a completely new jigsaw. Behind the Party's immediate political opponents his distrustful gaze discovered the contours of a still more terrible enemy, of forces that operated a worldwide, supranational conspiracy.

He writes in retrospect that he found his situation at this time 'uncomfortable'. The SD had been founded before the assumption of power, and in the course of its growth the NSDAP, a party radically opposed to the prevailing system, met similarly radical opposition from the same system. At that time the SD did not 'have any executive opportunities but, on the contrary, endured the opposition of the executive'. However, this disadvantage turned out to be 'a blessing for our general development' because it necessitated 'exhaustive rethinking on all fronts'. The SD's most important task remained none other than 'investigating hostile elements theoretically and practically by means of the Intelligence Service, without at first any hope of executive powers'. Heydrich saw as his chief opponents those hostile forces which were 'publicly' and visibly organized in the German political parties, above all the Communist, and Socialist Parties, the Catholic 'Centre' and the German People's Party and the German Nationalist Party.

But he saw as much more dangerous for the realization of National Socialism's goals the 'ideological opposition forces' at work 'behind the scenes': the political Church, Freemasonry, Jewry, Marxism 'and so on'. Finally he confirmed that 'these same spiritual forces of opposition are working towards one universal goal'.[4]

Heydrich had laid the foundations for the SD with one or two files from Himmler and the idea of forces working 'behind the scenes', behind all manifestations of political life. He was fascinated by the prospect of trying out his talent for Intelligence work on this rough and ready basis. He started work with energy, thirsting for action and with a real determination to succeed at last in his new career and prove himself to Himmler.

Heydrich's 'Ic'-Service was not, however, the only Intelligence and counter-espionage organization at the NSDAP's disposal, nor the only one to have its HQ in the 'brown house'. The political landslide of the September elections in 1930, which transformed the National Socialists at one blow from a splinter party into a mass party and made them the second largest group in the German Parliament, had increased the security needs of all the Party organizations. National Socialists everywhere saw that power was almost within their grasp. Now it was important for them to have more than superficial information about opposition organizations. On the other hand the Party itself, practically overnight, had become a threat to the government, and at the same time the most powerful and dangerous rival of the other major people's parties. Consequently official agencies strengthened their clandestine information gathering on the NSDAP just as much as did Hitler's rivals in the Communist, Socialist and the right-wing middle-class Parties, as well as the German Nationalist Party.[5]

The result, apart from a general fear of spies in the Party ('Everybody thought everyone else was an informer'[6]), was, above all, the foundation or revitalization of the Party's own counter-espionage organizations. Heydrich and Himmler's 'Ic'-Service was just the newest and, at first, the smallest of these. Rauscher, the *Gaupropagandaleiter* (SS-Regional Propaganda Officer) for Munich and Upper Bavaria, and his assistant Schumann had begun, in that same summer of 1931 and also in the 'brown house', to build up a secret Intelligence service for the NSDAP whose duties were not only defensive, but also offensive, in that it sought to disrupt opposition organizations.[7]

Although Rauscher seemed to be professional enough as regards the work in his own HQ in Munich, and to be effective in his appraisal of incoming reports, his attitude towards the organization of his Intelligence network was decidedly amateur. He did not bother to instal his own independent agents, but indiscriminately regarded every Party functionary and *Bezirksleiter* (District Officer) as his agent. For this reason both the authorities and the Bavarian left-wing and centre newspapers had quickly acquired a fairly thorough knowledge of Rauscher and Schumann's Intelligence work. The *Münchener Post*, for instance, carried several pertinent reports on 'intimate revelations from the brown house'.[8]

The SA had also reorganized its enemy reconnaissance and Intelligence department after the palace revolt of the left-revolutionary SA-leader Stennes. In that same summer of 1931 Röhm, the new SA-Chief of Staff, had appointed Dr Graf Karl DuMoulin-Eckart, a Munich lawyer, as head of the SA-Intelligence Service. He set up a network of SA-agents *(Sab)* who reported mostly on the opposition paramilitary organizations, such as '*Stahlhelm*' and '*Reichsbanner*', the Communist Party (KPD), and the Army.

Bungling and superficial as his National Socialist rivals in the Party and SA might have appeared to the new SS-Secret-Service chief Heydrich, he could only note with envy how much better provided for they were in terms of personnel and finance. By comparison the SS-'Ic' was not even recognizable as an embryo. But after the top SA spy, DuMoulin, had been exposed by the Social Democrat *Münchener Post*, and had been involved in two trials, the chances of the 'baby' of the National Socialist Intelligence services improved by leaps and bounds.[9] Admittedly a 'retired naval Lieutenant, Heyderich [sic]' was mentioned in the newspaper article, with the postscript, 'This is the man who has to set down great thoughts on paper in painful detail,' but nothing else emerged about 'Heyderich'. The Political Department of the Munich police force also got to know the name Heydrich very early on. For scarcely two weeks after taking up his position in the 'brown house' he had to give a short report at a conference of SS-leaders, about which the Political Department of the Munich police was soon informed. But Heydrich's exact function remained unknown to the regime's spies.

In his report, Heydrich explained the task of disrupting political opponents and announced a plan to build up the SS's own counter-espionage section.[10] This was a first indication of his talent for both instructing and unsettling the Party and his superiors.

Developments now followed thick and fast. At the beginning of September came a secret SS order to compile 'an "Ic"-report without delay'.[11] The first information about the opposition soon started coming in as well as confidential reports on their own units. The files on Heydrich's kitchen table were piled higher and higher. Shortly afterwards he scored his first big success in the contest with the rival National Socialist Secret Services, which also brought the first preliminary decision in favour of *his* office. Heydrich uncovered the source of treachery within the 'brown house' which had been helping the Political Department of the Munich police to get reliable information. Heydrich unmasked one of the Party's 'Munich putsch veterans' as an officer in the Criminal Police and a spy. He put pressure on the man whose cover he had broken and succeeded in converting him. From November 1931 the eye of the Bavarian Political Police in the SS was blind, while on the other hand, Heydrich received regular reports from Munich police HQ.[12]

SS-*Reichsführer* Himmler was satisfied with his 'intelligence man'. He was convinced that he had made the best move on the board in deciding on the former naval Lieutenant. At the end of 1931 it was decided to withdraw completely Heydrich's department from the 'brown house' and to instal it in a private flat where it could be screened better and where its work would be less disturbed.

At the same time Heydrich was allowed his first three assistants. The Nazis' 'Secret Police' chief moved into his new office with them, along with his files and the rudimentary index of hostile elements which he had set up and managed himself ('At that time all the opponents of the NSDAP still fitted into a few cigar boxes!'[13]). Two rooms were taken in the flat of a Party member, Viktoria Edrich, a widow, in the fourth storey of No. 23 Türkenstrasse in Munich. 'Mother Edrich', as she was soon known to Heydrich's assistants, proved to be a particularly loyal and dependable National Socialist. The '*Blutfahne*' (bloodied flag) which had been carried in front of the NSDAP on 9 November 1923, was kept hidden in her wardrobe during the ban on the SA and SS.[14]

But the SD's pitiful equipment was not improved by the move. Heydrich had the same old furniture as before and still no typewriter. If one was particularly needed it had to be fetched by tram from SS-Major Hildebrandt and taken back again when it was finished with. Himmler showed his satisfaction with gestures that did not cost anything. Heydrich was promoted to SS-Captain at the time of the move and had therefore theoretically by-passed his old rank in the Navy. During the Christmas holidays of the same year he married his fiancée, the twenty-year-old Lina von Osten, from the island of Fehmarn. As a wedding present the SS-*Reichsführer* promoted him again. On 25 December 1931 Heydrich became SS-Major.[15]

The young couple took up residence in one of the two rooms rented from the widow Edrich, while Heydrich's three assistants worked on the index of opponents and the dossiers on members of their own Party in the other room. Heydrich's three helpers, unemployed SS-men, were only paid occasionally, and were mostly fed by 'Mother Edrich' on stews, for which the newly-married Heydrichs were sometimes grateful as well.

At the beginning of 1932 the Heydrichs managed to lease a real flat of their own, for which they paid 180 Reichsmarks a month in rent. The flat was in the Munich suburb of Lochhausen, in house No. 55. His widow remembers it as 'a partitioned-off hutch on the first floor, with gaps between the floorboards the width of your finger. But my husband had given everything a good coat of paint.' Every day the head of the SS-Secret Service went to his office in Türkenstrasse, which now consisted of two rooms, travelling third class on the railway, which cost him 3.10 marks a week. A passport photograph of that period shows him still dressed in a civilian suit that was too small for him, with his hair cut short and parted in the middle in the standard haircut of the German Navy.[16]

Heydrich set great store by always describing the two rooms in the Türkenstrasse as the 'department', as if the SD was already a government body.[17] With a restless thirst for activity he completed his index there. The first objective was to note, without having exactly delineated the concept, everything that seemed threatening in their opponents' political work and above all everything that could be recognized as a cross-connection 'behind the scenes'. The index cards in the SD's cigar boxes were arranged by opposition groups: communists, Social Democrats, political Catholics, bourgeois conservatives, representatives of the aristocracy hostile to

National Socialism, Freemasons, Jews. Those people with multiple entries were of particular interest. Social Democrats who were also 'known' as members of a Masonic Lodge, aristocrats who had close relations abroad, and Jewish communists were put in a special 'poison index'. Jews and Freemasons were only of interest if they were prominent politically. 'Automatic opponents did not exist at all at that time. Jews interested him as part of a political problem, not in a human or racial sense.'[18]

Heydrich's surveillance work was centred at first on Munich, then took in the whole state of Bavaria, and then spread in loose and sometimes incomplete concentric circles over the whole Reich, noting also connections abroad. Weak members of his own Party were entered in a special index. Those with too many debts, those who had homosexual affairs or mistresses to hide, those with previous convictions who had not admitted them on joining the Party, and those who were closely connected to opponents by friends or relatives all became 'cases'. It was also a matter of routine for the 'Ic'-men of the SS-sub-districts to report on the personalities, mood and development of the Army.

At the end of February Heydrich was rudely awakened from this undisturbed surveillance work. The police in Oldenburg had arrested an agent of the 'Ic' of the Brunswick SS-sub-district. He admitted to the police that he had passed on information from the fortified area at Wilhelmshaven 'to the Intelligence Service of the SS'. The records stated that the Intelligence Service was just being formed and that his task was to gain information on 'the propaganda, meetings and paramilitary organizations of the opposition parties' and also on 'the political attitudes of the population, particularly of officials and the Army'. The agent reported to a 'Herr Kobelinski'.[19]

Luckily for Heydrich the police did not manage to find out any more about this Herr Kobelinski, who was the Intelligence man of the Brunswick SS-sub-district or, even more important, about his boss. Nothing came of the affair. But Heydrich immediately realized that he would have to organize his Secret Service quite differently if he did not want to suffer a fate similar to that of his rival DuMoulin, whose cover had been broken. The main initiates and 'Ic' people from the SS-sub-districts would not in future be simply appointed by the respective SS associations as a matter of routine, without having been thoroughly screened by HQ, and without having the personal confidence of the boss.

Instead of the agents of the various sub-groups, Heydrich wanted to cultivate an independent organization of assistants under his personal, central command, which would be able to make use of the existing organizational structure of the Party and the SS while not forming any part of them. He withdrew all counter-espionage agents and informers from the SS and made them directly answerable to himself. The SD was not only to remain the Intelligence department of the SS, but also to evolve into an independent entity which was indeed part of the SS but as autonomous as possible. It was to be exclusive and at the same time an SS within the SS.[20]

The political developments of the next four months provided the ideal background for this operation. When the SA and SS were banned in April 1932 Heydrich was forced into pantomime by the government of the Weimar Republic. The 'Ic'-Service, like countless Secret Services before and since, had its name changed to Press and Information Service (PID), while its boss and his assistants submerged ever deeper. The first commandment for self-preservation was to distance oneself as far as possible from the banned SA and SS. While DuMoulin's SA-Intelligence Service was not resurrected in the autumn, when the ban was lifted, Heydrich's secret organization emerged with greater strength.[21]

As early as April Heydrich set out on an extensive tour of Germany. He wanted to choose his future sub-district officers personally. His yardstick for picking his assistants was based on the practice of the British Secret Service, the supreme example by which he wanted to judge his own Secret Service and to which he still remained true after 1933. 'They were his example, their's were the standards he wanted to reach,' testified his wife, Lina. He thought it a 'fundamental German failing' to regard all Secret Service work as something improper. German politicians since the time of Bismarck had had to operate in the dark because they had never had an effective Intelligence Service. The Party for whose security he was now responsible should not suffer the same fate. According to Heydrich the British and their Secret Service had always promptly 'recognized all politically relevant trends and climates of opinion'. For this reason British politicians had always developed many more initiatives and, in the last analysis, had always been more successful than the Germans. It had always been the fate of the latter to lose the initiative and hence the battle. Heydrich believed that the British level of perfection could only be attained if more than one lifetime were spent on it. Looking around the Party in Munich he was most distressed by the problem of personnel. 'To this end he could use only highly intelligent people and not the blockheads the Party normally made use of.' What particularly impressed him about the British Secret Service was that so many intellectuals worked for it. It went without saying that members of the British elite worked for the Secret Service everywhere in the world and in every occupation, 'and all this on an honorary basis'.[22]

Right from the very start he intended to take account of this basic feature of the work of his idolized British example when building up his own Secret Service. It therefore comes as no surprise that the first staff that Heydrich succeeded in bringing home from his expedition through Germany were almost exclusively academics. First he won over Leffler, who was later to become SS-Sergeant-Major in the SD. After his matriculation Leffler had studied at the Technical Universities in Berlin and Brunswick, seen service as a naval pilot and following the war had passed his examination as certified hydraulic engineer 'with credit'. He had been a soldier and an officer in the *Freikorps* (Free Corps), then a technical assistant at the Technical University in Brunswick, before becoming the manager of an industrial concern. The economic crisis forced him into the uncertainties of being self-employed.[23]

Leffler was joined in Heydrich's net by Dr Herbert Mehlhorn, a lawyer and political economist who had graduated *magna cum laude* and was a barrister in Chemnitz. He was a member of the NSDAP and the SA, and became the most trusted member of the Press and Information Service in Röhm's SA. He was followed by Dr Wilhelm Albert, an engineer and *Freikorps* fighter from Franconia, and Dr Johannes Schmidt, a lawyer in Thuringia. He became the 'Ic'-man of the SS there.[24]

Leffler himself informs us that Heydrich took particular care over the assistants who were to be installed at important points in the SD network. He not only had their pasts, political histories and economic situations investigated but also included their wives in the enquiries.

True to his British example, Heydrich favoured primarily academics on his recruiting trip. Most of them had completed their studies with distinction and were also successful professionally, at least until the world economic crisis of 1929. But other candidates presented themselves who might also be useful to Heydrich in the great future he was planning for his Secret Service. Amongst these mention must chiefly be made of Carl Albrecht Oberg, a merchant from Hamburg, with whom Heydrich worked closely after 1933. Even his past was typical of the criteria that influenced Heydrich's selections. Oberg came from a professorial family in Hamburg, and until shortly before his matriculation had attended the famous schools of smart Hamburg society. He volunteered without finishing school and after the war became a merchant and a *Freikorps* fighter, before getting a job with a firm of fruit importers. He was also made unemployed by the world economic crisis, bought a cigarette business and joined Heydrich in 1932.[25]

Heydrich wasted no time in manning his control points throughout the Reich with engineers and lawyers, with chemists, merchants, political economists, accountants and former officers. There grew up in Munich a small, elite team with which he systematically filled out the framework of the SD in the nine months before Hitler's seizure of power, under conditions of the greatest secrecy, not only during the period of illegality but even after the ban on the SA and SS had been lifted.

Himmler rewarded the zeal of his young counter-espionage chief. In July Heydrich was officially named director of the SS-Security Service, and the PID finally became the SD. That same month Heydrich was promoted again, to SS-Colonel, and a move to a bigger office was indicated.[26]

But his first muster of the regional staff and the section heads of the Munich HQ still took place that summer in the two rooms in Viktoria Edrich's flat. During this conference Heydrich and Himmler clarified their programme. Heydrich once more affirmed the shining example of the 'Service' and the *Deuxième Bureau*. One of the participants in the conference remembers that, like them, the SD was to gather and evaluate 'comprehensively and in broad outline, sound and valid material about the goals, methods and plans' of political opponents at home, to report, when necessary, on improprieties within their own ranks, and to inform the Führer, the Party leadership, and later the National Socialist government, of anything of interest. But the representatives and additional personnel of the Service were never to form an organization of 'paid agents and informers'. Only 'people of irreproachable and unimpeachable character' could be made use of. The number of HQ staff was to be kept to a minimum. Outside their HQ the SD could rely only on an organization of honorary 'trusted people who acted purely from the best of motives and enjoyed the respect of the community by virtue of their achievements, their professional ability and their objective and sober judgment'.[27]

In September the SD moved from Türkenstrasse and the Heydrichs from Lochhausen to a small villa at No. 4 Zuccalistrasse in Munich. The house stood at the end of a cul-de-sac. 'The position was ideal for a Secret

Service' according to Heydrich's wife Lina. It was surrounded by a longish garden and was 'in the best position' in the Nymphenburg district. The rent was 180 Reichsmarks. Later it served Reinhard Heydrich exclusively as an official residence when he was chief of Munich's Political Police Division. After the war the house was favoured by film stars, amongst whom was Ruth Leuwerik.[28] In the last year of the Weimar Republic, however, it consisted of a small official flat for Heydrich and his wife and offices for seven assistants. These formed the HQ of the SD.

Despite this comparatively rapid development in the year after Heydrich took over, which had taken the SD from half an office and a borrowed typewriter in the 'brown house' to a villa in the fashionable Zuccalistrasse, the financial position was and remained precarious. The ban on the SD and SS, the high costs of maintaining the SA residences, the growth of the Party apparatus and the drop in the Party's income had overtaxed the Party's financial resources. Admittedly the principle of the SD was unpaid assistance, but the HQ staff in the central office had to be paid. But the SD came right at the bottom of the scale of priorities for Party funds. The SD had permanent money worries because of the SA, to which the SS was still subordinate, and was therefore dependent just as much on Röhm as on the Party and Rudolf Hess. The monthly wages for its chief, 'C' as Heydrich, with one eye as always on the British Secret Service, liked to be known,[29] were very seldom paid on time. The telephone was disconnected on one occasion because the bill had not been paid. Every time the married men went home on leave Heydrich had to consider whether he could let them come back. Heydrich's wife says of this situation:

At that time I was the maid-of-all-work in the villa, which had the rather grandiose title of SD Central Office. I was look-out, cook and housewife. I had a good view of the street from the kitchen. That was my observation post. I cooked the routine meals for the whole house. Every Wednesday the elite team of the SD played 'Aschinger', which was named after the Berlin eating-house. We could very seldom buy meat and fish, so every Wednesday we had an 'Aschinger salad'. It consisted solely of potatoes, other vegetables and spices. Strohmeyer, an SS-man and Secretary of the SD, would fetch beer for everyone. And that was the high point of our social life at that time.[30]

Heydrich attached more and more importance to the Party's most secret of Service Services, and since the flow of money was becoming increasingly scanty, he decided to make an energetic attack on Röhm. 'Himmler was never averse to leaving the begging to his dogsbody.' Until then Heydrich and Röhm had only made superficial contact on an official level and through the recommendation of Baron von Eberstein. As far as Röhm was concerned the SD was not much more than one 'of the odds and sods' which were then sheltering under the roof of the Party and the SA. He did not know very much more than that this department was surrounded by a certain amount of secrecy. Only after receiving Heydrich's begging letter did Röhm decide to have a look at the SD. Hess was to accompany him.

One activity which took place on the day of that great inspection by Röhm and Hess gives an impressive illustration of the mixture of official and family activity which at that time characterized the embryonic SD. It shows both how little influence and power the 'chief' enjoyed at that time in the Party, the SA and the SS, and how much trouble he took to please his superiors, particularly Röhm. Heydrich's widow reports:

On both sides of the hall in the house in Zuccalistrasse stood tiled coke stoves which every morning the SD's factotum, that is myself, had to light and keep going. And every morning, with great regularity, the matches that lay on a ledge on one of the stoves had disappeared. And then, just as regularly, the SD's factotum had to buy new ones, which had disappeared again by the next morning.

Then the factotum ran out of patience. 'C's wife, who was then twenty-one years old, decided to have her revenge. She bought a box of exploding matches which made a particularly loud noise at a joke shop in the Viktualienmarkt in Munich. So the 'culprit' would soon give himself away. She put the matches on the ledge of the stove and awaited events. In the course of that same morning Heydrich came down the stairs from the first floor where his office was, in a state of great excitement, 'glowing with eagerness and enthusiasm'. 'Himmler has just called. Röhm and Hess are already on their way and are coming to inspect us.' They had not expected such an exalted visit. Secretary Strohmeyer was quickly sent to the shops with a few marks out of the housekeeping. He was to buy a small bottle of port and two cigars – one for SA-Commander Röhm and one for SS-*Reichsführer* Himmler who was known to 'enjoy smoking the odd one on special occasions'.

The exalted visitors arrived. On their findings ultimately depended the financial security of the SD and therefore its future. The assistants were presented to them. They were shown the index file of the opposition and the principles of the SD's work were explained. Röhm must have been very impressed by what he heard, for Heydrich's request for financial support was granted. One thousand marks was promised in the first instance. Admittedly only half that amount was actually received, but Heydrich was elated. For the first time his Secret Service had risen above its worst financial worries. Rent or wages were assured, at least for a few months.

The agreement was celebrated with a glass of port. Secretary Strohmeyer hurried in with the two cigars, took his matches out of his pocket and offered a light first to Röhm. 'There followed an explosion. The *Reichsführer* looked round for cover, Röhm went as white as a sheet. Of course it was still a time of violent clashes and the pistols of the SA and their red opponents sat loosely in their holsters.'[31] It was only after the SD's factotum, a beautiful young woman as yet unknown to Hess and Röhm, had explained the story of the exploding matches that their expressions relaxed. 'Röhm found it amusing.'[32] From that time on, Heydrich cultivated his contacts with Commander Röhm, though privately he did not think much of his two superiors. There was something 'pretty queer' about Röhm, he confided to his wife. But then his smartness and soldierliness compensated for any other failings. Röhm also took more notice of the promising 'young man' after the inspection in Zuccalistrasse. When Heydrich's first son, Klaus, was born in June of the following year, Ernst Röhm was his godfather.[33] From that time on they used the intimate form for you, '*du*', in their conversations.

Heydrich's relationship with Himmler became more and more distant. Outward appearances gave a picture of earnest servility: 'Of course, Reichsführer, of course!' Heydrich was well aware of what was healthy for his career! He had come unstuck once because of insubordination. He intended to avoid failure in a second career at any price. 'In the Navy he had learnt how to agree even if he was of the completely opposite opinion.' He always said 'Of course' to Himmler as well, even when he thought the *Reichsführer*'s explanations were illogical and pure hot air. He is supposed to have remarked to his wife: 'I simply think to myself: how does he look in his underpants. Then everything's all right.' However much he was at pains to see progress in his work and to make a good impression on Himmler, privately he put Himmler in the same bracket as the hated 'small-minded schoolmaster' in the Navy, the future Admiral Raeder. He often compared the two of them: 'In them the German nation has lost two excellent schoolmasters.'[34]

The *Reichsführer* was systematically cut off from the daily work of the SD by Heydrich. He only got to see the results, or the parts that Heydrich showed him. The separateness from the 'normal' SS and the autonomy which was so characteristic of the SD after the seizure of power took root during this period. Right from the start Heydrich was very anxious that all the threads should come together only in his hands. His discussions with individual specialists were always private. None of them knew what the others were working on. The individual pieces of the jigsaw that the specialists picked out of the daily pile of Intelligence material provided only 'C' with a clear picture. Only he could fit them together: the agents were bound in secrecy even among themselves. Even regular private intercourse of the assistants with each other was forbidden.[35]

This method of working was, of course, objectively justified, but it also suited Heydrich's strongly introverted, taciturn character. It became clearer and clearer that he was far more suited by nature to Secret Service work than to a career as a naval officer of the Weimar Republic. In the long run Heydrich would have woken from his dream of becoming an Admiral to the sober recognition that he could never realize his own potential as a naval officer, notwithstanding the scandal about the elder daughter of a naval superintendent and the disgrace of an unceremonious dismissal. His 'inner self' could not have found his 'outer self' in a naval uniform. Dr Werner Best, his future assistant, whose inside knowledge has provided the most reliable picture of Heydrich's character, described it as follows in his post-war evidence. 'The specialization of functions, the dependence on the chain of command, the confined space on the ships and the promotion by seniority must in the long run have become unbearable to an impetuous nature which always wanted to press forward and upwards.'[36]

Heydrich took to the Secret Service like a duck to water. The *Reichsführer* observed his metamorphosis with astonishment. Heydrich drove his Security Service on with an insatiable curiosity, with dispassionate coldness, and with a burning ambition to wipe the floor with the other Secret Services, firstly in the Party, then throughout the Reich. He seemed to have been predestined for the work by his harshness and his cynicism, by a very loose attachment to prevailing morality, by his unusual talent for piecing things together, and above all by his sharp instinct, his 'sixth sense'.

The battles over the political direction of National Socialism only interested him as an Intelligence man and hardly at all as an ideological Party member, so that he remained free of ideological fanaticism. He pledged himself to the fanaticism of success. The twenty-nine-year-old Reinhard Heydrich longed for the National Socialist movement to seize power. For only power, undivided power, could take him where he wanted to go: right to the top.

Chapter 6

THE ALLEGED JEW

Perhaps I stood and cheered on the wrong platform.

Reinhard Heydrich, 1932

The year 1932, the 'fateful year' of the Weimar Republic, also provided the turning point in Heydrich's life. Exactly a year before the seizure of power and a year after his entrance into the SS, his own career was at a half-way point. The short time since the establishment of his SD had seen the achievement of considerable status, both for the Party's Security Service and for its young leader. Certainly the Party could have survived without him, but Heydrich made steady upward progress in the Munich leadership, the most important in the Party. A memorandum of March 1932 placed him in twenty-seventh place out of thirty-five, but a standby list included in this memo already accorded him fourteenth place.[1] On 1 December 1931 he was promoted to SS-Captain, on 25 December to SS-Major, promotion to SS-Lieutenant-Colonel could not be far off. The 'military career' which was his dream seemed secure.

And then, on 8 June 1932, Gregor Strasser, then the *Reichsorganisationsleiter* of the NSDAP, received a letter from the *Gauleiter* of Halle-Merseburg, Rudolf Jordan, in which he revealed his findings that 'A Party member called Heydrich' was in the 'Reich leadership' and that his father lived in Halle, in Jordan's area of responsibility. In his report to Munich the excited *Gauleiter* declared: 'There is reason to believe that the Bruno Heydrich in Halle, indicated as his father, is a Jew.'[2] An extract from Hugo

Riemann's music dictionary of 1916 was included as 'proof'. Bruno Heydrich was mentioned in this, with a note appended to the effect that his name was 'really Süss'.[3] Strasser, who until then had had few dealings with Heydrich, realized at once the significance of this message: it involved the most secret activities of the NSDAP's Secret Service. Had Hitler entrusted the security of the Party to, of all people, an agent of the 'Jewish world enemy', when it was the very feeling of anti-semitism which most convincingly united the diverse Party factions?

The Party's chief genealogist, Dr Achim Gercke, was immediately called into action. At the end of two weeks he was able to quell the rising panic of the Party leadership with the following report: 'It can be seen to emerge from the enclosed genealogy that . . . Heydrich is of German origin and free from any coloured or Jewish blood.'[4]

The 'Bruno Heydrich . . . indicated as his father' was therefore not Jewish. But according to the family, 'one of his musical rivals spread the rumour that he was. The artist paid no attention. It was a matter of indifference to him.'[5]

The rumour had arisen because of the second marriage of Heydrich's paternal grandmother, Ernestine Wilhelmine Heydrich, *née* Lindner, to the journeyman locksmith Gustav Robert Süss: according to Gercke, 'as the mother of the large family by her first husband Reinhold Heydrich, she had often chosen to call herself Süss-Heydrich'.[6] To the xenophobic bourgeoisie of Halle, whose ideas still bore the mark of the world as seen by Richard Wagner and his son-in-law Chamberlain, the name of Süss conjured up Jewish origins. But there was no direct line of descent from Süss to Reinhard Heydrich and, as the racial investigator Gercke could not fail to notice, the locksmith Süss was 'in any case . . . not of Jewish origin'.[7]

This 'testimonial on the racial origins of former naval First Lieutenant Reinhard Heydrich' was placed before Strasser, as well as *Gauleiter* Jordan, the chairman of the court of enquiry and arbitration, Heydrich himself, and most important of all, Himmler. Thus the matter was settled officially, but it was by no means at an end. There were still rumours in Halle about Heydrich's father. There was one other name to be considered as well as Süss: that of Isidor. Reinhard was not the only one affected by the rumour. In 1923 a students' association in Halle had refused to accept his brother Heinz on the grounds of the same suspicion.[8] Even after the war, former citizens of Halle clung to their conviction, which they claimed was common knowledge in the town, 'that Bruno Heydrich was half Jewish'.[9]

It was impossible to scotch the rumour and on more than one occasion Heydrich resorted to judicial proceedings in order to re-establish his good name. Among those he prosecuted for slander, as late as December 1940, was a thirty-three-year-old baker, Johannes Pabst. The German press gave banner headlines to the announcement 'a year's imprisonment for the slanderer'[10] when Pabst was accorded this sentence on 12 December because he had spread abroad the claim, already shown to be false, that '. . . Heydrich and his father were of non-Aryan descent'. It was pointed out as reason for the judgment that as a high functionary in the movement and the state, Heydrich required 'special protection against such character defamers' and indeed the punishment had only been so mild because Pabst, an invaluable Party member, had only spread this false claim with the best of intentions. Once, at a railway station, in the company of the future press officer Dr Schmidt, Heydrich is said to have met an acquaintance from Halle called Rühle and to have said to him: 'I've won the case about my origins. Now let anyone dare to claim I'm a Jew. I'll destroy him.'[11]

Later Heydrich was to confide in only his closest colleagues that 'circles in the Party opposed to him' had declared him to have Jewish blood in his veins. 'Certainly the name Süss appears in his genealogical table, but there is no reason to suppose that it was a Jewish Süss.' It was far more likely to have been a name of German trades family origins; in any case he was not in a direct line of descent from it.[12]

The further one departed from the entirely convincing genealogical explanation of the affair submitted by Gercke, the wilder and more outrageous became the speculations, with the result that by the end of the Third Reich they were transformed into almost pathological stories. The former SD-officer, Dr Wilhelm Höttl, saw fit to impart in his memoirs[13] the information that in a series of raids Heydrich had all incriminating genealogical evidence removed from official records. He is said to have removed the gravestone of his 'Jewish grandmother, "Sarah"' from the Leipzig cemetery and to have replaced it by one bearing the less embarrassing inscription of S. Heydrich. As late as 1945 this view of Heydrich was common currency in the Berlin HQ: Dr Wilhelm Stuckart, then former Secretary in the Ministry of the Interior and SS-General, was to recall that Heydrich had been considered 'Jewish or partly Jewish'.[14] Field-Marshal Milch surmised him to have been 'quarter Jewish'.[16] In one statement the former Berlin Counter-Intelligence worker, pianist Helmut Maurer, laid stress on the fact that in 1940 he had removed incriminating evidence about Heydrich's origins from the Halle record office.[16] According to Maurer 'if his memory served him right, Heydrich owed his Jewish connections to his father's side of the family'. This material procured by Maurer was said to have been saved by Canaris, kept out of Heydrich's reach and even to have enabled him to blackmail his rival in the SD!

Gossip about the Heydrich family reveals that 'his powerful hooked nose' also gave cause for concern about the otherwise ideal SS-man.[17] Yet the explanation of this was quite harmless. Heydrich had acquired his hooked nose by breaking it while taking part in the pentathlon held by the Army sports school, and again while out on a private ride.[18] In the jargon of the *Spiegel* he was indeed attributed a 'nordic body, but a slit-eyed, battered face', and it was said that 'nothing vexed him so much as his origins'.[19]

Best of all were the recollections of the former masseur and personal physician to the *Reichsführer,* the inscrutable Finnish medical adviser, Felix Kersten,[20] whom Heydrich had always suspected of being a spy for the Allies.[21] Kersten alleged that he had learnt from Himmler that both he and Hitler had been informed about the Jewish origins of their security chief shortly after the seizure of power in 1933. Hitler is reputed to have had a personal interview with Heydrich and to have said afterwards to Himmler 'this Heydrich is a highly talented, but also highly dangerous man whose abilities we must retain in the movement. Such people can only be allowed to operate if they are kept under tight rein; to this end his non-Aryan origins arc admirably suitable. He will be eternally grateful to us for retaining him rather than throwing him out and will obey us blindly.' This, Himmler is said to have confidently added to his story 'was then the case'. The SS-*Reichsführer* apparently confided in his masseur that Heydrich 'was in a permanent state of torment because of this knowledge of his inadequate origins', that he 'was unable to relax for a moment, his sense of inadequacy gnawed continually at him. I discussed the matter with him often and attempted to help him, and this in spite of my convictions to the contrary, by admitting the possibility of a conquest of strains of Jewish blood by finer Germanic blood, even using him as an example.'

Certainly this paternal chat from the *Reichsführer* did help, according to Kersten, for Heydrich 'had soon conquered the Jew in him on a purely intellectual level and taken up an extreme position on the other side. He was convinced of the damning nature of the traces of Jewish blood he possessed and hated this blood which played him so false. Indeed the

Führer could have found no better man for the struggle against the Jews than Heydrich; he offered them no mercy.'

The former American prosecutor in the Nuremberg trials, Robert M W Kempner, also referred to Kersten's statement, inferring from it that the genealogical table produced by the National Socialist Dr Gercke was of no consequence, since it had 'obviously been drawn up in accordance with the decision, previously approved by Hitler and Himmler, to provide a cover for Heydrich'.[22] Kempner failed to notice that Gercke's report was produced in June 1932, but that, if credence is given to Kersten, Hitler took the part of the 'Jewish half-caste, only after the seizure of power, at the earliest in March 1933, almost one year later'. In the event, Kempner had been influenced by evidence discovered in the fifties; in the Israeli edition of his book we find his support for the Jewish thesis.[23]

Just when the previously popular tale about the Jewish grandmother was found to be no longer watertight, a British journalist, Charles Wighton, appeared from the wings with an even less likely discovery.[24] If nothing could be made of the paternal line of descent, perhaps something could be done with the maternal one? Thus it was that he smelt a rat in the fact that Gercke's report had not delved deeper into Heydrich's maternal lineage. Admittedly Heydrich's mother, Elisabeth Maria Anna Amalia Kranz, daughter of the Dresden *Hofrat,* Professor Krantz, had been included, but not her mother or her grandmother. The journalist concluded as follows: 'The significance of the missing grandmother is clear: The Nazi inquisitor researching Reinhard Heydrich's Aryan blood discovered only too much about this grandmother and her predecessors, certainly far too much for it to have been included in the secret Party records of the SD-chief.'

Following on from this it became clear that Gregor Strasser 'and his more sinister disciple Martin Bormann' possessed 'other and far more secret records' which they kept in their safe. Admittedly the contents of Bormann's safe were never found, but Wighton still had sufficient proof: first, 'the first name of this secret grandmother was Mautsch', secondly, 'she was the one who had brought money into the family'. Nevertheless, Wighton refrained from swearing to the truth of this assertion, taking refuge in the formula 'of a strong *prima facie* case'.

All these stories seem fantastic, but they were transmitted, and embroidered on with relish, becoming the stuff of history. For example, the respected British historian, Professor Hugh Trevor-Roper, bases the secret of Heydrich's restless activity on apparently nothing other than

Kersten's tales. 'Fear of blackmail was behind Heydrich's success,'[25] proclaimed the Professor 'with all the authority that I possess,[26] for despite his blond hair and blue eyes he was, as Himmler and Hitler were fully aware, of Jewish origin.' The opinion of German colleagues was no different: in a testimonial used by the German court to throw light on the historical background, and which led to a final pronouncement, the Kiel historian, Michael Freund, also claimed that Hitler and Himmler had known that Heydrich 'had Jewish blood in his veins' and for this very reason had been 'chosen . . . expressly' for the extermination undertakings.[27] The historian of the Intelligence Service, Gert Buchheit, revelled in his claim: 'His Aryan passport was a forgery.'[28]

It was generally held as self-evident that Heydrich, 'the prime mover behind the extermination of the Jews', did not himself fulfil the 'biological postulates of the National Socialist leadership in its most important respects' (by this is understood its obsession with racial purity and pedigree). Even in standard histories of the Third Reich, on the lines of Karl Dietrich Bracher's *Die Deutsche Diktatur* (The German Dictatorship), Heydrich's Jewish origins are so clearly exposed that one hardly dares believe that they could ever have been concealed.[29]

Yet all this is outdone by the polished arguments trotted out by West German historians. The unusual hardness, so much a feature of this man Heydrich's character, was, if we select an example from the writing of the Berliner Joachim C Fest, less 'based on a penchant for sadistic cruelty, than a case of the contrived lack of conscience of a man who had lost his peace of mind', for, and here lies the solution to the puzzle, 'Reinhard Eugen Tristan Heydrich suffered from a fatal blemish, he was in a condition of mortal sin which rendered him vulnerable: he had Jewish ancestors.'[30] Heydrich's shrill outbursts against the Jews are instantly credited to a motive of 'self-purification', the destructive dynamism which fulfilled him indicates a ceaseless attempt to break free from the 'conflicts between ancestry and ideological demands'.

What was the reason for such abnormally obstinate support for the thesis attributing Jewish origins to a man whom even the British historian Reitlinger felt obliged to describe as 'the most fanatical of all the racialists'?[31] What caused otherwise serious historians to content themselves with spurious information sources produced by journalists with little regard for the truth? How could historians let themselves be carried away by an almost wanton desire to make ingenious psychological assessments without being aware that they were thereby branding Heydrich as a sacrifice to that very theory of which he, as the man behind the 'Final Solution', was the chief proponent, namely the Nazi racial theory? How was it possible for the historian Reitlinger for example, himself a Jew, not to feel embarrassment when he explained Heydrich's hounding of the Jews as a 'pathological Jewish hatred of his own blood',[32] or for the chronicler of the Theresienstadt ghetto, H G Adler, to declare that Heydrich desired to conquer 'his hated Jewish core . . . through the murder of all Jews within his reach'?[33]

Could, then, the ceaseless tension and the unappeasable, even morbid ambition, such patent characteristics of this figure Heydrich, have indicated a 'paranoid fear of discovery',[34] as was maintained as late as 1971 in a diagnosis by one of America's most famous psychiatrists, Friedrich Hacker?

The 'amazing obstinacy'[35] with which so many historians, and to an even greater extent high SD and Gestapo officers and even Counter-Intelligence men clung to the thesis of Jewish origins betrays the impossibility of encompassing, in all its many dimensions, the undoubtedly richly complicated figure presented by Heydrich, one of the 'greatest criminal figures in history',[36] and the impossibility of reaching a true estimation of his historical role. Furthermore it reflects the demand to discover behind the mask of nordic superman, which fulfilled all the clichés of the Nazi ideal in such uncanny perfection, a monstrous flaw, an inner conflict, an explosive secret which would shrink Heydrich to the convenient format of all the front-rank Nazi leaders: to the single-minded pursuits of a Himmler, the blinkered doctrinal outlook of a Rosenberg, to the shallow bragging of a Göring.

There was doubtless a deep rift to be discovered in this personality, a personality which became even more opaque after Heydrich's death. This rift split Heydrich into two pieces, which sat uneasily with each other. Even in photographs of Heydrich remaining with us today there seem to be two different faces staring at us. The slightly slanting eyes, even a little Mongolian in appearance, and long asymmetrical nose comprise two badly fitting halves of a face. The former Swiss League of Nations Commissioner for Danzig, Carl Jacob Burckhardt, remarked after a conversation with Heydrich that his face seemed to be composed of two quite different halves. 'I said to myself that it is as if two people were looking at me at the same time.'[37] Furthermore, the rather fantastic claims made to Burckhardt by SS-men in the SD-chief's staff are given credence: namely that one day, under the influence of drink, Heydrich had staggered into his bathroom and stared at his reflection in the large mirror. Then he is said to have suddenly drawn his pistol and fired two shots at his mirror image with the cry, 'I've got you at last, you ass!' Assuming that this extraordinary event had really taken place, Burckhardt commented, 'this divided personality had shot at his other half, he had tackled the man which half of his face represented, but only in the splintered mirror; yet this did not rid him of it – he was obliged to spend the rest of his life in its company'.[38]

Figuring in the gossip from *Reichsführer* Himmler is the rumour, for whose transmission the masseur Kersten is predominantly responsible, that even Himmler himself had given his opinion on this split personality, more or less on the following lines: Heydrich had been a wretched creature, completely split in two, 'as is often the case with half-castes'.[39] This, then, was the catchword which alone facilitated the rationalization of something incomprehensible. The supposed flaw in his origins, which weighed more heavily on an SS-leader than a mortal sin, that was the solution to the puzzle. And it is almost with pleasure that the banner of this alleged genealogical flaw has been flown to this very day.

Admittedly there had to be some breach in Heydrich's defences and in the words of the *Zeit* historian, Heinz Höhne: 'What was more plausible than to detect this breach in the alleged stain on his origins?'[40] And in truth the key to this question may well lie in Heydrich's connection with the Jewish theme, long before he came face to face with the hatred for the Jews maintained by this most anti-semitic of political parties, and ultimately with the plan known as the Final Solution. In one respect at least the speculators in history and psychology were correct: Heydrich had a complex!

As we have already seen, whilst a schoolboy at the Halle *Reform-Realgymnasium*, Heydrich was often mocked because of his physical weakness and his high voice; his self-confidence was only partially developed. And most important of all: he had to suffer, when only ten or twelve years old, a jeering crowd pointing a finger at him, maliciously yelling 'Isi, Isi' behind his back.[41] 'Isi' stood for Isidor, and Isidor meant Jew. This was the extent to which the gossip about the Jewish or half-Jewish background of Reinhard's father, the conservatoire director Bruno Heydrich, had spread.

Thus was Reinhard set apart while still a vulnerable youth. He was caught in the trap of the Jewish question, a trap from which he was destined never to free himself. Furthermore he felt himself ostracized by a bourgeois, nationalist society which, particularly in that area of central Germany, attached a great deal of importance to the racial question. The man behind the Final Solution was himself in a ghetto – and he suffered unspeakably because of it.

Chapter 7

'O SANCTA SECURITAS'

When the immediate object was achieved, our opponents seemed to most of the comrades-in-arms suddenly to have melted away with the suppression of the rival political organizations. All search for them was in vain, because most of them had come over to us . . . Unable to uncover our opponents in their new situations, they dissipated their energies in senseless, undirected, individual acts of illegality.

Reinhard Heydrich, 1935 (on the NSDAP after 1933)

On 30 January 1933 Adolf Hitler and his National Socialist movement came to power. The following weeks and months brought the leading Party members close association with the Führer and the dignity of office. It was only for Heydrich and his boss Himmler that the 'new era' did not offer a task at national level. Ironically, it was Heydrich, for whom power and success were the most important things in life, who was left empty-handed after the seizure of power. While Göring in his position as Minister-President of Prussia held the reins of executive power in two-thirds of the Reich, while the National Socialists Frick and Goebbels were both promoted to Reich Minister, Heydrich was not even summoned to Berlin where all policies and decisions were made.[1]

Instead of being included in the general share-out of power, the little influence that Heydrich had had in the Security Service during the years of struggle was now forfeit. As early as 27 January he had been instructed by Himmler to give up his duties as SD-Chief of Staff temporarily, so that on the same date he could become SS-General 'with special duties', on the staff of the *Reichsführer,* at that time divided into four 'offices': Operational Staff, Administration, SS, and Race.

Heydrich was not put in charge of any of these offices but, seconded 'for special duties', he was now Himmler's maid-of-all-work.[2] He was to be the brains behind the ensuing phases of the seizure of power, the planner who dealt with the future of the SS in the new National Socialist state, and the sounding board for the *Reichsführer*'s own ideas. Heydrich now had to take part in all important discussions, and all SS offices had to include him in their circulation lists. In spite of this special position in which, though he compared unfavourably with the heads of the various offices, he rose to be Himmler's closest confidant, there was not the slightest sign to indicate his later development as the all-powerful police and Secret Service chief.

Instead of the unrestricted power which he had dreamed of, and which was to be the foundation for the unlimited extension and consolidation of his Secret Service, Himmler caused him one disappointment after another. While SS-leaders in Prussia, which was now Hermann Göring's domain, were already enjoying the fruits of power, Heydrich was still knocking vainly on closed doors. He was sent to Berlin by Himmler to confer with SS-Lieutenant-General Kurt Daluege, who was already installed in the Prussian Ministry of the Interior, and there he was forced to acknowledge that Berlin was entirely unmoved by the entreaties and suggestions of Himmler's Bavarian group. The telephonists in the Prussian Ministry of the Interior had even been instructed not to put the tiresome visitor through. White with rage about this off-hand treatment Heydrich sat in the luxury Savoy Hotel near the Berlin Zoo and tried, with obsequious ingratiation, to counter the rebuff he had suffered. He wrote the following letter to the 'esteemed SS-Lieutenant-General Daluege':

Since Thursday I have been trying without success to penetrate the 'protective screen'. I have telephoned no less than six times. Since I have to travel back today, I beg you to recognize this as a token of my visit and hope that the opportunity for a personal visit will present itself in about ten days. I remain your most humble and obedient servant, R Heydrich. Heil Hitler![3]

Nor was it only the triumphant SS-leader Daluege who scorned a visit from the head of the SS-Security Service. When Heydrich was dispatched on a special mission by Heinrich Himmler to the Foreign Office, always the butt of SS jokes, an official sent him packing like a schoolboy trying to see an X-rated film. This incident also highlights the discrepancy between the treatment Heydrich and his boss Himmler experienced in the first weeks of the Third Reich and the significant future role they were to play.

Again in February, Heydrich was sent to Geneva with SS-leader Friedrich Wilhelm Krüger (who was later to pacify defeated Poland).[4] On 2 February the Second International Disarmament Conference had started up again, after a long intermission. Heydrich and Krüger were attached to the German delegation, led by Ambassador Nadolny, as 'police and security experts'. In a Geneva already impregnated by League of Nations idealism, a mixture of détente diplomacy and the impact of the first reports from German émigrés produced an atmosphere that was hostile in temper to the Third Reich and in which Heydrich was naturally a foreign body. Both the atmosphere in Geneva and the German delegation's reserved and compromising negotiating technique produced an almost physical discomfort in him, to which he reacted with all the irrational hostility of a man who is thrust as an outsider into an alien world. He was aware of the contempt with which Nadolny, the professional diplomat, encountered him day after day. Heydrich, the conqueror who always had to be on the attack, was lost in the politics of 'shabby compromises' which he considered mean, namby-pamby and petit bourgeois. The thought and manners of the SS and the diplomacy of détente were irreconcilably opposed.

Krüger and his inspiration, Heydrich, wanted to show what they thought of the whole affair by making a particularly forthright and arrogant gesture. After all, they had not seized power just to pussyfoot around in Geneva! Heydrich understood the conference languages, English and French, but even so he could not grasp what was being discussed.[5] For him the conference hall was nothing but another of those 'gossip shops' which were currently being done away with in Germany. 'Why don't we have any orators here?' complained Heydrich. 'Of course these fatheads can't urge the German point of view!'[6]

Heydrich had little contact with the other members of the German delegation. Erich Kordt, who was later to be an ambassador, listened to him 'out of politeness' as he explained the principles of the SD's work – with scarcely disguised threats against the 'fashionable' bourgeois, non-National Socialist Foreign Office. 'We are very well aware that the members of the Foreign Office would like to see our government disappear again as quickly as possible. But they are deluding themselves. We have ways and means of staying in power.'[7] Ambassador Nadolny was noticeably more annoyed by the arrogant and hostile behaviour of the police specialists. Even foreign diplomats were said to have turned up their noses at Heydrich's behaviour in the luxury hotel where the delegation was staying, and in bars and restaurants. Kordt was instructed by Nadolny to drop the odd-man-out Heydrich a gentle hint to the effect that he was not in the company of other National Socialists there, but of foreign diplomats who showed only distrust and repudiation for the Third Reich.

But instead of changing tack, Heydrich brought matters to a head. He was annoyed that the manager of the German delegation's hotel was flying the flags of all the countries participating in the conference with the exception of the Third Reich's new German flag, with its swastika. Heydrich complained to the management but got a cool reception and his demand was passed on to Nadolny, the head of the German delegation. Heydrich ('The Swiss are a nation of inn-keepers') wanted to teach a lesson to this Swiss inn-keeper. Through SD-agents in Geneva, he had a huge blood-red swastika flag made and hung it from the rooftop of the hotel one dark night. The next morning the flag of the Third Reich flew for the first time on the shores of Lake Geneva. Now it became very clear exactly who was in charge in the German delegation. Without more ado Ambassador Nadolny sent Heydrich home.

Heydrich may have indulged in escapades like the swastika affair in Geneva less often in the following years, but in all the tactical calculations behind his rise to power in those years there was always a small residue of uncontrolled boyishness, a mixture of spontaneity and recklessness, of sycophancy and arrogance. Of course, any judgment must take account of the incredible youth of the leaders of the SS and SD. Heydrich was twenty-seven when he took over the SD, Himmler was SS-*Reichsführer* at twenty-nine. Heydrich was in charge of Munich's Political Police at twenty-nine, and at thirty-one he was head of the Secret State Police and the National Criminal Police. The same went for all his leading colleagues. Gunter d'Alquen was editor-in-chief of the SS-newspaper *Das Schwarze Korps* (The Black Order) at twenty-five. Dr Werner Best, perhaps the most intelligent of the SD leadership, was its chief administrator at thirty. At twenty-six Dr Franz Six was director of the SD Central Department for the Press and Publications. Walter Schellenberg, who began his career in the SS at twenty-four, became at thirty-one the youngest SS-General.

'At that age one can't expect wisdom,' said Heydrich's widow in extenuation for his escapades. 'In all seriousness, he was still very youthful at that time.'[8] Once, when his wife's silk handkerchief fell in the water on a Sunday outing to the Starnberger See, Heydrich jumped in after it in full uniform. By that time he was already head of the Bavarian Political Police. As his wife commented: 'He enjoyed that sort of thing; he had no false dignity.'

It was only when the National Socialists took over power in Bavaria that Heydrich's and Himmler's situations were actually altered. The background was briefly this. After Prussia had been brought into line with National Socialist centralism on 6 February, and after the smaller states with clear National Socialist majorities in their governments, such as Thuringia, Lippe and Mecklenburg had followed suit, the alarm bells started ringing in the Bavarian state government. In Munich, Minister-President Heinrich Held of the ultramontane Bavarian People's Party (BVP) addressed his 1933 election campaign solely to the struggle against the 'Prussian menace'. No Reich Commissioner from Berlin, that is, no representative of a strong centralizing power, was to be allowed to cross the line of the Main unpunished. On 6 February, President Hindenburg had given a consoling answer to an anxious enquiry from Held on this subject, to the effect that no such Commissioner should cross the Bavarian line. In consequence of this the BVP declared at election meetings that any Reich Commissioner who flouted Hindenburg's promise and entered Bavaria would immediately be arrested.

For their part, the Reich Minister of the Interior, Frick, who was himself from Bavaria, and even Hitler intervened: 'I did not let people get the better of me while in opposition and now, as representative of the power of the state, I still have the energy to protect the unity of the Reich.' And the unity of the Reich remained the camouflaging formula for bringing Germany into line under National Socialism. On 1 March Held himself was summoned to Berlin and given a sharp warning by Hitler about any monarchist, clerical or separatist plans.

In the national elections of 5 March the NSDAP again became the strongest party in the Reich, with 43.9 per cent of the votes. But this 43 per cent did not give it the majority necessary to form the government of Bavaria. However, under the emergency decree of 28 February it was possible for Berlin to encroach on the powers of the authorities of individual states 'for the protection of the people and the state'. This was the background against which the Bavarian *Gauleiter*, Wagner, together with Röhm and Himmler, demanded from Held's government on 9 March that General Franz Ritter von Epp should be appointed State Commissioner for Bavaria. SA and SS formations formed up outside the Bavarian State Chancellery. The Bavarian Ministry head refused to comply, and had investigated, but in vain, the possibility of bringing in units of the Army or State Police. In the meantime Epp's letter of appointment had been ready and waiting in Berlin for a long time, and at about 7 p.m. on 9 March the Bavarian Ambassador in Berlin was informed of it. The Bavarian state government in Munich was also to be informed by telegram of the turn of events and any further resistance on their part to the appointment of Epp broken. If Held had continued on his anti-National Socialist and anti-Reich course, in spite of the telegraphed instructions from Berlin, he would have been acting illegally. Therefore, everything depended on whether he actually received the telegram or let it go missing via a government official sympathetic to the BVP. The 'brown house' was obviously afraid of this. One SS-leader was particularly distrustful. He made his way to the Munich telegraph office at the head of a raiding party. Pistol in hand he himself delivered the Berlin telegram which contained a communication of such importance for the Bavarian National Socialists. That SS-leader was Reinhard Heydrich.[9]

The same night Epp formed a provisional state government in which *Gauleiter* Wagner became Minister of the Interior and *Reichsführer* Himmler became Chief of Police for Munich. Now the twenty-nine-year-old Reinhard Heydrich moved into the Police HQ with him, as director of the Political Department VI. This was the first handhold on the power which Heydrich had desired for so long.[10]

From that point on things developed at a cracking pace. A few days after their conquest of the Political Police in Munich Heydrich and Himmler were also attached to the Police HQ in Nuremberg-Fürth, in Franconia. Finally on 1 April Himmler was made Chief of the Political Police for the whole of Bavaria. And Heydrich started to build up a Bavarian Political Police force at his own pace. On the directions of Wagner, the Minister of the Interior, the Chief of the Political Police took command of 'all political sections of the state police authorities and police offices, all political police sections in local government, district offices and municipalities and all formations of the political auxiliary police for the executive; the concentration camps, whether already in existence or still to be established.'[11]

This was the start of the secret executive triangle of the SS or SD, the Political Police and the concentration camps, which formed the force-field that enabled Himmler and Heydrich to create what was later called the SS-state. The instrument was provided and the musician Heydrich knew how to play on it.[12] He took well-trained people from every office of the Munich police administration for the newly formed authority: officials from the criminal service and government officials and employees from professionally appropriate police authorities. In addition there were one or two long-serving SS-leaders, making a total of at least 150 employees. Within a few weeks the work-force was approximately doubled.

First of all Heydrich instituted a purge of the existing manpower. Politically objectionable and professionally incompetent officials were removed. The pragmatic way he went about this, which mirrors exactly his technocratic character, is best illustrated by the cases of two officials who had up until then worked in the Political Department of the Munich police, Police Inspectors Heinrich Müller and Franz Joseph Huber. Both belonged by origin and political conviction to the extremely anti-National Socialist Bavarian People's Party, which was regarded with equal hate by the NSDAP.[13]

After the war Huber himself testified that in March 1933 he was sacked, but that a few days after receiving his notice he was summoned to Police HQ in Ettstrasse by Heydrich. His heart was pounding when he arrived there. Heydrich asked the dismissed official which Huber he was, and consulted a list of names, beside several of which there was a small cross. After a short discussion he was sent back to his post. From that time on Huber gathered information against NSDAP heretics like Strasser zealously and expertly. He subsequently became Austrian section head. And in the later Berlin Gestapo Franz Joseph Huber even rose to the head of the office for right-wing opposition, reaction, and the Churches. Until that notable discussion with Heydrich in March 1933 he had hunted down the Bavarian NSDAP, the SA and the SS. Now he was pursuing their opponents with, if possible, still greater zeal.

Heinrich Müller, who was later known as 'Gestapo-Müller', had even said, when an SS-troop, with Heydrich at their head, had occupied the Police HQ during the sudden seizure of power in Bavaria by Wagner, Himmler and Röhm: 'Just let them come, we'll take care of them.' And together with Huber he had even tried to put up real resistance. But at least

Müller had not been directly involved in combating the NSDAP before 1933. His specialist field had been the communist movement and in particular its underground, espionage and terror apparatus. Huber was well qualified by his invaluable knowledge to fulfil the same function under Heydrich, for one of the main tasks of the newly created Bavarian Political Police was precisely the complete destruction of the communist apparatus.

Real professionals, technocrats, were prized by Heydrich. In this context their political past was relatively insignificant as long as they did not constitute security risks, and as long as the results of their work at any given time provided credible proof of their loyalty to the new rulers.

But it was just this unideological attitude of Heydrich's which was a continuing and growing source of difficulties with the Party. For years the Munich NSDAP stuck to their spiteful judgment of Huber and Müller. A personal assessment stated that Huber had been 'a malicious opponent of the movement' and that, as a member of the Political Department of the Munich police, he had lost no opportunity of 'holding forth about the movement in a cynical and sarcastic manner to National Socialists who had been arrested or brought before him'. The usual consequence of such behaviour, and of his 'ultramontane convictions', would without doubt have been his final dismissal from government service.

It was indeed admitted that Müller had combated the left-wing movement 'extremely vigorously, even partially disregarding legal rules and regulations'. His political convictions, however, had moved between the German Nationalist and the Bavarian People's Party, and he had never sympathized with the National Socialists at all. Moreover he had married the daughter of the publisher and editor of the official BVP paper *Würmtalbote* (The Wurmtal Messenger).

It was not the only conflict that Heydrich had to endure with a Party which was in his opinion politically shortsighted and small-minded. Within the closed circle of the SS Heydrich had even suggested that, now they had seized power, the Party, and with it the SA, should be dissolved. Both of them had fulfilled their tasks with the seizure of power. 'Now,' so Heydrich thought, 'the main thing was to consolidate their power and not to keep eternally pressing forward.' Only hours before his death, after the assassination attempt in Prague, when he was in a state between dreaming and waking 'where he spoke what he otherwise only thought', he kept on saying, according to his widow's statements, 'The stupid SA, the stupid SA'. His main concern in those months in 1933, the period of consolidation of power, had been 'What should we do with the SS to prevent it becoming another SA?' He wanted to map out for the SS a task for the future, and he saw that only in its function of protecting the new state, as a police force.[14]

What was true of the SA was also true of the Party. What he saw of it in Munich he thought to be a 'combination of mediocrity and pretensions to be our sole representative' and therefore also potentially explosive for internal politics. Nor could Heydrich understand why Hitler 'from a sort of Nibelungen-like loyalty kept on numerous good-for-nothings in spite of experiences of the worst kind, and many complaints'.

These views did not remain private: they soon contributed to the rejection of the young upstart, 'vertical take-off' Heydrich, by the long-serving Party functionaries. *Gauleiter* Wagner, who had been a co-conspirator with Himmler and Heydrich against the provincial government as recently as the March days, was soon dismissively calling the Chief of the Political Police 'the beer-ometer of the German Reich'. All he did was to reproach them about their way of life, which he saw as un-National Socialist, and about their drinking too much beer. Even today his widow recalls: 'My husband could get really furious when he went to one of the Munich beer halls with me or a guest, and regularly saw *Gauleiter* Wagner sitting there holding conceited and ostentatious court.' Then Heydrich would stand up, give the *Gauleiter* a critical, contemptuous look and move to another beer hall.[15]

Relations between Police HQ and the 'brown house' now became formal, but were naturally maintained. For in order to carry out his duties in the Bavarian Political Police Heydrich was directed, at least for the time being, to work together with the Minister of the Interior, *Gauleiter* Wagner, whom he secretly despised so much. For the real or potential opposition to National Socialist power in Bavaria was now instantly broken by Heydrich. The arrest of thousands of opponents from lists compiled by the SD, among others, began on the very night of the National Socialist takeover, 9 March. The prisons were soon found to be inadequate and it was decided to set up a concentration camp for the Bavarian prisoners. The legend that Heydrich was the creator of such concentration camps for the use of the police has been repudiated by the Israeli historian Aronson as 'completely without foundation'.[16] It first saw the light of day in Zurich, in 1945, in Heinrich Orb's memoirs, and since then has been frequently repeated, for instance in Eugen Kogon's *The SS-state*.[17] In reality the foundation of the camp at Dachau can be traced to a suggestion from the Minister of the Interior, Wagner, to the Minister of Justice, Frank ('Poland Frank'). Wagner recommended that 'the same methods be used which were formerly used against the victims in the mass arrests of the National Socialists. As is well known they were confined within empty walls and nobody cared if they were exposed to the inclemency of the weather or not.'[18]

Although Heydrich was neither the founder nor, so to speak, the 'landlord' of Dachau concentration camp, or 'KL' as it was still called at that time, he still made immediate and systematic use of its existence. From 1 April the camp came under the command of Himmler, who appointed as successive commandants SS-leaders Wäckerle and Eicke. It was only with difficulty that Heydrich got on with the two of them, both being superior to him in rank. But he knew that power struggles would creep in because a Political Department had been set up in the camp which was controlled by the Bavarian Political Police (BayPoPo) and therefore by him. As the head of this authority it was also Heydrich who had to determine who went to Dachau and who left again. He had no influence, however, on what happened to the prisoner while he was inside the camp.

Opponent after opponent was dealt with, almost exactly according to the outline plans he had made long before 1933. First came the communists. After they had been destroyed Heydrich turned his attention to the apparatus of Socialist Party officials and to the Marxist trades unions. Finally, at the end of June, he began an operation against 'political Catholicism', which in Bavaria meant the BVP. All its officials were first of all taken into 'protective custody' in Dachau. Statistics given by Heydrich to the Minister of the Interior on the 'development of the numbers in protective custody' reveal Heydrich's use of the protective custody method. From 1 to 31 July 1933, that is during the BVP operation, 2097 persons were taken into protective custody. During the same period, however, 1820 persons were set free. In December of the same year, the number of those released was far greater than the number of those taken into custody, the figure being 1008 to 600. Finally Heydrich made it known that for the whole of 1933 a total of 16,409 protective custody orders were made and 12,554 detainees were set free again.[19]

It is clear from the large number of releases and the short terms of custody of most of those detained that Heydrich saw the object of protective custody as a means of dissuading from action those elements which were regarded as 'hostile to the state' and as an instrument to threaten and terrorize particularly obstinate opposition party functionaries. A closer analysis of the range of people affected led Aronson in his doctoral thesis to the conclusion that the operation was organized:

> . . . so that in every town and village some people were affected, who disappeared, and then returned after a short time depressed and intimidated. This produced an atmosphere of terror which paralysed the resistance of possible opponents. People feared what they heard of the reality of the terror, and there arose a legend of terror which sometimes exceeded the reality.[20]

This was the formula which Heydrich confidently and repeatedly applied: later, when he was responsible for security policy for the whole of the Reich; in his later policy towards the Jews when he wanted to bring about their wholesale emigration from Germany; and after 1941 in his pacification measures as Protector of Bohemia and Moravia.

But at first it was only in Bavaria that the formula was put into effect. After the political parties it was the turn of those forces who, according to Heydrich, had been active 'behind the scenes': the troublesome portion of the clergy, mostly the lower clergy, whom Heydrich understood how to separate from the Church bureaucracy very skilfully.[21] And after the clergy the Jews. In the middle of July Heydrich put a prohibition on the activities of all Jewish organizations whose aims were not 'purely religious' or 'purely charitable'. The object was obviously the depoliticization of the Jews, their removal from society and their latent intimidation. At that time Jews were not imprisoned in Dachau by virtue of their being Jews but because of their having been politically active opponents of National Socialism, or communists, or journalists hostile to NS or 'reactionaries'.[22]

Reactionaries constituted a further group in Heydrich's catalogue of opponents. Louis Strassner, for example, a shoe manufacturer from Eggenfelden in Bavaria, was taken into protective custody on 10 February 1934 because he would not acquiesce in the new social conditions created by the NSDAP. Heydrich himself commented on this case: 'There is a large degree of animosity amongst the workers in the firm of Louis Strassner because the workers . . . are paid below the standard rates. Although the wage agreement which was in force at the time was brought to Strassner's attention he ignored it.' Strassner had apparently insisted 'that he was master of his own factory'. According to Heydrich, Strassner, in addition, was known as 'an exploiter of the workers', and it could be disputed whether he had 'any social understanding'.[23] The zeal for arresting and detaining people, demonstrated by the Bavarian Political Police under the leadership of Heydrich, who was at last able to give full rein to his innate hunting instinct, soon led to more political prisoners being taken into custody in Bavaria than in all other states of the whole Reich, including Prussia. Even Reich Minister of the Interior Frick, a convinced National Socialist, was uncomfortable about the high proportion of prisoners in Bavaria and complained about it to Himmler, though without success.[24] Even he had not yet grasped the fact that the Heydrich–Himmler team intended to use their Bavarian empire as a huge training ground on which to try out their conception of a Reich police force controlled by the SS. Their intention was also to test the capacity and suitability of the triangular relationship of SS–Police–concentration camps for the struggle against both the enemies of the state and at the same time against opponents of the SS in the administration and the judiciary, the party and the SA, who were otherwise loyal to the system. A political system like that of National Socialism which made such total claims on the unity of the nation and which was preparing itself to overcome particularism and federalism for the first time in modern German history, even against the opposition of those hostile to the Reich, needed as one of its strongest bonds a unified police force covering the whole new Reich. By bringing this into existence its creators were bound to secure a special place for themselves in the permanent power struggle which characterized the Führer state. Seen in the long term, the Reich Police was bound by the internal laws of Adolf Hitler's Reich to move more and more into the centre of power and to draw in Heydrich and Himmler and their SS as well.

The question of who exactly prompted the thought in whom that the SS, and the Reich Police which was about to be created, should be merged in one state protection agency, of whether it was the fussy but cunning Himmler who set his 'dogsbody', ever thirsting for action, on the one-way street to power, or whether it was the latter who did the same for his often hesitant *Reichsführer*, can only be guessed at. But probability points to Heydrich.

SD-Major Höttl testifies that the idea of elevating the SS to be the Third Reich's police power had been born in Heydrich's head.[25] The author's impression of the characters of the two 'inseparables' points to the young 'rocket' Heydrich as the originator of the conception of a Reich Police controlled by the SS. It is more likely to have been Heydrich, with his insatiable restlessness and his all-devouring intellect, who hit upon such a modern idea as that of a unified police force, than Himmler, who was admittedly intelligent but also incredibly impractical. Even Heydrich's widow attests: 'My husband forced the idea of the Reich Police on Himmler. He was always shoving Himmler along in front of himself. There was often no other way. For Himmler had a reputation with the old Party members and even with Hitler.'[26] Heydrich himself was 'of no account in the Party', he was 'a young puppy'. 'For this reason he had to carry Himmler in front of himself like a shield. It didn't matter whether he could stand him or not, or whether he thought him intelligent or not.' As long as he lived Heydrich remembered one anecdote about Himmler which he himself had experienced. The *Reichsführer* announced that he was going to visit Heydrich's house in Fehmarn. Since his pedantic passion for gardening was well known, Heydrich's wife spent days weeding the garden. By the time he arrived they were convinced that the garden was completely free of weeds. But Himmler managed to find one and pointed it out, saying: 'That will have to come out!' Heydrich commented: 'Himmler would have done much better to have been a professor. But what would happen if we were to instal German professors as our leaders?'[27]

It was in the nature of things that there should be plenty of cause for clashes between them, for differing conceptions of direction and pace. But Heydrich apparently avoided these clashes with the utmost self-control. According to his widow, 'He knew that without Himmler he would be completely written off as far as the circle of Munich putsch veterans was concerned.' But Himmler must have quite often lost his temper, despite Heydrich's acting the humble yes-man all the time. SS-officers testify that if the two of them were alone in an office there were quite often 'very fierce rows'.[28]

Lina Heydrich also comments: 'Whenever Himmler was dissatisfied with one of my husband's measures, he would be summoned. But each time, my husband's arguments would demolish him and drive him into a corner until he could not choose but give in.' Sometimes Himmler would explode with curses: 'You and your damned logic!'[29] Often the *Reichsführer* even had to shelter behind apparent orders from the Führer in order to be able to reverse decisions which he had sanctioned in the course of such conversations, influenced by the force of Heydrich's arguments.[30]

81

But, in practice, these budding differences of opinion had no significance. On the contrary, the diverse talents and characteristics of Himmler and Heydrich seemed to complement each other excellently in the struggle for power. And speed was of the essence in this race. For success on the Bavarian training ground counted little against developments in police affairs outside the Bavarian frontiers. In Minister-President Hermann Göring's Prussia, the biggest state in the Reich, covering almost two-thirds of the total area, the Prussian Premier had already made himself boss of the Political Police. In the high-living Dr Rudolf Diels, who was not a National Socialist, Göring had found a man who had already been active as a Principal for the Political Police of the Prussian Ministry of the Interior. He had therefore managed to organize very quickly a highly effective Political Police force in Prussia, which he had purged of opponents of the regime and led into battle on behalf of his boss against the unpopular rivals from the isolated Bavaria.

Diels transferred 250 officials from the police authority of Weimar-Prussia (as the Prussia of the Weimar Republic was called) to his office, which was given independent powers exempt from the old Prussian police authority laws. These had stated, among other things, that the police could only take measures which fell 'within the framework of existing laws'.[31] Diels' police apparatus also separated itself physically from the residual police force. A former art school at No. 8 Prinz-Albrecht-Strasse in Berlin was taken over. At the end of April Göring legitimized Diels' troop by a law making it a special state authority, answerable only to Göring himself. It was christened with the name 'Secret State Police HQ' (Gestapa).

Heydrich and Himmler were given numerous examples of how stubbornly their adversary Göring knew how to protect his domain, one such being their own repeated lack of success. They dared not hope for an eventual victory over the Gestapa from the tiny bridgeheads which remained to them. One of the few officials in Diels' empire who were close to Himmler and Heydrich was Police Captain Arthur Nebe, the head of the 'Executive'. Tongue-in-cheek, Göring and Diels made a harmless concession: SD-Captain Heinz Jost was permitted to be liaison leader between the Supreme Command of the SS (RFSS) and the Gestapa. Göring exulted: 'Himmler and Heydrich will never get to Berlin.'[32] There was no love lost on the other side either. Heydrich grumbled about Göring's way of life: 'We always reproached the Weimar bigwigs, and with reason, that they made their profits from the people's misery. And now it's Göring!' But none of this was any use: Heydrich could not get anywhere near the 'Reichspompführer'.[33]

Unexpected aid came at the end of 1933 from the Reich Ministry of the Interior. The Minister of the Interior, Frick, wanted to flatten the last obstructive remains of independence amongst the German states and set up an administration for the whole Reich which was competent to give directions to the states. The cardinal point of the plan was naturally the ticklish question of the police. Whereas up until that time the sixteen states of the Reich had each controlled its own police force, these were now, for both practical and political reasons, to be subordinated to the Reich. But the large territory administered by Göring and his Prussian police and Gestapa stood in the way of Frick's plan. Where Frick demanded control over all German police authorities it was denied to him on his own doorstep in Berlin, and in a fairly drastic way too.

In November 1933 Göring promulgated a law that completely removed the Gestapa from the control of the Ministry of the Interior. Frick, who did not have his own power-base within the Party, had no chance of prevailing against Göring. According to Heinz Höhne, the chronicler of the SS, his gaze then turned 'to the man who had declared that he would drive the Gaufürsten [the big "Party Barons" of the regions] from the levers of power in the police. Heinrich Himmler – he promised salvation.'[34] He and his assistant Heydrich, motor and ignition combined, were also seeking to create a single police force for the whole Reich. And they had already proved in Bavaria how skilfully they could deal with the administration and state authorities. Frick decided to hold the stirrup for the combination of Heydrich and Himmler. With the additional firepower from Frick's Ministry, the political police of one state after another were taken over. On 27 October the press announced Himmler's appointment as Chief of the Political Police in Lübeck and Mecklenburg–Schwerin. Hamburg followed in November, Baden and Württemberg, Anhalt, Bremen, Thuringia and Hesse in December, and finally Brunswick, Oldenburg and Saxony in January. With the exception of Prussia, Himmler and Heydrich had control of all the Political Police forces of the German Reich. Eventually, with the spectre of an approaching conflict with the restive SA, hungry for revolution, on the horizon, Göring realized that even he could not force the issue about the sovereignty of the Gaufürsten. Negotiations soon followed with Frick's Ministry and with the SS-Reichsführer.

The extent to which the mysterious story of the frustration by Heydrich's SD of an assassination attempt might have encouraged Göring to negotiate cannot be determined. Apparently at the end of 1933 one of Heydrich's SD-agents is supposed to have picked up the trail of a Trotskyist conspiracy in Strasbourg, which was planning an attempt on Göring's life. The agent must have told Heydrich personally, who immediately grasped the opportunity that it offered. If he could inform Göring of the discovery by the SD of an assassination plot, that would bring into question the quality of Göring's own Gestapa, and of its leader Diels. In fact a Trotskyist circle was finally discovered in Berlin by the SD, which put Göring under an obligation of deep gratitude to Heydrich.[35]

In any case Göring eventually gave in to pressure from the alliance between Himmler, Heydrich and Frick and was prepared to compromise about the Political Police. His confidant Diels was removed to a senior government post in the Rhineland and simultaneously protected from Heydrich's immediate revenge. Himmler was appointed Inspector of the Secret State Police. But it was Heydrich who on 22 April 1934 took over the direction of the Gestapa.[36] Now the Political Police force of the whole of Germany was at his disposal. The opportunities this position offered him were inexhaustible. And Heydrich knew how to exploit them.

He had hardly gained a foothold in Berlin before he took steps to transform the organization. This was despite all opposition from the government bureaucracy, which was hostile or at least cool towards the SS, despite budding attempts at legalization from Frick's Ministry of the Interior, and despite braking manoeuvres by Göring, who had not conceived the surrender of the Gestapa to Heydrich as being quite so total as Heydrich wanted. He appointed to the most important executive positions in his new 'Gestapo' his own officials from Bavaria, who had proved their loyalty to him personally. In the meantime Flesch, a former professional with the BayPoPo, and colleague of Müller's, had also made the transition from Saul to Paul, just as Müller and Huber had done, and all three, having joined the SS and SD and been promoted to SS-Second Lieutenant, now moved to Berlin.

In October 1934 a plan of the division of duties in the Gestapo laid down the distribution of functions. All existing Departments became Divisions, Offices became Departments, and so on. Heydrich himself ensured by this plan that his own importance was enhanced. At the same time the chain of command was put on a military footing. A position previously described as 'personal adviser' in Diels' time, was now called 'Adjutancy'. Heydrich filled this position with a man who was loyal to him personally, an assistant from the SD who had quickly been promoted to SS-Lieutenant-Colonel.[37]

Three posts were now established.[38] Division 1 (Administration, Organization, Law) was soon taken over by SD-leader Dr Werner Best, a lawyer who had already proved his worth in Bavaria and Württemberg. Best, one of the most intelligent and cultured of all the intellectuals in the SD, was also a clever administrative lawyer and a convinced orthodox National Socialist. He cleared away the administrative and legal obstacles which might have hindered the workings of Heydrich's security apparatus. The core of the Gestapo, however, lay in Division II. Heydrich at first retained its effective direction for himself. For this reason he was safely able to entrust its most important sub-department (II 1) to Flesch and Müller, whom he could trust to work closely together.

In sub-department II 1 A Müller was able to pursue his old passion without the annoying restrictions that had always hindered the Weimar police. Gestapo-Müller, as he was soon called, was to combat what were seen as the leading and most dangerous opposition groups to the Third Reich, the left-wing radicals, who included all shades of communists and Marxists and all their subordinate and related organizations. In another section of this sub-department II 1 A, Section C, Franz Josef Huber was demonstrating how justified Heydrich had been a year earlier in not committing him to Dachau but allowing him instead to prove his trust-worthiness. He was now in charge of prosecuting reactionaries, the conservative opposition, and was the expert on Austria. In Section H another official from Heydrich's Bavarian squad was keeping an eye on the right wing. Josef Meisinger, an old National Socialist, was watching his own Party and its organizations. In Section B, Flesch was investigating opponents of the system in the denominational associations and among the emigrants, and was keeping an eye on Jews and Freemasons. It was only in the service sections, such as those dealing with filing, archives and identification, that former appointees of Diels were allowed to remain.

But in the third Division, which dealt with counter-espionage, Heydrich saw to it that everything remained firmly under his own control. Dr Gunther Patschowsky, a trustworthy SD colleague from the pre-1933 days, whom Heydrich had already placed opportunely in Diels' Intelligence Service, was appointed to this department.

With this apparatus filled with new experts who were either loyal to him personally or owed him a debt of gratitude, Heydrich started the business of realizing his plan, first conceived in 1931, of an all-out struggle against the forces hostile to the state and its ideology. The foundation stone for this altar to divine security was laid.

Colleagues and observers noted with astonishment how well this amateur got on in his new profession: although he was head of a national office, he had never himself been in state employ, never had any training in administration or police work, and was younger than the average age of his officials. After the war Werner Best recalled his astonishment 'that Heydrich's subordinates feared him, just as much as they respected and to some degree admired him'.[39]

This fascination also sprang from the fact that Heydrich got right 'into the thick' of any task he turned his hand to. The dexterity of his enquiring mind, together with an acute instinct for the work, made it possible for him rapidly to separate the essential from the unimportant in any task that confronted him. 'He took no time at all to get into his stride, no matter what he was doing.'[40] Many office heads, who had prepared themselves excellently for making reports to 'C' (as Heydrich was soon known in the Gestapo as well) 'because they knew how hard and wounding he could be if he noticed faulty workmanship',[41] were confounded by this faculty. An adviser would often be interrupted after only a few minutes, having hardly begun his report, with: 'That's quite clear, I can see the problem. So you would like to suggest . . .' And Heydrich would frequently hit on what his official was about to suggest to him as the result of long deliberations on the subject.

His phenomenal memory proved useful to him here. He knew every telephone number by heart. He amazed his experts by remembering events which had occurred months before and being able to give file numbers off the cuff which even the experts involved had to look up.

His own restless nature served to spur on his officials too, to make the fight against all opposition ever keener. And the list of the opposition grew longer and longer. Where communists and Marxists had been the prime targets for Diels' Gestapa, Heydrich now opened a whole new catalogue. Alfred Schweder, one of Heydrich's colleagues, in a commentary on the Political Police in 1937, defined an 'enemy of the state' as 'anyone today who consciously works against the people, the Party and the state, their ideological foundations and their political actions'.[42] A more precise definition was given in an internal document: 'in particular we mean communism, Marxism, Jewry, the politically active Churches, Free-masonry, political malcontents (grumblers), the nationalist opposition, reactionaries, the Black Front (Strasser, Prag), economic saboteurs, habitual criminals, also abortionists and homosexuals (who from the point of view of population policy are prejudicial to the strength of the people and defence, with homosexuals there is also a danger of espionage), traitors to the country and the state.'[43]

A newly developed system of registration and investigation afforded the Prinz-Albrecht-Strasse a permanent, up-to-date and flawless coverage of these opposition groups. Once they had been 'found', they were to be retraceable at any time.

This, for Heydrich, was the *raison d'être* of the Political Police. He reproached the party, the SA and even the 'regular' SS with narrow-mindedness as far as the political Security Services were concerned.

When the immediate object was achieved, our opponents seemed to most of the comrades-in-arms suddenly to have melted away with the suppression of the rival political organizations. All search for them was in vain, because most of them had come over to us. The situation arose in which many people unfortunately still find themselves today. Unable to uncover our opponents in their new situations, they dissipated their energies in senseless, undirected, individual acts of illegality . . . Unfortunately they only fight what they can actually see, that is, the opposition parties. They have not realized that the parties, in keeping with the circumstances, are just the most acceptable outward manifestations of spiritual forces which still intend to fight the Germany embodied by the Führer and the NSDAP, which still intend to destroy Germany with all its great strength of blood, spirit and territory.[44]

Heydrich could not hope to fulfil his security objectives with the executive and surveillance apparatus of the Gestapo alone. Therefore an organization was developed along another channel, parallel to that of the spy organization of Müller and Flesch – the SD, which had been somewhat neglected in the confusion accompanying the seizure of power, and whose leadership Heydrich had temporarily given up. As early as the summer of 1933, Heydrich had once more elevated himself, in addition to being Chief of the Bavarian Political Police, to the direct leadership of his own creation, the SD, and set himself to build up an organization kept hermetically sealed from all public inspection. Neither the Ministry of the Interior with its interfering reminders of legal limitations on Heydrich's authority, nor the Ministry of Justice could impose on him here.

It was only on 9 November 1933 that the SD officially became a proper SS-Branch, the fifth in fact.[45] But in practice a register of addresses of 30 May already shows Heydrich, who in the meantime had been promoted to SS-Major-General, to be the head of his own 'Security Branch' with its offices in the Mittelsbacherpalais in Briennerstrasse in Munich.[46] The lawyer mentioned above, Dr Werner Best (administration and law); retired Majors Julius Plaichinger (economics); Walter Ilges (Jews and Free-masons); and Wilhelm Patin (Catholicism) made up the small SD apparatus in the first year of power, combined with the small old cadre of the SD (left over from the days when Heydrich himself was still being chased by the Weimar Political Police), and also including Leffler, and Oberg, the son of a Hamburg merchant.

The striking organizational parallels with Diels' Gestapa in Berlin were later on to lead to many difficulties over spheres of authority between the SD and the Gestapo which could only be removed in 1939 with the foundation of a Reich Central Security Department (RSHA). The second characteristic of that phase can be best illustrated by the bizarre figure of Dr Wilhelm Patin. Heydrich gave him the job of investigating and analysing the tendencies of political Catholicism. Patin was of 'a very good family', had studied theology and been ordained as a priest. After inter-vening periods as a divinity teacher and a canon in a Bavarian court seminary Patin added an LL.D to his D.D. He had published a book about Liceta, the Bishop of Reversiana, and a study of the Bavarian lay and ecclesiastical decorations – and was incidentally cousin to Himmler. Later this doctor twice over and ordained priest became Adviser on Catholics in the RSHA. The attraction of the Black Order for brilliant academic figures and prominent and recognized experts in their fields who were unable to resist the temptations of Heydrich's SD is perhaps most remarkable in Dr Patin.[47]

In November 1933 another lawyer, Dr Hermann Behrends from Oldenburg, entered the SD. According to Aronson, the historian of the SD, Heydrich at this time took particular pains to win over lawyers. 'He wanted the new SD-leaders, who were to have an academic training, to have the intellectual equipment of highly qualified civil servants, so that they could help him to run and to modify the machinery he had taken over from the Weimar Republic.'[48] The shining example of the British Secret Service certainly played a part here too.

But other academics also felt attracted by the intellectuality and the fascinating atmosphere of clandestine societies and the Secret Service. They naturally wanted to work for the new Third Reich in important posts, but not in the plodding SA or the Party jungle. One example of this is the historian and philologist Dr Wilhelm Spengler, who was to write one of the best appreciations of Heydrich and the SD in 1943. Spengler had graduated *'summa cum laude'* in 1931 and had passed the state examination for the Advanced Teaching Diploma (first class) in 1932. Although he was not a Party member Spengler had entered the SD in November 1933 and built up a literary office based in Leipzig, where he examined all new publications in the Reich for their relevance to the SD's investigation of hostile elements.[49]

In a short time Heydrich's SD became 'the reservoir for the most intelligent men that National Socialism was ever able to attract'.[50] There was Reinhard Höhn, Professor of Constitutional Law in Berlin who, at only thirty-two, was the head of the central department for *'Lebensgebiete'* (spheres of life) of the Inland-SD. He won over Otto Ohlendorf, a lawyer and political economist, from the Institute for World Economic Affairs in Kiel and eventually Professor Franz Six. After graduating *magna cum laude* in political science, history, political economy and journalism, the latter was teaching at the University of Berlin as Professor of Foreign Studies. In the SD he specialized in investigating Freemasonry and Jewish Politics under Höhn. One of his pupils was Eichmann, who had stumbled into the SD by mistake.

The baby of the squad of intellectuals that gathered round Heydrich was Walter Schellenberg, jurist and political scientist, who was only twenty-four years old. The SD, as Heydrich had conceived it as early as 1931, seemed in fact about to rise to be the Intelligence Service of the Reich in the truest sense of the word.

This development in intellect and personnel which gave the SD a charmed life, largely undisturbed by attempts at control by government agencies, also had organizational parallels. By order of the Führer's deputy Rudolf Hess, the SD finally obtained, in June 1934, the desired exclusive role of the Party's only Intelligence Service. The core of the 'internal Intelligence Operation' of Alfred Rosenberg's Foreign Office, which had been forlornly working in parallel with the SD, was to be merged with the SD within a month. There were to be no more instances of private Secret Services, belonging, for instance, to the SA, to any *Gauleiter*, or to the German Labour Front.[51]

Also in 1934, round about November and December, the SD finally moved to the capital from provincial Bavaria, which was somewhat remote from the centre of power. It moved into a new residence at 102 Wilhelm-strasse in Berlin. Heydrich's Secret Service began to consolidate. What it still lacked as much as ever, as Heydrich had already complained in the days before the seizure of power, was an executive arm. But now his new Gestapo, which was connected to the SD through the overlap in personnel, stood ready to fill that gap. Heydrich could play this new piano excellently. If the Gestapo represented the white keys, the SD was the black ones. All in all, any piece could be played on this keyboard.

Yet Heydrich was not satisfied. The hated officials of the Ministry of the Interior were still able to put enough pressure on the pedals to put a damper on Heydrich's plans for his twin offices, which seemed either too severe or too ambitious. Moreover, Reich Minister of the Interior Frick tried at this point to get rid of Himmler and Heydrich, whom he had earlier employed to reinforce his struggle against Göring's sovereignty, but he was now confronted by the all-too-powerful coalition of Göring, Himmler and Heydrich. They all had the same basic goal, however. Frick, just like Heydrich and Himmler, wanted to see the establishment of a united German police force covering the whole Reich, at all levels. But while Frick, as a civil servant, could only imagine such a police force in the hands of the Ministry of the Interior, Heydrich and Himmler were aiming to merge the new force with the SS.

Again it was Heydrich who shoved his *Reichsführer* in front of him in the battle that was now under way. In May 1936 the SD boss was conducting verbal preliminary negotiations with officials from the Ministry of the Interior, the results of which were included in an outline for a Führer decree on 'The Unification of Police Power in the Reich'.[52] *Reichsführer* Himmler was to be promoted to 'Inspector of the German Police' but as such to be subordinate to the Reich Minister of the Interior. Naturally that was of no use to Heydrich and Himmler. Therefore on 9 June 1936 Heydrich presented counter-proposals in which he declared that the Führer wanted Himmler's official title to be 'SS-*Reichsführer* and Chief of the German Police'. Accordingly Heydrich's new draft contained the following proposals, which defined the scope of this appointment:

1. In order to bring together the police functions of the Reich in one hand, a Chief of the German Police will be appointed who will be charged with handling all police affairs which come under the jurisdiction of the Reich Minister of the Interior.
2. SS-*Reichsführer* Heinrich Himmler will be appointed Chief of the German Police. He is answerable personally to the Reich Minister of the Interior and to the Prussian Minister of the Interior.
3. The Chief of the German Police has the rank of a Reich Minister and takes part in meetings of the Reich cabinet.

But Frick did not admit defeat so easily. That same day he intervened with Hitler. But he lost on points. Only with regard to according Himmler cabinet rank did he have any success. Himmler was only to be called in as a State Secretary. Frick still attempted quietly to remove the title 'SS-*Reichsführer*' from the new designation. But Heydrich, who still had good reason to make himself useful to his *Reichsführer,* forced it to be reinstated in a sharp and uncompromising debate.[53] But even the nominal subordination to the Reich Minister of the Interior very soon became a farce. It was established that the *Reichsführer* was the permanent representative of the Minister even when the latter was actually present and that in every case his decisions were ministerial decisions. The historian Buchheim commented in a post-war judgment[54]: 'The position of the police chief was interpreted not so much in the sense that it accorded the Minister rights over the disposition of the police, but rather in the sense that the rights of the Minister passed to the police chief.'

On 17 June 1936 the following position had been reached. All the advantages Heydrich had managed to negotiate were laid down in the 'Decree of the Führer and Reich Chancellor on the appointment of a Chief of the German Police'. Not only had the advantage of centralization on a nationwide scale been achieved, but also the actual and personal union of the Party function of SS-*Reichsführer* with the governmental office of Chief of the German Police. This now became law.[55] The struggle for control of this newly created and legalized Reich Police of the SS immediately sprang up around and under Himmler. Heydrich's SS comrade Kurt Daluege also fought for the decisive share in the Black Order's spoils.

Daluege, who was already an SS-General and therefore two ranks above Heydrich, had until then commanded the Prussian Police, with the exception of the Gestapa. But a decision of the newly appointed Chief of the German Police soon made clear which individual branches of the police were to belong to which department. The German Police was split into two main departments, two great columns which were supposed to provide the security support for the National Socialist Reich. These were on the one hand the Order Police (regular police) and on the other the Security Police.

Heydrich reaped a record harvest. The *Reichsführer*'s gratitude for his stubborn and skilful conduct of the proceedings against Frick certainly played a part. As head of the Central Security Department of the SS (Sipo) Heydrich got the lion's share. In addition to the control of the Secret State Police for the whole German Reich he was given control of the Reich Criminal Police, the Frontier Police and the Counter-Espionage Police. Daluege had to settle for what was left. To his Central Office of the Order Police was added the Protection Police (the ordinary civil policeman), Traffic Police and finally the Police Administration. Heydrich moved up several ranks.[56]

Clearly, it could be said that the German Police was divided between a security function and a combat function, as Best wrote in an essay in the journal *Deutsches Recht* (German Law) in 1936: 'The police function has a splinter combat function . . . that is of disarming the internal political and criminal enemy.'[57]

Typically, the combat function was taken over by Heydrich. Never before in German history had so much power been concentrated in the hands of one person as was concentrated in Heydrich's hands in 1936 with the unification of the 'ordinary' and 'political' secret police. He now possessed an apparatus which even corresponded in its range and pretensions to the opposition's conception of the supreme policeman. The new Security Police became in his hands the instrument for combating both criminal and political 'enemies of the people and the state'.

There arose a completely new conception of the police. The thirties saw a wide-ranging discussion which was neither started by Heydrich nor centred on him in the course of which there developed an image of the police which diverged more and more from that of the protective force of the 'liberal welfare state'.[58] Heydrich and his police lawyer and theorist Werner Best were always discussing the same point with lawyers and government officials, with specialists in public law, and with the professionals from the public prosecutor's office. Best affirmed that the new social order bore as little resemblance to the old, liberal, bourgeois, constitutional state as to an absolutist police state. The enlightened ideas underlying the Prussian General Code of Law of 1794, which saw the police force as having a purely protective function, were quickly done away with. In 1936 the prominent National Socialist lawyer Dr Walter Hamel was of the opinion that the German Police had 'been given a political and national task, namely to adapt the individual to the interests of the national community'.[59] According to Heydrich's own adaptation of these ideas, while 'the liberal welfare state saw to it that peace and security were maintained in order to guarantee the freedom of the individual', the police of the National Socialist state would take over not only the duty of providing security 'but also the job of building up the national community on the foundations laid by ideology and the political leadership'.[60]

In the conception of Heydrich's star lawyer, the idea of the political and non-political secret police in the National Socialist state was likened to that of an institution 'that monitors the state of health of the German nation, promptly recognizing every symptom of illness and identifying each destructive germ – whether these are due to internal corruption or have been intentionally implanted by external infection – in order to eliminate it by the appropriate means'.[61]

In this idea of the police Heydrich saw himself as a doctor whose preventive surgery on each identifiable seat of infection was instrumental in saving the whole organism. As Romain Rolland once said of the French writer Charles Péguy, he was like a '*ci-devant* Communard who had put holy water into his petrol'. This prudent doctor wanted not only to heal but also to prevent disease. According to Heydrich the organizational development and contact between the Secret State Police (Gestapo), the Criminal Police (Kripo) and the SD in 'organic and logical configuration' would have one single goal:

The complete apprehension of opponents in their basic intellectual element, the total identification and detection by the police of their organizational form and personnel, and finally the systematic control, destruction, crippling and elimination of these opponents by means of executive force. While the old police were restricted to single cases which naturally could only be dealt with after the completed act, the crime, the basic idea for the Security Police and the SD was prevention, both in the criminal and political sectors.[62]

Selling these ideas to the old hands in the Criminal Police, even to those whose attitude towards the new system was reserved, was like carrying coals to Newcastle. For a long time they had been demanding that habitual criminals should be taken into preventive custody so as to avoid new offences, new 'attacks on the nation's health'. Preventive custody was indeed theoretically possible in the Weimar Republic, but a custody order could only be made by a properly constituted court. And that was precisely the difficulty. For the courts, which worked by precedent and were rather liberal by inclination, were very loath to make use of this possibility. The police felt that they were the ones to suffer from this 'liberalism' by having to catch a criminal again after an offence which they had long expected him to commit, but which they could not prevent. Heydrich helped the officers of his Security Police to overcome the scruples that the courts felt before 1933. Heydrich declared whole groups of people to be social parasites purely from the point of view of the police, and his Security Police were given the authority to take them into preventive custody on the principle that 'a loving gardener isn't afraid to weed'. That meant sending them to a concentration camp. The reason given was that 'A court can only judge how dangerous an offender is on the basis of one offence, while the police are equipped with all the knowledge of internal and external circumstances for a comprehensive assessment of a criminal.'[63] Dr Werner Best, Heydrich's head of Law and Administration, was able to provide a single legal foundation, based on 'national justice'. According to this interpretation of the law, both the authorities and all fellow Germans were organs of one nation which were to work together according to the national will as laid down by the Führer. On the one hand the function of the police would be active and on the other 'the criminal taken into protective custody would cooperate passively'.[64]

One group of 'social parasites' after another was lined up for this involuntary cooperation, one group of 'social outsiders' after another landed in the concentration camps (KZs). Regular batches of people who had served three or more sentences in prison or penitentiary were caught, mopped up and put in safe custody as 'habitual criminals'; beggars and tramps, prostitutes and pimps, homosexuals, racketeers and profiteers, psychopaths and obstinate delinquents went on the wanted list as 'anti-social elements'; and anyone who had turned down several offers of work without a justifiable reason was regarded as 'workshy'.

In the concentration camps they met 'social parasites' of a political nature: communists, politically active clerics, Marxist trade union leaders, journalists and individualists who were hostile to the system, suspected spies, both actual and potential opponents of Adolf Hitler's new Third Reich.

The range of this catalogue of enemies of the state and 'social parasites' allows one to judge the power Reinhard Heydrich possessed after 1936, only five years after he had taken a badly paid post of little social status in the SS, having recently been an unemployed naval officer. It was now at his discretion who, from among the millions in Germany, was delivered into protective custody. Since he had the authority to impose or repeal this protective custody and since it was not subject to any judicial ratification or examination, he now ordered protective custody instead of police custody whenever the internal and external security of the Reich seemed to him to demand it, 'in order to avoid the necessity for a judicial examination of police measures' as he remarked in a Gestapo order in 1937.[65]

It was in vain that the lawyers of the Reich Ministry of Justice, who although they were National Socialists still thought legally, attacked this system. The Gestapo chief stubbornly extended his legal system with its police bias. He was convinced that the sanctity of law should be replaced by the concept, which he himself was to define, of the security of the Reich. And according to his concept, anyone who remotely endangered the security of the Reich belonged in a KZ. Bearing in mind this rigour in the cause of security, which he had personally championed and practised, it comes as no surprise that he tried to take over control of the camps themselves as a remedy against threats to the state.

Reichsführer Himmler was irritated by the irresistible expansion of his young man's power: he wanted to deprive him at least of this final means of SS coercion. He stubbornly refused to give the KZs to his Sipo chief. Instead he appointed Theodor Eicke, an Alsatian SS-Brigadier of dubious character (he murdered Röhm), as Inspector of Concentration Camps directly responsible to himself. Professor Eugen Kogon, in his post-war bestseller which is held to be the standard work on the SS, persistently portrays Heydrich in every edition,[66] as the inventor and founder of the KZs, despite Aronson's banishment of this idea to the realm of legend in his doctoral thesis.[67]

In reality Heydrich, while still head of the Gestapo and Security Police, struggled in vain against the head of the KZs, who was given the agreeable name of 'Papa Eicke'. He had incriminating material secretly gathered on the way in which Himmler's protégé Eicke was running the camps. Heydrich's officials began to find fault with the treatment of prisoners in the camps, 'admittedly on grounds of political competence rather than of humanity' in the opinion of SS expert Höhne.[68] Nevertheless, as early as 1935 Heydrich's Gestapo had laid down guidelines for a KZ-*Kommandant* to report immediately to the state prosecutor's office if any prisoner's death involved suspicious circumstances. And Eicke complained querulously to the *Reichsführer* about other SS comrades poking their noses in. The Gestapo was of the opinion 'that the concentration camps were in such a mess that it was time to hand them back to the Gestapo'.[69]

Chapter 8

HIS FAVOURITE TARGET: ROME

Is it not the case that this skilled and subtle attempt to undermine the unified political will of the German people is even more dangerous than any high or state treason perpetrated by the communists, precisely because it is not immediately obvious to one and all?

Reinhard Heydrich (on political Catholicism)

Heydrich's only major written political statement consisted of a small series of articles and pamphlets entitled *Die Wandlungen unseres Kampfes* (The Fortunes of our Struggle) which appeared in 1935. It is by no means without significance that in these articles political Catholicism is given primary importance among all the forces deemed to be opposed to National Socialism. Heydrich's prime consideration was 'The Church's abuse of its political power'. In comparison with this central theme even Freemasonry was overshadowed, and reduced by Heydrich to the role of a cover organization for international Jewry. According to Heydrich, all substantial opposition could be condensed into two spiritual and organizational fields: 'the Jews, and the politicized clergy' (in other words, the Jesuits).[1]

The chief of the SD was convinced that both these opposition groups were conducting their fight on two levels employing 'at one and the same time, both above board and open tactics, and concealed, underhand methods'. But the Church was Heydrich's chief target, taking precedence over the Jews and the Freemasons, who were hated and reviled throughout the Nazi Party. This was confirmed by his widow: 'He considered the Church to be the most dangerous of all the domestic enemy groups. For him political Catholicism was the major enemy because it defied capture.'[2]

The series of articles mentioned earlier reveals a great deal about Heydrich's attitudes. In writing it he did not, of course, fail to subscribe to the obligatory canons of National Socialist philosophy. Expressions of condemnation of 'corrupting' Jewry and a display of conviction about the struggle for world power by the Freemasons are present, as is familiarity with German history 'particularly with the eighth century, so crucial for the development of Germanic civilization'. As a man of letters, however, Heydrich quite certainly viewed the eighth century with little sympathy. It can be inferred that his treatment of this subject, a source of embarrassment on the most superficial of readings, was an entirely opportunistic acquiescence to the Germanic cult professed by his superior, *Reichsführer* Heinrich Himmler. When writing *Die Wandlungen unseres Kampfes*, Heydrich could not possibly forget his own career, which still depended on pleasing his superior.

What Heydrich wrote on political Catholicism, however, was tinged not only with careerism but also with the passion that only appears in writing of absolute conviction. Strongly mirrored here is his own relationship with the Church, the result of a Catholic upbringing in an atmosphere made particularly fanatical through his father's conversion. Never discussing belief in Christ, Heydrich confined himself to an analysis of the political power of the Church and her 'tribes', of 'anti-state and anti-*Volk* [nation] intentions, and the consequences of denominational struggles'.

There was a double meaning for Heydrich in this picture he painted of the church in 1935; one aspect of which was purely personal, the other political:

Originally the Churches were intended to serve as intermediaries between God and the people. According to their founders the Kingdom was not to be of this world. Yet an entirely politicized and materially ambitious priesthood has reversed the teachings of the Churches' founders. Nowadays they all proclaim that only *they* and *only their Church* have the omnipotence of God in this intermediary role. Independently of any justification of this claim all of them conduct their *secular* political affairs from *this* position of total power.

Not content with endeavouring for centuries to destroy the racial and spiritual values of our people they now assume an outward show and fake the preservation of these values, proclaiming themselves saviours of the world. *Instead of being genuine, selfless intermediaries, they have conquered one secular position of power after the other, using religion as their protection.*[3]

After this 'thorough', 'historical' outline Heydrich turned his attention to the more topical problems of the two years since the seizure of power:

Then Church supporters organized themselves politically to secure and substantiate these secular positions. Before the seizure of power the basic party structures (the Centre Party and the Bavarian People's Party) clearly betrayed their politically secular nature. Those groups founded earlier, with a great deal of foresight, to prepare the way for religious politics, have been transformed into supporters of political parties (Catholic Action etc.). In this way the Church is penetrating all aspects of the lives of our people. Whilst Germany's religious press denies the political nature of these groups, *the same Churches abroad openly admit to it.* We find that the clearest evidence of this assumption of secular influence is probably provided by statements the Church has made, along with attempts at sabotage of the legislation on sterilization and race. After the seizure of power, religious indoctrination of large numbers of unordained assistants, the so-called laity, was set in motion, with the express purpose of widening the Church's secular sphere of influence. These assistants were subjected to treatment in hundreds of spiritual retreats. This implies that they were taught to do everything mechanically, thereby systematically losing awareness of their own physical or spiritual potential.

With the victory of the National Socialist movement the Führer had finally achieved the union of Church and state 'in one large community'[4] which resulted in the negation of the concept of the political Church.

The secular ambitions of the political clergy had prevented their taking this into account. Since open political or social disruption was impossible, an effort was made to save face by the sudden revival of an old Church complaint, using the slogan: *Our beliefs are endangered.*

In this way the community united by the Führer is being disrupted by mistrust and doubt and we are faced with an attempt to sow discord between Party and State. This fight *purports* to be against godlessness, and for the rescue of Christian virtues and the preservation of German culture. *It is impossible to make these assumptions* which are made by the credulous in the Church, assumptions that in the past these Christian virtues were guaranteed by the political leaders of the religious community. We can prove the opposite by a thorough investigation of that leadership. Documentation gives the lie to their moral and cultural foundations and reveals the emptiness of their arguments. It is not in reality a positive fight for the preservation of religious and cultural values (which are scarcely in danger) but a continuation of the old bitter struggle for secular control of Germany.[5]

Heydrich put pen to paper more often when he felt he could wipe out the 'political caste of priests' at a stroke. This was during the period of Nazi *Kulturkampf* (culture struggle) against the Catholic clergy, who were subjected to a series of judicial enquiries on matters of morality and illegal dealings in foreign currency.[6] A Hitler Youth song of the period went as follows: 'Heavily laden with foreign currency the nun slips across the country. Her face is pious and holy and so she remains above suspicion.'[7]

There were counsels of moderation from all sides, in the struggle with the Church. But Heydrich considered conflict to be unavoidable and never missed an opportunity of openly fighting political Catholicism, using the Gestapo and the SD, and not restricting himself to 'reasons of security'. In April 1936, a few days before the biggest morality trial in Germany began in a division of the Koblenz court, a trial in which the accused were 276 ordained brethren from Westphalia and the Rhineland,[8] Heydrich wrote a newspaper article giving his opinion of the 'subversive activity' of political Catholicism: he was of the opinion that Church protests against compulsory sterilization of the mentally handicapped were hypocrisy.

Is it not a masterpiece of hypocrisy when on the one hand all the important laws are revealed as irreconcilable with the teaching of the Church, but on the other hand, in the interests of the Church, the foreign currency laws are simultaneously repudiated, regardless of the harm done to people or state?

Heydrich's next question is full of his vehement hatred of the Church:

> Should the Church not concede that she is acting in her own interests
> by violating the laws of the land and the people, when, at this very
> moment, over 100 monks are on trial for the most evil and repulsive of
> crimes?[9]

The depth of Heydrich's feeling against the Church is here clearly
evident. Bernhard Lichtenberg, a former Centre Party deputy, then
serving as Dean of Berlin Cathedral, sent a letter to Göring, protesting
about events in the Esterwegen concentration camp, at the same time as
Heydrich was writing *Die Wandlungen unseres Kampfes*. Göring handed
the letter of protest over to the Gestapo. Heydrich allowed his legal
adviser, Dr Werner Best, to reply that shooting, occurring 'during escape
attempts', was later subjected to judicial enquiries 'and found to be in
order'. Attached to this reply was a statement from Eicke, the 'inspector of
the concentration camp'. There was no further comment but the letter was
doubtless approved by Heydrich since it interpreted precisely his own
hatred. Lichtenberg's protests were described as outrageous lies. It was
always 'the same rabble-rousing clerics in their guise of spiritual clothing
throwing mud at others, crying "there's dirty work afoot!"' If the 'gutter
apostle' Lichtenberg kept his own altar as clean 'as the responsible SS keep
their own affairs' then all would be well in the Third Reich.

> But as long as these voles continue to gobble up German foreign
> exchange, leaving their dirt behind on the altars and as long as their
> greedy political slobberings disturb the altar candles, these ultra-
> montane, destructive powers have no right to concern themselves
> with matters of state.[10]

This 'international Church, opponent of the state, preaching hatred and
destruction'[11] was Heydrich's favourite target. Hitler himself had to call a
halt when he zealously suggested infiltrating the seminaries with agents of
the SD, in order to undermine the powerful structure of the Church from
within and bring about its downfall.[12] The greatest self-sacrifice he could
have made in obedience to the Führer and his goals would have been to
have passed himself off, not as a communist nor as a Jewish Freemason, but
as a Catholic. The extent of his self-denial can be measured by the standard

formula he would use to appease any growing unrest in his spies and agents: 'Should it prove necessary, I am personally prepared to carry a candle in the procession on Corpus Christi Day!'[13]

His ruthless ardour in pursuit of Catholic activists brought him into conflict even with his own family: his mother would have no more to do with him after he had the Bishop of Meissen arrested. And this was the son on whose SS career she had laid so much importance.[14]

It is not difficult to discover the reasons behind the particular vehemence with which he pursued the Catholic movement – this persecution which became his own personal passion, totally distinct from his other campaigns, be they against the communists or, in those early years of the Third Reich, the Jews. Like his *Reichsführer*, Himmler, Heydrich had been subjected to a strong Catholic upbringing, in his case verging on the fanatical. His father, whose conversion had been merely opportunist, was quite willing to have an eternally pious atmosphere in the home. But this atmosphere had no more been able to enslave the young Heydrich than had the stick which was used as retribution when he broke the rules of his Church.

His interest in the Catholic creed had been only superficial, and when he was introduced to the biologically inspired philosophy of Himmler and the SS, he dismissed certain central points of religious faith without any deep struggle. As an enlightened technocrat with an interest in science, his attitude to the Immaculate Conception was one of complete scepticism; as a modern vitalist he could dismiss the doctrine of original sin scornfully. Even as a young naval officer the concept of human equality had held no attraction: to the SS-officer it appeared 'contrary to nature'.[15]

It was obvious that the doctrines of the SS and Catholicism were incompatible. As early as 1934 the Church had taken a resolution on this incompatibility, forbidding priests and other ecclesiastical dignitaries to become members of the SS; from 1937 this ban was extended to the Nazi Party as a whole. In 1934 Heydrich's religious adviser in the SD, the Catholic cleric Geiste, had been excommunicated.[16] Heydrich's ties with the Catholic Church had been further loosened by his marriage to Lina von Osten, who had been christened in the Lutheran Evangelical Church and brought up in a particularly north German Protestant atmosphere, only superficially Christian. Indeed, the final break was harder for him than for Lina. Although formal affiliation to neo-paganism was beneficial to the career of an SS-officer even in 1934 and 1935, Heydrich took his stance as a dissident only after his wife did so. Not until the spring of 1936 did he officially declare his secession, before the Berlin – Lichterfelde lower court.[17] Perhaps consideration for his narrow-minded Catholic mother played a part in this.

Another motive undoubtedly at work here originated in the ambivalent attitude Heydrich had towards the Church's role as a powerful international organization. It was an organization which, by means of its 'unscrupulous domination of minds, its techniques of using power, and its rigid organization, was to build up its position over two thousand years'. Heydrich's leaders, Himmler and Hitler, shared this unfortunate passion, as did Goebbels, of whom Heydrich had a very low opinion. What the leadership of the SS found particularly fascinating was the effectiveness of tightly organized orders like the Jesuits. This was worth investigating, with the aim of imitating the successful methods employed. Accordingly, those Catholic organizations felt by Heydrich to constitute the major threats to his own claim to power took up positions of increasingly uncompromising antagonism.[18] There were no illusions on either side: this struggle was for power pure and simple, not just for power over the Germans' souls, but for political influence, economic power and control of press and property.

In 1935 Heydrich's SD edited a report on corruption in the world of letters,[19] which indicated that this hatred was less inflamed by philosophical differences with the Catholic movement than by very effective, intentional similarities in organization. In the operations and strategy of his opponents in black cassocks Heydrich discovered exactly the degree of cunning and tactical recklessness displayed in his own schemes for the SD. According to the report, by means of 'embarrassing falsification and opportunist exploitation' of National Socialist concepts and vocabulary, 'the bitterest opponent' (as political Catholicism was clearly defined) wanted 'to make capital for its own cause'.[20] Countless pieces of evidence were extracted from ecclesiastical publications of the years 1933 to 1935, predominantly from Jesuit and Franciscan authors. Although merely embarrassing to read now, they were used by Heydrich's SD as further proof of the danger of Catholic Action. Excerpts from the *Little Library for Franciscan Youth* and the extract, which is quoted below, from the second pamphlet written by the Franciscan Father Kauffner with the title *Francis, Leader of Youth*, were considered by the SD researchers to be particularly interesting and noteworthy:

In Francis, an ideal leader [Führer] is lit up for the world . . . At this very moment Francis stands in the front line as a leader . . . Why is the entire world pursuing you, Francis, why is it you whom youth follows *as their leader* and ideal . . . out of thousands of youthful eyes beams the earnest desire . . . Francis is the patron saint of Catholic Action.[21]

With great indignation the SD researchers recorded how value was placed on St Francis 'as a leader' and also on St Sebastian, this last seen as representing the 'greatest of soldiers'.[22] In addition the Jesuit Muckermann compared his creed to 'a flag, which had fluttered in the wind during the great battles of world history'.[23]

Evidence was prepared from Catholic writings especially for 'C', Chief Heydrich, to demonstrate parallels between the Third Reich and its opponent, between the thought of the religious orders and SS units. The SD selected fatal evidence from a Catholic brochure on 'The Jesuit and German mind'. In this text Heydrich's analysts read that after the abolition of the Society of Jesuits in 1774, 'an absolute allegiance to the Pope' had resulted in its re-emergence and the unbelievably rapid re-assumption of its work in the world during the following 120 years. The sentences below, taken from this brochure, must have electrified Heydrich:

The speed and certainty shown in the occupation of important fields of organization recalls the speed with which . . . the supporters of the Third Reich manipulated all important positions in government, in financial organizations and in Germany's schools and colleges.

The religious tract then continued by saying that the work of the Jesuits was characterized 'by the unconditional obedience of a soldier, by submission to their General's leadership, speedy preparation in action and fast occupation of key areas of operation'.[24]

As a man convinced of his own effectiveness against the opponents of the Third Reich, Heydrich must have been aware that the greatest opposition came from Jesuitism, essentially parallel to the Reich in its principles of development and organization. He saw that cadres like the SS and his own SD on the one hand and the Society of Jesus on the other fulfilled the same function in the power struggle played out, in the first instance, between the people and the Nazi movement, and in the second, between the people and the Church. In both camps selection from the community took place with the primary aim of indoctrinating a special group – 'a sort of elite'.[25] This indoctrination, based on 'comradeship and authoritarian leadership, founded on discipline, reliability and trust',[26] played an essential part in achieving the goals of both sides.

Heydrich was aware that Catholicism made a quasi-totalitarian claim similar to that of National Socialism. After the obliteration of communism in Germany only in Catholicism did National Socialism find an equally dangerous opponent. The creed of National Socialism was not merely to seek toleration by the people, but to penetrate totally all areas of life, both public and private. As far as Heydrich was concerned, 'the glasses through which he sees his God' were 'a matter of individual concern for each German'. But any public demands made by the Christian Church or even any attempts at influencing politics were definitely to be 'prevented'.[27]

According to Heydrich's report only the National Socialist movement could take an active part in politics, and although Catholicism claimed to stop short of politics, clinging fanatically to its old goals, and asserted that its aim was merely the dissemination of Christian doctrine, in fact, through its fight for denominational schools it wanted to retain a hold over education and training. Furthermore it was concerned with both private and public morality and aimed at the 'Christian formation of all aspects of life'.[28]

'None of our other opponents can be accused of the subtle game played by the Catholic movement,'[29] continues Heydrich's report. But he envied so much 'subtle dialectic'.[30] 'Of all the supranational powers,' he admitted, 'political Catholicism has shown itself time and again as our major opponent.'[31] Judaism and Freemasonry were here clearly relegated to a secondary position. These evaluations of the differing degrees of danger offered by various opponents were top secret. They were to be kept under lock and key and circulated in limited numbers only. Heydrich, however, gave the public a unique glimpse of his interpretation of the growing dangers of political Catholicism. In the *Völkischer Beobachter* (the Nazi newspaper) he put the following rhetorical question:

Is it not the case that this skilled and subtle attempt to undermine the unified political will of the German people is even more dangerous than any high or state treason perpetrated by the communists, precisely because it is not immediately obvious to one and all?[32]

Despite his deep involvement in the secrets of power, Heydrich's evaluation of Catholicism remained completely superficial. His judgment of the Church was restricted to organizational concerns; as ever in Heydrich's case, the philosophical questions behind these were of little consequence. The technician of power took more interest in the Church's instruments of power than in its means of grace.

It was only the growing crisis in relations between the Nazi state and the Church in the years after the seizure of power which made this pursuit of his favourite opponent conceivable. Had it not been for the conflict between Hitler and his henchmen, Rosenberg, Himmler and Goebbels, on the one hand, and the Catholic Church on the other, the problem posed by Catholicism would have taken quite a different form even for Heydrich. But there is no doubt that, even had he never belonged to the SS, his reaction to his intensely Catholic upbringing would have resulted in an increasing indifference to the Catholic faith. The idea of religion held no attraction for him. According to his widow, 'all spiritual politics were anathema' to him. Besides, the Church did not belong to the 'new era' in which the technocrats of the SS found their fulfilment. 'The Church is only a shell left over from the past.'[33]

The Chief of the Security Police and the SD never missed an opportunity of attacking this shell. As early as 1933 he had instructed the executive of the Bavarian Political Police 'to keep a close look-out to ensure that the permitted activities of the religious . . . groups and unions do not deteriorate into political action'.[34] The long chain of Heydrich's 'measures' extends from the early months of the Third Reich until his death.

The murder of the ministerial adviser Klausener during the so-called 'Röhm putsch' may be attributed to Heydrich. In this case he dropped the anonymity of the putsch set-up, in which he normally acted only as the transmitter of orders, dealing with lists written by others. The Röhm putsch, a reckoning with the old SA guard, was intended to settle various feuds, both personal and political, between the SA and the SS, Göring, and even Hitler himself. Those shots fired against Röhm and his group of expedient SA-leaders were to act as a cover for those aimed at other dangerous opponents of the Third Reich. There were also some accidents on 30 June 1934, and Gestapo chief Heydrich was only partially responsible for these events. The shooting of religious adviser Klausener was quite another matter, however. The presence of his name on all lists to be 'settled' on 30 June was in keeping with Heydrich's carefully considered strategy and was to deal a considerable blow to Heydrich's most hated opponent: Catholic Action.

Even before 1933 ministerial adviser Dr Erich Klausener was head of this organization.[35] During the early struggles of the Nazi movement he had made a name for himself as one of its strongest opponents, through his position as head of the police division in the Prussian Ministry of the Interior. After the seizure of power he was consequently removed to the Ministry of Transport by Göring. There he was politically neutralized and indeed seemed to have got off lightly.

His leadership of Catholic Action made him particularly interesting to Heydrich. Klausener had taken up the fight against Nazi politics at public meetings of Berlin Catholics. He became an embarrassment, and both Göring, and Klausener's successor in the police, SS-leader Daluege, attempted to have him legally silenced. Consultation of the files showed 'that no serious criticism could be made against him for his handling of office'.[36] Heydrich saw as a particularly provoking action on the part of the 'Catholic rabble-rouser', Klausener's appeal for a 'special awareness of the social teaching of the Church' at a church service on, of all days, 1 May 1934. This was designated sabotage of the Mayday holiday. Shortly afterwards, on 24 June, Klausener voiced opinions said to be 'against the interests of the state' whilst delivering an improvised and probably very animated speech in the Hoppegarten at the *Katholikentag* (a biennial meeting of Catholics).

Police Superintendent Meisinger was among the Gestapo observers who were to report back to Berlin on the meeting (he was to achieve even greater significance in the Blomberg-Fritsch crisis of 1938). The report these officials made about Klausener must have given Heydrich great cause for excitement.[37]

The time when Klausener was moving into the picture as a particularly dangerous opponent coincided with the moment when various drafts of the liquidation lists arrived on Heydrich's desk; these were duly 'settled' on 30 June. On his own initiative Heydrich put Klausener's name on one of these death lists. According to Göring, in Nuremberg, the Klausener matter had been 'a completely mad action on Heydrich's part'.[38] On 30 June 1934, six days after Klausener's appearance on the *Katholikentag*, Heydrich, in his office in the Prinz-Albrecht-Strasse, gave orders to SS-Captain Gildisch: 'You are to take over Klausener's case and shoot him yourself.' Gildisch carried out this order to the letter. He shot Klausener in his office and then informed Heydrich by phone. 'C' instructed him to pass off Klausener's death as suicide. Only on his return to Prinz-Albrecht-Strasse did the SS-Captain learn of Klausener's identity and the reason for his death. 'He was a dangerous Catholic leader,' was Heydrich's explanation.[39]

On the same day Adalbert Probst, Reich leader of the Catholic sports organization *Deutsche Jugendkraft* (German Youth Force) was shot while trying to escape.[40]

Behind Heydrich's decision to include Klausener among the victims there possibly lay a deeper reason than the simple desire to eliminate a rising opponent. On 25 June, the day following Klausener's speech, the long-delayed negotiations between the Reich government and the Catholic episcopacy had been reopened. The aim was to determine finally Article 31 of the concordat between the Vatican and Berlin and thereby establish the status of the Catholic organizations. Four days later a provisional agreement had been reached, guaranteeing continuation of the Catholic youth organizations, including one previously dissolved by the secret police. But the shooting of Klausener caused the Catholics to break off negotiations, and they were never resumed.[41] For Heydrich this was doubtless an achievement: the cessation of negotiations left the fate of the Catholic groups even more in his power and his secret police could now pursue them at their leisure.

The war was to provide the ideal climate for Heydrich's anti-Church politics. 'Exigencies of war' provided an excuse for measures impossible to implement in peacetime. In October 1939 Heydrich sent Hitler a memorandum in which his intentions were clearly stated. He claimed that it would be easy to bring the Church congregations round to positive cooperation. Opposition to 'Führer and Reich' came in the main 'from certain rabble-rousing pastors'. The influence of the Church had shrunk in recent years; there was a distinct absence of new membership and no decisive, united leadership. The German-Soviet non-aggression pact had caused a certain amount of confusion among the Catholic clergy. Some saw in it the possibility of 'converting Russia and bringing the greater part of Eastern Europe back into the Catholic fold'. Others feared the end of the Church in Europe 'should France and England not succeed in destroying the Nazi rulers in Germany'.[42] But behind their public declarations of solidarity, Heydrich's memorandum went on, the clergy were still bent only on sabotage. His hatred for the Church made Heydrich suggest that 'rabble-rousers and saboteurs' be sent to concentration camps without any regard for their ecclesiastical rank. He wanted to reduce state financing of the Church, and forbid pilgrimages and large religious gatherings on the grounds of reduced transport facilities. Religious newspapers should be kept to a minimum 'in view of the paper shortage'. 'There must be no possibility of the Churches regaining their old positions of power.'[43]

Throughout the war, as chief of the Secret Service, Heydrich was to sustain his interest in the Churches: those ordained or holding office in the various denominations were no longer permitted to travel abroad, and any contact between the evangelical Churches, world Protestantism and leading figures in England were observed. The SD were to take strict measures at the customs: 'All material providing evidence that the Bishops were making use of the diplomatic bag in their dealings with the Vatican is to be carefully collected. All episcopal and Vatican courier lines are to be found and infiltrated.'[44] It was said in Gestapo circles that by 1942 at the latest the Jesuits were to be 'shut up in camps in the East'.[45] In October 1941, Heydrich, now designated Protector of Bohemia and Moravia, ordered 'the completion of the communications network so that all proof of Church opposition to the state should be to hand on the day of reckoning'.[46]

It was indeed Heydrich's ceaseless energy and unflagging hatred which had stiffened the Nazi struggle against the Church during the period of persecution. As a colleague was later to testify, the Christian Churches were rid of their toughest opponent on Heydrich's death in 1942.[47] The official Church history also states that 'the murder of Heydrich in 1942 led to a certain improvement in the situation of the Churches.'[48] When Heydrich died, his network of Church specialists in the Gestapo, and the SD, and their informers (including a significant number of junior Catholic clergy), became a vehicle without propulsion.

Chapter 9

THE DUTY TO EXCEL

Regarding liability for military service, we must provide the armour-bearer of the nation with the best recruits, in the field of sport we must always be amongst the first, in the professions the consciously political SS-man must be the most expert.

Reinhard Heydrich, 1936

Heydrich seemed to work twenty-four hours a day. None of his numerous offices seemed to occupy him completely, nor any of his many commitments to exhaust him. His subordinates commented enviously that the 'boss' could do everything 'with his left hand' while his rivals feared that with his right hand he was already secretly taking on new offices. The more incompatible the latter appeared the better they seemed to please him. In 1940 his election as President of the International Criminal Police Organization had been added to his functions as head of the Reich Central Security Department (RSHA), chief of the Security Police and the Gestapo, and his appointment as an active pilot in the Luftwaffe. The acquisition of this new, international function in the August of that year deserves particularly close examination, since it is in equal measure bizarre and characteristic of Heydrich's methods. The accumulation of offices and the combination of numerous, even contradictory functions were indeed commonplace occurrences in the Nazi state. Such accretion of personal influence and power by specially favoured and 'safe' National Socialists indicated a characteristic weakness of the system. It lacked leaders who combined professional competence with loyalty to the regime.

Apart from Göring, who was, properly speaking, overtaxed in all his offices and especially so by being simultaneously Commander-in-Chief of the Luftwaffe and Reich Plenipotentiary with responsibility for the four-year economic plan, it was Heydrich in particular who accumulated one office after another. When there was no other way, he proposed himself as principal, president or some similar post of responsibility.

Such was the case at the Bucharest congress of the International Criminal Police Organization (ICPO) which took place at the time of the annexation of Austria.[1] Although one might think that Heydrich was heavily occupied as chief of the SD detachments in the critical weeks of the annexation, he still found time to take part in the Bucharest congress in his capacity as the superior of the chief of the German Criminal Police. Thirty-three countries were represented at the congress, including Great Britain, France, the USA, Sweden, Japan and Switzerland. The ICPO had also come to be known as Interpol. It had been founded on the initiative of Schober, then Police President of Vienna, and was the second attempt at making the work of the criminal police international, the first having been brought to an end by the outbreak of the First World War.

During the Bucharest conference it was proposed that the seat of the organization should be transferred to a neutral country because of the annexation. This failed through the sharp intervention of Heydrich. He explained to the conference that Skubl, the former Austrian Secretary of State, had been elected President of the Organization for five years. And, since Austria had in the meantime become part of the Reich, the presidency passed to Skubl's successor in office, SS-Brigadier Otto Steinhäusel, the new Police President of Vienna (who was naturally Heydrich's subordinate). Therefore neither a new election nor the transfer of the seat of the ICPO to another country were necessary. There was no serious opposition to Heydrich's interpretation of the situation. And when Steinhäusel 'departed this life' (as the official Party obituary put it) under mysterious circumstances in June 1940, Heydrich assumed control of the organization himself with the consent of its members. Thus from 28 August 1940 he became head of the only international police organization which was still functioning, and functioning surprisingly well even in the second year of the war. In the meantime only England, France and a few of the smaller countries which had been overrun by the Wehrmacht (German Army) had ceased to cooperate.[2]

Heydrich transferred the seat of the organization from Vienna to Berlin and issued a self-satisfied communiqué to the German press in which he commented that his taking over the office promised that the organization would 'operate in a well-planned and successful fashion in the future'. The new President, 'whose organizational talent had already made the German Criminal Police into a forceful instrument', would now also 'open new avenues for international cooperation of the criminal police authorities under his direction, bring into being a powerful organization and a criminal police network that will make escape more difficult for criminals throughout the world and serve to hinder crime'![3]

At the same time, therefore, as his task forces were beginning to 'pacify' Poland in their own way, Heydrich had succeeded in donning the magic cloak of legitimacy for what appeared as his fight to prevent internationally organized racketeering. He had catapulted himself into the presidential chair of the international police authority without so much as arousing the suspicion of the delegates from what still amounted to nearly thirty states, even receiving for the most part their unhesitating acclamation. This may admittedly have been intended more for the desired improvement in the technical effectiveness of Interpol.

There were, in fact, under Heydrich's control, such highly developed and, as it were, 'neutral' establishments as, for example, the Institute of Forensic Science of the Security Police in Berlin, which was among the leading institutes of its type in the world. Heydrich's presidency raised expectations that the use of such establishments, as well as numerous other initiatives from Heydrich and his specialists from Criminal Police HQ under Arthur Nebe (for example in the field of detective work), would give new impetus to intensifying the international fight against drug trafficking, prostitution, fraud and smuggling rings, and would raise the general success rates.[4] The murders by Heydrich's task forces in Poland, in so far as they were known of at all, fell 'outside the province of' Interpol. Our awareness of the schizophrenic cynicism of Heydrich's approach is made all the more oppressive in retrospect by knowledge of one of the meetings convened under the auspices of this organization. Heydrich, on his assumption of the presidency, had pressed on with his plan of finding 'worthy accommodation' for the ICPO in Berlin. Suitable quarters were eventually found in a spacious aristocratic villa on the Grosser Wannsee. It offered on the one hand 'sufficient room to accommodate the international card indexes and to accomplish the executive work of the international office. On the other hand the house provides the members of the organization, whose personal contacts represent one of the most important prerequisites for flourishing international cooperation, with a comfortable home of superior taste which is equally suited to work and to social intercourse.'[5]

On 20 January 1942 there took place in this house, in the agency for the combat of international crime, the conference of the State Secretaries of the most important German ministries, called by Göring to prepare the organization of the 'Final Solution of the Jewish Question'. It bore the title 'Wannsee Conference' and thus, with Heydrich in the chair, gave a place in history to the Interpol house, but in a context far removed from its intended purpose.

But in 1940 it was, to begin with, the special representative of the 'President' (as Heydrich, with that ambiguity characteristic of his thinking, occasionally let himself be known), SS-Colonel and Principal Dr Zindel, and the Executive Manager and General Secretary, the real Hofrat *Regierungsdirektor* (Government Director) Dr Dressler, who carried out their duties there. They probably never dreamed of the bloody work to which their department was to be put about a year later. Heydrich himself valued this prestige success at international level, which he had won so easily, as a recognition of his personal achievement, and emphasized his newly acquired, high-flown title when it seemed useful to him. Shortly before the start of the Russian campaign, for example, he was still signing his articles with the full title 'Chief of the Security Police and the SD, President of the International Criminal Police Organization'.[6] But Interpol came to concern him less and less as Germany's deepening isolation in the war soon eroded the efficiency of its worldwide function.

The war provided the proper climate for Heydrich's principle of excellence. He was now able to demonstrate that the officers of the SD, who were sometimes looked down on by the serving Wehrmacht, 'were not mere pen-pushers concerned with papers and files',[7] that they did not only 'arrest unarmed civilians' but that even at the front the SS were the bravest, the most resolute and the most daring.

Despite all the opposition, voiced above all by Himmler and Hitler, Heydrich decided to 'detail' himself for action at the front as often as possible. Characteristically enough the service he chose was not the Navy, in which he had originally served, but the Luftwaffe. Already an enthusiastic pilot in civilian life – he had taken part in aerobatic flying competitions in his little Deaky aircraft and flown from Fehmarn to Berlin on a good many Mondays[8] – on the outbreak of war he requested permission from Luftwaffe-General Loertzer to fly with the Luftwaffe, at first only as a crew-member. His first combat mission on 12 September 1939 was as a gunner in the Bomber Group KG 55.[9] But Heydrich was not satisfied with being simply a crew-member. Before going on duty he would practise in the dawn light on the Staaken airfield and after a while he passed the fighter pilot examination.[10] He saw his first action as pilot of an ME 109 in the Norwegian campaign and made reconnaissance flights over England and Scotland in an ME 110 fitted for aerial photography. Between missions he returned to Berlin time and again on the night plane in order to conceal his absences from the RSHA as much as possible from Hitler and Himmler, who naturally only with very mixed feelings allowed the head of their most secret Secret Service to indulge in skirmishes over England with the Royal Air Force.[11] On 5 May, while making flights over Belgium and Holland as Luftwaffe-Captain he sent a consoling field postcard to the peevish Himmler, saying that he would be 'back on duty in a week'.[12] The *Reichsführer* was mollified and of course also rather grateful that it was Heydrich instead of himself who represented the SS leadership at the front. 'I think of you a lot . . . and again wish you good luck and all the best,' he wrote back to the 'Luftwaffe-Captain in the Western Campaign'.[13] In addition he kept himself informed of Heydrich's daily welfare by telex from the KG 55. Heydrich returned to Berlin in the middle of May with a newly awarded bronze bar for combat missions on his chest.

He found the next opportunity to put his soldierly readiness for action to the test in the Russian war. Although grounded categorically by Hitler and Himmler he still managed to sneak off. He kept his cover until the time when he was forced to make an emergency landing to the east of Berezina, following a dogfight behind the Soviet lines, and could only be got out again by a German combat patrol.[14] The Luftwaffe rewarded him with the silver bar for combat missions and the Iron Cross, First Class. The insubordination of the ambitious all-rounder came out when Hitler noticed the fresh decorations while Himmler and Heydrich were making their report at the Führer's HQ. He escaped, however, with a ticking-off in front of the assembled team before being reminded of his duties by Himmler.[15] At the same time Heydrich was also chasing after success in another field with which he was associated: sport.

An ardent and talented competitor, particularly in sabre fencing,

Heydrich had already been a highly placed sports official before the war, in his position as 'Inspector of Physical Training', under Chief of German Police, Himmler. As inspector of sport for the SS, he had thought of founding a 'Reich Physical Education Training Centre', a 'Reich School of Marksmanship' and other teaching institutions for the Black Order. Now he announced that it was his aim 'to raise it [sabre fencing] to that high level to which, on account of the stature and power of the Reich, it was entitled even in the international arena'.[16] Since German sport seemed to him to be a deserving cause, he started to look for an international office for his next coup.

This time he combined sheer intimidating terrorism with intrigue: he wanted to become President of the International Fencing Federation, the 'Fédération Internationale d'Escrime' (FIE). The Federation was based in Brussels, and it was not looking for a new President. It already had one in Paul Anspach, a Belgian who had given great service to fencing.

Anspach[17] had been elected President of the FIE in Merano, in September 1939, for the period until 31 December 1940. His successor should have been chosen at a congress planned for the spring in Brussels, but which never took place because of Germany's Western Campaign. On 17 May the Mayor of Brussels surrendered his town to the German troops, and everyone had concerns other than the presidency of the international fencing administration to think about. Not so Heydrich. Among the many other senior Belgian officers in the Gestapo's Brussels prison there was the *Auditeur Général*, the senior military prosecutor of the defeated Belgian army. His former superior, the head of the military Security Service, had been involved in the deportation of Germans and real or suspected German sympathizers before the invasion by the Wehrmacht. Some of the deportees had been murdered in a cellar in Abbéville where their transport had halted.[18] At the subsequent hearing it was established that Anspach, although under suspicion, had had no part in these proceedings. During his interrogation, Anspach's high place in the world of fencing had also emerged. 'So you're a fencer,' the Gestapo official at the hearing said to him. 'That will certainly interest our boss as well.' The boss was indeed interested. Quick as a flash he seized the opportunity and on 9 August 1940 he dispatched a detachment led by SS-Second Lieutenant Holzhauser with directions to seize the archives of the FIE in Brussels and Ghent.

Anspach got off with a fright, was set free and received a meticulously detailed list of all the files, monies and items which had been seized, together with the news that everything had been taken to the Prinz-Albrecht-Strasse in Berlin and placed 'at the disposal of SS-Lieutenant-General Heydrich'. After the war he recalled: 'Immediately after my release I turned to the then *Reichssportführer*, von Tschammer und Osten, in the hope of getting my archives back with his help, and asked him if he could possibly intervene in my favour. As early as 19 September 1940 I received an answer in the affirmative from Tschammer. He would attend to the return of the files and was ready to intervene again if nothing was received in the near future.'[19]

In October and December Anspach repeated his requests, but naturally without success. Neither he nor von Tschammer had grasped what Heydrich was aiming at: the presidency of the FIE! A first important step towards his goal was the assumption of the highest German fencing office to which one could be appointed. He was given responsibility for fencing in the Reich, in the middle of December, under the Nazi Reich Association for Physical Training, with effect from 1 January 1941. Von Tschammer did not want to get on the wrong side of the powerful SS leadership, which by now had a finger in every pie.

And in addition, Heydrich had in the meantime become a well-known and recognized figure in German competitive sport. 'SS-Lieutenant-General Heydrich is well known as an active sabre fencer who belongs to the Reich special class,' the Düsseldorf newspaper, *Mittag* (Noon) commented. 'He recently led the Berlin SS team in its successful start in the German team championship. The great boom in SS fencing which, as is well known, provided the winners in all three weapons in this year's [1940] German championships, can also be ascribed to his work.'[20] Heydrich's position as the highest German fencing official now gave him a completely different authority for dealing with Anspach. On 5 February 1941 he requested Anspach, through the Brussels office of the Gestapo, to place himself at Heydrich's disposal in Berlin. It was with very mixed feelings that Anspach accepted the 'invitation': he had only a vague memory of Heydrich himself, who had been presented to him briefly about 1935, at one of his routine inspections of the national fencing associations. But he still remembered exactly what had been said to him at a meal in the Berlin Hotel Adlon following that inspection, in which, amongst others, the German Olympic fencer Casmir had taken part. There had been talk of the growing influence of the SS in German fencing, including of course, Heydrich, about whom Anspach had enquired. The reply consisted of the ominous sentence: 'Watch out, that man is dangerous, very dangerous.' It was of this that Anspach was reminded when, immediately after his arrival in Berlin, he was taken to the Prinz-Albrecht-Strasse and shown into Heydrich's room.

Heydrich received him cordially, jumping up and coming to meet him. 'It's a great pleasure to see you again, Herr Anspach, especially now, when our nations are discovering their mutual Germanic stock. You yourself are the very picture of a Fleming.' But Anspach, who had made up his mind not to accommodate his host in anything, repudiated this advance with the remark that he was not a Fleming but a Belgian. 'As you wish, Herr Anspach, but in any case you are Germanic.'

This affable elevation to Germanic status was indeed not without cost: Heydrich informed his unwilling guest that he was in fact already in possession of all the documents of the FIE and declared himself ready 'to revitalize the activities of the FIE'. The archives were 'of course' at Anspach's disposal again and 'under no restrictions', but they would remain in Berlin 'for practical reasons'. Moreover, during wartime, international fencing activities could only take place through Germany's good offices, since it was only from Berlin that contacts could be established with other European capitals 'because of the censorship'. When Anspach did not appear in the course of the conversation to be sufficiently receptive to these arguments, Heydrich reminded him of the fact that his, Anspach's, term of office had theoretically already expired on 31 December 1940, and that he was only entitled to carry on FIE business because the war had made a fresh election impossible. A happy state of affairs for Heydrich, which he exploited right away in inviting Anspach to transfer the presidential powers to himself, the patron of German fencing, immediately if possible, and for as long as it would take Heydrich to call a new congress to elect a new president properly.

Heydrich had of course already made up his mind that he needed Anspach's help and intercession on the international stage if he was to realize his ambitious prestige plan. He therefore suggested the two SS-officers Dr Hoops and Talman as liaison officers between Heydrich in Berlin and Anspach in Brussels. Anspach wavered because he considered Hoops and Talman, whom he had known personally since before the war, to be highly skilled fencers of personal integrity and international standing. But, after the twenty-four hours delay Heydrich had suggested for him to think the matter over, Anspach turned down the Gestapo chief's request and informed the two liaison officers that the only acceptable solution would be for 'all documents to be returned and the presidency to remain where it was'. Anspach naturally knew what the Gestapo was. He was after all already acquainted with Heydrich's Gestapo prison in Brussels. Anspach's refusal to give in seems all the more courageous since this was a question of principle rather than of vital interests. As so often happened, Heydrich accepted a firm and resolute attitude in this instance too, simply because he encountered one so seldom in those around him. Anspach was able to return to Brussels unharmed.

But the affair was not yet over. On 17 February Talman appeared in Brussels to deliver a letter which had been drawn up by Heydrich and which, as the distinguished German fencing champion asked him, not without embarrassment, Anspach needed only to sign. Heydrich expected his opponent to sign a text the essence of which ran as follows:

Dear Heydrich, as you no doubt know, my mandate and that of my office expired on 31 December 1940. It is impossible for me to convene a congress to settle on my successor on account of the war situation. For this reason the work of the FIE has come to a complete halt . . . As an enthusiastic fencer and founder member of the FIE it is only natural that I should see Germany provisionally taking over the direction of the FIE as the only possible solution . . . and I therefore want to ask you in particular to look kindly on the suggestion . . . that you, by virtue of your personal standing and in your capacity as *Reichsfachamtsleiter* (Reich head of fencing), might take over . . . the presidency for the time being, until the matter can be finally settled at a later date.[21]

That was too much! Anspach reacted furiously with a letter to Talman, a copy of which he also sent to the President of the International Olympic Committee for his information.[22] Heydrich pricked up his ears and parried with an *ad hoc* alliance with Dr Basletta, the Chairman of the Italian Fencing Association, with the aim of reducing the impression of desire for personal glorification which his ambitions created in others. Basletta was known to be a friend of Anspach's, so it looked very like a compromise move when Heydrich informed his 'Dearest Mr Anspach' in a personal letter of 25 June 1941 (the Russian Campaign had been under way for three days!):

With regard to the management of the International Fencing Association, I have reached the following agreement with Dr Basletta, the President of the Italian Fencing Association: for the duration of the war I shall carry on the direction of the affairs of the FIE in consultation with Dr Basletta. The question of the ultimate direction of the FIE for the next period of office can only be settled after the end of the war. I have appointed SS-Captain Talman as my liaison officer with you.[23]

Anspach's renewed protests, which were not without their aggressive undertones, strike one as almost suicidal obstinacy.[24] But Heydrich in fact left him alone this time as well, not replying to any of his letters. Indeed, he had what he wanted. In addition to his position as President of the International Criminal Police Organization, he had now become for the second time the *de facto* top official of an international organization.

The ruthlessness of his acquisition of the fencing appointment immediately calls into question the sportsmanship of Heydrich the sportsman. The answer to this question offers one of the best insights into the difficult and complex character of the man. To begin with there is testimony from the sporting camp. Herbert E von Daniels, a top German sports official, who had effortlessly made the transition from Weimar after 1933, wrote a commemorative article in the specialist newspaper *Leibesübungen und körperliche Erziehung* (Physical Training and Education) in the summer of 1942 on 'Reinhard Heydrich as a physical educationalist' in which he recalled an event in Bad Kreuznach in August 1941:

For the second time the wartime German fencing championships have come to an end. The Reich special class, the best twelve, have formed up and been honoured. In fifth place in the ranking stands an SS-General and General of Police. It is Reinhard Heydrich.[25]

As to Heydrich's attitude he asserts:

He receives with pleasure all the congratulations but his whole attitude expresses his modesty in victory. Those who know him are aware that he will not relax even now. His base attitude towards sport, as much as towards work, is one of incessant activity, always pushing himself and striving to improve.[26]

Except for 'his modesty in victory' this is an astonishingly accurate assessment of Heydrich's character, with the principle of excellence as the driving force behind his restless, glory-seeking activity. Even twenty years after his death a German sports magazine admitted in a rather embarrassed review of Heydrich's role in German sport that 'it can hardly be denied' that he was, 'as far as achievement goes, an acceptable sportsman', a 'top sportsman'.[27] In fact Heydrich demonstrated his stature as a competitive sportsman again and again. For instance when, in December 1941, one of the fencers chosen for the German national team for the international match between Germany and Hungary dropped out, Heydrich stepped into the breach at short notice. He had no opportunity to take part in the training with which the team was supposed to build up its performance for the difficult contest against the superior Hungarians. A few days before the match the only possible time he had to get himself into form was between 4 and 6 o'clock in the morning; during the night he exchanged, as it were, the RSHA for the fencing arena. But in spite of this he emerged as the best of the Germans and second best overall in the sabre-fencing part of the contest. 'An almost unimaginable result when one considers the amount of other work he still managed' a sports journalist commented, with justification, in a review.[28]

Of all the different sports in which he took part, fencing, which he admitted to be his passion, was most suited to his constitution. In the words of Heinz Höhne, an historian of the period, 'watching suspiciously and parrying an opponent's intentions, reacting with lightning speed to unforeseen situations'[29] were second nature to him. In addition he was also a keen horseman, skier, swimmer and modern pentathlete. For his subordinates at the RSHA, whom he often pressed into service as tennis partners, an invitation to play was more to be feared than looked forward to.[30] And finally Heydrich was even more enthusiastic about flying, sailing and shooting. So all in all he was an uncommonly all-round sportsman.

In the obituary notice quoted above, Daniels wrote of the sportsman:

One only really got to know comrade Heydrich on the days following such successes. However pleased he himself might be about his victories, he didn't make much fuss about them. Now and then he would encourage his comrades with a joke if they had not been as successful as himself. The hours spent training with him or in his company after the bouts were unforgettable.[31]

Heydrich apparently never talked about the companionship of sport: it was supposedly so much second nature to him that he was a living embodiment of it.

Admittedly this verdict was given in 1942, after Heydrich's death, so one must allow for opportunism or caution on the part of the author. Can we not on balance accept Heydrich as a good sportsman? Former SS fencing aces reported that their boss had always acted naturally with them, unaffectedly, even modestly, and generally as an uncomplicated sporting comrade. Even today they unanimously testify to the natural authority he gained through his achievements. They extol with conviction his open manner towards 'civilian' fencers. This was apparently not noticed by the civilians themselves. 'He was always reserved, impenetrable and unpredictable towards them.'[32]

Because of this his participation in contests apparently led frequently to uneasiness and uncertainty, and everyone breathed a sigh of relief 'if he left without . . . causing any ill-feeling'.[33] The civilian fencers are even supposed to have submitted a memorandum to the Reich Head of Sport on Heydrich's 'practices' which was apparently destroyed immediately, at von Tschammer's request. It may have dealt with the complaint that Heydrich took it as his special duty to entice promising fencers into the SS whenever they appeared, or if this did not work, to try to get them assigned to the SS. Obviously he wanted to build up an SS team of the best fencers in Germany, or to make it look as if such men were best off in the SS.

On the other hand, if one is to believe them, his SS fencers went through thick and thin for him; they had everything to gain by it. Even requests of theirs that contravened official Nazi orthodoxy were approved. For instance, when they asked him to protect Paul Sommer, the former German champion, who was Jewish in the sense of the Nuremberg Laws, Heydrich made it possible for him to emigrate to America. It is also reported[34] that the Polish Olympic fencers were protected during the war at the express wish of Heydrich. Kantor, a Polish Jew who had taken part in the 1936 Olympics, was even received in Berlin when he fled from the part of Poland under Soviet occupation. Heydrich pumped him about training methods in Poland and the Soviet Union and provided him with papers and money before finally allowing him to return to Warsaw.

On the other hand his civilian fencing masters and referees often clashed with him. For instance, when the special referee in Berlin wanted to introduce a competition restricted to the SS, on the grounds that, as professional soldiers, they could no longer be regarded entirely as amateurs, Heydrich was so scathing about him that none of the SS fencers dared to speak to him openly again. The following story is told about this referee:

> This courageous man wanted to clarify the matter and therefore sought out Heydrich in his HQ in Prinz-Albrecht-Strasse. Heydrich tried to intimidate him with the power of his office. But when the shabbiness of using such pressure was pointed out to him, he gave in. It was the first argument between the two of them: many were to follow, when the one became director and the other sports manager of the Special Department for Fencing. Heydrich respected the professional ability of his sports manager and also his firm denial of many of the SS's special requests.[35]

Moreover, it was to be observed with surprising frequency that, as long as the right moment was chosen, the facts were unassailable, and the applicant courageous and uncompromising, Heydrich would be visibly impressed, and give in again and again, making decisions which diverged considerably from his original ones.

The top fencing official himself is unanimously portrayed as a talented and extraordinarily gifted fencer. His fencing style could be characterized as 'hard', a style that is practised by most of today's successful fencers.[36] He had learned a lot from frequent lessons from top-class masters. But whenever the decision went against him in a bout, he seemed for a long time to be a bad loser. Sometimes during contests he would forget himself and dispute the judges' decision excitedly. He had installed many of his fencers in Office I of the Services Sports Department. There Head-of-Office Streckenbach often heard the gruff comment about Heydrich: 'He can never lose, only complain.' By this was meant complaints about proper or questionable decisions by the judges.[37] It was only when his undaunted fencing master took him on one side afterwards and reminded him of his role as a model for the SS fencers that he appreciated his misconduct and pulled himself together. Just how much it mattered to him to be seen as truly fair and sporting is shown by the fact that he expressly asked his fencing master to warn him immediately if his conduct in any competition could be seen as unsporting. It was important to him to give public proofs of his 'sporting disposition'. His ability to endure public contradiction on such occasions is established by an incident that took place during the eliminating rounds for the sabre in 1940. When he started grumbling again at a decision by the judges, the referee publicly reprimanded him with the words: 'On the fencing strip the laws of sporting fairness apply and nothing else.' Heydrich was speechless – and submitted. All this provides an illuminating character sketch of Heydrich which reflects on his actions in other spheres. It does not, however, explain the motives and incentives for his mania to excel in sport and his outstanding performances.

Without doubt he took pronounced and uncomplicated pleasure in his ability to beat others and an almost vital joy in battle and victory. This did not, however, seem to fulfil him but to exhaust him, through his boundless, indeed morbid ambition. More and more he filled the ensuing emptiness by submitting himself to further tests of his ability. The 'competitor of conviction' was forcing the 'sportsman for pleasure' more and more into the background. His conviction was that the new SS was superior in spirit to the 'bourgeois', 'reactionary', 'old' armed forces, and particularly to the Navy, which had treated him so badly. He wanted to be the living proof of how much could be achieved if one belonged to the Black Order 'properly' and not inadvertently like the *Reichsführer* whom he satirized often. As early as 1936 the still inexperienced Chief of Security Police had recorded his conviction that 'self improvement' was in direct proportion 'to the efforts made' and that SS members had to 'gradually become the best in all fields'. 'Regarding liability for military service, we must provide the armour-bearer of the nation with the best recruits, in the field of sport we must always be amongst the first.'[38] As the 'model for all other SS-men', in Himmler's words, he tried to do justice to this conviction in all fields of life: as 'armour-bearer' in the Luftwaffe, as the best in sport.

There was more than the usual obituary pomposity in the Prague newspaper *Der Neue Tag*, which commented on his contribution to sport in its summing-up three days after his death:

> His sporting achievements were meant, above all, to set an example to the men under his command, to prove to them by his example that even the heaviest claims of one's official duties do not prevent one being purposefully and systematically active in sport at the same time.[39]

Thus amongst other things, he had on 9 November foisted on the *Reichs-*

führer an order which obliged top SS-leaders to learn to fence with the light sabre.[40] The 'synthesis of sportsman and soldier' had sounded a chord in Heydrich, his 'conviction of the *duty to excel*', and it was precisely in this that he was so important for the Nazi conception of sport.[41] The same catchwords with which Heydrich had camouflaged the bloody work of his task forces were now used for the innocuous theme of sport, such phrases as 'the duty to be tough', the 'thankless task which we *must* carry out'.[42] Who is not reminded of Hitler's objective by this example?: 'I want my youth to be strong and beautiful. I shall have them trained in every physical exercise . . . In this way I shall eliminate the thousands of years of human domestication.'

Hitler wanted a young generation 'which will make the world tremble with fear'.[43] Reinhard Tristan Eugen Heydrich was the larger-than-life prototype for such a conception of sport, for seeing the discharge of one's duty as subordinate to an overriding political necessity or as the mere technique of achieving an ultimate goal. Thus the contradiction between the sports comrade and top sportsman on the one hand and the Gestapo chief and proponent of the Final Solution on the other was more apparent than real as was demonstrated at the very climax of Heydrich's sporting achievement. Reinhard Heydrich resolved it in the principle of technical accomplishment and in his own contradictory personality, which stood, as it were, in the middle. 'Whatever he did, he did it thoroughly,' his widow said about him, 'which is a legacy from the Krantzes on his mother's side.'[44]

Chapter 10

THE CHIEF
SUSPICION-MONGER

People think that the Gestapo can find a solution for everything. Thus, to put it facetiously we are everything from 'the maid-of-all-work' to the 'dustbin of the Reich'.

Reinhard Heydrich (on German Police Day, 1941)

Heydrich's passion for doing everything thoroughly was felt by the enemies of the regime more and more each month as the chief of the Security Police and the SD established and extended his power. Right from the start he strove to make the fight against adversaries worldwide, and was not satisfied to confine reconnaissance and pursuit within the borders of the Third Reich. On the contrary, the more communists, pacifists, socialists or other opponents of the regime who sought to escape his clutches by flight, the more Heydrich's thousand eyes were turned abroad. The enemies of the regime were followed more and more closely across the borders by the SD's spies and collaborators.

The emigrants, who were able to carry on abroad, undisturbed, the same activity which had long ago landed those of like opinions inside the Reich in concentration camps, appeared particularly dangerous to the SD. For instance, Heydrich was 'particularly satisfied'[1] that the journalist Carl von Ossietzky, a pacifist already imprisoned by the Weimar courts as a traitor, and the same man who for years had revealed to the rest of the world and to the opposition inside Germany how the Reichswehr had evaded the disarmament regulations of the Treaty of Versailles, was now in the

Esterwegen concentration camp. However, the reports that friends of Ossietzky were playing the same old game unhindered just beyond the German frontiers would not let him rest.

One of them was Ossietzky's longstanding collaborator Berthold Jacob-Salomon, who had written well-informed articles directed against the Reichswehr and its secret rearmament in the left-wing journal *Weltbühne* (World Stage) with the attribution 'By an old soldier', before moving abroad at the beginning of March 1933. He settled in Strasbourg, where he carried on collecting news about German rearmament and published it in the *Unabhängiger Zeitungsdienst* (Independent News Service) which he edited himself.[2] His information about the formation of new regiments, about weapon and vehicle production and personnel movements was so precise that Heydrich was burning to interrogate the hated emigrant in Berlin about his Intelligence sources.

A suitable tool soon turned up in a report by the German Embassy in London, which, in reply to a routine enquiry from the Gestapo about 'persons in emigrant circles who are suitable for collaboration', suggested a certain Dr Hans Wesemann. A Social Democrat journalist on *Vorwärts* (Forward) and the *Sozialdemokratischer Pressedienst* (Social Democrat Press Service), he had left Germany in 1933 and was keeping his head above water in London with casual work. On 28 June 1934, von Bismarck, a member of the Embassy staff, reported from London that Wesemann was prepared to cooperate with Heydrich's office. In the autumn of 1934 Wesemann travelled to Heydrich's HQ on a passport which had already been extended by the London Embassy on instructions from Berlin. The new Germany made a great impression on him. 'I understood that I had betrayed the German cause and determined to do penance,' he explained later.[3]

First of all Wesemann was to approach the communist propaganda specialist, Willy Münzenberg, who was directing a propaganda centre in Paris with great skill. But the amateur Wesemann was no match for the experienced Münzenberg. In the meantime, however, the file on Berthold Jacob was growing and growing in Heydrich's filing cabinets. Since Wesemann had known the pacifist, who was now operating in Strasbourg, since the days of the Weimar Republic, and since Jacob had even been Wesemann's witness 'when the latter married Herta Meyer, the little Jewess from Leipzig', the raw secret agent for the Gestapo was set up as a lure for his former friend.[4]

Contact between the old acquaintances in London and Strasbourg was soon re-established. Wesemann provided Jacob's news service with 'information' – material fabricated by the Gestapo – he got subscribers for him and was soon helping him out with small amounts of money. Wesemann always gave receipts, in order to prove to his customers the authenticity of his work. So for a short time Jacob was supported by Heydrich, whose only aim was his destruction.

But Heydrich was prepared to invest. In October 1934 he had Wesemann travel from London to Strasbourg and build up Jacob's expectations 'of a wider sphere of activity in the context of anti-fascist propaganda', chiefly so that he could explore the possibility of abducting Jacob to the Reich.[5] But the Gestapo did not think Strasbourg was suitable for the attempt. Neither did it prove feasible to entice the victim into the Saar, where the referendum was at that time in full swing. In Trier, at the Gestapo office, Wesemann was instructed by Heydrich's assistants Dr Richter and Manz that Jacob 'was to be lured into Germany at all events'.[6]

After some thought Basel was decided on. From there it was scarcely ten minutes by car to German territory. At the end of 1935 Wesemann and Richter met in the Basel hotel 'St Gotthard' and devised the abduction plan. From there Wesemann went back to Strasbourg and took his 'friend' a bundle of 'good news'. Apparently an English edition of Jacob's News Service was assured and the false passport, which the pacifist had asked for, would be procured. A trusted person would arrive in Basel 'who did not want to compromise himself by a visit to France'. For this reason Switzerland had been chosen for a meeting which was arranged for 9 March.[7]

At six in the evening Jacob arrived at the 'St Gotthard' as arranged and was sent on by the porter to the restaurant 'Zum schiefen Eck', where the gentlemen were already waiting for him. The restaurant was one of the last houses in the town. The German customs post of Klein-Hünsingen was only a few hundred metres further. But in his pleasant anticipation of the promised help from a friend and the false passport, this did not occur to Jacob. Nor did he suspect anything underhand when Wesemann greeted him in the 'Zum schiefen Eck' and informed him that a gentleman from Liechtenstein would soon look in about the false passport. This 'gentleman from Leichtenstein' who was in fact the Gestapo collaborator Manz, soon arrived too. The three of them drank again and again to the future, perhaps with the intention of making Jacob slightly befuddled. Then the 'gentleman from Liechtenstein' showed them some blank German passports and suggested filling one out, not there in the restaurant but in his own house which was nearby. A taxi was called and was on the spot straight away. In fact it was a hired car from Zurich and the driver was Gestapo Commissioner Gustav Ott, from the frontier village of Lörrach. The party took their places and after a journey of a few hundred metres – the German barrier was open – the car was stopped by German frontier police, appropriately enough in Adolf-Hitler-Strasse. Jacob's passport had expired, so he was arrested, while the others were able to return to Switzerland. The trap had closed on Berthold Jacob-Solomon, 'the old soldier'.[8]

The following day Jacob was being interrogated in Berlin. On 12 March his friends Dr Robert M W Kempner, a lawyer, his partner Aschner, and the author Walter Kiaulehn were arrested; the Gestapo suspected them of being informers for the abducted pacifist.[9] 'Heydrich himself took part in the interrogation,' recalls Kempner, 'and held forth maliciously. He said he wanted to have a look at this collection of "shady Barons".'[10]

Jacob, however, did not name any informers but maintained that he had procured his own information, and demonstrated this to the horrified officials:

> He proved to them that he could deduce the establishment of new regiments and divisions quite legally by means of publications which communicated the promotion and transfer of colonels and generals. From the *Reichsanzeiger* (Reich Gazette) he showed which new stock and limited companies had been formed and what the aims of these new concerns were.[11]

Even so, Jacob's future in the hands of the Gestapo was not rosy. He was lucky, however, for in the meantime Wesemann had been arrested and had made a confession to Swiss authorities, who were infuriated by the abduction. In a note to the Foreign Office the Swiss demanded that Jacob be returned and that the German officials responsible be punished. The Gestapo initially told the Foreign Office that they had had nothing to do with the abduction, and the Swiss were only successful at the second attempt. After vehement insistence on the existing arbitration agreement, the Wilhelmstrasse came to the conclusion that only the return of the Gestapo prisoner Jacob could prevent further uncomfortable disclosures and appease the Swiss authorities. Reich Foreign Minister von Neurath received a ruling from the Führer through Hitler's Chancery Director

Lammers. Hitler, furious about the uproar, and intent upon preserving the appearance of peace because of the annulment of the military restrictions of the Treaty of Versailles which was just going through, decided to hand Jacob over to the Swiss authorities. He was set free on 18 September 1935.[12]

Heydrich was annoyed. In the first place he had to swallow a defeat when Jacob was set free, and in the second place the amateurish execution of the plan had not exactly enhanced the professional reputation of his sleuths. This was all the more important since another abduction from abroad had ended in a fiasco in January of the same year.

It was 9 January when Heydrich summoned his factotum, SS-Second Lieutenant Alfred Naujocks, to his office and silently held a photograph out towards him. It showed a young man 'with a most likeable face'.[13] 'That is Rudolf Formis. He has gone underground and is making broadcasts against National Socialism,' explained Heydrich and gave Naujocks the order: 'Bring Formis to Berlin. Alive!'

Heydrich told him that the transmitter in question had been located by means of radio direction-finding fifty or sixty kilometres (about thirty-five miles) south-west of Prague, near the small town of Příbram. Formis was making two broadcasts a day which were hostile to the Reich and the Party and which were best received over the whole of south Germany. The programme made open propaganda for the 'Black Front', the organization of Otto Strasser, the left-wing National Socialist and opponent of Hitler, who had escaped to Prague.[14] It was well known that Formis had been a pioneer of radio, an engineer and former technical director of Radio Stuttgart, and that he had attached himself to Strasser, for whom he was now transmitting propaganda against the Third Reich.

As cover Naujocks took with him a girlfriend of his fiancée, procured himself a false passport in the name of Gerber,[15] and crossed the border into Czechoslovakia in a black Mercedes. He soon found what he was looking for, but more by chance than from professional skill. The pirate transmitter was located in a room in the hotel Záhoří in the village of Dobříš, and the couple travelling under the name of Gerber also registered there.

Naujocks took a wax impression of the key to Formis' room and telegraphed to the SD head office 'found'. Then he left his 'wife' behind for the skiing while he flew from Prague to Tempelhof to get new instructions. Heydrich repeated that his mission was to deliver Formis alive and to destroy the transmitter with phosphorus. A sedative was made up for Formis, and Gert Gröthe, a colleague from the SD, was sent along as a reinforcement. The two returned to Dobříš and got ready to strike on the night of 23 January.

But everything went wrong. The bottle of chloroform broke while they were trying to surprise the engineer. Formis was able to draw a pistol and wounded Naujocks slightly with three shots. Gröthe shot back, hitting Formis in the head and killing him. The two SD-men found time to damage the transmitter with phosphorus before beating a retreat. After an adventurous flight they arrived at the border and reached Berlin at mid-day on 24 January. In the Berlin office Heydrich raged about the amateur methods 'straight out of a gangster film' with which his colleague Naujocks had messed up the mission.[16]

But however discouraging foreign actions such as the attempt at Jacob's abduction and the Formis escapade were, they still pointed to the new sphere of action into which Heydrich and the SD were slowly feeling their way, pursuing opponents of the system beyond the frontiers, the sphere of foreign espionage.[17]

Just as the SD had extended its network of eavesdroppers over the whole of Germany, where soon no area of public, business and in many cases private life was left uninvestigated, just as it registered every beat of the nation's pulse by means ranging from the system of informers to ordinary public opinion polls,[18] so it infiltrated further and further into the jungle of the Secret Services. Reports from abroad were gathered systematically in SD offices in frontier areas, and every conceivable SD section, as well as individual SD-leaders, cultivated their own information networks. The Jewish Section of the SD, for instance, maintained its own Middle East network and kept up contacts in Palestine through a journalist not only with the Zionist leader Feifel Polkes but with the Arabs too.[19]

Officially, SS-Brigadier Heinz Jost's Central Department III 2 was responsible for espionage, though he was distinguished neither by professional soundness nor by the ability to get things done.[20] 'But the more the SD expanded into the undergrowth of Intelligence, the more it met with opposition from military Counter-Intelligence *(Abwehr)*', as Canaris' biographer Heinz Höhne observed.[21] Above all the first Counter-Intelligence chief, Admiral Canaris' predecessor, naval Captain Conrad Patzig, found it impossible to get on with Heydrich. Patzig, 'primarily a naval officer' and 'without much inclination for Secret Service work', was a man of limited diplomatic ability who was at home in the conservative circles of the Army and for this very reason distrustful of the Secret Service of the SS. He was quite unable to defuse the open hostility between Counter-Intelligence and the SD.[22] In late autumn, 1934, Patzig told his friend Canaris quite clearly that he was fed up with emotional difficulties with Heydrich and wanted to leave. The Counter-Intelligence chief was getting into more and more trouble through concerted harassment by Heydrich:

> The head of the SD has found an excuse for getting rid of me. We made some reconnaissance flights over Poland whereupon Warsaw sent a diplomatic note to the effect that they regarded such flights as a breach of the German-Polish non-aggression pact of 26 January 1934. This would have remained a diplomatic incident if Heydrich, who had been informed about it, had not intervened with Blomberg (the Reich Minister for War) and expressed his disapproval, for he said that such an incident was damaging to the good name of the National Socialist system.[23]

Blomberg in fact took the matter up and a suitable successor for Patzig was sought and found in December 1934, in the person of Admiral Wilhelm Canaris. Blomberg's decision in favour of Admiral Canaris was influenced at least by the fact that the Admiral also knew Heydrich 'very well' and that this old acquaintance could make relationships between the head of Counter-Intelligence and the head of the SD easier.[24] In fact, while he was a sea cadet, Heydrich had been under the command of Wilhelm Canaris for nearly two years in Kiel, when the latter was the First Officer of the training cruiser *Berlin*. Cadet Heydrich had spent many evenings in Canaris' house playing music with his wife Erika. Canaris informed the Wehrmacht commanders that after taking up his office on 1 January 1935 he intended to strive for better cooperation between the SD under Heydrich and Counter-Intelligence 'in friendship and in frankness'.[25]

His attempts to reach an agreement were at first rewarded with success. At the end of January the first conversation between the old acquaintances took place in Berlin in the exclusive restaurant 'Horcher'.[26] Heydrich was obviously delighted at seeing his respected former boss again and even Canaris acted towards Heydrich 'with the affability of an older comrade'.[27] Contrary to speculation about 'animosity at first sight' between the two

Secret Service chiefs, supposedly due, above all, to Heydrich's 'aggressive-ness towards naval officers' because of his discharge in 1931,[28] Heydrich and Canaris agreed immediately on close cooperation, which was to last for many years and prove both professionally productive and personally very congenial.[29] After the war, Vice-Admiral Gustav Kleikamp, formerly a member of the Court of Honour which tried Heydrich, who also knew Canaris, testified to this, and also attributed it above all to the fact that 'Canaris was also one of those highly gifted and somewhat awkward naval officers who felt that they had been passed over by Raeder'.[30]

Canaris and Heydrich continued the rediscovered relationship in private as well. Moreover, they became neighbours quite by chance. On moving from Swinemünde to Berlin the Admiral had taken a flat in Döllestrasse in Berlin-Südende. At the same time the Heydrichs too had bought a house in Döllestrasse. Heydrich's widow Lina recalls: 'During a walk one Sunday in the spring of 1935, we met a couple whom Reinhard greeted with surprise and pleasure. It was Canaris and his wife . . . We looked in each others' prams and arranged to meet. Soon there was a lot of coming and going between the two families.'[31] On Sunday afternoons the Canaris family moved into the Heydrichs' garden to play croquet and in the evenings Canaris would return the favour with his home cooking. A year later the families moved still nearer. In August 1936 Canaris bought a house in Dianastrasse in Berlin-Schlachtensee and at the beginning of 1937 the Heydrichs moved into Augustustrasse, just round the corner. Now they were next-door-neighbours with adjoining gardens.

> The old game began again. We saw each other. We visited each other . . . We arranged musical evenings. Erika Canaris and Reinhard played second and first violin. A musical winter, a sort of middle-class visiting with instruments followed this beginning. It was a lovely peaceful time. The men would arrange to meet and go riding together in Grunewald, sometimes taking colleagues along as well.[32]

The official relationship between Counter-Intelligence, the Gestapo and the SD was also rendered more peaceable, and the working atmosphere more temperate, by the personal bond between Canaris and Heydrich. Agreement was even reached on the boundaries between their various areas of authority. After protracted negotiations which were conducted on the one side by Canaris himself and on the other by Heydrich and his head of the Counter-Espionage Police, Dr Werner Best, a ten-point agreement defined the competence of the Counter-Intelligence Department and that of the Gestapo and SD.[33] 'The Ten Commandments', as the agreement was soon known, assigned foreign espionage and Counter-Intelligence solely to the Counter-Intelligence Department, while the Gestapo maintained as its domain the 'investigation of actions punishable under Para. 163 StPO [treason] and any necessary enquiries'. Since Counter-Intelligence did not possess its own police force in peacetime, the Gestapo was to be called in as their executive organ. Nevertheless one of the 'Commandments' gave precedence to Counter-Intelligence in doubtful cases.[34] It was agreed that exclusively political investigation should be left to the SD.[35]

Nevertheless the seed of new friction lay in this new agreement. For, since the borderline between political and military information-gathering is very fluid and since any military Intelligence Service which did not take account of the political situation would be a very imperfect organization, the Counter-Intelligence Department was not prepared to do without a certain degree of investigation and information-gathering in the political field. Accordingly Canaris did not allow the 'Ten Commandments' to prevent him from leaving the borderline unclear. On the pretence that he had to keep in the picture both militarily and politically, he carried on tapping those sources of information both at home and abroad which he held to be necessary, even when the 'Ten Commandments' were replaced by an agreement much less favourable to Counter-Intelligence, which Canaris and Heydrich signed at Prague Castle in May 1942, only a few days before Heydrich was assassinated.[36] Conversely, the Gestapo's concern with cases of treason and enquiries about political opposition groups led to more and more foreign espionage. So in practice investigators and agents were obliged to violate the peace treaty between Counter-Intelligence and the SS.[37]

But the core of the rivalry between Canaris and Heydrich lay still deeper. The political alignment, method of operation and personnel of the two Secret Services were so opposed to each other in so many respects as to almost preclude their long-term harmonious cooperation. It was above all because Heydrich and his organization were driven to extend their activities further and further by the dynamics of the National Socialist system that those centrifugal forces developed which signalled dissension rather than unity between the rival departments.

Moreover, the estrangement between Heydrich and Canaris was

accelerated by an affair in which the SD infringed the jurisdiction of Counter-Intelligence in great style and which at the same time marked the transition from defensive to offensive investigation. The SD learnt of the Soviet military opposition's plans for the violent overthrow of Stalin through General Skoblin, a Russian émigré living in Paris, who acted as a double agent for Heydrich's SD and the Soviet NKVD.[38] The chief conspirator was said to be Marshal Mikhail Nikolaievich Tukhachevsky who was known to be 'pro-Western'. Skoblin was ordered to Berlin. The intrigue had its origin in a parlour in the Adlon Hotel. Heydrich received useful information from the Russian General not only about Tukhachevsky's intended putsch but also about the Marshal's attitude towards Hitler's Third Reich. Apparently Tukhachevsky had, together with the British and the French military, discussed the idea of a preventive war against the rearming German Reich.[39]

On Christmas Eve Heydrich and Himmler reported to the Führer on the information collected from Skoblin and the SD-staff on the ablest soldiers of the Soviet Union. And, more important, Heydrich told him how he proposed to make use of the information. If they succeeded in warning Stalin of the Soviet military's intended putsch, then the dictator would surely be provoked into making a final destructive stroke against the Army leadership. After a discussion of the pros and cons of this plan to cripple the Red Army, Hitler endorsed Heydrich's proposal.[40]

The warning from SD-officers that Skoblin was a double agent and that it was possible that Heydrich was allowing himself to be used by Stalin, were in vain. 'C' promptly decided: 'If Stalin suspects the officers of the Supreme Command of preparing a conspiracy he will doubtless look for proof of their treason. If, however, such proof does not exist, it must be supplied.'[41] Up to March 1937 Heydrich had some documents forged, which contained correspondence between officers of the German Army and Tukhachevsky and were produced mostly by Franz Putzig, the SD's engraver, under Naujocks' supervision. The forgers found genuine examples of Tukhachevsky's signature in Army documents from the years when the Reichswehr and the Red Army were working in close cooperation. Letters were prepared using these signatures which even imitated the Soviet Marshal's peculiarities of style. The German officers' signatures were copied from cheques and genuine German stamps could be obtained without any trouble.[42]

At the beginning of May, SS-Colonel Hermann Behrends, the SD-

Führer-East, passed the Tukhachevsky documents to the NKVD who handed over in return three million gold roubles, which afterwards proved to be, for the most part, as genuine as the doctored papers. In the middle of May the dossier arrived in Stalin's hands. The interpretation of Soviet affairs expert, Robert Conquest, is that Stalin had already intended dealing with the Army Commanders, whom he considered to be too independent, in the course of the giant 'purges'. But 'this final "proof" of treason apparently made Stalin decide to take action against the Generals'.[43]

The importance of Heydrich's intrigue against the Soviet Army is still uncertain today. But it was certainly a factor in the massacre of the Soviet military leadership, which began with Tukhachevsky and his 'accomplices' being shot on 12 June 1937 for 'collaboration with a power hostile to the Soviet Union' and ended with the liquidation of approximately 35,000 Soviet officers, half of the entire officer corps. It was only during one of their rides together that Canaris himself was informed of the long-range intrigue by the head of the SD. 'The news was of great concern to him,' Canaris' biographer Heinz Höhne surmises, 'for an adventurism that could one day hurl the whole Reich into the abyss revealed itself to his gaze.'[44]

Meanwhile another side of Heydrich's complex character had disclosed itself to his friend and rival Canaris through this affair of the Commanders of the Soviet Army. The policeman's thoroughness, the sportsman's need for achievement, the compulsion to climb ever higher and an insatiable ambition constituted only one half of Heydrich's split personality. The other half revealed itself more and more clearly to be a mixture of cunning and reserve, of mistrust and a malicious duplicity which sought out its own kind in the twilight world of the secret police. Consequently when Adolf Hitler's Third Reich could be helped by intrigue, Heydrich was involved. When, hardly a year after the Soviet dictator had got rid of his military, Hitler's dynamic foreign policy also came into conflict with obstructive elements in the leadership of the Wehrmacht, Heydrich's police instruments placed themselves at the dictator's disposal. In the crisis about Reich Minister-for-War Blomberg, who had not only inadvertently married a prostitute but also invited Hitler to be a witness, the Gestapo saw to it that the scandal became known.[45] Also, Heydrich turned a blind eye to an intrigue by Göring against von Fritsch, the Commander-in-Chief of the Army, who was accused of being a homosexual, and was hostile to the SS, even though von Fritsch's innocence had long before been established.[46]

135

As if under compulsion he worked out traps and stratagems and considered the most devious ways to be the most effective. Just as he himself secretly saw every step he took simply as a prerequisite for his next move, which was meant to bring him closer to his final goal, so he imputed to everyone else the same habit of directing their thoughts to hidden goals. The distrust that is a professional obligation for every Secret Service chief was second nature to him. His colleague Best declared: 'Because of this he approached everyone in that enquiring, mistrustful way which immediately struck one as his dominating characteristic.'[47] Nor did he make any secret of the fact that he regarded mistrust as a necessary virtue, or have any objection to his SD-officers giving him the nickname of the 'chief suspicion-monger'. To Heydrich's ears this was not criticism but praise.

But Heydrich's constant contemplation and pursuit of objectives had unhappy consequences for his conduct towards other people. Both inwardly and outwardly he created a tense atmosphere full of mistrust and friction. In every event which was caught in the searchlight of his apparatus – the SD or the Security Police – he looked for well-hidden objectives, a stubborn struggle to realize them and sophisticated camouflage – in short all the characteristics and activities which he would have developed in such a position.[48]

He projected his own characteristics on to the real or suspected enemies of the state and then attacked them accordingly. According to Best:

By this means, he confirmed, strengthened and made more concrete the theoretical and doctrinaire assertions about enemies of the state that came from Hitler and Himmler. Whatever attitudes and activities were designated 'from above' to be theoretically hostile to the state, Heydrich would certainly find real champions of them who appeared as dangerous to him as he would have been in their place.[49]

This led on the one hand to phenomenal successes in the actual fight against opponents and on the other hand to obsessions and unusually zealous application of his methods. 'Even in his lifetime,' his widow recalls, 'I had heard all the names of 20 July from my husband. Even most of those who at that time had not yet taken any practical action against the Third Reich had already been actually noted as security risks, as "shady

Barons", to use his own expression.'[50] If they were invited to a social occasion in Berlin Heydrich went through the guest lists beforehand and warned against getting into conversation with this or that guest who was 'a shady Baron'.[51]

The huntsman in Heydrich followed up the scent of worthwhile prey into the remotest spheres of life. When, in the course of the war, international firms in Belgium, Holland and Norway were taken over by German Commissioners, Heydrich straight away had the archives 'monitored for the security services'. In the files of Unilever for instance he found evidence of the political danger to the state of the 'multinationals' – thirty years before it became fashionable in the whole of Western Europe to suspect a 'world conspiracy' in them.[52]

His distrust did not even stop at fellow Party members and government notables. For the prosecution 'of the case of cases' he gathered information about the extravagant love-life of Joseph Goebbels, he observed the corruption in Göring's circle, he had Alfred Rosenberg's correspondents watched, and even Himmler's and Hitler's pasts held no taboos for his compulsive enquiries.[53] In Berlin he had the high-class brothel 'Salon Kitty' taken over by the SD, which he did not for love but for the information he hoped to gain from the visits of state and Party chiefs by means of listening devices and tape recorders.[54] In this case, his interests soon waned. He confided casually to the press chief of the Foreign Office that 'he was surprised how little emerged. Was it perhaps just a popular myth that secrets are given away in bed?'[55]

The ever quickening pace at which European politics were moving towards war constantly brought Heydrich new areas of responsibility, specific single actions or organizational changes. Above all the annexation of Austria to the Reich, followed by the annexation of the Sudetenland and finally, in March 1939, the occupation of Bohemia and Moravia, led not only to a considerable extension of the areas of responsibility of the chief of the Security Police and the SD in a territorial, that is, in a purely quantitative sense, but also to the establishment of Sipo and SD offices 'on wheels'. During the invasion of these regions and shortly after their annexation, the interests of the security and Intelligence services were looked after by so-called 'task forces'.[56] An advisory outline on the subject in the SD head office directs: 'Where possible the SD follows directly behind the invading troops and takes over the security of political affairs analogously to its duties in the Reich.'[57]

As to what this meant in practice, we have Heydrich's own testimony from a detailed memorandum on the necessity for task forces belonging to the SD. In all previous operations the task forces had followed directly behind the advancing troops 'on the special orders of the Führer and, by virtue of preparatory work, had systematically dealt heavy blows against those elements in the world from the camp of emigration, Freemasonry, Jewry, the political opposition of the Churches and the 2nd and 3rd Internationals, who were hostile to the Reich, by means of arrests, confiscation and securing the most important political material'[58] – and all this 'for the political and ideological security of these new areas'.[59] Apart from securing material of importance to the Intelligence services, secret archives and files on political opponents, the *Völkischer Beobachter* gave a hint of what this security obviously entailed when it wrote, shortly after Heydrich's detachments had entered the Sudetenland, that the men of the Gestapo and the SD had 'immediately begun to purge the liberated areas of Marxist traitors of the people and other enemies of the state'.[60]

The war of course brought a further intensification, a higher degree of unscrupulousness. Even before the outbreak of war Heydrich had had to provide for the eyes of the world an exactly timed excuse for the German Wehrmacht to begin hostilities, by staging an attack by Polish troops on the radio transmitter at Gleiwitz (now Gliwice) in Upper Silesia, an event, of course, which could have no real influence as a cause or reason for the war.[61] Nevertheless the operation still gave a taste of what actions Heydrich might become capable of in the case of war. His widow thinks that he considered the Gleiwitz escapade to be 'an excellent stratagem. He had no scruples about it. It even seemed to amuse him a hell of a lot.'[62]

A second security commando action corresponded exactly to his conception of 'active Intelligence work'. Even before the war started an SD-agent had managed to penetrate the British Secret Service network in neutral Holland, where it was very active, and succeeded not only in deceiving the British but also in gaining information about the contacts with the British of the conservative military opposition to Hitler in Germany. The SD-agent was soon on the best of terms with Captain S Payne Best, the legitimate agent of the British Intelligence Service, who appeared to interest Heydrich so much that he decided to have a good close look at him. Walter Schellenberg, who was given the role of a 'Captain Schemmel' from the opposition group in Army High Command, in what Heydrich himself called his 'play',[63] was given the task of enticing or abducting Best across the border. The abduction, one of the most spectacular operations in the history of the European Secret Services, was to take place on 9 November. (This was one day after the unsuccessful assassination attempt on Hitler in the 'Bürgerbräukeller' in Munich, by the lone joiner Georg Elser, whose attack was suspected by Hiter as having been inspired by the British Intelligence Service.)[64] Schemmel-Schellenberg asked the chosen victim to meet him in a café in the Dutch border town of Venlo. Best was accompanied by a Major Stevens and a Dutch Secret Service officer called Klop. Taken by surprise, the Allied Secret Service officers were snatched across the border by Schellenberg's agents. Klop was fatally wounded in the ensuing gunfight. The international scandal seemed at first to outweigh the benefits for the Intelligence services. It was only two and a half years later that decisive evidence about the Counter-Intelligence officer and master spy Thümmel (A54) emerged from the statements of the British captives, who had been interrogated in part by Heydrich himself. This evidence finally led to Thümmel's cover being broken by the Gestapo.

While playing at spies, Heydrich still found time for the biggest reorganization of the German security apparatus. On 27 September 1939 Hitler signed the decree for the creation of a Reich Central Security Department (RSHA) which formally united the police of the Third Reich and the Security Services of the SS. The unsupervised flow of measures between state authorities and Party officers which Heydrich had started therefore received official sanction. In addition Walter Schellenberg and Dr Werner Best were instructed by Heydrich to institute a section for internal Counter-Intelligence (IV E) and to coordinate the military and political sides.[65] The Janus-like character of Heydrich's apparatus became most apparent in the first weeks of the Polish campaign. While Heydrich, Schellenberg, Best and Six were discussing at their desks the organization of the RSHA they were to create, the task forces of the Security Police and the SD were on the move again – and this time they had instructions to kill thousands of people. Hitler had decided to decimate the ruling class of his Polish opponent even before the fighting was over. The explosions of the Stukas' bombs and the artillery's bombardments were supposed to drown out the volleys directed against the representatives of Poland's future resistance. Heydrich, 'the maid-of-all-work' as he acknowledged himself with a trace of bitterness, had once again become the 'dustbin of the Reich'.[66]

Shortly before the start of the Polish campaign six task forces were formed, each designated by Roman numerals and each destined for one of the five Armies that were standing to, except for the one reserved for West Prussian Posnania, which Hitler intended to re-incorporate into the Reich from which it had been annexed after the Versailles peace.[67] The instructions for these task forces were, according to Heydrich himself, 'extraordinarily radical' and concerned 'an order to liquidate numerous Polish leaders, amounting to several thousands'.[68] Polish professors and divines, high officials and officers, nationalists and above all the members of the chauvinistic Polish Western March Union, which saw Poland extending in the West as far as Berlin, were shot in turn by Heydrich's death brigades.

Among them were also, for the first time, large numbers of Polish Jews, even though there were still no general instructions for shooting Jews. Summary murders of Jews depended on the zeal of SS-General Udo von Woyrsch, the leader of the back-up special duty task force, and soon stopped after protests from the Wehrmacht.[69] But these events turned a new page, and brought closer a gruesome aspect of the future which linked the name of Heydrich with the Jews – the 'Final Solution of the Jewish Problem'.

Chapter 11

FROM POLICY-MAKER TO EXECUTIONER

The danger of Judaism for Germany is not averted by the Aryan legislation.

Reinhard Heydrich, 1936

The Jewish policy of the Third Reich was characterized from the outset by incessant jostling and competition between the most diverse institutions of state and Party. Apart from the 'will of the Führer', to represent which the offices of the 'Führer's Deputy' and the Party Secretary competed, along-side the Ministry of the Interior; other departments, in frequently changing coalitions, meddled by turns in Jewish policy. These included the Racial Policy Office of the Party, the Reich Department of Justice, the leaders of the Jewish communities and the Central Office for Community Policy of the NSDAP. In addition, the department of the Special Foreign Relations Offices, under Joachim von Ribbentrop, the Foreign Office under Alfred Rosenberg and the Department for External Affairs of the NSDAP, under Ernst Wilhelm Bohle, all had a special interest in Jewish questions, which led to recurrent bouts of interference and conflict with the official Jewish policy of the Reich.[1]

While all these agencies were always dependent on the 'approval' of the Führer's Deputy, whose interests by no means corresponded with the aims of all the other Party offices, this restriction hardly applied to the last group to have a hand in the Jewish policy – the SS. Himmler and Heydrich had carved out a position of power for the Black Order which made it fully a match for the Party. The separation of the SS from the command structure of the SA after the events at the time of the Röhm putsch, and the SD's exclusiveness as the Party's only Intelligence Service, granted by Hitler shortly before, followed by the creation of a unified police force under an 'SS-*Reichsführer* and Chief of German Police', linked to the SS at every level, and not least the establishment of the Reich Security Central Office (RSHA) – these were the stages by which Himmler and Heydrich gained the power to implement their ideas.

The fateful significance which the SD and Heydrich's Gestapo were to acquire for the Jews in the German sphere of influence was grounded both in the particular functions which were initially marked out for the Political Police in Hitler's state, and in the way in which Heydrich exploited this scope through the projection of his own vision of the concept of a Political Police force. Thirdly, through Heydrich the SD had been 'scientifically' concerned, since its inception, with 'international Jewry' as an ideological opponent. Heydrich therefore felt ideally placed to assist in solving the Jewish question.

'The inspiration behind the opposition', Heydrich himself had written in 1936, 'remains forever the same: world Jewry, world Freemasonry and a largely political bureaucracy of priests which abuses religion.'[2]

The SD-chief complained about Jewry in the same tone and with the same words as was usual in the whole nationalist movement at that time (leaving aside the individualist *Stürmer* editor, anti-semite Streicher, as a special case). For Heydrich too, the Jew was 'the deadly enemy of all nordic and racially healthy peoples'. 'His aim was and remains the domination of the world by a more or less visible elite. To achieve this aim, any means and any form of organization is appropriate, however stupid and ridiculous it may outwardly appear. The method is always the same.'[3] This was no mere lip-service to the spirit of the age embodied in the Third Reich. Heydrich's widow, Lina, testifies: 'Reinhard was deeply convinced that the Jews had to be separated from the Germans. In his eyes the Jews were . . . rootless plunderers, determined to gain selfish advantage and moreover to stick like leeches to the body of the host nation.'[4]

National Socialism, however, had, from the start, totally transformed 'the Jews', from the ideological or political opponent, as Heydrich understood the term, into 'the public enemy'.[5] This resulted in an almost limitless increase in the number of people at the mercy of the Political Police, whose powers increased correspondingly. Under Göring and their first President, Diels, the Gestapa (as it was then called) had already been able to act without supervision, unhampered by legal norms. But it took a man of Heydrich's incisive thoroughness to accomplish the 'reorganization of police law', supported by professionally distinguished and radically National Socialist SD and Gestapo lawyers – chief among them the Gestapo legal expert Dr Werner Best and the later Harzburg 'Management-Trainer', Dr Reinhard Höhn.[6]

From now on the police were no longer primarily concerned with maintaining the public peace, security and order, but had to act exclusively in accordance with the 'needs of the community'. Heydrich's police were no longer to be jailers, but the agents of the Führer's will. To the police leadership squad put together by Heydrich, this was not a point of law, but a 'question of destiny'.[7] From this self-image it was but a short step to presuming absolute knowledge of the Führer's will, and from there to shaping it. 'And we', said Heydrich, 'will be the ideological shock troops and the *Schutzstaffel* of the Führer's mind.'[8]

The central starting-point for executing the will of the Führer was doubtless offered by the fate, quarrelled over amongst the power-hungry authorities, which National Socialism had intended for Judaism. For Heydrich's security agents, moreover, the Jew had been an opponent from the beginning and was therefore an object of particular interest. The projection of the Jew as an ideological, political and police enemy, which increasingly made him the preserve of the SS, was facilitated above all by the amalgamation under Heydrich of the state force, the Security Police, including the Gestapo, and the Party force, the SD. By means of a constant flow of measures and exchange of personnel between the technical and bureaucratic Security Police and the ideologically based SD, Heydrich effectively integrated the state and Party forces.[9] In the Gestapo, immediately after his appointment as its chief, Heydrich had converted Department II F2 ('Jews, Emigrants, Freemasons'), as it was known under his predecessor, Göring's protégé, Diels, into Department II 1 B2 ('Jews, Freemasons, Lodges, Emigrants'). At the same time Heydrich also re-grouped his SD: within the Inland-SD (office II) he set up the Department II 1 12, which devoted itself exclusively to 'Jewish affairs'.[10] Both departments were eventually to be combined in Adolf Eichmann's Jewish Department IV B4 in the Reich Security Central Office (RSHA).[11]

By these means Heydrich managed to beat a path through the tangled maze of Nazi Jewish policy which led both to the enhancement of his own power and to establish himself as the champion of the Führer's will. The road to that form of Final Solution subsumed under the heading 'Auschwitz' was certainly not so inevitable as was claimed after 1945. For example, his predecessor in the Berlin Gestapo, Rudolf Diels, thought after the war that the Final Solution had matured 'in the minds of Himmler and Heydrich'.[12] In the opinion of the Chief Interpreter for the Foreign Office, Paul Schmidt, it had emanated from the Himmler, Heydrich, Streicher group.[13] Heydrich's first biographer, the British journalist Charles Wighton, even brought up the rumoured 'Jewish extraction' again, and wrote that he felt 'that he himself had been betrayed by his ancestors, and that for his own justification he must obtain racial absolution by taking revenge on the cause of his psychosis [the Jews].'[14] And of the summer preceding the outbreak of war the journalist reported, 'All the pent-up hatred which Reinhard Heydrich cherished against the Jews was concentrated on the opportunities which war would offer to his venom.'[15]

Even well-informed historians such as the French scholar, Léon Poliakov, asserted that Heydrich had been the first National Socialist official to be working for the annihilation of the Jews before war broke out;[16] and Poliakov's American colleague, Henry A Zeiger, reported that Heydrich had won Hitler over to the idea of killing every available Jew in Europe, and only then had Hitler and Göring decided on the Final Solution.[17] German members of the fraternity came to a similar conclusion. Professor Karl Dietrich Bracher of Bonn, for example, in his standard work *The German Dictatorship*, tersely announced that whether alternatives to the planned annihilation of the Jews had ever had a chance was 'doubtful'.[18]

Nevertheless, however deeply the *Schutzstaffel* and Reinhard Heydrich were implicated in the frightful decimation of European Jewry, it is quite wrong to believe that the perpetrators of the greatest mass crime in German history were also its authors. For a decade there has been a growing tendency among researchers to attempt a dispassionate explanation of that process, free from the immediate horror of the post-war period and the haze of murder and destruction. The *Spiegel* articles by Heinz Höhne, which in 1966 were the first to paint a comprehensive and unprejudiced picture of the Death's Head Order, contradicted the general image which many contemporaries had created of the origins of the so-called Final Solution.

The interpretation that the SS and especially Heydrich had deliberately driven Nazi anti-semitism along the road to Auschwitz lacked concrete evidence for Höhne.

> It is virtually based solely on the reasonable reflection that the men who plunged millions of Jews into an orgy of blood, destruction and sadism could not have turned from peaceful citizens into mass murderers overnight as it were – in other words, that the annihilation of the Jews was already implanted in the hearts and minds of the SS before the command to destroy was given. Against that there is evidence that the decision to murder the Jews originated from outside the SS leadership. Up to early summer 1941 . . . there is no document of any SS organization which provides for the physical destruction of European Jewry.[19]

And in 1972 the historian Uwe Dietrich Adam, probably the foremost authority on Jewish policy in the Third Reich, demolished the thesis of a preconceived plan and with it the thesis of a formal anti-semitic continuity under the SS symbol, as well as the conspiracy theory, which inspired the entire Nuremberg Trials and a large part of the post-1945 generation of political scientists and contemporary historians. Again and again, according to Adam, the mistake has been made 'of making an *a posteriori* interpretation of the Jewish policy of the Third Reich and perceiving a thread running through the whole'.[20] In doing so, the fact was overlooked that the Führer state was more like an 'authoritarian anarchy'[21] and that 'there was just as little National Socialist Jewish policy as there was National Socialist foreign policy, but the concurrent interests and motives had to be considered and evaluated separately.'[22]

And in this question of jurisdiction Heydrich by no means played a leading part. Particularly in the first two years of the Third Reich, other Nazi groups decided on the line taken at any given time against the Jews. In the first months after the seizure of power it was doubtless Streicher's anti-semitism which determined the anti-Jewish stance of the regime. The boycott of Jewish businesses on 1 April 1933, the bloody riots against Jews in March, and the decrees banning Jews from swimming-baths and concert halls, 'all this bore the unmistakable mark of Streicher'.[23]

The first wave of terror against the Jews did not die down until 1934. More moderate anti-semites, not a little concerned for German prestige and the reputation of National Socialism abroad, took command. The prominent Nazi jurist Hans Frank already spoke of a 'certain termination' of further differences with the Jews. To tens of thousands of Jews also, who had fled across the frontiers, the worst seemed to be over. In May 1935 the Nazi newspaper, *Völkischer Beobachter*, reported that almost 10,000 of them had, in the meantime, returned to Germany.[24]

It was for this very reason that the rabid anti-semites sounded the alarm again and mounted a campaign against the 'returning stream', this 'typical piece of Jewish insolence'.[25] Tirelessly, *Stürmer* editor Streicher worked up a mood of pogrom. Even in the most remote communities *Stürmer* showcases were set up by which the people were to be infected with a campaign of atrocity stories about the deadly Jewish enemy which intensified weekly. In February 1935 a newly founded sister-paper of the *Stürmer*, the *Judenkenner*, joined in the Jew-baiting with headlines such as 'Beastly Racial Morals', 'Jewish Women Wallow in Butter', or 'Jewish Lust for German Women'.[26]

The pornographic and criminal verbal orgies were not the end of the matter, however. This time it was Goebbels who took up these widely disseminated diatribes and attempted to convert them into political demands. At the end of April his newspaper *Der Angriff* (The Attack) was already predicting a fresh wave of anti-semitism,[27] and in June he polemicized against 'stupid and foolish phrase-making by bourgeois intellectuals to the effect that the Jew is also human'. 'We no longer want the Jews!', was his irrevocable conclusion.[28] The coarse anti-semitic utterances and propaganda attacks had created a climate of frenzy that Frick's Reich Ministry of the Interior itself had difficulties in allaying. At the end of April it announced a revision of state citizenship, the granting of which was to depend on racial conditions. The ministries therefore began to respond to pressure from the gutter, making concessions to the anti-semitic radicals who were rapidly restricting the 'living space' of the German Jews.[29]

The German states were instructed not to certify non-Aryan candidates of medicine, veterinary science, dentistry or pharmacy, 'pending a final regulation'. Shortly afterwards Jews were no longer allowed to enter any state examinations in these subjects.[30] In May the new Combined Service Act also barred the Jews from the armed forces: they had to leave the Wehrmacht and the Labour Service.[31] And to wind up this process of repression the first race laws in German history came into force, the 'Nuremberg Laws', which stamped the Jews as second-class citizens.[32]

During this campaign against the Jews Reinhard Heydrich's Gestapo took part in anti-Jewish activities for the first time, in their self-imposed role as 'champions' of the Führer's will. Through a circular of February 1935 addressed to all Gestapo regional HQ's, for example, Heydrich forbade the Jews something which they probably seldom desired – the right to hoist the swastika flag. Another decree of April of the same year instructed the Gestapo throughout the Reich, in jargon typical of Heydrich, 'on their own authority, with reference to local circumstances, to subject the teaching by Jewish tutors at the German universities to a thorough overhaul'.[33] Heydrich himself wrote that it could not be tolerated 'that people who do not belong to the German nation as a whole should prepare young Aryan compatriots for examinations by means of Jewish tricks'.[34] The hidden meaning of Heydrich's invented term, 'overhaul', scarcely needed interpretation: in plain language it meant house-searches, intimidation and finally the prohibition of Jewish participation in university teaching.

Besides his ambition to gain recognition in the sphere of 'positive influence on the shaping' of National Socialist Jewish policy, these encroachments by Heydrich particularly reflected the intention of the police not to leave any area unregulated which could conflict with the ideological conceptions of the SS, and also the endeavour to appease the widespread dissatisfaction of many National Socialists with the relative restraint displayed by the police bureaucracy so far.[35] The Heydrich-Himmler team was still struggling painfully for recognition and had no wish to antagonize any of the competing groups within the power jungle of the Führer state, which might prove inimical to this very recognition.

In the following year, 1936, the wave of anti-Jewish persecution receded again. For the German Jews there ensued a period of outward quiet and even a certain legitimate security. Certainly, the basic anti-semitic attitude of the system remained latent, and by introducing new measures Heydrich and Himmler repeatedly sought to re-activate the Jewish question. On the instruction of Gestapo HQ, in late 1935, all regional HQs had to record the Jews of their district in a central Jewish register. In January 1936 the same office forbade the Jews to wear the state decoration for sport, and in January 1937 Heydrich also ordered surveillance of the half-Jews, the 'first degree cross-breeds'.[36] The general outlook was milder than in previous years, however. The murder in Switzerland of Wilhelm Gustloff, a prominent Party figure, by the Jew David Frankfurter, was exploited to some extent in the press, but in Hitler's commemorative address any invective directed against 'international Jewry' was avoided.[37] Historians see the explanation of this in the impending occupation of the Rhineland and in the Olympic Games, which forced restraint on the system.[38]

Besides this, the anti-Jewish measures taken so far had already resulted in the removal of Jews from the most important political and cultural walks of life under the Third Reich, though their elimination from the German economy, demanded particularly and with passionate hatred by Goebbels,[39] had by no means progressed very far. 'On the contrary,' confirmed Aronson, the Israeli Heydrich scholar, 'Jewish businesses and firms continued to flourish up to the eventual turning-point in November 1938.'[40] And Hermann Göring, head of the economic four-year plan at that time, who adhered only with reservations to the group of anti-semitic agitators, evidently still hesitated to expel the Jews from this last area altogether.[41]

This complex, vacillating game played by the rival anti-semitic groups of the Third Reich met with no approval from the intellectuals of Reinhard Heydrich's SD, dedicated as they were to good sense and rationality and continually urged on by their chief himself to the principle of efficiency. If Judaism, as Heydrich was convinced, was a 'three-dimensional', 'demoniacal' and unfathomable ideological opponent, then aimless messing around could not suffice. 'The Jewish threat to Germany is not averted by the Aryan legislation,' reported Heydrich.[42] The Jewish 'subversive organizations' with all their 'international connections' were working as ever, in his opinion 'for the destruction of our people and all their values'. Spheres of life such as art, science and the economy were 'still very far from free of the enemy'.[43]

At the same time his Jewish Department in the SD clearly defined Jewry as 'the opponent of state and Party'. The Jew 'as a person, proved by the difference of his race and of his national characteristics', had always been 'one hundred per cent opposed to National Socialism'. In the past as in the present, Jewry had known how to express its inherent mentality, 'in liberalism, especially Freemasonry, in Marxism and not least in Christianity'.[44] For Heydrich's SD anti-semites it was a fact that this Jewish mentality which had thus come to light was 'hereditary, therefore ineradicable and indivisible'.[45]

Up to now, in Heydrich's judgment, the fight against political and cultural organizations and their influence had merely been directed against the symptoms of the disease. What mattered was the removal of its carriers.

If this failed, the SD-chief expected the worst: 'Either we eventually vanquish the opponent or we perish.'[46]

But how was one to remove the Jews? That was the central question for the whole of Nazi anti-semitism, and on it opinions were divided. Heydrich and his young men, who he had been able to place in positions of authority in the SD, were similarly perplexed. One thing appeared certain, however: the *'Stürmer* methods' with their mixture of blind hatred, political pornography and coarse vituperation, disgusted those black-uniformed intellectuals, who hoped to combine 'respectable behaviour, uncompromising National Socialism and common sense in their organization'. 'Before the primitive recipes of the official Party Jew-bashing policy,' attested the historian Höhne, 'they demonstrated an evident horror.'[47]

Uneasiness about the anti-semitic horror propaganda – broken window-panes, Jews beaten up by the SA mob and all the abuses in stark contrast to the sober and rational behaviour of the SD – was expressed in various ways. Gestapo officials condemned as 'crude mischief' pamphlets and propaganda posters whose anti-semitism appealed to the lowest instincts.[48] In a memorandum, the SD Jewish expert, Herbert Hagen, declared that the *Stürmer* book for young people, *Der Giftpilz* (The Poison Mushroom), highly praised in Party circles, was simply unsuitable for juveniles, and the chief editor of the SS-newspaper *Das Schwarze Korps*, Gunter d'Alquen, who conducted a lively exchange of ideas with Heydrich, printed a headline speaking of 'Anti-semitism which harms us'.[49] Searching for a course of his own which could lead him from the wrangling of the anti-semitic power groups along the route to the rationally based 'elimination' of the Jews, Heydrich soon encountered a dispute which divided the Jews in Germany themselves. The mass of German Jews, in spite of their experiences in the early years of the Third Reich, still clung firmly to their aim of assimilation with the German people and – with or without the retention of their Mosaic faith – merging with them. Opposed to this majority were those Jewish nationalists who hoped to achieve their aims in their own state. The policy of sticking it out held by the assimilationists was in stark contrast to the Zionist policy of leaving Germany and setting out for Palestine. Although the assimilationists mostly wanted to obliterate their Jewish identity as quickly as possible, to the spokesmen of Zionism anti-semitism appeared to be constant proof that a solution to the Jewish question was only to be found in emphasizing racial, cultural, historical and religious differences. 'No hiding-place will conceal us any longer,' wrote the young Zionist Rabbi Joachim Prinz, 'in place of assimilation we desire something new: the confession of faith in the Jewish nation and the Jewish race.'[50]

In this dispute Heydrich discerned the means by which his Jewish experts hoped to reach the solution to the Jewish question. If there were already Jewish forces at work which were striving for the removal of the Jews from Germany, why should not emigration be the aim of the German enemies of assimilation too? On the look-out for a suitable man to develop this plan and take over the newly created SD-Department II 1 12, Heydrich came across an SS-officer just two years older than himself, whom he appointed as first Jewish expert of the SD and head of the small Department II 1 12 – the Prague-born nobleman, Leopold Itz von Mildenstein. As a qualified engineer and contributor to a Berlin newspaper, *Börsenzeitung* (Financial News) he had gained a reputation as an expert on the Middle East, and through journeys abroad and personal relationships had made numerous contacts with Zionist organizations. As Mildenstein related after the war, Heydrich's attention had been drawn to him by a series of 'pro-Zionist articles' in the *Börsenzeitung*[51] and through a report of a journey to Palestine in Goebbels' newspaper *Der Angriff*,[52] and in the autumn of 1934 he had invited him to join the SD. This was the hour of birth of the SD's independent Jewish policy, which admittedly could only be implemented insofar as the Castor and Pollux of the Black Order, Heydrich and Himmler, were successful in building up their uncontrollable, sprawling machinery of power parallel with the development of the vacuums created by the overweening dictatorship of the Führer. In the summer of 1936 at the latest, when Himmler was appointed Chief of German Police and Heydrich was made Chief of Security Police, this freedom of action was institutionalized.

The aim of the Jewish policy of the SD, which bore Heydrich's personal stamp much more strongly than did the Gestapo,[53] was described by the formula 'solution by emigration'. The tactical paths which were to lead to this objective were simple. While Heydrich allowed the Zionist organizations working for emigration a certain freedom of action, the opportunities available to those Jews who still believed in a basis of existence, albeit restricted, in Germany, and did not think of themselves as travellers to Zion but as Germans of Jewish faith, had to be totally destroyed.[54] The provisional objective was summed up in a memorandum to Heydrich from

SS-Second Lieutenant Herbert Hagen, who replaced Mildenstein in 1936, 'First: suppression of Jewish influence in all areas of public life (including the economy). Second: furtherance of Jewish emigration.'[55]

This policy of Heydrich's was swiftly implemented. The Bavarian Political Police gave instructions, for example, that 'the activities of the Zionist youth organizations' lay 'in the interests of the state leadership'. For this reason, it was given out to the state police that the members of the Zionist leagues 'were not to be treated with that severity which is necessary towards adherents of the German-Jewish organizations'.[56] The Jewish expert, Mildenstein, had tried to ward off troublesome influences on the part of ministerial bureaucracy by contact with the Jewish expert of the Ministry of the Interior, Bernhard Lösener. His request for a joint petition to Hitler's Deputy, Hess, against the defamation of the 'half-breeds' had been assured by Mildenstein of his support. And Heydrich had ratified this by a handwritten note, 'Agreed, C', in the margin of the memorandum.[57] 'C' stood for 'Chief', the abbreviation cultivated by Heydrich, which connected him, at least in this way, with the Chief of the British Secret Service, his great model.[58]

Heydrich pressed on, unhindered, towards his ambitious target: no longer always to be the agent, but to make his own policy. While the state authorities were still thinking along the lines of a purely legal solution to the problem, and in Party circles the fire of violent anti-semitism smouldered on, Heydrich had a clear-cut plan and a definite aim in view. In his opinion the Jewish problem was only to be solved by controlled emigration directed towards Palestine.[59]

'As a National Socialist,' he announced in intimate circles, 'I am a Zionist.'[60] And even in his manifesto, *Die Wandlungen unseres Kampfes* (The Fortunes of our Struggle), he wrote that one should not allow oneself to be deceived by Zionism over the 'basically' hostile attitude of the Jews. But in contrast to the assimilationists, 'who disown their Jewish race', he was ready to praise the Zionists. First point in their favour: 'The Zionists advocate a strong racial standpoint.' Secondly: 'By emigrating to Palestine they aspire to the creation of their own Jewish state.'[61]

Unconcerned by the objections of other agencies of Nazi Jewish policy, especially of the Foreign Office, which out of consideration for England did not consider the creation of an independent Jewish state in Palestine to be compatible with the interests of the German Reich, the SD continued to pursue its efforts in this direction.[62] Although from 1933 to 1937 only

24,000 Jews had been able to emigrate to Palestine,[63] the turning-point arrived at the beginning of 1938. In spite of the scruples of the Foreign Office and the Department for External Affairs of the NSDAP, on 1 February 1938 Hitler also declared himself in agreement with the promotion of Jewish emigration to Palestine.[64]

Preparations had already been made by Heydrich's Jewish expert, Mildenstein, Hagen, his successor, and their unobtrusive assistant, Adolf Eichmann. The training-camps maintained by Zionist organizations, in which the future emigrants received preparation for the agricultural work and trades needed later in Palestine, were encouraged by Department II 1 12. The Zionist leagues were also scrutinized to determine how much they might contribute to the SD in urging more and more Jews across the frontiers of the Reich.[65] The men of II 1 12 spread their tentacles into the HQ of the Zionist movement itself. In February 1937 Eichmann was able to greet an emissary of the Zionist secret organization 'Haganah' in the person of 'Commander' Feifel Polkes, who came to Berlin from Palestine in order to discuss mutual ideas, including the potentialities of a Palestinian Jewish state, with the men of the *Schutzstaffel*.[66] In the autumn the visit was returned, in the form of a picturesque trip to Palestine by Jewish expert Hagen and his assistant Eichmann – with Heydrich's express approval.[67] As Hagen summed up the outcome of the negotiations with the Haganah representative in a report for Heydrich, 'in nationalist Jewish circles there is great satisfaction' with radical German emigration policy, 'because the Jewish population in Palestine is augmented to such an extent that in the foreseeable future the Jews will outnumber the Arabs in Palestine.'[68]

The Jewish policy of the SD now gained steadily in significance. In the tangle of innumerable overlapping briefs and disparate interests the SD – and Heydrich also – slowly rose to a position of importance 'which in questions of Jewish policy made it a recognized authority'.[69] Even the Ministry of the Interior was now prepared to make concessions. Should Jews desiring to emigrate need a police certificate for example, then in order not to hinder emigration, previous convictions no longer had to be entered. In May 1938 the Ministry of Economic Affairs requested the SD for the first time to put forward a complete reorganization of all the regulations pertaining to questions of emigration. And in June, in *Das Schwarze Korps*, SS-members were requested by SS-Second Lieutenant Hagen to make no further incursions into the Jewish question until such time as the SD and the Ministry of Economic Affairs had reached agreement as to how finance for the emigration should be provided.[70]

The first great test for the plan was provided by the annexation of Austria by Germany. The territories were scarcely united before Eichmann, the rising star in SD Jewish policy, hurried to Vienna, and as Jewish expert to the Inspector of Security Police and the SD set up a first 'Central Office for Jewish Emigration' in the former Rothschild Palace in the Prinz-Eugen-Strasse.[71] The system of indirect pressure which had characterized the emigration policy of the Heydrich machine up until then was replaced for the first time by the large-scale use of direct force.[72] The disparate legal systems and the general confusion after the annexation were deliberately exploited by Eichmann, who had meanwhile been promoted to SS-Second Lieutenant.

In order to increase the emigration quotas of the Austrian Jews, Eichmann above all required money. For since most of the 300,000 Jews in the country were not well-off, and on the other hand all the countries of destination only accepted those Jews who could show a required sum of money, Eichmann took remedial measures after his own fashion. He confiscated Jewish assets illegally or compelled the richer Jews to transfer part of their property to the Central Office.[73] Heydrich himself later summarized this procedure, 'The way we did this was to present the Jewish community with a demand for a certain sum to be levied from the rich Jews who wanted to emigrate. The problem was certainly not getting rid of the richer Jews, but of the Jewish rabble.'[74]

Eichmann was soon able to report increasingly magnificent figures to his superiors. By the autumn he had expelled 45,000 Austrian Jews.[75] However much this emigration resembled expulsion, however much it contained elements of extortion and humiliation, the result of the SD's Jewish policy must go on record as having alleviated the Jewish problem inflamed by National Socialism. At the end of 1938 it was felt by the Ministry of the Interior that the importance of the Nuremberg Race Laws was receding and that the necessity for supplementary laws was removed. The State Secretary in the Ministry of the Interior, Wilhelm Stuckart, wrote in an article that the significance of these anti-Jewish laws would recede as 'the achievement of the ultimate aim in the Jewish question' drew near.[76]

But the very achievement of this aim, the silently bureaucratic deportation of Jewish people, and the whole Jewish question itself across the frontiers of the Reich, upset the extremists in the Party. They were already annoyed that Heydrich's SD had monopolized an area which the Party claimed for its very own. Once again it was Streicher who, in the spring of 1938, at the politically most unfavourable moment, unleashed a new campaign of agitation. The SD, extremely concerned to prevent any interruption to its emigration procedure through shrill tones and foreign disquiet, immediately detailed Eichmann to restrain Streicher's scandal-sheet from its activities. But in vain. At the end of June, Eichmann's chief, Herbert Hagen, was forced to report that the mission to Streicher had 'failed miserably'.

It was inconceivable to Heydrich's Jewish expert that the 'pleasing fact that very many Jews in Vienna are returning to their jewishness' should be regarded as undesirable by the *Stürmer's* chief editor, Hiemer. 'When I hear stuff like that I tear my hair – what do they expect exactly? Perhaps the *Stürmer* subscribes to the radical solution of making them a head shorter, so that they can't hit upon the pleasing idea of declaring themselves Jews in the first place.'[77] Relations with Streicher sank to an all-time low, and Heydrich abruptly ordered that further contact between the Jewish expert of the SD and the *'Frankenführer'* (Party leader in Franconia, Streicher) must stop for the time being.

But Streicher was not alone. Propaganda Minister Goebbels, who had been instrumental in stirring up enmity towards the Jews from the beginning, also intervened. In the April boycott of 1933, and then during the wave of anti-semitism in 1935 and on all subsequent occasions, he tried to bring the Jewish question to a head. In 1937 he tried to persuade Hitler to put pressure on Mussolini to carry out Jewish legislation in Italy as well, and in 1938 he pestered the Minister of Economic Affairs, Funk, finally to expel the Jews from the economy. Goebbels had been seen less often on the pinnacle of power in the months immediately preceding this move. Family difficulties, his various love-affairs, especially his liaison with the Czech film-star, Lída Baarová, had soured his relations with Hitler. His press control policy had also been criticized. Goebbels was thus desperately seeking for a way of proving himself indispensable to the Führer once more.[78]

The opportunity was provided by a controversy which the governments of Germany, Switzerland and Poland were conducting over the Jews. In August the Swiss had already pressed in Berlin for a reduction in the flow of Jews from Germany, and the ensuing negotiations between the Swiss authorities and Heydrich's deputy, Dr Werner Best, resulted on 5 October in the passports of German Jews only remaining valid if they were stamped with a 'J'.[79] The next day, the Polish government enacted a similar measure, clearly intending to rid themselves of their Jews of Polish nationality living in Germany by a piece of trickery. To remain valid the passports of Polish citizens likewise had to be stamped by the Polish authorities, otherwise the holders were to be refused entry to Poland. As the stamp could only be issued in Poland until the end of October and the mass of Polish Jews in the Reich were obviously making no arrangements to acquire it, Heydrich reacted in his own manner. The number of Jews awaiting compulsory emigration was not to be increased by Jews of Polish nationality. Heydrich therefore ordered the 15,000 Jewish holders of Polish passports living in the Reich to be arrested, in order to push them across the Polish border as unwanted aliens. When the Polish border authorities refused to accept this large number of Polish Jews, they were forcibly driven across the border into Poland by Heydrich's Security Police during the night of 29 October.[80]

Caught up in this first, great, mass deportation of the Third Reich, a master tailor named Grynszpan, who had been arrested in Hanover, was wandering around in the no-man's-land on the Polish-German frontier. In Paris, Grynszpan's seventeen-year-old son Herschel heard of the fate which had befallen his father. On 7 November he felled an official at the German Embassy in Paris, Third Secretary Ernst vom Rath, with five pistol shots, injuring him severely.[81] On the following day the *Völkischer Beobachter* was already threatening that it was clear 'that the German people will draw their own conclusions from this new deed'.[82] Admittedly, it was by no means certain at the time whether Herschel Grynszpan had fired the shots from the obvious motive of revenge for his family's fate, or because he sought the German diplomat's life for other reasons.

Whatever drove the young emigrant to his action, it was as if Goebbels had only been waiting for the shots from Paris as his cue. On 9 November, like all the Party veterans, he travelled to Munich for the annual commemoration of the failed Hitler putsch of 1923. In his traditional speech in the 'Bürgerbräukeller' beer hall Hitler did not once refer to the attempt on the German diplomat's life. But when the Party veterans were about to sit down for their evening meal, towards 8.30 p.m., a telegram announced that Embassy Secretary vom Rath had died of his wounds in the afternoon.[83] According to the testimony of the Munich SS-leader von Eberstein, Heydrich's godfather, Hitler was so overcome that he refused to speak.[84] At this moment Goebbels clearly saw his chance to show the

Führer whom he could really depend on. No-one was to be allowed to outdo him on such an opportune occasion! With masterly vagueness he delivered a stirring speech suffused with hatred of the Jews, before an audience of SA and Party members, in which he said little that could later be held against him, but from which the vast majority of his listeners gained the impression that 'acts of vengeance were about to be perpetrated against the Jews'.[85] He had reported to Hitler, Goebbels blurted out, that in many places spontaneous action had already been taken against the Jews. The Führer had decided 'that such demonstrations were neither to be prepared nor organized by the Party. So far as they arose spontaneously, however, steps were not to be taken to prevent them.'[86]

The Party representatives, firmly convinced that they had listened not just to a speech but to a briefing, instructed their local subordinates accordingly. In the course of that same night the pogrom developed which has gone down in history as the *'Kristallnacht'* (Night of the Broken Glass): synagogues went up in flames, SA-men drove the Jews from their houses, Jewish shops were destroyed, department stores demolished. The stench of Streicher's *Stürmer* lay over the land.

Heydrich, held to be the instigator of the *Kristallnacht* until long after the war,[87] was surprised by Goebbels' campaign when a synagogue went up in flames close by his room in the 'Vier Jahreszeiten' (Four Seasons) Hotel in Munich.[88] He and his Gestapo legal adviser Dr Werner Best were still puzzling over the cause of the synagogue blaze as a telephone call from Regional Gestapo HQ in Munich brought an explanation. One of Goebbels' propaganda agencies had informed the Gestapo that 'pogroms against the Jews had been ordered, in which the Gestapo were not allowed to interfere'.[89] When the dumbfounded Heydrich requested clarification and orders from *Reichsführer* Himmler, the latter only passed on an order from Hitler which implied nothing other than that the SS had to keep out of it, and that Heydrich's Gestapo merely had to safeguard Jewish property. Heydrich obeyed. In an express teleprinter message at 1.20 a.m. he instructed the Gestapo and SD offices throughout the Reich to intervene in the destruction according to Hitler's orders: the Gestapo were therefore to make contact with the appropriate political agencies 'by telephone, and arrange a discussion on carrying out the demonstrations'. The political organizers were to be informed that they would have to 'adjust' their 'measures' to restrictions imposed by the SS. These laid down that

'German life and property' were not to be endangered, shops and houses were only allowed to be 'destroyed, not plundered', non-Jewish businesses were to be protected against damage, foreign Jews were not to be molested.

The police were instructed not to hinder the demonstrations, but to see that the restrictions were observed. 'Historically valuable material' from the synagogues was not to be destroyed, but handed in to the appropriate SD offices.

In conclusion Heydrich ordered that 'in all districts as many Jews – especially wealthy ones – are to be arrested as can be accommodated in custody'. Heydrich's scrupulous attempt to distance himself from the outrages in which he did not wish the Gestapo and SD to be involved, is evidenced by his order that 'particular care must be taken to see that the Jews arrested on account of this [i.e. his!] order are not ill-treated'.[90] The consequences of the riots were devastating in every respect. Clearly blaming Goebbels' address, Heydrich notified the provisional result on 11 November: 815 shops had been destroyed, twenty-nine department stores demolished, seventy-six synagogues and 117 houses destroyed and a further 191 synagogues set on fire, thirty-six Jews had been murdered and another thirty-six seriously hurt.[91] The Party Supreme Court later counted a total of ninety-one 'killings', as it termed them.[92]

But far and beyond the murders and destruction of property, the Goebbels campaign – whether previously decided upon with Hitler or only subsequently sanctioned by him – signalled a disconcerting renunciation of the old policy. Himmler and Heydrich saw clearly that their concept of discreet emigration had suffered a severe defeat, and they began to prepare for fresh difficulties. In a memorandum Himmler called the Goebbels campaign 'empty-headed',[93] and Heydrich spoke of an 'almighty mess-up'.[94] Weeks later, in an address given to the Wehrmacht National Political Training Course, Heydrich publicly laid the blame for the pogrom on the Propaganda Ministry and thereby 'dissociated himself from the Jew-baiting'.[95] Hitler's opponent, the Counter-Intelligence officer, Grosscurth, made a note about Heydrich in his diary; 'Privately he declared that the Jew-baiting was the worst blow to state and Party since 1934.'[96]

It was certainly not humanitarian considerations which drove Heydrich and Himmler to protest against the Goebbels coup, but revolt against the irrationality involved in the events of the *Kristallnacht*, and probably also the circumstance that 'such noisy action conflicted with their trusted practice of silent bureaucratic terror'.[97] This was already evident on 10 November when the Jewish emigration organizers of the SS struggled to break new ground in a changed political situation. On that day Himmler anticipated a decree already in preparation and forbade the Jews to possess any weapons.[98] The hostages captured during the large-scale action against the Jews were transferred to the concentration camps, but they were soon released again, and Heydrich determined to speed up the emigration of those Jews who had been arrested.[99]

These were only reflex measures, however, of slight relevance for the future course of events. Henceforth, it seemed, this would no longer be laid down by Heydrich and Himmler, but by the Goebbels-Hitler partnership. In fact, Goebbels was the first to be informed of what was to follow by way of further measures. On 10 November he was able to intimate to the Minister of Economic Affairs that Hitler would now order Göring to remove the Jews from the economy.[100] On the same day a discussion took place between Goebbels, Göring and Hitler. Goebbels suggested imposing a levy on the Jews, which was eventually set at one thousand million marks, and Hitler now ordered Göring 'to carry out the economic solution.'[101]

Göring invited representatives of all the departments concerned, over one hundred participants altogether, including Heydrich, to a session in the Reich Ministry of Aviation on 12 November. [102] Four points soon crystallized as the outcome. First: As a 'fine' for the assassination of vom Rath and not least in consideration of 'the critical state of the Reich's finances', one thousand million Reichsmarks were in fact demanded from the Jews. The damage caused by the Nazi mob during the *Kristallnacht* had to be compensated for by the insurance companies, but the money was to be confiscated.

Second: A start was to be made on the compulsory 'Aryanization' of the German economy by the compulsory purchase of Jewish businesses at prices below their value, and their re-sale at the true market price for the benefit of the Reich's finances, and by the encashment of shares and other securities in Jewish possession.

Third: Goebbels insisted on discriminating still further against the Jews in Germany and forcing them into 'apartheid': Jews were no longer to be allowed to enter German theatres, cinemas and circuses, German bathing-pools or even the 'German woods'; in railway carriages special 'Jewish compartments' were to be set up. Without hesitation Heydrich agreed to these proposals.

With the fourth point, however, it was again Heydrich who referred to the main problem, namely that the ultimate aim of all these measures must always remain the emigration of the Jews from Germany. 'However thoroughly we remove the Jews from business life, there will always remain the basic problem of getting the Jew out of Germany.' Heydrich then held up Eichmann's activities in Vienna as an example of successful emigration so far. 'On the instructions of the Reich Commissioner we have established a Jewish Emigration Office in Vienna by means of which we have brought 50,000 Jews out of Austria, whereas in the *Altreich* during the same period, only 19,000 Jews were able to leave.'[103] (By '*Altreich*' Heydrich means the territory of Germany before the 1938 *Anschluss*.)

His proposal to set up a similar Emigration Office in the *Altreich* also was at once approved by Göring. In connection with the emigration Heydrich finally drew attention to the obvious danger of 'Jewish pro-letarianization' inherent in the planned exclusion of the Jews from the economy. As a way out he recommended that the Jews should certainly be isolated by the creation of prohibited areas, but that they should retain their own restricted sphere of activity in the economy. 'To assist their identification' he proposed that they should carry a particular distinguish-ing mark, though he rejected Göring's suggestion of Jewish ghettos.[104]

The Foreign Office made renewed attempts to oppose this and in a circular about 'The Jewish Question as a Factor in Foreign Policy' declared that in its view any solution which could lead to an independent Jewish state in Palestine was unsuitable.[105] But on 24 January 1939, decidedly won over to the side of the SS by Goebbels' enterprise of 9 November, Göring ordered that the emigration of the Jews should be furthered and advanced by every possible means. A 'Central Office for Jewish Emigration' was to be established in the Ministry of the Interior as Heydrich had suggested, to function as a clearing-house for all agencies involved in the expulsion of the Jews.[106] The following tasks were detailed more precisely:

It is the business of the Reich Central Office, in the entire Reich: 1. to make all preparations for stepping up the emigration of the Jews, including the establishment of a suitable Jewish organization to prepare emigration applications, taking all steps to ensure the pro-vision and, where appropriate, the realization of funds held at home and abroad, and, in collaboration with the Reich Emigration Office, to locate suitable destination countries for emigration; 2. to *control* emigration, among other things providing for the emigration of the poorer Jews; 3. to speed up the emigration procedure in *individual cases*, by fast and smooth provision of the required state papers and certificates through the centralized processing of applications and supervision of the completion of emigration.

Thus, after the setback marked by the *Kristallnacht*, Heydrich's concept had again triumphed. This also found expression in the fact that at the end of his directive Göring appointed the Chief of Security Police, i.e. Heydrich, as *Leiter* (Leader – a Party post) of the Reich Central Office, with the proviso that he was still required to consult Göring 'before taking fundamental measures'.

As H G Adler – surely the most committed chronicler of the fate of the Jews in the Third Reich – commented one generation later, in 1974: 'Many phrases in this directive appear very promising and almost humane, but they remained phrases among which people's lives were often crushed and ruined on account of the grit which officialdom scattered in the works to achieve fast and smooth provision.'[107] However, it was precisely Heydrich's emigration policy which, in retrospect, seen against the terrible background of Auschwitz, turned out to be a sort of large-scale rescue operation for hundreds of thousands of Jews, even if the objective facts of the case certainly bore no relation to the subjective motives of the leadership of the SS.

At all events Heydrich used the *carte blanche* given him by Göring to impose his concept of the solution to the Jewish question, as far as it went, on the state authorities concerned. On 11 February 1939 he advised the heads of the Foreign Office, the Ministries of Economic and Financial Affairs and the Ministry of the Interior of the establishment of a Central Office, and on the same day a conference took place between Heydrich and representatives of these authorities, during which Heydrich once again stressed the necessity of emigration and its acceleration.[108]

In addition to the Central Office for Emigration in Vienna, further Central Offices were planned, first of all for Berlin, Frankfurt-am-Main, Hamburg and Breslau, where Jews were concentrated. Another Central Office was later set up in Prague, under Eichmann's direction, for Bohemia and Moravia. Currency difficulties were to be relieved by a fund made up of compulsory contributions from rich Jews. Heydrich again named Palestine as the main goal towards which the Jewish experts of the new Central Offices were to guide the stream of emigrants. The 'suitable Jewish organization' requested by Göring to work in conjunction with the Central Office was to prepare the emigrants for their future problems, establish Jewish schools and undertake welfare work.[109]

Nevertheless it took until July 1939 for the 'Reich Association of Jews in Germany' to come into being as the compulsory Jewish partner of Heydrich's Central Office. All German and stateless Jews who had their 'customary domicile' within the Reich became compulsory members of the society. As aim and object, this society was also given the task of 'furthering the emigration of the Jews'. The responsibility for this too lay with Heydrich.[110]

With relentless pressure the Jewish leaders were now forced to prepare their people for the required exodus from the Reich. As manager of his Central Office, Heydrich had appointed the chief of Gestapo Department II, SS-Colonel Heinrich Müller ('Gestapo-Müller') from Berlin, who succeeded Eichmann in October; the latter continued his own meteoric rise to power, the wave of emigration having already passed its peak.[111]

First, however, in the summer, the Gestapo demanded an ever higher tribute to be paid to the chief object of the SS Jewish policy, mass exodus. For example, without regard for individuals, the Jews of Berlin were required to produce a daily list of seventy families ready for emigration.[112] As Heydrich saw it, 'the incisive measures' against the freedom of movement of the Jews and their increasing elimination from the economy would 'increase the wish to emigrate'.[113]

In effect, the Reich Central Office was soon able to announce a real record: the emigration figures for the *Altreich* were almost doubled, from 40,000 in 1938 to 78,000 in 1939. In addition, Eichmann, working in Prague, achieved the figure of 30,000 Jews 'out of the country'.[114]

The functional alliance which Heydrich's Jewish experts in the SD had formed with the Haganah emissary Feifel Polkes, which had merged the interests of radical Zionists with those of the radical Jewish emigration organizers in the SD, now really bore fruit. According to the total reconstruction in 1955 by the two British journalists, Jon and David Kimche,[115] two delegates from the Jewish secret organization 'Mossad', linked to the Haganah, had already sought contact with Heydrich's Jewish specialists. Mossad had set itself the task of illegally smuggling Jews into Palestine from all over the world, against the rapidly stiffening resistance of the British, who were hostile to the Jews entering that country. The two Mossad emissaries, Pino Ginzburg and Moshe Auerbach, offered to assist the SD in transporting the Jews earmarked for emigration by the Black Order. Ginzburg took up quarters in Berlin, and Heydrich pressed on with sending, week by week, 400 Jews to Palestine. With no illusions of mutual esteem the representatives of both sides now worked to deport the German Jews and increase the Jewish population in Palestine. Together Mossad and the SD sought to outwit the ever-more-vigilant British, who arrested thousands of illegal immigrants, captured ships and, in retribution, soon reduced the legal immigration quotas, already cut to a minimum, to nil.[116] But Ginzburg's and Heydrich's transporters were even more successful. Thousands of German Jews were smuggled into their land of hope in the summer of 1939. For October Heydrich had even approved direct transport from the harbours of Hamburg and Emden, Mossad had already chartered further ships, when the outbreak of war abruptly deprived the alliance between SD and Zionism of its future. 'Under the hail of fire from the Stukas and guns the last great chance to save German Jewry perished,' as the chronicler of the SS, Heinz Höhne, described the event.[117]

It is true that there was still a trickle of immigrants to Palestine and other countries during the early years of the war. On 24 April 1940 Heydrich's RSHA issued a decree to the authorities concerned, announcing that emigration was 'to be intensified during the war'.[118] And on 20 May 1941, one month before the Russian campaign, Heydrich's Deputy, Schellenberg, signed an order to all SD and Gestapo offices with the same wording. The emigration solution was limited to the Jews in Germany and Austria, however; 'with regard to the inadequate exit possibilities', emigration from occupied Belgium and France was already forbidden, as it would mean a 'fresh curtailment' to the emigration of German Jews. 'In view of the Final Solution which is certain to come, the emigration of Jews from France and Belgium is to be prevented.'[119]

On 23 October, however, this last chance was also lost. Gestapo chief Heinrich Müller relayed an order from Himmler according to which the emigration of Jews from the Reich was to be halted immediately – except for those who paid for their freedom in foreign currency.[120] Nevertheless, about two-thirds of the Jews living in the entire Greater German Reich (the *Altreich,* Austria, Bohemia and Moravia) had been shipped abroad by then, through Heydrich's policy of expulsion, or had fled to safety across the borders. From the *Altreich* the number was 300,000, from Austria 130,000, from Bohemia and Moravia 30,000. About 70,000 of them arrived in Palestine.[121]

These figures imply that if the organizers of Jewish emigration under Heydrich had been given at least one or two more years for their campaigns of emigration and expulsion, the Jewish question would perhaps have been solved in this way, according to the requirements of National Socialism. However, the war which Hitler ordered against neighbouring Poland on 1 September 1939 upset anything verging on a world-scale solution to the Jewish question. There followed giant strides towards ever more unscrupulous solutions. There were three facts above all which were creating a completely new situation. First, the war had virtually closed the pathway to emigration, although the route via Scandinavia, Portugal and Japan remained open for a while longer. Secondly, it was the war which offered the tendencies latent in National Socialism unique opportunities for the kind of development which was only conceivable and only became feasible in the abnormal conditions created by international conflagration. In the Jewish question the war cleared the way for that 'constitutive element of dynamic force'[122] inherent in National Socialism. Thirdly and finally, the conquest of Poland and then of further countries increased the scale of the Jewish problem to previously undreamt-of dimensions. Instead of seeing the number of Jews concerned steadily decrease through the effect of the emigration policy, Heydrich was faced with figures which went up in leaps and bounds.

The fate intended for the approximately three million Jews in Poland was discussed between Hitler, Himmler and Heydrich, together with the Danzig *Gauleiter* Albert Forster, on 20 September 1939.[123] As Heydrich informed his task forces, and the leaders of the task forces of the Security Police whom he had hastily summoned, the following measures had been decided upon. The Jews still remaining within the Reich were gradually to be deported to Poland, to the new 'Wild East' of the Third Reich. The Jews from the provinces ceded to Poland after the Versailles peace treaty of 1919, and now repossessed by the Reich, were to be deported to occupied Poland within one year, and the Polish Jews themselves were to be concentrated in municipal ghettos,[124] 'in order to improve the practicability of control and deportation'.[125]

Heydrich ordered: '1. Jews into the towns as quickly as possible; 2. Jews out of the Reich into Poland; 3. the remaining 30,000 gypsies also to be sent to Poland; 4. systematic dispatch of the Jews from the (regained) German provinces by goods train'.[126] He indicated that these measures were merely the short-term aims of the new phase in Jewish policy, but that they already held out a prospect of 'the planned general measures' (i.e. the 'final aim').[127]

On 29 September Hitler laid down what was meant by the 'final aim'. The Jews were to be settled along with other 'unreliable elements' between the Rivers Vistula and Bug, on the new German-Soviet demarcation line. The 'final aim' therefore, consisted of a Jewish reservation to be set up under German guard.[128] On 6 October Hitler gave a clear indication that his 'final aim' in fact amounted to temporary or permanent concentration in a particular area. In a speech lasting several hours about the political solution of the future of Poland, he set forth six basic principles which he held to be unalterable conditions for a solution he would consider acceptable. In point number three this suggestion was made to the Western Allies 'in connection with an attempt to regulate and control the Jewish problem'. However, like all Hitler's other suggestions, this one drew no response and was overtaken by the Western Campaign of 1940.[129]

In the meantime, however, the SS under Heydrich's centralized control began methodically to pursue their plans for the attainment of the 'final aim'. Eichmann and SS-Major-General Dr Walter Stahlecker were sent into the proposed area to mark out the boundaries of the planned Jewish reservation; they found it south-west of Lublin. Said Eichmann later, 'We saw an enormous area, we saw the River San, villages, market-places, small towns, and we said to each other it was the very thing.' Eichmann chose the little town of Nisko am San as the 'metropolis' of his Jewish state.[130]

On 30 October the plan was set in motion. Himmler directed first of all that between November and February all Jews living in the provinces which had been Polish up to 1939 and were now part of the Reich again, were to be resettled in the Jewish Utopia on the San. While the unbroken succession of goods trains containing victims hastily selected by the Security Police began to roll, chaos developed. Trains were misdirected, accommodation was scarcely ready, and there was not even any certainty of food for the resettled.[131]

Ruthlessly, and as the result of the winter season, in frightful conditions, Heydrich's task forces now drove 87,000 Jews from the re-occupied territories, and another 6000 from Vienna and Ostrava, into the imaginary

Jewish state on the San.[132] At the same time Department IV D4 was set up in the Reich Security Office in Berlin with the special task of coordinating the deportation procedure, as yet unorganized, and taking over centralized control of the evacuation question, as Heydrich explained at a conference in Berlin on 30 January 1940.[133]

But the old basic rule of National Socialist Jewish policy, which stated that anyone in Adolf Hitler's Reich who felt called upon to do so might contribute his own measures to Jewish policy, soon brought a temporary end to the programme of rigorous expulsion pursued by Heydrich's officials. The Departments of War Economy and Armaments of the German Supreme Command had already deplored the evacuations on account of the loss of Jewish labour,[134] and the Governor of Poland, Hans Frank, also opposed the regular shipments to his 'Reich'. He was carrying out his own process of resettlement in occupied Poland,[135] but had no desire to accept in addition Jews expelled by the SS. In February 1940 he sought help from Göring in Berlin. The mania of Heydrich and Eichmann for resettlement was leading to chaos, the food supplies of the province were visibly threatened, and the economy of the country was upset. These arguments were successful. At the end of March, Göring, who in his position of responsibility for the economic four-year plan was concerned for his part that the pool of labour available for the German economy should not be reduced, forbade any further deportation to the planned Jewish state. The RSHA attempted to cover up this fresh defeat and temporarily stepped up the emigration process once more. But on 13 April 1940, with the abandonment of Eichmann's shanty town of Nisko, the plan for a Jewish reservation in Poland was finally buried.[136] Hitler had meanwhile also lost interest in it. In conversation with the German writer Colin Ross, he remarked, 'the creation of a Jewish state around Lublin would never signify a solution either'.[137]

Once again it was the war which gave another merciless turn to the screw of Nazi Jewish policy. In place of the failed Jewish state in newly conquered Poland, there arose an even more fantastic plan, which promised Heydrich's Jewish specialists the realization of their wildest dreams. Since the end of the twenties[138] the name of Madagascar had turned up again and again in general discussion about a homeland for the millions of Jews. The island in French colonial possession became a Philosophers' Stone for all Jewish politics by anti-semites from the Netherlands, from France and soon also from Germany. In a pamphlet of 1927, the Dutch Egon van

Winghene, from Rotterdam, had been the first to suggest Madagascar or another island ('The opportunity for control is greatest there and the fear of contagion the slightest') as the future home of world Jewry.[139]

In 1934 Heydrich had read Winghene's writing also,[140] and the argumentation which connects Heydrich's 'pro-Zionism' with that of the Dutch anti-semite is almost identical. Winghene also sets his face against the assimilationists but confesses to Zionism, to a 'Total Zionism': 'This race must be given a large enough land of their own.'[141] Only two 'radical solutions' to the Jewish question were considered possible: 'Physical destruction and extermination', which Winghene excludes as being as much 'un-Aryan' as 'impractical',[142] and secondly 'clear-cut separation'[143] from the respective host nations and 'creation of the Jewish state by assignment to, and enforced settlement of a large enough territory (island) under Aryan control'.[144]

The plan was first taken seriously after the *Kristallnacht* of 1938. The French Foreign Minister Bonnet had confided to Reich Foreign Minister Ribbentrop in December that France was thinking of 'getting rid of ten thousand Jews somewhere' and had the island of Madagascar in mind.[145] Since then the plan had been sporadically taken up by the Nazi anti-semites, and in the Foreign Office a counsellor of the legation, Franz Rademacher, first made notes on a 'Madagascar Project' on 3 June 1940, when preliminary work was beginning for a peace treaty with France.[146]

Hitler had expressed no objection to such a plan, and it now seemed to Heydrich that another great opportunity had arrived for a large-scale solution to the Jewish question. Once more the chance presented itself of formulating grand and audacious policy. On 22 June 1940, with the armistice between France and Germany and the hoped-for peace treaty, it was clear that the island assigned as Jewish territory could for the first time be demanded from the French. Heydrich pressed on with the necessary steps. Two days later, on 24 June, under the stamp of Eichmann's Department IV D4, he wrote a letter to 'dear Comrade von Ribbentrop':

In January 1939, in his capacity as Deputy for the Four Year Plan, the Field-Marshal [Göring] charged me with carrying out Jewish emigration from every part of the Reich. In the following period, in spite of great difficulties, Jewish emigration was successfully continued, even during the war. Since my office took over the task on 1 January 1939 up to the present time, over 200,000 Jews have emigrated from the

Reich.[147] *The whole problem* – there are already about three and a quarter million Jews in the territories *at present* under German sovereignty – can, however, no longer be solved *by emigration*. A final territorial solution is therefore necessary. I make the request to be allowed to take part in the forthcoming discussion dealing with the Final Solution to the Jewish question, should such discussions be planned.[148]

Heydrich did not wait for Ribbentrop's reply. At his urging, all further preparations were begun in the RSHA immediately. The plan was taken up 'enthusiastically'.[149] The day after the dispatch of Heydrich's letter a member of the RSHA staff, Jagusch, informed a representative from the 'Reich Association' that there was now a plan for the complete solution of the Jewish question with the removal of the Jews from all European countries. As destination Heydrich's man named 'a colonial territory which would serve as a reservation'.[150]

Jewish expert Eichmann was sent to the Tropical Institute in Hamburg for information about the climatic conditions on the promised isle,[151] and Eichmann's assistant, SS-Captain Theodor Dannecker, travelled to Paris to study the files on Madagascar in the Colonial Museum there.[152] A plan was worked out in detail. Dannecker committed it to paper. And on 15 August 1940 Heydrich transmitted it direct to Ribbentrop. The management of the gigantic enterprise was to be the responsibility of the 'Chief of the Security Police and the SD', that is, Heydrich himself. 'After the end of the war' about four million Jews were accordingly to be shipped off to the Jewish reservation within five years. Production and trade were to be built up 'under German supervision' in separate German and Jewish businesses. The form the 'advance contingents' were to take was laid down in detail. The first shipments were mainly to consist of 'farmers, builders, craftsmen and workers' families up to the age of forty-five, as well as doctors'. 'The Jews may bring up to 200 kilos of unsealed luggage per person. Jewish farmers, craftsmen, doctors, etc., *must* bring, as far as is available, the complete equipment necessary to practise their profession.'[153]

Heydrich again divided the enterprise into a 'short-term plan' and a 'long-term plan'. The 'short-term plan' implied the concentration and assembly of all the available Jews in occupied Poland, and the 'long-term plan' – that was Madagascar.[154] Of course, it was generally believed impossible to carry out such a comprehensive plan during the war. But it was reckoned that the war would be over by the middle of 1942 and the required measures could then be taken.[155]

'However unreal and in the light of the subsequent course of the war, however ridiculous' (in the words of the chronicler of the Final Solution, H G Adler) the Madagascar plan may appear, it would be wrong, however, 'to dismiss it as mere abstruse talk'.[156] The version put forward that the Madagascar plan had simply been 'camouflage' to hide the planned extermination,[157] has also been repudiated by research.[158] That Heydrich, of all the various solutions to the Jewish question, advocated most 'persistently' the Madagascar plan, is confirmed both by his objective critics and his apologists.[159]

But just as had happened earlier to his plan for the solution to the Jewish question by means of emigration, the further development of the war now caused the welcoming shores of the enormous 'ghetto island' to recede into the distance. Without waiting for the end of the war as the signal for the 'Big Lift' of European Jewry to the African island, the expulsion of the Jews from Germany was already being intensified. In October 1940, on Hitler's instructions, about 6500 Jews were deported from Baden and the Saar Palatinate to unoccupied France; the Reich Governor in Vienna, Baldur von Schiarach, was permitted to have 'his' Jews driven into occupied Poland; and in January 1941 the RSHA began the expulsion of a quarter of a million people from the German eastern provinces – still strongly opposed by the Governor of Poland, Hans Frank.[160] And still it was Heydrich who assiduously gave orders to his officials, thus translating into action decisions which had frequently been taken outside his own sphere. From the Jewish policy-maker he became the mere jailer, from the driving force behind a partly presentable permanent solution he became the precise executor of commands.

On his orders more and more Jews were herded together in Poland, into an enormous 'waiting-room' for the impending Final Solution, which for him was still a territorial one. Not until the spring of 1941, with the preparatory stages of the Russian Campaign and the strained transport situation connected with it, did a certain calm enter into the hectic concentration of the Jews. 'It was the calm before the storm,' wrote the German contemporary historian, Adam.[161] Heydrich still did not know that he was filling a waiting-room of death. He still did not know that the postponement of the Madagascar plan until the end of the war signalled the end of his emigration policy. The spectre of mass murder was raising its ugly head.

Fresh grounds for that last horrific interpretation which the National Socialist enemies of the Jews attached to the phrase 'Final Solution', were provided by the war. While the planning preparations for the Madagascar project were still taking more concrete form, in the winter of 1940/41, Hitler's plans for military confrontation with the Soviet Union were coming to the fore. In March 1941 the means by which he intended to conduct this war against the 'ideological opponent' became clear.[162] Following an early preliminary discussion on 3 March, General Alfred Jodl, Chief of Staff, German Supreme Command, noted, 'The Jewish-Bolshevik intelligentsia, as the previous oppressor of the people, must be removed.'[163] Ten days later, in the 'Guidelines on Special Areas' in 'Directive No. 21' (*'Barbarossa'*) in passage 12b, edited by Hitler himself, it was already indicated that the SS-*Reichsführer* was entrusted with 'special tasks in preparation for the political administration' in the operational area of the army. These 'special tasks' resulted from the 'struggle which is finally to be decided between two opposing political systems'.[164]

Within the limits of these tasks the SS-*Reichsführer* was to act 'independently and on his own responsibility'. In distinguishing between the competence of the Army and that of the SS in the operational area it was merely laid down that 'The SS-*Reichsführer* is responsible for ensuring that in carrying out his tasks the operations are not hampered.' The Army High Command was to work out the 'details', 'directly' with the SS-*Reichsführer*.[165]

Negotiations opened between the Chief of the General Staff of the Army, Major-General Eduard Wagner, and the Chief of the Security Police and the SD, at first represented by the Gestapo-chief Müller, then – as Heydrich was dissatisfied with his handling of the negotiations – by Heydrich himself. The latter had already confided to Wagner at the beginning of the negotiations how he envisaged the organizational framework of the special tasks ordered by Hitler. As in the Polish Campaign, only on a grander scale and with extended powers, 'task forces of the Security Police and the SD', still to be formed, were to follow in the footsteps of the troops in the Russian Campaign also.[166] After considerable argument over the question of how far the special commandos should be subordinate to the fighting troops, on 26 March Army High Command issued a draft order, which Wagner submitted to Heydrich at the beginning of April.[167] Apart from a few qualifications – 'danger in delay' and 'to avoid interruption of the operations' – Heydrich was given a free hand. In the words of the order the task forces were to carry out their 'particular tasks of security policy' in the operational area 'on their own responsibility' and were also authorized 'to take executive measures on their own responsibility against the civilian population in the course of their assignment'.[168]

In the entire order there was certainly no mention of mass executions. On the contrary, Heydrich and Wagner had agreed on two prominent functions for the special commandos. In the Army service area, behind the immediate battle zone of the troops, these included the 'taking into custody, prior to the commencement of operations, of stipulated objects (materials, archives, files of organizations hostile to the Reich and the state) as well as of particularly important individuals (leading emigrants, saboteurs, terrorists, etc.)'. In the Army rearward area, even further back, Heydrich's troops were to assist military Intelligence in 'investigating and fighting the tendencies hostile to state and Reich' as well as briefing the military commanders in the Army rearward areas 'on the political situation'.[169]

On what level and with what approach Hitler intended the 'special tasks', only briefly outlined here, to be tackled, was first revealed in an address on 30 March, for which he had assembled the supreme commanders of the three sections of the Wehrmacht and about 200 senior officers in the New Reich Chancellery in Berlin. In the impending campaign, he explained, it was a matter of a relentless race war. This fight left no room for outdated notions of chivalry. The supporters of the Bolshevik cause, including the secret police and the political commissars, following their murderous excesses in the occupation of the Baltic states, in the Soviet aggression against Finland and in their invasion of eastern Poland and the territories seized from Rumania, now found themselves outside the jurisdiction of the regulations governing the treatment of prisoners-of-war. They were therefore to be rendered harmless. 'We do not wage war to preserve the enemy,' he shouted, and, 'In the East, by being hard now we are being kind to the future.'[170]

What kind of war he gave the SS-*Reichsführer* and Heydrich's RSHA task forces concrete orders for is not clear from any of the extant records, documents or statements.[171] Heydrich, too, practised the same discretion. Not until two weeks after the start of the war against Russia does a written order emerge, in which Heydrich informs several high-ranking SS and police leaders of the basic directives to the task forces. Besides the conventional work of the Security Police, the arresting and placing in custody, the investigating and surveillance, in Point 4, under the heading 'Executions', the text runs:

> To be executed are all functionaries of the Comintern (as are the communist professional politicians in general); the senior, middle-ranking and radical low-ranking functionaries of the Party, the Central Committees, the District and Area Committees; people's commissars; other radical elements (saboteurs, propagandists, snipers, assassins, agitators, etc.); Jews in Party and state posts.[172]

The fact that, as well as those Jews who were also Bolshevik office-bearers, the Jewish civilians accessible behind the front were also to be executed, first emerges from the relevant progress reports of the task forces *after* the beginning of the war, and from the reports submitted by surviving leaders of the task forces after 1945.

According to these, Heydrich had passed on to the prospective leaders of the special commandos only a small part of what Hitler had ordered. When, in April, he summoned the divisional heads of his RSHA for the first time, to announce the new special assignment, there was only talk of a 'hard task'. The problem was 'to secure and pacify the Russian zone'.[173]

When Heydrich became more outspoken the SD intellectuals and the rationalistic bureaucrats of the Gestapo pulled long faces. The SD-*Inlands-Chef* and lawyer, Otto Ohlendorf, the SS-Major-General Dr Walter Stahlecker, the smooth and always charming Walter Schellenberg, the chief administrator Bruno Streckenbach, the Gestapo boss Heinrich Müller, and finally SS-Major-General Dr Dr Rasch, holder of two degrees, and the Professor of Politics, Dr Franz Six – none of them was prepared of his own free will to undertake the bloody assignment.[174] Only the head of Reich Criminal Police HQ, Arthur Nebe, the subsequent collaborator in the resistance movement of 20 July, volunteered.[175]

Under pressure from Heydrich, and partly also – as in Ohlendorf's case – in order to avoid any further charges of cowardice, the leadership of the *Osteinsatz* (Eastern mission) was assembled. Enlisting the troops for Heydrich's death brigades was no less difficult. When about 3000 men were eventually drummed up, in May 1941, they were a motley crew. Out of officials from the Gestapo, deserter-hunters from the Criminal Police, men from the SD and from Daluege's regular police, out of soldiers from the *Waffen-SS* and foreign auxiliary policemen, Heydrich formed four task forces, subdivided into task force commandos and special commandos. Task force A, led by Dr Stahlecker (after his death in a partisan raid, Heinz Jost succeeded him) was to follow Army Group North closely as far as Leningrad; Task Force B, under the Criminal Police chief, Nebe (and later, SS-Major-General Werner Naumann) advanced with Army Group Centre until just outside Moscow; C and D under command of SS-Major-General Dr Dr Rasch (later Dr Thomas) and SS-Colonel Ohlendorf (and later SS-Brigadier Dr Bierkamp) spread out through the enormous area of Army Group Centre from Kursk and Kiev to the Black Sea.[176]

For the time being, however, shortly before the beginning of the war, they were bent on the destruction of the Bolshevik opponent. In the Frontier Police School in Pretzsch on the Saxon Elbe, and in the little town of Düben on the Mulde, Heydrich twice gathered his special unit together in the middle of June; but here also, he spoke only of a mission which demanded 'unprecedented severity'.[177] To the heads of the task forces he spoke more plainly however; 'in the Führer's view' Eastern Jewry, which was the 'reservoir of Bolshevism', had to be wiped out, as the task force commando leader, Dr Walter Blume, recalled after the war.[178] In an appeal for mercy to the Nuremberg Tribunal, referring to what Heydrich had said at that time, Ohlendorf wrote that he had transmitted the 'Führer's command', according to which 'Communist functionaries and activists, Jews, gypsies, saboteurs and agents are basically defined as elements which endanger the troops by their existence and are therefore to be executed without further ado.'[179] And in the Nuremberg Trial, to the question as to what directives had been issued for the treatment of the Jews, he replied, 'The directive was issued . . . to liquidate the Jews . . . in the same way as the political commissars of the Soviets.' When the judge asked Ohlendorf, 'When you use the word "liquidate", do you mean "kill"?', Ohlendorf's unequivocal reply was, 'By that I mean "kill".'[180]

The 'incident reports' which Heydrich regularly called into the RSHA in Berlin, illustrate most clearly what assignment the manhunters of the Black Order were carrying out. From villages and ghettos, from prisoners-of-war camps and the cities of the East they were herding their victims together. Extracts from reports drawn up by the task force and commando group leaders, penned in a sober, military style, illustrate what was understood in this merciless ideological war in the wide-open spaces of the East, by 'executive measures against the civilian population', as the Heydrich-Wagner paper bloodlessly paraphrased it.

A report of 19 December from Task Force B mentions an operation in Mogilev and explains, 'In checks on the exit roads from Mogilev carried out with the assistance of the regular police a total of 135 people, most of them Jews, were seized. 127 people were shot.' According to the report, a nearby transit camp for Soviet prisoners-of-war was 'searched for Jews and functionaries. 126 people were transferred and shot.' The same report states that at Parichi, near Bobruysk, 'A special operation was mounted, in the course of which 1013 Jews and Jewesses were shot.'[181] A report from Riga on 30 November 1941 from Task Force D states laconically, '10,600 Jews shot.'

Shot, shot, shot – the import was always the same, even if the expressions varied. An incident report from the Crimea declares, for example, '1000 Jews and gypsies put to death.' A report by Task Force B from Lithuania implies that the concentration of Jews in concentration camps had begun, 'and thus about 500 Jews, among other saboteurs, are currently being liquidated every day'. In Lacoisk '920 Jews' were '. . . executed. The town can now be declared free of Jews.' More and more Jews were 'disposed of', 'rendered harmless' or simply 'seized'.[182] All social groups and all offences which were to be dealt with, on Heydrich's written instructions, by execution, were mentioned again and again in the incident reports. One example is the report of Dr Rasch's Task Force C from Kiev, which brought higher authority up to date with their activities by notifying more than 51,000 executions:

> The executions carried out by the squads are directed against the following: political functionaries, plunderers and saboteurs; active communists and political ideology-mongers; Jews who have wormed their way out of prison camps by giving false statements; agents and informers of the NKVD; persons who gave false information and influenced witnesses in order to have ethnic Germans deported; Jewish sadism and lust for revenge; undesirable elements, anti-social persons, partisans, politruks; the danger of infection and contagion; members of Russian guerilla gangs, irregular volunteers, the suppliers of Russian gangs with provisions, insurgents and agitators, degenerate youth.

And then came the all-embracing expression, 'Jews in general'.[183]

More and more it was the 'Jews in general', as opposed to the other political, social or criminal victims of this ruthless thoroughness, who formed the main contingents of those 'disposed of' in the mopping-up operations by Heydrich's death troops. From 6 to 30 March, according to Incident Report No. 194 by Commando Group 8, 'special treatment' was meted out to '20 Russians for communist intrigue, sabotage or member-ship of the NKVD, 5 Russians for theft, housebreaking, embezzlement, 33 gypsies, 1151 Jews'. During the period under review in November 1941, as stated in Report No. 143, Commando Group 5 killed '15 political func-tionaries, 21 saboteurs and plunderers, 10,650 Jews and 414 hostages'.[184]

Russian Jewry was mercilessly decimated by the shooting of the task forces. Up to New Year 1942 Task Force A reported 249,290 Jews killed, Task Force B reported 45,467 Jews liquidated, and in conclusion Forces C and D accounted for 95,000 and 92,000 Jewish victims respectively[185] – including partisans and peaceable shopkeepers, prisoners-of-war and civilians, butchers from Stalin's secret police and orthodox believers, the rebellious and the submissive.

The figures reported to Berlin by one or other task force, according to Ohlendorf's testimony at the Nuremberg Trial, were sometimes manipu-lated on their way to the top, but even with this reservation scholars reach the figure of about 300,000 Jewish victims in the first year of the German expedition to Russia alone.[186]

The world had not experienced such a massacre since the extermination of the American Indians by the white settlers, or perhaps since the genocide perpetrated by the Turks against the Armenians during and after the First World War. Nevertheless the final stage of the National Socialist persecution of the Jews had still not been reached. As the Tübingen contemporary historian, Adam, sums up the latest research, 'The extermi-nation measures, doubtless based on Hitler's wishes, did not yet represent the definitive order for the Final Solution.'[187] Rather, the massacres by the task forces appear to him to be only a more horrific copy of what was going on in Poland, one in which 'Hitler's bent for destruction revealed sharper outlines through his conception of the political and ideological enemy, with measures interpreted more clearly and directly than in Poland as a novel dimension of the "nationhood struggle".'[188]

Contrary to the unanimous opinion of historians up to the end of the sixties that the decision in favour of the Final Solution had already been made with the task forces' instructions to destroy the Jews[189] – closely contemporary with the Commissar Order – Hitler's task force assignment to Heydrich lends itself to the following most likely interpretation:

> to exterminate speedily and ruthlessly every possible and imaginable opponent under cover of the war, to achieve his and Himmler's pipe-dream of a settlement in the East . . . This was an untidy and relatively short-term concept which almost certainly excluded detailed plans extending beyond this period, such as that for mass destruction, demanding an enormous amount of manpower, time and planning.[190]

However vigorously the Jews of Soviet Russia were being decimated by the murderous zeal of the task forces at this time, it nevertheless appears that a systematic plan for the extermination of European Jewry did not in fact exist at this point. The most important circumstantial evidence for this is that only on 23 October, through an order from Himmler and secondary measures by the RSHA, did Hitler issue a general prohibition of the evacuation of Jews from any of the occupied European countries, to take effect immediately.[191] In May 1941, while Heydrich was dredging up the ranks of his task forces, the order was given that the extent of the emigration from the Protectorate of Bohemia and Moravia was to be 'kept up during the war'.[192] In May, in the journal *Böhmen und Mähren,* Heydrich himself defined the term, 'Final Solution', with the formula, 'inducing the Jews to emigrate'.[193] And at the beginning of August, internal 'Guide-lines for the Treatment of the Jewish Question' were still being produced by the Reich Security Office, the starting-point of which was that the Jewish question, 'after the war at the latest, will be solved for the whole of Europe generally'. Some of the draconian regulations, which subjected the Jews to constantly increasing harassment and deprivation of their rights, west of the Soviet Union too, reveal the degree of inhumanity which already characterized the treatment of the Jews at this time.[194]

Nothing, however, pointed conclusively to whether the same fate which was intended for the mass of Soviet Jews was also being prepared for the rest of European Jewry. The main aim still seemed to be the territorial Final Solution as Heydrich had formulated it; the Madagascar plan still haunted the minds of Heydrich and his assistants. In October 1941 for example, Eichmann held discussions in this direction with his deputies for the individual provinces.[195] Even in February of early March, in spite of the crisis nature of the persecution of Jews, the RSHA seems once again to have expressed its desire to assign an island to the Jews after the war.[196]

In the summer of 1941, as an interim solution, the concentration of the Jews in Russia, which it was believed would shortly be conquered, was openly under discussion.[197] And on 4 February 1942 Heydrich himself was still making final reference to this plan. In a secret confidential address to the heads of the Security Police in Prague he touched on the Final Solution – without the constraint of propagandist considerations or camouflage. 'In the future development of the polar region', he argued, 'where the concentration camps will henceforth make an ideal homeland for Europe's eleven million Jews', efficient Czech skilled workers who 'cannot be Germanized', and whom he wishes to evacuate from Bohemia and Moravia, might perhaps be employed 'as foremen and overseers, etc., provided they show positive evidence of a pro-German tendency'.[198]

We do not know, and will probably never find out what the final aim of Hitler's enmity towards the Jews in the summer of 1941 might have been. At this point, however, it was certain that all the Jews in the German area of responsibility were provisionally to be assembled in the wide-open spaces of the East, pending a form of Final Solution acceptable to Hitler. For such a vast undertaking legal and administrative provisions had to be made.[199] On Hitler's instructions Göring thus supplemented the decree pertaining to the Final Solution of the Jewish question in Germany already issued by Heydrich in January 1939, and extended it in a letter of 31 July 1941 to include the whole of Europe. He authorized Heydrich:

. . . to make all necessary preparations in organizational, practical and material respects for a general solution to the Jewish question in the German sphere of influence in Europe. As far as the competences of other central authorities are concerned, these are to be shared. I further charge you to present me promptly with a general draft of the organizational, practical and material provisions for carrying out the hoped-for Final Solution to the Jewish question.[200]

In the relevant documentation and statements there is an almost consistent stress on the fact that this directive represents the actual order to carry out the Final Solution in the sense of an extermination 'industry', and that Heydrich hence became a conscious planner of the murder of millions of Jews of all Europe. Even this is very doubtful, however.[201] In the most recent scholarly evaluation of all the available documentary material that

1 Heydrich (in middle) with Hess (far left), Himmler (next to him) and
  Todt (to Heydrich's right) at an official function
2 Heydrich with his friend and rival Wilhelm Canaris in 1936

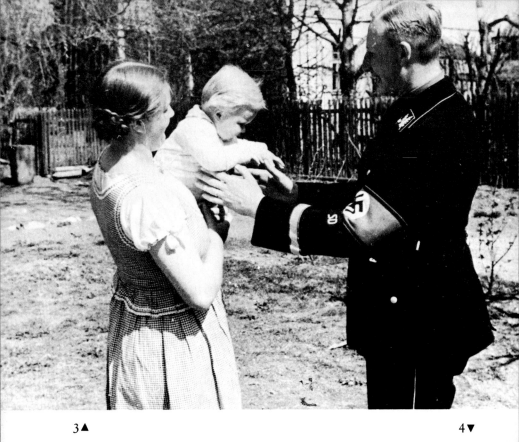

3▲

4▼

3 Heydrich, his wife and his first son at his home in
  München-Nymphenburg in 1934
4 Heydrich at his first meeting with President Hácha of the Protectorate
  government, at Prague Castle, at the end of September 1941
5 Heydrich (on the left) with fellow SS officers after a fencing practice

6 Heydrich at a ski-ing competition in the Tirol in 1941
7 Heydrich (left) with his deputy in the Protectorate,
  SS-Lieutenant-Colonel Karl-Hermann Frank
8 The scene of Heydrich's assassination in Prague

7▲ 8▼

9 Hitler speaking at Heydrich's state funeral. Generals of the SS,
   Luftwaffe and Police mount the guard of honour. Immediately after this
   Hitler ordered the destruction of Lidice as a reprisal

DEUTSCHES REICH

REINHARD HEYDRICH
✝ 7. III. 1904 ⚔ 4. VI. 1942

60
+440

BÖHMEN UND MÄHREN

BUDWEIS

10 Stamp produced for the first anniversary of Heydrich's assassination.
It shows the death mask made by the Berlin sculptor Professor Rotter

we have to hand, it is asserted that even this directive was 'certainly not an instruction to carry out what came to be understood under the term "Final Solution" after the war'.[202] With the authorization bestowed on Heydrich Hitler was more likely to have been thinking of a radical expulsion of all Europe's Jews. Only when it became clear at the end of August that the expected speedy overthrow of the Soviet Union had foundered, did he make up his mind to issue the first great deportation order, in September 1941, 'driven by the fanatical desire to purge his sphere of influence of the hated opponent whatever happened'.[203] 'The Führer wishes', ran a note written by Himmler on 18 September, 'that the *Altreich* and the *Protectorate from the West to the East should be cleared* and *freed of Jews* as soon as possible.'[204]

The first deportation orders, issued by Himmler, carry the signature of Heydrich's rival, Kurt Daluege, the chief of the regular police. In September a first shipment went to Lódź, in October a second brought 50,000 deportees to Minsk and Riga. While those deported to Lódź at first remained unmolested, after numerous delays and halts at intermediate stations the Jews from the shipment of 24 October fell into a prepared death-trap when they were unloaded at Riga: on the notorious 'Riga Bloody Sunday', 13 December 1941, they were shot.[205]

The previous month of November, at the latest, would therefore seem to have been the point 'at which the final decision concerning the physical destruction of European Jewry was pronounced'.[206]

The full import of that notorious conference which inextricably links the name of Heydrich with the extermination of the Jews, is only established with this discovery. It is a fact that although Heydrich had been appointed to supreme responsibility for the Final Solution by Göring in July, he only recalled the authority vested in him when under pressure from the altered situation in November. In accordance with his instructions to involve the other 'central authorities', he issued personal invitations to a conference 'with breakfast' on 9 December 1941 in the rooms of the Interpol villa at Grosser Wannsee, later postponing the meeting to 20 January 1942.[207]

As a copy of the minutes reveal, apart from Eichmann who was responsible for writing them, there were also present several functionaries from the SS offices concerned, from the Party Chancellery, the Ministry for the East, the Ministries of the Interior and Justice, and representatives sent by Göring, the office of the *Generalgouverneur* of occupied Poland, the Foreign Office and the Reich Chancellery. Heydrich took the chair.[208]

After referring once more to the instructions issued by Göring, which demanded the 'parallelization of policy decisions' of all the offices concerned, Heydrich again indicated that 'centralized control in the handling of the Final Solution' now lay, 'without regard for geographical boundaries', with him. For the benefit of those present, the previous stages in the solution of the Jewish question were recapitulated. First, their 'exclusion from particular areas in the life of the German nation', then their removal from German 'living space', by which Heydrich understood the 'intensified and systematically' pursued 'evacuation of the Jews from the Reich'. 'The object of the exercise was to purge German living space of Jews by legal means.' What Heydrich has to say about the resulting friction with the authorities of the 'destination or immigrant countries' sounds almost like a justified complaint addressed to foreign lands. 'Financial difficulties such as the increase in the deposits and landing-charges required by the various foreign governments, lack of suitable shipping, regularly tightened-up restrictions or total embargoes on immigration, all these made the evacuation efforts extraordinarily difficult.' Nevertheless, Heydrich pointed to the 'credit balance', the fact that 'from the assumption of power up to the target date of 31 October 1941 a total of about 537,000 Jews' had been 'induced to emigrate' from the Greater German Reich. After mentioning the ban on emigration imposed by Himmler the previous October, 'in view of the possibilities in the East', a new stage of the Jewish policy had been reached: 'Instead of emigration, there is now a further possible solution . . . the evacuation of the Jews to the East.' These 'operations', however, were only to be regarded as an 'alternative possibility', yet here already 'that practical experience [would be] gained which is highly significant in view of the coming Final Solution to the Jewish question'.

According to an estimate (which proved to be exaggerated) made by the RSHA, Heydrich said about eleven million Jews would be involved in this form of Final Solution; curiously enough, Heydrich included the Jews of England, Ireland, Portugal and Spain along with those of Sweden and Turkey. This has given rise to speculation up to the present time whether, in addition to the Final Solution familiar under the heading of 'Auschwitz', a territorial solution had not perhaps also been intended.[209]

However, the decisive paragraphs of the minutes leave few doubts, in spite of all camouflage, as to where the essential message lay. The two most important sections read:

In the course of the Final Solution the Jews, managed accordingly, are to form a suitable labour force in the East. In large labour gangs, with segregation of the sexes, the able-bodied Jews will be led to these regions building roads, whereby a large number will doubtless drop out through natural wastage.

And secondly:

And others still surviving at the end, since they will doubtless be the hardiest, must be treated accordingly, bearing in mind the process of natural selection, they must be regarded on their release as the nucleus for the regeneration of the Jewish strain. (See the lesson of history.)

What was to happen to the Jews who were unfit for work in the first place was either not mentioned by Heydrich or, because it would have gone far beyond the limits of a written record, was left out of the minutes.[210] But either his audience was well aware that the extermination of the Jews had already begun, or in his unrecorded remarks Heydrich left no room for doubt that 'natural wastage' and 'must be treated accordingly' were only rhetorical euphemisms for the biological destruction of all Jews within reach. That there was awareness of the issues at stake is shown, for example, by the statement noted in the minutes by the State Secretary for Poland, Dr Bühler, to the effect that his office would welcome the beginning of the Final Solution in occupied Poland, for 'of the roughly two and a half million Jews in question, in the majority of cases they were unfit for work'. Finally, the expression in the minutes speaks for itself when it says that 'alarming the population must be avoided'. Also, in the Eichmann trial of 1961, Eichmann himself, as a former participant in and recorder of the Wannsee conference, interpreted the term, 'possible solutions', as referring to the various 'possible ways of killing'.[211]

Heydrich was satisfied with the result of the discussion. There had been agreement on the form the evacuation of all Europe's Jews to the East was to take. The only exceptions were to be Jews over sixty-five years of age, severely disabled ex-servicemen and holders of high military honours from the First World War. None of the representatives of the 'central authorities' had raised substantial objections. Heydrich had again smoothly carried out an assignment from the Führer. According to Eichmann, he later entertained an intimate circle to 'a glass of schnapps'.[212]

The measures which followed this session formed the keystone of Jewish policy in the Third Reich and were at the same time the last role which Heydrich was to play in the drama. Eichmann now began his systematic combing of Europe, delivering the victims to the extermination camps, first recognizable as such in the autumn of 1941 and now greatly enlarged.[213] It is true that Heydrich's death a few months after the meeting at Wannsee, and especially the stricter responsibility taken for the extermination by Himmler, kept the chief organizer himself away from the mass murder, practised on an industrial scale, which is linked with the camp names of Treblinka, Sobibor and Auschwitz. In his standard work on the SS as an instrument of domination, the contemporary historian Hans Buchheim noted this fact: 'While the deportation of the Jews and the mass shootings by the task forces of the Chief of the Security Police and the SD were wholly the responsibility of the RSHA (that is, of Heydrich), the gassings in the extermination camps were expressly ordered by special command of Himmler.'[214] This is true both of the direct instructions from Himmler to SS-Major-General Odilo Globocnik for the destruction of Polish Jews, who built the camps of Blezec, Maidanek, Sobibor and Treblinka for that purpose, and of the special assignment, 'between ourselves', given to the commandant of Auschwitz, Rudolf Höss, and finally also to the Chelmno extermination camp.[215] This reservation is not without significance, for it gives a completely different picture of Heydrich from that of the fanatical driving-force behind the extirpation of the Jews, which has been drawn by a particular school of contemporary history and since then constantly repeated without verification. At the same time it corrects a mental attitude which constructed the fiction of a National Socialism resolutely bent on destruction and which took Heydrich as its personification.

Nevertheless, enough evidence remains of Heydrich's strong complicity. If there was any justice at all in the Nuremberg Trials, then Heydrich would certainly have been among those more convincingly accused. A death sentence against him would not have smelt of the vindictiveness of the victor in the same way as the sentence against Field-Marshal Jodl or the lifelong revenge on Rudolf Hess.

Yet a review of the connection between Heydrich's performance of his office and the development of the various stages of the National Socialist Jewish policy raises the question of the subjective concern this man felt for the fate of his victims. Only ten years separate the doubt he expressed in

1932, that in devoting himself to National Socialist anti-semitism he had 'perhaps been barking up the wrong tree', and the round of schnapps to celebrate the smooth running of the Wannsee conference. In between, on the one hand, lie his recognition of the independent Jewish state in Palestine, his sympathy bordering on admiration for the rediscovery of the Jewish race and nation by a large part of the Zionist movement, his revulsion at the *Kristallnacht* and finally his earnest furtherance of the Madagascar rescue plan. In unfathomable contrast, on the other hand, are the managerial perfection of his fulfilment of the Führer's command to liquidate the Jewish-Bolshevik world enemy supposedly revealed in Russian Jewry, the massacres perpetrated by his task forces, and finally the immense round-up operation, carried out with all his organizational flair, into the jaws of destruction.

What were the feelings of the man who was able to say of himself that as a National Socialist he was a 'Zionist'? We do not know the complete answer to this question. But from the little on record, the impression remains that the bloody part of his fateful encounter with the Jews did not satisfy his thinking, founded as it was on purposefulness and rationality, nor did his collaboration in the mass killings win from him any degree of inner approval.

On the contrary. The SS-*Reichsführer* repeatedly noted the lack of any proper insight into the necessity for hardness, as a passage in his later commemorative address for the dead Heydrich testifies. From countless conversations with Heydrich, he knew, said Himmler, 'what it cost this man to be outwardly so hard and severe despite the struggles and suffering of his heart!'[216] Divisional head Streckenbach confirms that the task forces' order to kill had been 'the worst order in his life', for Heydrich.[217] Another man present at the task force conference in Pretzsch even claims that it could be deduced from what Heydrich said there how ill at ease he had felt about the extent of his assignment. After a rousing speech Heydrich had dismissed his task forces with the words, 'Be hard where you must be hard, and be kind where you may be kind.'[218] And his childhood friend, Schultze, who visited Heydrich again in Prague in 1942, bears witness: 'The radical measures against partisans and subversive elements, against agitators and saboteurs – Reinhard felt all that was necessitated by the war, but to "bump off!" all the Jews into the bargain, that got him down.'[219]

The architect of the Final Solution, torn in all directions, took refuge in 'necessities of war' whenever the doubts became overwhelming. By resolving all Jews into one 'dangerous enemy' to be removed by the radical 'preventive' measures of his police, he silenced his own conscience. Eventually he was saying that 'the Jews had already declared war on us before 1 September'. Therefore their restriction of movement and installation in concentration camps and also their identification were all 'necessitated by war'.[220]

The pretext constantly quoted by Heydrich had been provided in the middle of August 1939 by the President of the Jewish Agency, Chaim Weizmann, when he held out the prospect in Geneva of Jewish participation in any impending war. In a Note of 29 August, as *The Times* reported, he in fact assured the British government that 'we Jews stand on the side of Great Britain and will fight for democracy', and he promised 'that all Jewish-human resources, their technology, their means and all their facilities would be usefully employed'.[221]

One week after the outbreak of war the *Jewish Chronicle* reiterated this obligation and without doubt involuntarily supplied ammunition to the advocates of an ever-more-radical solution to the Jewish question in Germany.[222] The chronicler of the Final Solution, Adler, accused Weizmann of this after the war: 'The most deplorable aspect of it is the short-sightedness with which the belief in a unified Jewish world power was fostered, which haunted National Socialism as the arch-enemy.'[223]

But of course Heydrich was fully aware that even the fictitious state of war between 'world Jewry' and the German Reich could not justify the activities of his task forces and Hitler's liquidation orders. The only justification that remained was his steadfast adherence to the 'duty to be hard', the power-hungry ambition which demanded blind obedience as the primary requirement for the pilgrimage to the pinnacle of power. 'He always assumed', broods his widow, 'that he had to perform his tasks to the bitter end.'[224] That did not alter the fact that he increasingly felt these 'tasks' to be 'negative', that the role of 'maid-of-all-work' and 'dustbin of the Reich' did not satisfy him. Since the summer of 1941, since the task force massacres directed by him, he had been seeking an escape route, another way to fulfil his duty, another way to achieve power – but it had to be a 'positive' one.

Chapter 12

A FRESH START?

At long last a positive task. At long last a change from being the dustbin of the Reich!

Reinhard Heydrich, September 1941

In September 1939 Heydrich had slipped into the giant role of establishing and directing the Reich Security office as though it had been designed with him in mind. But scarcely two years later it was evident that the suit which had once fitted him perfectly now restricted his movements. He neither wished nor was able to give it up, but he occasionally liked to let his subordinates, grown powerful in their own right, try it on for size, while he looked round for something new which might fit him better. He found what he was seeking in September 1942, in the provinces of Bohemia and Moravia, annexed to Greater Germany before the war, where a large majority of Czechs were averse to being part of the Reich and would not reconcile themselves to their lot as a German protectorate. In the summer months Heydrich's Security Police and SD built up for him a picture of Czech loyalty which grew steadily gloomier, reflecting the dangerously mounting passive and active resistance of the Czechs.

Since the outbreak of war against Russia the attitude of the Czechs towards the German authorities of the Protectorate and the Germans resident there had distinctly hardened. The acts of resistance, the mass demonstrations and a spreading movement of strikes and sabotage were directed on the one hand by the exiled Czech government in London of Dr

Edvard Beneš, with the help of BBC broadcasts and an extensive system of couriers, and on the other, since the pact between Hitler and Stalin had become meaningless, had gained a militant thrust from the professionals of the communist underground and Party apparatus. The time was now past when the communists polemicized less against the German authorities than against the 'bourgeois and reactionary Beneš clique'.[1] In the spring the organs of the illegal Communist Party were still writing about the Beneš government-in-exile to the effect that it represented those forces 'which, in spite of all protestations to the contrary, had first introduced the system of national oppression in Czechoslovakia, directed at that time against the Germans and the Hungarians'. In March 1941 leaflets were still being distributed in the Protectorate which, wholly in accordance with the Moscow-Berlin alliance, insisted that Beneš' policy was condemned to failure, for he had 'allied himself with the forces of reaction, with those forces which in the interest of monopoly enterprises had even risked war'. The main thing was not liberation from the Germans, but liberation 'from the dictatorship of bankers, monopolist masters and landowners'.[2] In the summer of 1941, when the Soviet Union was badly hit by Hitler's attack, when Stalin's hopes could no longer rest on the strength of his military forces alone, communist tactics changed radically. At a time when the German Army was fighting its way closer and closer to the heart of the Russian empire by the greatest war of annihilation in history, when two million soldiers of the Red Army were taken prisoner, it became vital for Stalin to weaken German might in the place where it was most susceptible – in the Protectorate of Bohemia and Moravia.

For the classic 'Bohemian square' was the bastion of German strategy. It was the turntable which connected both geopolitical and military strategic areas of influence from which the German war against Russia had to be conducted. The Prague-Berlin-Warsaw triangle is one of these areas. Whoever possesses it can control the Baltic. The second is the Prague-Bucharest-Sofia triangle, i.e. the Danube basin and south-east Europe. Bohemia was also the 'marshalling-yard' for transport within the German Reich as a whole. Railway lines and roads from Vienna to Berlin and from Nuremberg to Wroctaw (Breslau) went through Prague. The civilian and military traffic, and more particularly the arms shipments, went through the 'turnstile' of Prague. But most important of all, in this second year of the war and two and a half years after its union with the Reich, Bohemia had become the most vital centre for the German armament industry after the Ruhr. With the Škoda works in Pilzen and the arms factories at Brno, the German Reich had two of the largest and highest-quality armament manufacturers at its command. In addition, a considerable amount of German war production was increasingly transferred from the western areas threatened by air-raids to Bohemia. A third of German tanks, a quarter of the lorries of the Wehrmacht and forty per cent of light machine-guns were built in Bohemia.[3] The evacuation trend of the armament industry was also followed in wide areas of public administration and the Reich authorities.

A side-effect of this transfer from north to south, from west to east, was a sharp increase in the German section of the population in the Protectorate. In August and September 1941 alone, about 3000 German officials and industrial executives, together with their families, moved to Prague.[4] On the one hand they noticeably strengthened the German minority vis-à-vis the Czech majority, but at the same time they had the effect of aggravating the security problem.

The strength of German might was also its weakness: any disturbance of the status quo in the Protectorate, any setback to armament production was bound to have a severe effect on the German front in Russia. Every act of sabotage to the supply-lines of the Bohemian turntable, to the property and rolling-stock of the railways, every drastic reduction in agricultural production was at once a challenge and threat to the Reich, to be removed whatever the cost.

The Western Allies and their new partner, Russia, were well aware of the vulnerability of the Reich's military strength and war economy in its own hinterland, the Protectorate. In the summer of 1941, London and Moscow together inspired and organized, for the first time, a new wave of resistance against the German masters of Bohemia.

Klement Gottwald had previously talked about communism on the Moscow radio, but, after 22 June, he began to quote from patriotic Czech poems, and to praise the national and religious convictions of Hus.[5] The leaflet propaganda of the communists increased rapidly. If the Gestapo had only been able to seize 377 illegal communist publications in the Protectorate in June, in July the number had already increased tenfold, to rise to more than 10,000 in October.[6]

An appeal from the 'Pan-Slav Congress', which had then convened in Moscow, was circulated, in which 'all Slavs' were called upon to undermine the effectiveness of the German Wehrmacht by every means in their power. In particular, telephone and telegraph connections were to be cut, trains derailed, supply dumps burnt down and brake-cables severed. The workers were urged to work slowly, to produce as much waste as possible and to commit sabotage in every form.[7] The Czech section of the London BBC urged exactly the same. Hourly they broadcast their appeal, '*Pomalu pracuj*', 'work slowly!'[8]

As a result, the morale and productivity of the Czech work-force fell sharply. The propaganda from the resistance and the government-in-exile fell on fertile soil, as the food and supply situation in the Protectorate was severely impaired. The rations, even for armament and manual workers, were smaller than in the *Altreich*, and it was often impossible to distribute the quantities which were actually allotted. The main culprits were innumerable black marketeers and profiteers who sprang from all ethnic groups in the Protectorate – Czechs, Jews and Germans. They were responsible for the drastic bottlenecks in the meat and fat supply, but also for the shortage of worker-allowances such as cigarettes. Even German Party functionaries took an active part in the black market.

Since even Reich Germans had to produce an entry permit for the Protectorate, and such permission was most easily obtained for Party functionaries, they made up the greatest number of the many visitors who returned with a 'black' goose or a 'black' ham to Berlin. The middlemen were mostly Czech innkeepers and butchers, who were doing the best business of their lives. Among the working population all this naturally caused bad feeling. On a higher level there was added the conflict between the indigenous and the incoming profiteers, which was constantly resolved in favour of the incomers. 'In the Aryanization of Czech industry it was seldom a Czech who made the running, almost as seldom a Sudeten German from Liberec (Reichenberg) or Cheb (Eger), but it was always a German from Wuppertal or Düsseldorf, from Frankfurt or Cologne,' comments one of the foremost experts on conditions in the Protectorate at that time.[9]

The economic discontent was sharpened and given a political slant by the excessive chauvinism of the Germans towards everything Czech. They now repeated all the mistakes which the Czechs had previously made in their treatment of the Germans in Czechoslovakia. If a Czech Sokol parade in Cheb had earlier been a provocation, the provocative element was thoughtlessly repeated by German policy. For example, according to a language decree, German names were invented for towns in the purely

Czech region, which were to take precedence over the Czech ones.[10]

For all these reasons the slogans of the resistance and the BBC met with widespread approval in the summer of 1941. The first signs of an incipient strike movement were noted. The results spoke for themselves. From June to September 1941 armament production in the Protectorate fell on average by eighteen per cent, and in some factories by as much as thirty-five per cent.

In Berlin, and in the Führer's HQ the alarm bells shrilled. In proportion as the armament production declined, the number of acts of pure sabotage increased, to such a level not hitherto achieved. The highest incidence was of telephone wires cut, railway carriages set on fire and their brake-cables severed, and machines in arms factories deliberately damaged – just as the slogans of the resistance had urged. Resistance arsonists set supply dumps and factory buildings on fire, including, in August, a petrol dump containing 100,000 litres of fuel.

During the week from 14 to 21 September, in accordance with a call from London, the Czech Protectorate press, which was under German supervision, was boycotted. The boycott was so widespread that more than half of the editions went back to the respective publishers. The resistance stiffened more and more. On 20 September the climax was reached in Letovice, near Brno, when a home occupied by eighty-four German children evacuated from the towns was attacked with explosives.[11]

It became clear that if the German authorities wished to avoid a further increase in the resistance which, here in the hinterland of their own Eastern Front, threatened to turn into open rioting, then they would have to change their policy towards the Czechs in one way or another. At the time of the victorious German advance in Russia and the heavy Allied defeats, a liberalization was obviously out of the question. At this point the question of the fate of Bohemia crossed the path of Reinhard Heydrich. On account of the critical security situation he had already strengthened the offices of the Security Police and SD in Prague and Brno in July.[12] The reports which he received in Berlin transmitted to him 'the picture of a storm which was brewing over the Protectorate'.[13] Via Heydrich's office, the extract of the reports from the SD-regional HQs was also passed on to Hitler and Bormann. In a report from the office of the Reich Protector there was also talk of preparation of rebellion and general strike slogans for 28 October 1941. As soon as possible therefore, a conference was to take place in the Führer's HQ to discuss strategy. It was set for 22 September.

On 17 September the German State Secretary for the government of the Protectorate, the Sudeten-German SS-Lieutenant-General Karl-Hermann Frank, had already held a meeting with the most important SS and police leaders of the Protectorate. The meeting was unanimous in its criticism of the Reich Protector at that time, von Neurath. The career diplomat and former Minister for External Affairs was accused of handling Czech resistance too mildly. It was decided that Frank 'should read a paper on the dangerous situation' in the HQ of the Führer himself.[14] The day before, von Neurath had not permitted the draconian measures demanded by the Gestapo – who had made an extraordinarily precise survey of the organization of Czech resistance – to be carried out against well-known resistance circles. Representatives from the SD and military Intelligence took part in the meeting. The Intelligence officer and spy in the service of the Czechs, Paul Thümmel, was able to radio to London on 21 September 'The Gestapo demanded draconian measures, but von Neurath has rejected them.'[15]

How far the SS really wanted to take action, or whether it was perhaps more important to them to bring von Neurath, whom they disliked, into political discredit by demonstrating as many omissions as possible, is uncertain. At all events, it was evident that von Neurath had no nose for the beginnings of a 'situation', as he had previously shown in the student unrest of 1939. And even if he had, his position within the web of political forces in the Protectorate and also in Berlin would probably have been too weak to enable him actually to carry out energetic measures.[16]

Heydrich had ensured that he had been carefully prepared for the impending conference by the commander of the Security Police and the SD in Prague, Böhme. In particular, details were laid before him of the collaboration which the Gestapo had uncovered between the Czech government of the Protectorate under General Eliáš and the government-in-exile in London, which went on practically under the nose of the German Reich Protector von Neurath.

In the course of the morning of 21 September, State Secretary Frank arrived at the Führer's HQ in Rastenburg, the first of the invited delegates to the conference.[17] He delivered his speech to Hitler and was then invited to be present for the mid-day meal. Here too, the situation in Bohemia was the main topic of conversation. Hitler asked Frank, 'what the attitude of the Czechs was to the collapse of Russia'. They must realize that 'there is no escape from the present state of affairs'.

On the same day Heydrich was also ordered to Rastenburg, where he arrived in the late afternoon. Together with Himmler and Frank, with the aid of the material assembled by Böhme, he now explained to his Führer the causes for and the organization of the Czech resistance. What Frank had merely indicated, Heydrich was able to describe down to the last detail. Hitler was fascinated by the broad canvas of police reconnaissance work spread out before him. The discussions were continued on 22 September. Reich Protector von Neurath did not arrive in Rastenburg until the afternoon of 23 September, two days after Frank and Heydrich, as bad weather had caused him to miss his aeroplane connection in Berlin.

By the time von Neurath arrived, he had already lost the battle. On the strength of Heydrich's and Frank's reports Hitler had already decided 'to take drastic action'. For the Czechs von Neurath had 'only been a kind-hearted old gentleman'. 'Kindheartedness and peaceableness', said Hitler later, eventually became 'weakness and stupidity'.[18]

Heydrich had called von Neurath a 'court appeaser' and declared of the German policy in the Protectorate that it was characterized by two grave errors: there was no sense in rubbing the Czechs up the wrong way with the left hand, by the nationhood policy and provisioning for example, while stroking them with the right. The solution lay in the formula, 'Less provocation together with less tolerance.'[19] Heydrich's interpretation eventually carried the day.

Hitler told von Neurath point-blank that he now wanted to take a stronger line in the Protectorate, since the deterrent measures taken up until then had obviously not been adequate. For this line, however, he had less need of 'the experience of diplomacy'. For this reason he wished to entrust someone else with the performance of the office of Reich Protector 'for some time' – Reinhard Heydrich.[20]

Heydrich had quite plainly striven single-mindedly for the appointment. For the first time he had dared to bypass Himmler and entered into an alliance of convenience with Bormann. To be sure, he had valuable information on the 'Brown Eminence' in his armoury; but that did not exactly preclude his making use of him to pass on such material to Hitler as would make him see the extent of the Bohemian crisis so clearly that it was finally only a question of agreeing to the line demanded by the SS. Other representatives of the SS were also demanding a stronger line from Berlin, headed by SS-Lieutenant-General Karl-Hermann Frank, who might also have had a personal interest in it. He had possibly already imagined himself as von Neurath's successor, as he was much more familiar with the political and national peculiarity of the Bohemian sphere, and he knew Czech. And yet the choice fell on Heydrich. The first reason was that in Hitler's eyes Heydrich 'stood for a programme', but secondly, he had been able to produce a picture of Intelligence Service and Security Police reconnaissance work so convincing in its tight and detailed construction that he had easily been able to trump Frank's knowledge of the area.

The casting vote seems, however, to have been given by Bormann. The idea was prompted by a suggestion from Bormann's confidant, a senior ministry official, Heinrich Heim. By order of Bormann he had been the first to record Hitler's 'table-talk', as well as a minute chronicle of all the important events at the Führer's court. After Heydrich's death he noted, 'At my suggestion Heydrich was appointed Reich Protector at that time.'[21] In reality, however, he had merely remarked to his mentor that it would be best to entrust Heydrich with the policing of the Protectorate right away, and Bormann had taken up the idea at once and spoken up for Heydrich to Hitler.[22] His motive, according to Heim, was to separate SS-*Reichsführer* Himmler from his dangerous partner Heydrich, who far outstripped him in singleness of purpose, just when the conflict between the Party and SS was beginning. What was better than to remove the most dangerous potential adversary and commit him to responsibility at the same time?[23]

The appointment to Deputy Reich Protector, *de facto* therefore the sole wielder of power in one of the most important provinces of the entire German Reich, the appointment to probably the most complicated and difficult task of that time, which implied a mixture of Security Police and anti-terrorist work, Intelligence, administrative and diplomatic activity together with great executive powers – this was the fulfilment for Heydrich of a long-cherished dream. After ten long years of having to accept Himmler, 'the schoolmaster', inferior in intelligence and thoroughness, as his chief, he wanted to hold the reins of power himself. From the second rank of the hierarchy of the Third Reich he now wanted to advance to the front rank; he could tolerate no-one above him other than Hitler. He wanted his own territory, in which he could rule with unrestricted powers. And finally, having reached the limits of Security, he wanted to make policy himself.

He had felt himself to be the 'dustbin of the Reich', had carried out orders with ghastly thoroughness according to the slogan, 'Someone must be the bloodhound' – orders the logic of which escaped him and was unlikely ever to appeal to him. The more sensitive side of his nature had often enough been perplexed by the cold perfectionism of the mechanical side, when it was a question of carrying out orders; often he had been irritated by the split in his own personality. Often, at moments of depression, pity for his own predicament (pity he showed towards very few of his victims) got the better of the outwardly hard, even cruel prototype of the 'superman' of the SS.

Finally, he wanted to demonstrate that by means of the policies he intended to put forward, there too 'was order to be created where the methods of the Foreign Office had failed'.[24] On the evening of his nomination he told his wife with joy in his face that he was being 'appointed to Prague by the Führer, with the brief to restore order there after Herr von Neurath had, entirely in accordance with the methods of the Foreign Office, let things get so far out of hand'. Lina Heydrich was embittered.

It was terrible for me. He was never, never at home – or rather, he was only a visitor at home. I was married to Reinhard Heydrich for ten years, but I reckon he was not at home for seven of those years. Apart from his official duties he was on leave as an airman in the war. Then there were the many training flights, and his fencing too: at least an hour every morning, before the day's work began. And at the weekends there were the tournaments and preliminary heats.

His widow also said that there was at one time a serious marital crisis. So Heydrich's enthusiasm received a douche with the comments that they might as well separate, and 'oh, if only you had become a postman!'

Heydrich begged his wife on the telephone: 'Do try and understand what it means to me. At long last a positive task, at long last a change from being the dustbin of the Reich!'[25] The last ten years had ensnared him ever deeper in the aberrations and confusions of National Socialist politics, and had moved him ever further towards the very core of positive German guilt in this century – guilt which he himself had foreseen a decade before. But was a fresh start still possible?

Chapter 13

WITH CARROT AND STICK

My task is to teach the Czech people that they cannot deny the reality of their relationship with the Reich, nor avoid the obedience which the Reich demands.

Reinhard Heydrich, October 1941

Early in the morning of 27 September 1941, Heydrich arrived in Prague. The Germans and Czechs who awaited him had widely differing ideas as to what to expect. Common to them all, however, was fear. Heydrich already had a reputation as the head of a praetorian guard of Gestapo and SD, and a man who had never failed to carry out any command of the Führer's. The Czechs had mixed feelings: on the one hand they were afraid that Heydrich's appointment would bring a radical tightening-up of German policy; on the other, they felt some surprise to learn that Karl-Hermann Frank had been passed over. When the hated Sudeten-German Frank lost the appointment to the Reich-German Heydrich, who had no reason to dislike the Czechs, there seemed to be grounds for hope of a possible diplomatic gesture, almost a fresh start.[1]

'The Sudeten-German leaders', Heydrich complained in private circles, 'will never forget their old hatred of the Czechs, who have oppressed them, nor will the Czechs ever forget their hatred of the Sudeten Germans.' Frank could not have acted the 'new broom': he lacked that readiness to find pragmatic solutions. Matters were simpler between a Reich German and the Czechs. As far as the Reich-German Heydrich was concerned, he had never been in Prague in his life, except for one visit, after the outbreak of war, on the occasion of the occupation of the Protectorate. His widow later recorded that Heydrich had absolutely no preconceived notions about the Czechs.[2]

The opinions of the Germans within the Protectorate were equally divided. If, on the one hand, it was believed, especially among the Germans from Prague, that tough measures would now finally be taken against the Czechs, nevertheless, amongst the veteran campaigners for German nationalism the keynote was one of caution. After all, Heydrich did put Dr Walter Becher, the Sudeten-German leader, into a concentration camp, and other veteran nationalists of the *Kameradschaftsbund* (Comradeship Federation) with him.

The Party officials, according to Dr Walter Wannenmacher, Editor of the Prague newspaper *Der Neue Tag* (The New Day), trembled for Heydrich's distrust of the *Gauleiter,* his scorn for the Party generally as against the SS, and his disdain for the SA were well known. The Party men feared that Heydrich would weaken their position vis-à-vis the SS.[3]

Yet the general population of Czechs and Germans in Prague hardly noticed Heydrich's arrival. The day of the official assumption of his office was a sunny Sunday. People had gone out into the country. The war was hardly noticeable in Prague, where cinemas were showing the Ufa pot-boiler *Launen der Liebe* (Moods of Love).[4] But, for the first time, the black and white flags of the SS fluttered that day from Prague Castle (the Hradčany) alongside the red flags of the Party. Guards of honour composed of the Army, the *Waffen-SS*, police and units of the SD were assembled to greet the new 'Deputy' Protector. In a brief speech, Heydrich informed the gathering that Herr von Neurath was ill, and had requested the Führer to replace him. 'Under the circumstances, the Führer had no choice but to comply with this request,' he exclaimed.[5] Afterwards the new master of Prague Castle received a small and carefully selected band of future colleagues, German dignitaries and journalists, and issued a statement to them. He announced that in the next few days he would be explaining in greater detail the course which the Germans intended to pursue in Bohemia and Moravia; and it was to be clear from the outset that he, Heydrich, was interested in one goal only; that this area should exploit its full economic potential for war. Anything which endangered this aim he would suppress, whatever its origin or source. Anything which furthered it he would support.[6]

This speech caused many a long face among the Party functionaries, as one of the journalists who was present later remarked, a man who, even today, remains impressed by the coolness of Heydrich's first appearance. 'Heydrich', he said, 'looked like an English High Commissioner in one of the British Dominions, a completely cold individual who does precisely what he judges to be right in the light of the aims he has set himself. There is always *raison d'état* behind his actions.' Heydrich stood out in stark contrast to the familiar would-be supermen of the Nazi establishment.[7]

The following day reports appeared in the press. Under the headline 'Towards Self-Preservation' the chief editor of *Der Neue Tag* had written that the organism sensed internal and external threats and was forming antibodies in an effort to contain the danger. The isolation of the tubercular agent was quoted by way of analogy. Just as the body's defence system always prompted the organism to take the right action, so the German people had to put an end to the foolishness of Czech resistance. Heydrich was characterized in the report as the instrument of the preservation instinct. He had laid down a clear formula to serve as a guideline to his actions; he would do 'everything that serves a Europe controlled by *Grossdeutschland* [Greater Germany], opposing everything which harms it'.

The effect of these declarations and of the personality who was to implement them removed all doubt about the response required from every individual in the Protectorate.[8] It soon became abundantly clear that a new wind really was blowing. To tolerate less and to give less cause for offence, that was the resolution that Heydrich had brought with him to Prague. He embarked upon his programme unhesitatingly, and, without regard to long-term political ends, he created instant order, as Hitler had commanded. Among his immediate measures was included a harsh campaign against both nationalist and communist resistance movements, the intimidation of the Czech population and of the government of the Protectorate through terror, the neutralization of the Czech working class by attractive social policies and the disciplining of a sector of the German population inclined towards corruption.

On the very evening of his arrival Heydrich declared a state of emergency in the political centres of the Protectorate, in order, so it was given out, to be able to deal with 'unusual incidents'. Included in the state of emergency were the administrative areas of Prague, Brno, Ostrava, Olomoue, Kladno and Hradec Králové. Anything which threatened public life and security, or economic and industrial peace, or might do so, was subject to martial law. This included the illegal possession of weapons, ammunition or explosives, and any act of sabotage.[9]

This measure was announced on the radio throughout 27 September, from 8 a.m. onwards. It appeared the following day in the press and on posters in the streets.[10] In a second decree, illegal assembly, indoors or outdoors, was also made subject to martial law. On 1 October this measure was extended to include minor administrative centres as well.[11] The summary courts of justice had only three verdicts at their command; not guilty; referred to Gestapo; death. The death sentence was passed in about ten per cent of the cases tried: 404 people were sentenced and executed between Heydrich's assumption of office and the lifting of the state of emergency.[12] Many of the victims came from the middle class, the nationalist intelligentsia, the senior officer corps, largely drawn from the former legionnaire movement, and the activists of both types of resistance movement. The number of death sentences increased from six, on 28 September, to twenty on 29 September and fifty-eight on 30 September. Thereafter it declined.

Those executed in the first few days of Heydrich's office had, without exception, been arrested before his arrival; they were members of the resistance groups which had already been mopped up. All the victims were named, except for twenty-five, who appeared in the official lists of the condemned simply as 'persons'. In every case the reason for the sentence was published. For example, Dr František Kafka, the former Director of the Prague insane asylum, a social democrat, and the Party official Emil Feuerstein, originally a social democrat but latterly a communist, were both condemned as leading officials of a Czech resistance group especially concerned with helping people to reach the so-called 'Czech Legion' abroad, and with being actively involved in the gathering of Intelligence.[13] Among those executed were twenty-one officers of the former Czech Army, including six generals and ten colonels. They were accused of participation in a resistance organization directed from London.[14]

The list of civilian victims reflects all levels and classes of Czech society, with certain particular emphases. Peasants and workers were seldom represented. About ten per cent were described, apart from their professions and crimes, as Jews. On 29 September, for example, the communist functionary mentioned earlier, Emil Feuerstein, and one František Taussig, Secretary of the banned communist youth movement, were so described. Many death sentences were passed on charges of 'agitation'. On 15 October, Josef Dlouhý, a Prague newspaper editor, and František Dvořák, a police officer, were shot for jointly monitoring BBC broadcasts, and for distributing anti-German leaflets based on these broadcasts. They were charged with spreading disturbance and panic in wide circles of the populace by means of lying propaganda.[15] Four saboteurs were executed on the same day, a significant proportion of the day's victims. They were a teacher, an insurance agent, a driver, and a railway employee. According to the verdict of the summary court, they belonged to a resistance group: 'The task of your terrorist group was the planning and execution of acts of sabotage, particularly against the railways.' They had put sand and broken glass in the axle-boxes of goods wagons, which the BBC in London was constantly urging people to do.[16]

Organized national resistance was practically wiped out in the weeks after Heydrich's arrival in Prague.[17] By the end of that year only a few remnants still remained. This decline was due, not only to the deterrent effect of the executions, but also to a wide-reaching dragnet action of arrests, with which Heydrich was able to eliminate one chain of organized resistance fighters after another. The number of arrests in the months of October and November was between four and five thousand.

The Gestapo had been observing the resistance network for months, and informers had penetrated into their highest ranks. Directly after his arrival, Heydrich sent in his heavy squads. First of all the leaders were arrested. Through their statements, and with the help of the many filing systems that were confiscated, and the cracking of various codes, the Gestapo soon traced even the finest threads of the net. Section by section they were picked up. As well as the resistance groups, Czech communication with London was seriously disrupted. The organization ÚVOD alone lost a group of forty-one radio monitors. The arrested resistance leader, Colonel Josef Churavý, said in a statement that he had asked London to send out new encoding keys. These were delivered at the beginning of October by the first parachuted agent to arrive from London, whose name was Pavelka. He was to fall into the hands of the Gestapo three weeks later.

The scale of the Czech disaster was described by Heydrich himself in a secret speech:

When I say that our progress in the campaign against Czech resistance can be summed up, purely from the technical point of view, in the fact that in the last few days we have confiscated roughly ninety short-wave transmitters, and that the number of summary court sentences now totals between four and five hundred, while four to five thousand have been arrested, I must remind you also that we are dealing here with an organization of which it would be true to say that all the arrests and sentences of death involved exclusively people of high intellectual abilities. These were no fellow travellers, but the leadership structure itself. You can imagine what we might have had to contend with at their hands.[18]

So the nationalist resistance was practically paralysed for the next few months. Spying and sabotage were completely curbed by Heydrich's selectively applied terror. Beneš, too, says in his memoirs that after the arrival of Heydrich spying was more difficult than it had been under von Neurath.[19] The resistance groups that were still operational were largely connected with the Czech Communist Party. They had withstood Heydrich's strikes incomparably better than their nationalist rivals. This was partly due, no doubt, to their conspiratorial administration and their experience in underground work. They were much better designed for the job than the bourgeois groups. But, above all, it was thanks to the fact that the communists had entered into the resistance struggle only shortly before Heydrich's arrival, so that the Gestapo had not yet had time to infiltrate their ranks with informers. The dossier on the communists had more blank spaces than useful information in it.

Naturally, all these savage strikes against the resistance terrified the formerly uninvolved Czech majority. An eloquent sign of this was that more and more Czechs refused to support the resistance, even passively, and did all they could to remain absolutely neutral. Many of the Czechs got rid of their weapons after Heydrich's arrival: in October alone the Gestapo found 500 discarded weapons.[20] Heydrich's terror tactics did not stop short of the pursuit of high-ranking personalities. This was clearly demonstrated by the case of General Eliáš, the former Minister-President, who was subsequently sentenced to death. After Hácha, Eliáš was the highest representative of that 'semi-autonomous' state which Hitler had allowed the Czechs. General Eliáš was arrested only a few hours after Heydrich's arrival in Prague, so Heydrich's move must have been previously planned in Berlin. Although this case was part of Heydrich's overall strategy for the achievement of his immediate aims, it had been opened early enough to suggest that Eliáš was not condemned purely for reasons of expediency.[21]

Eliáš' name had been appearing regularly in Gestapo reports since the autumn of 1939, in connection with the nationalist Czech resistance, and, in particular, the collaboration between London and government circles in the Protectorate. Even government ministers were involved to some extent. The handling of the Eliáš case over the subsequent two years sheds some illuminating light on German policy towards the Czechs and on the procedures of Heydrich's political police.

In the autumn of 1939, the Gestapo had cleaned up an Intelligence organization led by people closely associated with Eliáš, chief among them Zdeněk Schmoranz, press chief of the Minister-President's office. Schmoranz asserted that he had always laid Intelligence reports before Eliáš, prior to sending them off abroad, and had always kept him informed of his relations with foreign countries. At about the same time, a leading official of the former Czech Intelligence Service revealed that he had handed over to Eliáš five million crowns from the secret funds of the Defence Ministry which had been saved from falling into German hands. A few days laters, another Czech, again a former Intelligence officer, confessed to the Gestapo that he had received money from Eliáš in support of the resistance movement. Then, in February 1940, the SD-agent, Schmalschlager, succeeded in penetrating a Czech espionage group which reported to English and French agents in Budapest, and was closely in touch with the French consulate there. By these means the SD got hold of a report on the German coal market, and the supply of coal to the German–Italian region, giving precise dates and indicating opportunities for sabotage. According to the Gestapo, this document could only have been prepared with assistance from the top men in Czech economic circles.[22] Such reports existed only because of the excellent relations between the resistance movement and the Minister-President's office itself.

As a result of Schmalschlager's evidence, the Mayor of Prague, Klapka, was arrested. He, too, testified against Eliáš to the Gestapo. In the meantime, the Hungarian security police had uncovered one of the relay points for the Czech reports, in Budapest. The Hungarian government handed over to the Reich further information about Eliáš which thus fell into their hands. Then, on the occupation of Paris, French documents were seized by the SD, containing yet more proof of Eliáš' guilt. The Germans weighed up the question of his final dismissal and arrest. Karl-Hermann Frank, State

Secretary to the Protectorate, pressed Berlin for action. Heydrich, on the other hand, preferred to penetrate the Czech resistance further, and Hitler, in the end, decided in favour of delay on diplomatic grounds.

However, when Heydrich set off for Prague as Reich Protector, the situation was entirely changed. Now Czech resistance was to be annihilated. It suited Heydrich, therefore, that his Prague office could report to him that on 20 September General Eliáš had once again received a delegate from Beneš in London, who had passed on to him new instructions for the resistance to German rule. This courier, Count Bořek Dohalský, was arrested by the Gestapo, and on examination gave numerous details of the collaboration between Eliáš and London.[23] The arrest of General Eliáš was, therefore, one of the first demonstrations of Heydrich's policy of 'less tolerance'. On 25 September, at 6.30 p.m., while still in Berlin, Heydrich had called on the President of the People's Court, Thierack, at his home, and had informed him of his appointment as Reich Protector, and of his determination to take matters seriously in hand.[24] Thierack pointed out to Heydrich that in his opinion it would not do to condemn the chief minister of a state in a police court. Heydrich took his point and was ready to pass the case on to the People's Court: but he would not be dissuaded from his plan to make the charge himself, as Reich Protector. Thierack objected that under the law the official in charge of prosecutions for the People's Court was always the Chief State Prosecutor. This objection was brushed aside by Heydrich with a claim to have overall power. 'I have been given plenipotentiary powers by the Führer, and with this justification I shall order that in this case the charge will be made by the Reich Protector.'[25]

After the arrest of Eliáš, Heydrich wanted to proceed swiftly with the trial, and Thierack declared that he was willing to go along with his wishes. There were some reservations expressed by the Reich Ministry of Justice, which was not altogether free from anxiety about whether the reputation of the People's Court might not suffer through the neglect of a thorough preparation of the case, and the fact that the representation of the charge against Eliáš was not to be undertaken by the Chief State Prosecutor. They were worried, too, about whether Thierack realized that the name 'Heydrich' had particular implications. Thierack admitted that in the prevailing emergency preparations could not be as careful as usual. Initially, three weeks had been set aside for the preparation of the case. But since, as Heydrich and Thierack believed, this extremely urgent situation amounted to a state emergency, Thierack declared himself ready to allow the People's Court in Prague to act very swiftly indeed.[26]

So even before Heydrich arrived in Prague he had won his first power struggle. Without having to refer to Himmler, or even to inform him, he had checkmated a Minister of the Reich and State Secretary, Schlegelberger, as well as Reich Minister Lammers. Lammers had even prevailed upon Hitler, through Bormann, to intervene; but to no avail, as State Secretary Stuckart had warned him. When it was brought to Heydrich's attention that in the Eliáš case mercy was the province of the Reich Minister of Justice, Heydrich received the communication in silence.[27] Heydrich wanted to make an example of Eliáš as soon as possible. On 27 September he arrived in Prague. On 28 September Eliáš was arrested. On 29 September the press reported the arrest and the charge of high treason. On 30 September the First Senate of the People's Court, under Thierack, flew to Prague. On 1 October, at 10 a.m., the trial began, in the State Police HQ in Prague.

The prosecution accused Eliáš of failing to pass on to the authorities information he had about illegal religious organizations, and the Intelligence activities of Schmoranz and of Klapka, Mayor of Prague. Eliáš admitted that he had known about resistance organizations. Indeed the evidence accumulated by Superintendents Schultze and Bingel was so overwhelming that he had no alternative but to make a confession.[28] By way of excuse for his behaviour Eliáš explained that he had always been a patriotically devoted Czech and had found himself unable to betray his fellow-countrymen.

By 2 p.m. the People's Court had announced its verdict. Eliáš was sentenced to death, stripped of his civil honours. But sentence was not carried out. Heydrich told the informants from the Reich Ministry of Justice that the right to exercise clemency in this case was reserved for the Führer himself. Hácha twice asked Heydrich to pardon Eliáš, and, on 6 October, Heydrich told Hácha that the execution had been postponed because Eliáš' evidence was required in some other important cases.[29] At the same time, Karl-Hermann Frank was violently demanding that sentence should be carried out forthwith, threatening that he would intervene with Hitler otherwise. A speedy execution was necessary, he claimed, because the Czechs, who were quick to see historical parallels, would compare the military situation and world position of contemporary Germany with the situation of Austria-Hungary in the period 1917-18. At that time, the Czech rebel, Karel Kramář, had been pardoned beneath the very gallows by the Emperor Charles. It was Frank's belief that a pardon for Eliáš would encourage the Czechs in their resistance.[30]

But what the lawyers of the Ministry of Justice had already discovered for themselves, was now made clear to Frank. The new Reich Protector was called Heydrich: he had unlimited power and he intended to use it, not only against the Czechs, but also against any attempts to place obstacles in his way, as he felt the lawyers were doing (he described them as petty) and against the over-zealousness of the nationalists, who threatened to disrupt his plans. Thus, while Eliáš was not executed, he was not pardoned either. Heydrich was not going to relinquish without a struggle such a useful source of pressure upon the government of the Protectorate.

He suggested to Hitler that the execution should be postponed. Other members of the government, who knew about the activities of the resistance, or who had worked for it, escaped with their lives. The Minister of the Interior, Ježek, who, as Heydrich was aware, knew about many of the things for which Eliáš had been sentenced, was not even arrested. For, Heydrich pointed out, if the Germans had arrested everyone who was in the know, the number of arrests would have been great indeed. 'I have put only the key men out of action; as for the rest of those implicated, I have left them in office, pretending to be ignorant of their guilt. I preferred not to make a clean sweep; that would have left me no-one to work with.'[31]

The methods Heydrich used to strike down the most dangerous opponents of German policy within such a few days, destroying practically the entire underground movement within the space of a few weeks, far outdid all previous measures. They were ruthless and severe, but they showed a very rare and outstanding political instinct. In the combination of these two ingredients lay the success of Hitler's new Deputy in the Protectorate. As Karl-Hermann Frank told the RSHA, an outside observer might not have noticed any sign during those weeks, apart from the restrictions of the curfew, that he was witnessing the suppression of a carefully planned revolt.[32] There had been no Army units marching through the streets, nor police, nor any armed conflicts. And Heydrich's blow was deliberately not aimed at the large number of those who were helping the resistance. He 'sorted out the spearhead of the attack, the chief trouble-makers, without any respect for the offices they held'. From those very first days of his Protectorate, Heydrich thus prepared for himself an avenue by which he might approach the Czech people. After the waves of hatred between

Germans and Czechs which had overwhelmed the Protectorate time and again since 1939, this selective policy of terror opened a tiny crack into which ruthless and pragmatic policy and propaganda might drive a wedge, and slowly separate the 'good' from the 'bad' Czechs.

Meanwhile, the precisely calculated German policy of tough repressive measures against the 'ruling class' and its representatives in the government and administration gave Heydrich another means of applying pressure. He was well aware, however, that the ruthless employment of repressive measures alone would never suffice to make the people and the government of the Protectorate amenable to him in the short time that the war-economy aims of the Germans afforded, and to further which Heydrich had been sent to Czechoslovakia.

To make the government of the Protectorate amenable meant, first of all, to neutralize them by all the means available. To this end Heydrich had a long discussion with Hácha to try and gain acceptance for the German measures. He paid his initial call to Hácha the day after his arrival, informing him that his term of office in the Protectorate was a limited one. He had been entrusted with the role of Protector because the attitude of the last Minister-President, Eliáš, who had now been arrested for high treason, had been 'hostile to the Reich'. He reminded Hácha also of the

> . . . astonishing accumulation of acts hostile to and damaging to the Reich carried out by citizens of the Protectorate, acts which had been directed by a tightly organized resistance movement within the Protectorate, which was in the pay of enemy powers of the Reich and which, in systematically pursuing the line put out by enemy propaganda, was trying to stir up the essentially peace-loving population of the Protectorate and bring them into conflict with the Greater German Reich.[33]

Heydrich promised that he would make every effort to overcome the problems faced by the Czech population, 'chiefly lying within the sphere of food supply'. He admitted that there were shortages which were far in excess of those to be expected in wartime. During his term of office he would seek to ameliorate these conditions, given appropriate backing by the population.

Hácha, who right up to the morning of that day, after he had heard about the first martial-law sentences and the arrest of Eliáš, had been determined to resign, now decided to stay in office. He promised loyalty to Heydrich, 'in the name of the Reich as well as of the Czech people'. With this, the way was clear for Hácha's collaboration and for Heydrich's policies in the early months. He promised a gradual reduction of the reign of terror as a reward for Czech good behaviour. This good behaviour he attempted to secure with a mixture of 'negative' and 'positive' steps. If necessary, he would have taken a breach with the purged government of the Protectorate in his stride, for he was not interested in the bourgeois intelligentsia, but in the acceptance of his terror machine by the workers and small peasants of the Protectorate. He hoped that, since it was not directed at them, they would shrug it off as a necessary evil.

First of all Heydrich had to acquire a superficial reputation for justice. He began with tough measures: 169 of the 404 death sentences passed by Heydrich's emergency courts were aimed, not at political resistance, but against economic crimes. Racketeers, black marketeers and illicit meat slaughterers, those mainly responsible for the poor supply of foodstuffs to the population, were ruthlessly rooted out by Heydrich. One of the first special squads formed by the German Criminal Police, on 29 September, was to combat profiteers and black marketeers. In the press, on the radio and on wall posters Heydrich urged the Czechs to 'report to the police all cases of illicit trading, illegal slaughter, profiteering, hoarding, etc., known to them'. The 'enemies of the people who were putting the nutrition of the population at the gravest risk' had to be stopped at all costs. There was a reward for information leading to conviction.[34]

Heydrich's first appeal to the Czech people, via their stomachs, was an unqualified success. The pent-up fury against war-exploiters making a profit out of the general misery was released in a flood of denunciations. Heydrich made sure that drastic action resulted and that the death sentence was almost invariable. So it was that among the 404 victims of Heydrich's selective terror-apparatus there were twice as many butchers as intellectuals, and more racketeers than high-ranking officers. While the 'politicos' were shot, Heydrich had the 'economic pests' hanged. The official list of executions for a single day, 10 October, is a typical example. It runs thus:

Hanged: 22

Lerach, Vaclav, cattle-dealer	Zítek, Antonín, butcher
Blažek, Otokar, butcher	Stejskal, Stanislav, cattle-dealer

Elicer, František, municipal
government employee
Leiner, Karl, Jew, dealer
Klecka, Bohumil, teacher
Uzel, Josef, butcher
Lerach, František, mason
Trávníček, Antonín, butcher

Mikuláš, Arnošt, butcher
Mans, Josef, butcher
Kohout, Bohumil, butcher
Tychna, František, official
Vaníček, Josef, butcher
Four other persons[35]

Heydrich made a great deal of propaganda capital out of his drive against the 'economic criminals' and 'enemies of the people', and he skilfully linked it with his campaign against 'the idiots spurred on by London and Moscow'. The newspapers of the Protectorate, for example, obliged with headlines such as 'Fourteen black marketeers hanged, Germans and Czechs'; 'The fight against black marketeers and communists'.[36] After a very few days there was a marked and increasing tendency, especially on the part of the poorer class of Czechs, to support Heydrich's moves.[37]

Only a week after Heydrich's assumption of office it was noted with satisfaction at the Führer's lunch table: 'The Czech workers have accepted with equanimity the liquidation of the underground.' The working class were only concerned with food and their jobs. A worker had even written to Heydrich, giving his name in full, to say that in the whole of Czech history it had always been the same, that the lesson had had to be learnt all over again by each new generation. 'Nobody would mind' if 2000 more such 'enemies of the people' were shot.[38]

A particularly good impression was made by the fact that Heydrich neither spared the rich, nor was he intimidated by titles and high honours; above all, he directed his terror-campaign not only at Czechs and Jews, but also at Germans (admittedly in smaller numbers).

In a secret speech to the top members of the German leadership of the Protectorate, he announced in unmistakable tones his intention to apply savage measures 'in the same way to those trimmers profiting from the war' who pretended 'to be serving the Reich here, but were in fact only out for personal gain and were damaging the good name of the Reich'.[39]

On 4 November, for example, the factory owners Walter and Helmut Adam from Jihlava were hanged for 'economic sabotage': according to the testimony of socialist émigrés these two were actually 'keen Nazis', in whose factory 'only Party members were accepted'.[40] On 30 September the Reich-German chemist Joseph Melcher, who was connected with a Czech

Intelligence organization, was shot, and on 18 October the German butcher Josef Hertl from Prague was hanged for his trading activities as a 'middleman'.[41]

The 'chief suspicion-monger' Heydrich even suspected a close connection between the racketeering and the resistance, orientated towards London. (After Heydrich's death, Frank recalled that the 'active resistance front, and the passive resistance, ranged from the highest places in the autonomous government, down to the black marketeers'.)[42]

The execution of a Head of Department at the Ministry of Agriculture, Otokar Frankenberger, can probably be linked with this campaign of Heydrich's. He was accused of deliberately failing to inform German local authorities of economic crimes whose existence he had been aware of, and hence of hindering or preventing the discovery of these crimes. His aim had been to stoke the fires of resentment of the German occupation, particularly in the towns, by keeping rations short, thereby preparing the ground for action by the resistance. And it was precisely in order to dissipate this undoubtedly widespread disaffection, that Heydrich very early on put special emphasis on police activity directed against the black market.

But the execution of racketeers and black marketeers was only meant to form the backdrop against which Heydrich was to stage his 'positive' moves to improve food supplies. Among these measures were the direct surveillance of producers and the seizing of clandestine stocks.

Czech control over supply, surveillance and distribution of foodstuffs was consequently drastically curtailed. While the names of hanged black marketeers were filling the columns of the Protectorate's newspapers, Heydrich ordered on 2 October a new count of livestock and cereal supplies. All those who had submitted false figures in the cattle count of June and the pig count of 4 September, and who were now prepared to 'report retrospectively' were promised an amnesty. Even the German authorities themselves were surprised by the response. After only a few days Heydrich was able to report to Berlin that the figures originally calculated 'had been exceeded by thousands'.[43] When the final tally was completed, by 19 October, even Heydrich was flabbergasted: Frank reports that the number of pigs disclosed was 560,000.[44] In some cases farmers and cattle-dealers had not reported even half of their total head of stock. In three Moravian districts for example, only 45,000 pigs had earlier been reported, while now, on a single day, there were 33,000 'illegal' pigs 'belatedly' reported or discovered by search.[45] Heydrich ostentatiously ordered the supplies of foodstuffs confiscated from racketeers or black marketeers to be distributed to the canteens of large firms. The workers were supposed to be persuaded that the new Reich Protector was in fact not fighting the Czech people, particularly not the working class, but that his terror-machine was directed only at the activists of the resistance and the 'enemies of the people', who alone were supposed to be responsible for the bad state of affairs of the Protectorate.

And after all, their participation in Heydrich's course of action, or at least their neutral stance, it was suggested, would be for their own good. Every pig discovered on the premises of a racketeer, so they were to believe, was destined to end up on the plates of Czech workers. In this connection Heydrich promulgated the system of works canteens, so far unknown in Czech firms, but suggested many months before by Army factories and accepted in principle. He set 27 October as the deadline for the establishment of canteens. In these canteens meals were distributed in the work-force without requiring them to produce ration cards, and in those firms which lagged behind in establishing canteens the extra rations were simply handed out in their raw state. According to the unanimous opinion of all reports, these moves were given a 'hearty welcome'.[46] Morale-reports of the SD and the Prague armaments inspectorate confirmed that the combination of 'soup kitchen' action and a vicious attack on the black market had a beneficial effect on the morale of the workers, although the supply of food, while distinctly improved, had not really been very substantially increased.

There was a change of attitude in the working class, first of all (and exclusively, to begin with). According to a secret report, the workers seemed to be grasping the point 'that they would fare best if they went about their duties conscientiously'.[47]

In the next few weeks Heydrich made full use of this first noticeable change of mood to win the confidence of the workers completely. Two problems above all had to be resolved, and in such a way that the marked improvement in material conditions would be associated with trust in Heydrich's good will to achieve civil peace, tranquillity and stability. On the one hand there was the question of wages and of nutrition and clothing, and on the other the need to bring social welfare into line with the standards prevailing in the Reich. It was not that what had been done so far ran counter to Heydrich's rather poorly developed sense of social justice, but that it offended his reason. If the Czech workers were needed at all, Heydrich had argued, even while he was still in Berlin, then one had to avoid such elementary psychological mistakes as allowing different levels of rationing for Czechs and Germans, and above all the exclusion of the Czechs from categorization into normal, heavy, and very heavy labour (for rationing purposes). 'You can imagine how keen the Czechs will be to produce tanks for the Germans, for example, if they don't benefit in any way themselves.'[48] How much could be achieved by the opposite tactic was clear from the high numbers of those who, mainly for material gain, had opted for official German nationality. Tens of thousands of Czechs had registered themselves in 1941 as being of German origin. The Čiháčeks, Doskočils and Králs had turned into whole legions of Försters, Rotters and Schwarzes. In the racial twilight-zone of Bohemia, most people could claim a mixture of Czech and German blood in their ancestry. Popular slang soon invented a nickname for these 'transfers': they were known as 'Margarine-Germans' on account of the superior fat-ration the Germans received.

The unions served as an instrument to bring Heydrich's policy home to the masses. The National Central Trade Union Agency (NOÚZ), with its roots stretching back into the Czech Republic, was a multi-union body, with which the German Workers' Front enjoyed only a loose relationship. Contact between the two groups was maintained by a 'Liaison Office of the Reich Protector with the Unions', led by a high-ranking official of the German Workers' Front. The aim of the Czech union was to concern itself 'no longer with politics, but with workers' welfare, wages, social security and recreation'. Heydrich conveyed to his closest colleagues, particularly Frank and Burgdorff, that he wanted to de-politicize the population, in line with the class-principle devised by Othmar Spann: 'Structuring of society in non-political class-groups so that the energies of the small man are consumed by the practical and material concerns of his job.'[49]

He commanded that during October mass meetings should take place in the most important factories at which official speakers might convince the work-force that Heydrich's policy was not directed against them but that, on the contrary, the new Reich Protector was a friend of the working man. They should not allow this friendship to be forfeited through any acts of 'foolishness', such as toleration of sabotage. The speakers announced that they would shortly be enjoying the opportunity of putting the complaints and suggestions of the work-force to the Reich Protector himself. In the list of complaints the shortages of tobacco and fat took pride of place. In addition, the scarcity of industrial footwear and bicycles was emphasized, and complaints were made about the differing treatment of Czech and Reich-German workers, as well as about general pay and welfare problems.

On 24 October, at the end of the union campaign, when Heydrich had been in office as Protector for just one month, he met some forty representatives of the work-force, led by the union leader Stočes. It was the first time in Czech history that a workers' delegation had been received in the Emperor's Hall of the Hradčany Castle in Prague.[50] After the speakers had declared their loyalty and had described in detail the problems of the workers, it was Heydrich's turn to speak. He addressed the union delegates as his 'comrades at work'.[51] He requested their understanding for the difficult supply-situation prevailing in the Protectorate. First and foremost it was the 'racketeers and war-profiteers, the black marketeers and usurers' who were responsible, and they were being dealt with. (The speakers from the unions had previously expressed to him their support for his severe measures.) The meat and fat supply would be improved because of the large numbers of pigs only now being declared. Furthermore he intended to divert fat, at the rate of 420 grammes (15 oz.) each for two million workers, together with grain, from stocks in the Reich. And he was going to look into the questions of industrial footwear and child allowances.

His cordial relations with the State Secretary in the Ministry of Agriculture, Backe, stood Heydrich in good stead now. They dated from the Berlin days, when the Backe and Heydrich families and the doctor from the *Charité*, Professor de Crinis, had enjoyed regular social gatherings. State Secretary Backe had declared at a meeting between himself, Frank and Heydrich in Hitler's HQ that it was possible to supply this 'highly political' fat in sufficient quantities.[52] Thus by the end of October the fat-ration of workers in heavy, very heavy and long-shift jobs was in fact brought up to the levels in the Reich proper. With special ration cards the ration stood at 1040 grammes (2¼ lb.) per month.

Almost thirty per cent of the population of the Protectorate benefited from the drive to supply more fat.[53] Another immediate step that Heydrich took was to restore the flow of adequate supplies of tobacco goods, interrupted chiefly by irregularities in the German and Czech supply depots, by cigarette-hoarding and black-market activities: it was the miners who were worst affected.[54] By 'making use of funds confiscated from middlemen and racketeers' Heydrich was furthermore able to provide the Czech work-force straight away with 200,000 pairs of work-boots. They were distributed free to industry by Works Councils and unions.[55]

Although with hindsight these measures have the unmistakable stamp of piecemeal charity, they were viewed differently in those days of bottle-necks in every conceivable commodity, of the war-economy with its system of permits and rationing of clothing and food. But greater than their material value was their contribution to a gradual change in the political climate, their role in achieving a propaganda victory by modifying the mood of the broad mass of the people. For Heydrich margarine was not just a soft fat for spreading on bread, obtainable against the appropriate number of ration-coupons: fat, boots, cigarettes and cash, as he himself said, were 'factors in political influence'.[56] And he knew that the Protector would have to build up tremendous political influence if he was going to meet in full the war-economy demands which had brought him to Bohemia.

Among the measures intended to have a decisive influence on the political climate was the reform of social welfare and national insurance. The prevailing standard was still that of the Czechoslovak Republic, far behind that of the Greater German Reich. Heydrich had new regulations drawn up to improve the national insurance cover of the workers and miners, and to raise pension rights without a corresponding increase in contributions. These regulations came into force on 1 April 1942. Altogether the invalid and old-age pensions were increased one-fifth by these measures, the widow's pension by a third and the orphan's pension by seventy-five per cent. A compulsory unemployment benefit was intro-duced for the first time.[57]

The first and only Labour Day Heydrich was to see as Reich Protector, 1 May 1942, was used by Heydrich to stage, under his personal direction, a massive display of his 'pro-worker' sentiment. The first move was to change the holiday to a Saturday, so that the workers would have two clear days off. (At that time, Saturday was part of the normal, six-day working week.) Among the workers of Prague alone he distributed 116,000 free cinema tickets and 18,000 theatre tickets. Football games in the national league championships were specially transferred to the dates of the May holiday, and likewise tickets were handed out by an organization attached to the unions. To crown the whole enterprise Heydrich officially announced, to celebrate the May holiday, what had been revealed in the planning stage at the end of October: the conversion of luxury hotels in Luhačovice Spa into Recreation Homes for workers. On 1 May 3,000 Czech workers were granted recreational holidays: 7,000 received them during 1942. Selection of the lucky recipients was by the employer, in conjunction with the Works Council.[58]

One consequence of the whole enterprise was that Heydrich was raised out of the anonymity surrounding the mere provider of social welfare to take his place in the limelight as the 'friend' and benefactor of the Czech workers. The Czech Propaganda Minister of the Protectorate government, Moravec, announced over the radio and in the press that 'all honest men of toil' were Heydrich's own people.[59] 'For the first time', went the press consensus, 'the Czech work-force is being shown on a large scale the connection between productivity and welfare, with its implications in the purely human sphere, while previously the purely mechanical relations, of hours worked to pay, of effort to remuneration, were the rule.'[60] Particularly singled out for attention were the free holidays in the luxury hotels of Luhačovice Spa. Above all, this initiative on the part of Heydrich had demonstrated 'that such holiday facilities were no longer reserved for those who could afford the money and leisure to enjoy them'. Cash was no longer to be the sole criterion for such a privilege, but contribution to the economic war-effort. The organ of the official Czech Unions commented that Heydrich's policy was in keeping with 'the National Socialist concept of the value of the workers'.[61]

Other Czech papers compared the standing of the worker with his former social position under the Republic. To point to the 'social action' by Heydrich on this May holiday, it was stressed, was to remind many workers 'of how much *talk* about Socialism there had been previously on this day, about workers' rights and the significance of labour'. All this had been mere fine words, forgotten again once it was time to return to work. But today the fact was that 'the rights of workers are at a high premium. Today a genuine social policy is being carried out, as evidenced by the unparalleled measures undertaken by Heydrich.'[62] Radical social reform in Bohemia and Moravia had previously 'failed because of financial obstacles and for want of understanding among government circles at the time'.[63]

In contrast to his dismissed predecessor, von Neurath, who had looked for support to the Czech aristocracy, to the Bohemian Count Bubna-Litic and the 'aristocracy of money', the grand bourgeoisie, and had thereby lost control over the Czech people, Heydrich courted the favour of the working masses. This policy was carried right down to matters of detail. He concerned himself with wage-levels, he undertook goodwill tours to the big firms, where to the horror of his entourage he chatted, against all security precautions, with the Czech workers on the shop floor; he distributed extra incentive-money; he halted the flood of black-market geese in the direction of Berlin – and all this in such a way that the Czechs could not possibly overlook it.[64] He reduced the administrators to a state of confusion by ignoring official channels and paying out considerable sums in gratuities and pensions to the families and to wounded members of the Czech gendarmerie, which was operating against the resistance. A cab-driver who had helped enquiries into an assassination plot involving explosives, in the traditional trouble-spot of Kladno, was rewarded on Heydrich's orders, with a gratuity of 10,000 crowns from Protectorate funds. The same amount was paid out to the family of the gendarmerie Ensign Komínek, severely wounded in the explosion. The widow of a gendarmerie Lieutenant Ometák, shot by the resistance, was given by way of immediate aid the same sum of money, and beyond that, Heydrich ordered that her pension be set at the level of her husband's last full salary payment. Wounded Czech policemen were sent German pistols with his personal compliments, families with children received savings books 'containing respectable amounts'.[65]

The treatment of the case of Lažnovský followed the same lines. This 'Reich-orientated', actively collaborating journalist had been taken ill and died of poisoning after a meeting with Eliáš. Although Heydrich tried vigorously to represent his death, probably just the result of simple food-poisoning, as a case of assassination, a thorough criminal investigation produced no conclusive evidence for this. Nevertheless, Heydrich had Lažnovský given a state funeral, and his widow received the pension appropriate to a Section Head, although the journalist had not been a civil servant and had probably not died for political reasons.[66] Families of victims were all sent personal letters of sympathy by Heydrich. He identified so strongly with the role of 'father of the country' that he himself believed the sentiments he had uttered back in October at the reception for Czech workers: 'I have not come only to impose an iron regime upon you, but also to create a regime of social justice.'[67]

To find out whether his social-political efforts were really having the desired effect, and were not just being flatteringly reported by propaganda, which only told him what he wanted to hear, Heydrich had the results researched by his own SD. They were unambiguous: among the work-force the tide was beginning to turn in favour of Heydrich and his policy of de-politicization. The rape of the Czechs began to turn into a seduction. And it was perhaps Heydrich's spontaneous gestures that had the greatest impact, even more than the basic material concessions. It was a common subject of conversation, reported a representative of the Foreign Office to Berlin, 'That such a high-ranking person should hold out his hand to the ordinary workers and talk about the most personal affairs man to man.' The reception of the workers' delegation in Prague Castle, in particular, it was said, 'was noted with satisfaction', and 'created no slight impression'.[68]

The reports reaching Berlin even impressed the old Czech-hater, Hitler himself. Even as recently as January 1942 he had declared at table that 'Providence' had created Germans and Czechs natural enemies, and that there was no room for both of them in Bohemia and Moravia. 'One of us must go.'[69] One could not even call the Czechs Slavs. 'All you have to do is leave a Czech moustache unshaven, and you'll soon see the Mongolian blood by the way it droops.'[70] Yet, by 20 May, although still no Czech-lover, he told his table-companions in an obviously cheerful mood: 'it was possible to turn the Czechs into fanatical adherents of the Reich simply by feeding those gourmets double rations and not sending them to fight on the Eastern Front. Then they would accept it as their duty to work twice as hard in the munitions industry.'[71] In general he declared himself pleased with the state of affairs in the Protectorate, which nine months earlier had been Berlin's biggest headache. Hitler concluded that 'an attitude friendly to the Reich' would soon be universal among the Czech people.

'Is it merely a coincidence', asks one of the foremost historians of the Protectorate, 'that three or four days earlier Heydrich had sent Bormann two detailed reports on his own policy, to be passed on to Hitler?'[72]

In the reports sent on by the defeated remnants of the Czech resistance to the exiled government of Dr Edvard Beneš in London, the message must have been the same as Heydrich's to Berlin. For with dismay Beneš' colleagues noted at this time that Heydrich's new policy was showing every sign 'of corrupting the working class by means of ostentatious social reforms, bestowed with dramatic gestures'.[73] And Jaromír Smutný, Beneš' confidant and Head of Chancery, admitted 'there are a lot of collaborators at home, and our industry is today the greatest and keenest supplier of arms to Germany'.[74] In resistance circles, among the intelligentsia and the grand bourgeois, the workers were universally accused of corruptibility.

Astonished socialists and somewhat puzzled contemporary historians after the war were loath to attribute to Heydrich alone such a sure instinct for the working man's real concerns, the amazing ability to put himself into the frame of mind of a social class to which he did not belong by upbringing, the staggering knowledge of the effect of words and token gestures. The search for an 'adviser on social affairs' who was *really* behind the brilliant achievement of winning over the workers soon turned up a well-known socialist, Ernst Torgler, the former leader of the Parliamentary group of the German Communist Party in the Reichstag and chief suspect in the Reichstag fire trial. It was the ex-resistance fighter, Bernd Gisevius, who first committed the rumour to paper: it was said that Torgler had come to Prague with Heydrich's entourage, supplied with false documents and in the uniform of an SS-officer. Torgler had then, according to the rumour, acted as Heydrich's 'left hand' to drive a wedge between the Czech workers and their leaders and induce them to collaborate on a mass scale with the Germans.[75]

It is well known that after the war (1948) Torgler angrily attacked Gisevius as the 'corpse-looter of the Third Reich' and condemned his evidence as 'vile lies or at the very best stupid, empty gossip'.[76] He had never been in Prague in his life or in Czechoslovakia at all, for that matter, and had never set eyes on Heydrich. On the other hand Torgler himself does admit to 'a degree of collaboration' with the Anti-Comintern operation in Germany at that time and with its leader Dr Eberhard Taubert.[77] And in May 1940, he concedes, he was called before SS-Lieutenant-General Müller ('Gestapo-Müller'), who ordered him to compose a number of proclamations in the style of the communists, intended for use by German Counter-Intelligence during the campaign in France. Torgler did indeed compose 'over about ten days, six or seven communist leaflets . . . , urging French workers not to sacrifice themselves for the 200 families, i.e. the magnates who exercised decisive political power'.[78]

In fact, however, the collaboration was much more extensive. After the Reichstag fire trial, in which Torgler was acquitted, and after almost three years of 'protective custody', from which he emerged, amazingly enough, to take up an undisturbed civilian life in 1936, he was given an office of his own in 1938, where he worked on a 'special task'. At his own request he was allocated his former private secretary, Maria Reese. Frau Reese, a Communist like Torgler, had first joined the Trotskyites in Paris, after the Party's disastrous setbacks in 1933, and then returned to Germany. With his secretary Torgler wrote a book about the Party from the standpoint of an insider. Its line of argument was prescribed by National Socialist propaganda: it dealt with the justification for being a Communist before Adolf Hitler's National Socialist revolution had made the class struggle unnecessary and impossible. After this revolution there was nothing left for the Party to do. Aside from this, it gave many examples of the remote control of the German Communist Party by Moscow and its employment for the ends of Soviet foreign policy during the Weimar period.

Parts of the manuscripts were shown to Hitler, 'who liked it, but decided the book should not be published yet. The way was being smoothed for the Soviet-German agreement, and this should not be jeopardized.'[79]

Torgler was therefore already deeply involved in collaboration with the Gestapo and other organizations of the Third Reich when Heydrich began to take an interest in him. This came about at the latest when he included the name Torgler in a secret list of 700 names after the conclusion of the Soviet-German Non-Aggression Pact. The list included all those Communists whom Heydrich would have liked to interrogate in the Reich Security HQ, but who had escaped to the Soviet Union after 1933 and there disappeared into the toils of the Great Purge. Kurt Torgler was the youngest name on Heydrich's 'shopping list', with whose aid the Gestapo filed its requests with the Soviet NKVD for items it still lacked. Kurt, Ernst Torgler's son, was only thirteen years old in 1933 when Party comrades smuggled him to England after the Reichstag fire and arranged for him to stay with Ellen Wilkinson, later Education Minister in the Labour Cabinet. From there he went to the Soviet Union, where he first of all worked in an engineering works and then, still only a sixteen-year-old, was sentenced to ten years hard labour for 'participation in Trotskyist agitation'.[80]

It was Heydrich who had him released from the Soviet forced-labour camp. Together with other liberated prisoners he was handed over on the bridge over the River Bug in Brest-Litovsk. In contrast to all other prisoners, who, if they were Jews, were shipped off after interrogation to the concentration camps in the East, or, if non-Jews, sent to Dachau or Oranienburg for 'protective custody', Kurt Torgler was set free. He even became 'eligible for military service', and became a Sergeant and an interpreter. He was killed on the Eastern Front in 1943.

This is where the guessing begins. What other reason was there for Heydrich to show this special favour to the son, unless it were interest in the father? Another Czech historian, who has had access to Prague documents which are very difficult to get at and which have been partly sifted by Soviet experts since 1968,[81] maintains that these papers 'show indisputably' that Heydrich 'pulled in' Torgler to help with his social policies in Prague.[82] But this assertion, too, like Gisevius' story, is extremely dubious. The evidence available from the Berlin Employment Office and Torgler's original work record shows that at the time in question – September 1941 to May 1942 – he was working uninterruptedly as auditor for the property trust-company 'Cautio' in Berlin, and not for Reich Protector Heydrich in Prague – who appears not to have needed the help of a former Communist Party leader in the conduct of his resourceful social policy.

Chapter 14

THE FÜHRER'S WALLENSTEIN

Wallenstein's problem was Bohemia's problem.

Reinhard Heydrich, 1942

Prague is surrounded by gentle rolling hills stretching out from the Bohemian capital to the north, south and east. Every evening the Reich Protector drove through this pleasant countryside to reach his 'island'. Barely 20 kilometers (12 miles) away, half an hour's drive, stood the official residence of the Protector, the manor-house of Panenské Břežany, amid dense, shady forests. The manor-house, similar in style to the châteaux of the Loire, was surrounded by parkland and gardens, giving way eventually to woodland and a little village nearby.

The Heydrich family had moved into this house after a short interim stay in the town apartment designated for the Reich Protector in the Palace of Charles IV in the Prague Castle. Lina Heydrich had urged that they leave the city, to which she was a stranger, as quickly as possible, and that with the children, the two boys and their daughter Silke, they should 'move out to a place where they could live their own lives, where she need not be reminded all day long that she was the wife of the Reich Protector'.[1]

Panenské Břežany had been 'requisitioned' after the establishment of the Protectorate, having been the property of the Jewish sugar-millionaire Bloch-Blauer from Nestomice.[2] As the official HQ of Heydrich's predecessor, Baron von Neurath, the building had been completely re-decorated. Even today Heydrich's widow is capable of enthusing: 'It was

216

all beautifully fitted out. Herr von Neurath had it done. The AA [Foreign Office] people could do that kind of thing.'[3] It was the first time that Heydrich had derived any material advantage from his official position. He soon fell in love with the white manor-house. He even condescended to lend an ear to discussions about furniture, pictures and the management of the household, participating in domestic affairs which he normally considered 'unmanly'. For the first time in ten years something like a regular family life developed. Heydrich referred to it ironically as 'the bosom of his family', but he enjoyed it. It seemed to his wife that he was beginning to discover a new world. At this period he would often work eighteen, even twenty hours a day. Despite this he rarely spent the night in the town apartment at the Hradčany, but was driven back by his chauffeur, Corporal Klein, to Březany. Often he took the wheel of the dark green Mercedes himself and drove with the hood of the car down, even in rain and cold. 'That's how we keep a cool head, Klein.'

He tended more and more to take his papers home with him, in order to get back to Březany and his intimate family circle all the sooner. 'He liked being able to be less formal for once,' his widow reveals. 'He stretched out on the sofa and read, often into the small hours.' Frau Lina regards the time spent at Březany as the best part of her married life. 'It was wonderful.' The lady of the house had almost unlimited time on her hands, for what could rarely be obtained in Berlin in the third year of the war was still freely available in Bohemia and Moravia. Czech servants did most of the chores. 'Every servant had a servant of his own. It was all still very Austrian.'

Outside the walls of the estate, a guard was posted, on Himmler's orders. It consisted of a detachment of Security Police, later replaced, after Heydrich's death, by older 'Home Guards'. Heydrich grumbled about this guard, quartered in the neighbouring, main Czech village. 'His' Czechs, he was convinced, would never harm him, and even if anyone had the will to do so, he would not dare.

Heydrich came home even more frequently when he learnt, in November, that the family was expecting a new addition in the summer. 'He was rather awkward at first with the two boys, Heider and Klaus,' runs the account of his relationship with his children. 'He intended to start doing things with them later, when they were almost young men, sports, flying, shooting. But he was a proper Daddy to his daughter. It didn't matter whether an official meeting was going on in the house or there was a visitor, his daughter Silke was brought to him at six for her goodnight kiss.'

At this time it became noticeable that Heydrich was developing a new passion for history. In addition to documents, and the best-sellers of the period, from which his wife would occasionally read him short excerpts, he consumed historical novels, monographs and biographies. They were all about Bohemia and its relationship with the German Empire. Above all it was the figure of Wallenstein which cast a spell upon him. 'He read everything about Wallenstein that he could lay his hands on.'[4] 'His adjutants (aides) turned to historians and journalists for new Wallenstein material, which Heydrich read at Březany. On Sundays he made numerous trips to Friedland, Wallenstein's ancestral seat. All the outlying areas had to be visited, too, and in the course of time Heydrich formed an overall picture of all Wallenstein's properties, scattered throughout Bohemia.

But his historical interests did not stop there. He drove to Mělník, for example, visited the grave of St Ludmila, and was interested in the excavations at Prague Castle being carried out by the German University of Prague. But time and again he came back to Wallenstein. He was really enthralled by him. Even thirty years later the voice of his widow cannot hide her astonishment at this development in her otherwise cold and pragmatic husband. But for Heydrich, Wallenstein and Bohemian history were no simple return to the past. His preoccupation with the Duke of Friedland was for him rather an obsession with the burning issues of the present, and the problems which bore in upon him so intensely in this entirely unfamiliar province of Bohemia. He could not have prevented himself from developing an interest in the area, even if he wanted to. 'Bohemia, that was his problem. And Bohemia was Wallenstein's problem, too. That was where he saw the similarity.'[5]

For Heydrich, Wallenstein stood for the intimate relations between Bohemia and the Reich. His interest focused on the fact that Wallenstein, in 1618, as Colonel of a Moravian regiment during the uprising of the Bohemian and Moravian nobility, did not join the rebels, but – after being deserted by his regiment – fled with the campaign funds to Archduke Ferdinand, who the following year became German Emperor Ferdinand II; that Wallenstein raised a regiment of dragoons in Flanders and led it into action in 1619 and 1620 in the cruel suppression of the Bohemian rebellion; on the fact that Wallenstein's ultimate aim was to create exclusively *Imperial* military power; that he demonstrated the utmost toughness in maintaining discipline – all this led Heydrich to see the enigmatic generalissimo, that 'constantly misinterpreted' figure, above all as a symbol of Bohemia's loyalty to the Reich, and of the indissoluble bond between Prague and the Reich. For Heydrich this was more than mere propaganda calculated to win the Czechs over. In his view the 'powers that stood for order' in Europe had always drawn Bohemia into their sphere. 'Charlemagne did so, as did the first German Reich in the Middle Ages, the Habsburgs in modern times, and the creator of the Greater German Empire, Adolf Hitler.' With this sentiment Heydrich laid down his Bohemian 'credo'.[6]

Thus he aligned himself as a matter of conviction with the German school of historical thought which has always seen Czech history only in relation to German. Propaganda constantly reiterated the centuries-old dependence of Bohemia and Moravia upon the Holy Roman Empire and upon the house of Habsburg. By the same token, the part of Czech tradition represented by Jan Hus, the historian and politician František Palacký, by Masaryk and Beneš, was constantly decried. The periods of Czech history when Germans and Czechs were on a hostile footing were to be expunged from memory, or at least held accountable for all the catastrophes suffered by the Czech nation. By means of Heydrich's severe methods against Beneš' men, said the journal *Böhmen und Mähren* during these weeks, 'the seeds of Palacký's "no surrender!" romanticism, constantly germinating anew, were to be crushed once and for all'.[7] Time and again, it was claimed, the Bohemian heartland of the Reich had 'plunged a knife into the back' of German unity. It had begun as far back as Marbod, who had refused to take part in Arminius' war of liberation against the Romans.[8] Heydrich saw in the 'embittered historical consciousness of Palacký' (said the editor of *Der Neue Tag*) the malignant seed which, under Beneš in the twenty years after the First World War 'produced poisonous fruits as dangerous as they were seductive'. But he found the precise opposite in the 'mission of the Bohemian King Wenceslas, the historical link with his new concept of the Reich'.[9]

St Wenceslas, brought up by his grandmother St Ludmila, desired as King of Bohemia to establish Christianity as the national religion. Bohemia would become intimately linked by this process with the Unity of the Reich, in both the religious and the political sense. His brother Boleslav had him killed on 28 September 935. Wenceslas is honoured to this day as the patron saint of the Czechs. Heydrich exploited the deep-rooted affection of the Czech people for the figures of Wenceslas. The 'Wenceslas tradition' occupied a central place in his propaganda. A visit by Heydrich and Hácha on 19 November 1941 to the Bohemian Crown Jewels, among which the Wenceslas crown holds pride of place, was very much in line with this policy.

The German Heydrich managed to persuade the Czech President Hácha to participate in his joint demonstration, which was widely interpreted as a symbolic act of cooperation. The speech given on this occasion was designed to supply chapter and verse for the 'natural and God-given' bond between Bohemia-Moravia and the Reich, and hence was made a great deal of in the press of the Protectorate. At this ceremony, in the Wenceslas Chapel of St Vitus' Cathedral on the heights of the Prague Castle, the Head of State handed over on a velvet cushion the seven keys of the Coronation Chamber, in which the Crown Jewels were kept. 'These Coronation Insignia', said the President 'are the symbols of the loyalty of Bohemia and Moravia to the Reich'. Heydrich's reply was: 'As the representative of the Führer in the Protectorate I receive these keys into my hands and thereby also the task of guarding the insignia. As the Crown Jewels are the symbol of the loyalty of Bohemia and Moravia to the Reich, you, Mr President of State, are today . . . the guarantor for the bond and the faithfulness of the Protectorate to the Reich.' Then Heydrich returned three of the seven keys 'into the care' of the President, with the words 'Regard this as a token both of trust and of responsibility.'[10]

The interpretation put upon the ceremony in St Vitus' Cathedral by Beneš' counter-propaganda completely ignored the historical symbolism: 'We are shocked to the core when we think of the future of the Crown Jewels. They represent such a high value in terms of gold and precious jewels, that that corrupt Nazi official might easily arrange their "disappearance".'[11]

The real significance of the occasion was of course quite different. The dramatic presentation of the affair clearly showed how profoundly susceptible Heydrich was to the romantic and myth-building treatment of history characteristic of the SS. The address he gave to the Protectorate government and to German and Czech representatives bears witness to the same tendency. The symbolic event in St Vitus' Cathedral, explained Heydrich, had 'ended centuries-old uncertainties' and once again demonstrated the appropriateness of the 'Führer's deed of 16 March 1939'. Hácha's participation, which had made possible the 'peaceful return of the Protectorate', was in accordance with 'the spirit of the true Wenceslas tradition'. On the historical significance of the Wenceslas tradition, the amateur historian Heydrich expatiated: 'After the migration of a large part of the Germanic population other peoples penetrated this region from the East, to form the line of descent, with a strong Germanic admixture, of the present-day population. Culturally and politically this was a movement from East to West.' In the course of its political and racial development Bohemia had had to work out its proper relation to Eastern and Western neighbours. Culturally at least 'a dissociation from the East and an approach towards Western attitudes had taken place'. 'Geopolitical conditions necessitated an appeal to the Reich at various times, for help against neighbouring peoples in the East and the South-East, and that led logically to integration in and subordination to the Reich.' From this point on, the population of Bohemia and Moravia had constantly oscillated between East and West, between 'the political pressures for membership of the Reich and the drive towards independence'. Time after time a particular 'phenomenon' occurred. It had exercised its 'fatal' effect once again in the weeks preceding his, Heydrich's, arrival in Prague.

It was a bad habit of these people, unfortunately, to bow the head after military or political defeat, and to promise loyalty, only to continue faithlessly along their old path, when the leadership of the Reich, into which they had been incorporated, had accepted this promise on trust and withdrawn its forces. Sometimes it had been the kings and rulers themselves who were guilty of the treasonable act; sometimes their vassals, provoking rebellion and treason against the ruler, who had kept faith with the leadership of the Reich.

After this geopolitical outline Heydrich returned to the figure of Wenceslas. The fate of St Wenceslas and his brother Boleslav he called 'a tragic illustration of this pattern of events, but also a historical symbol of the clear lesson to be learnt for the present and the future'.

Wenceslas, recognizing historical necessity, had once and for all thrown in his lot with the Reich and thereby for the first time turned his face against the East. The rebels who, under the leadership of his brother Boleslav, took arms against the statesmanlike policy of Wenceslas, had failed to recognize the historical destiny of this area and its eternal involvement with the Reich, and out of genuine conviction had overthrown Wenceslas and his policy, murdered the king himself and attempted to restore a bastion against the West.

But destiny and geographical situation had been too strong, even then, so that Boleslav himself had been induced by experience of the East 'to take the path back into the Reich'.

In the same speech Heydrich demonstrated how successfully a propagandist exploitation of the Wenceslas tradition could be used as the basis of his own policy, how logical Heydrich's policy must appear if one once adopted the premise that his version of Bohemian history and of the significance of Wenceslas was completely correct. Hácha's decision in 1939 to capitulate without resistance to Hitler's annexation plan Heydrich called 'a decision in the spirit of the true Wenceslas tradition'. And the argument of the Wenceslas tradition was at hand to cover, too, his own selective campaign of terror against resistance circles. 'The rebels against the Reich during the days of September and October of this year were brought to justice because they not only failed to grasp the Wenceslas tradition, but because they reverted to ancient Eastern habits and stabbed the Reich in the back, in order once more to convert a bastion against the East into one against the West.' What they overlooked was that the leadership of the Reich had learnt the lesson of history and took the warning that it must be prepared for a recurrence of this phenomenon. 'The Wenceslas tradition', his speech concluded, contained the message 'that Bohemia and Moravia had only been great *with* the Reich, and would forever be weak *without* it'. But it also told us 'that the population – remembering that it numbered among its ancestors many of German stock – finally grasped the commitment of altering their attitudes and behaviour in the light of their historical experience'.[12]

None of this interpretation of Bohemian-German relations, of Wenceslas and the geopolitical shifts between East and West, originated in Heydrich's own mind. He had sifted it from memoranda by Karl-Hermann Frank going back to 1940, from the essays of Raschhofer in the magazine *Böhmen und Mähren,* from his reading about Wallenstein, and from discussions with the Reich-German and Bohemian intellectuals he occasionally invited to Panenské Břežany. What was original was the eclectic, panoramic view and the grand reduction of a historical process to a manageable essence: above all, the application of this to the practical political and propaganda task that faced him.

Like all the speeches he gave while Protector, the speech on the Wenceslas theme was written by Heydrich himself. It was always agony for him to deliver an address. 'It was always a disaster when he had to give a speech,' his widow confirmed. And it never occurred to him at all that somebody else might write his speeches for him. Here too he wanted to be perfect. He wanted to speak naturally and spontaneously. Most texts of his speeches are not manuscripts but notes taken by a secretary during delivery.

The Wenceslas speech had been practised, as was his wont, behind closed doors at his country retreat, with his wife to supply audience-reaction. After every lengthy subsection he demanded frank criticism. 'And she certainly rose to the occasion,' counting his hesitations and ruthlessly relaying them to him: 'eighty-seven "er . . . er"'s'. Like most soldiers he was a poor public speaker. Staccato, in fits and starts, he snarled out his words without using articles. In intimate company, on the other hand, he was a good talker, 'convincing, well-structured and logical'. Another eye-witness: 'In a small group he spoke not without charm, as clear as crystal, perhaps a bit frosty.' The more he was forced to speak in public, however, the more improvement could be noted in his performance. But there was always the tendency to make sudden leaps of thought and to lose the thread. 'The trouble was that his thoughts ran ahead of his speech.'[13] All the Wenceslas propaganda ('good old Wenceslas out of the fairy-tale', wrote Beneš sarcastically in London[14]) would have gone for nought if it had not been for the supporting wave of collaboration from Czechs which gave it genuine force. It took an army of Czech journalists and officials, together with the Protectorate government and first and foremost President Hácha himself, to create conditions receptive to the propaganda that would, hopefully, tip the scales away from the prevailing anti-German mood.

Heydrich knew how to handle Hácha. He knew that he had won when the ageing President failed to resign in protest, either on the day of Heydrich's assumption of office, or that of Eliáš' arrest, or, at the latest, during the days of the first, purely politically motivated martial-law sentences. Hácha was doubtless convinced right to the end that his remaining in office served to prevent even worse treatment of the Czechs under his care. Hácha's Czech Ministers, too, were almost to a man prepared to collaborate. Either they were simply conscientious experts in their field, blind to political issues, or they had been made aware of the fact that

Heydrich's SD and Gestapo had plenty of evidence of their previous collaboration with the government-in-exile in London. Heydrich kept this ace up his sleeve to guarantee their good conduct.[15]

His aim, after the dismissal of the government formed by Eliáš, now himself sentenced to death, was to create a new administration, assembled on a unique basis: on the one hand it must be receptive to Heydrich's policies, in other words it had to be prepared to collaborate very actively. On the other hand, it had to be preserved from becoming such an obvious puppet that it lost all credence as guarantor of Czech autonomy. It could not be allowed, either, to become a risk to Heydrich, thereby reducing his policy merely to force and terror. Heydrich knew that a system imposed purely by force could not accomplish his task, which was to exploit to the full the contribution of Bohemia and Moravia to the war-effort and to pacify the country until the end of the war. Another object he aimed at was to ensure that the government under Hácha compromised itself so completely in the eyes of the Allies and the government-in-exile that Beneš would of his own accord cut all lines of communication with the Czech government at home. For better or for worse, Hácha's government had to be made totally dependent on collaboration with Heydrich.

To produce this fabulous, rather improbable animal, the Czech government he needed, Heydrich was prepared to employ every means in his power: no concession was too great, no ploy too crafty, no move too complicated. It was not until January 1942 that Heydrich accomplished, after much tactical trial and error and long-drawn-out manoeuvring, what the old Sudeten-German nationalists had sought to obstruct because it was too great a concession, what was greeted with uncomprehending grumbles by hard-line factions within the Nazi Party, and what gave the Beneš government in London cause for the bitterest fear: on 19 January 1942 the new government of the Protectorate was firmly established, with a composition that both Hácha and Heydrich could interpret as the means to achieve their own ends. 'With the confirmation of the Reich Protector', the former Justice Minister, Professor Jaroslav Krejčí, became the Premier as well as Justice Minister once more. The seven remaining ministerial appointments were filled by the provincial President of Bohemia, Richard Bienert (Minister of the Interior); Dr Josef Kalfus (Treasury); Colonel of the Reserve Emanuel Moravec (Education, Culture and Information); State Secretary Dr Walter Bertsch (Industry and Labour); the Controller of Czech Railways, Dr Jindřich Kamenický (Transport and Technology);

and finally the Chairman of the Czech National Council for Culture, Adolf Hrubý (Agriculture and Forestry).[16]

With the exception of Bertsch all the appointees were Czechs. But in Bertsch, an outstanding expert, Heydrich had planted an informer within the government, whose regular participation at Cabinet meetings of the Krejčí administration effectively neutralized the government politically from inside. Heydrich's aim was 'largely to disarm the Cabinet as an instrument of political decision-making', as State Secretary Reichert of the Reich Ministry of the Interior explained.[17] In the person of Moravec, whom Heydrich characterized accurately as a thorough-going Czech 'advocate of annexation to the Reich', he had established a political bridge-head from which to make surprise sorties.

By confirming Hrubý and Krejčí in office, on the other hand, Heydrich went a long way towards meeting Czech wishes. Both saw themselves as salvaging as much as possible for the Czechs. Heydrich knew the views of both. An even greater concession towards the Czechs was the appointment of Bienert as Minister of the Interior. For he was a longstanding member of the anti-German and anti-Habsburg 'Mafia', originating in the Czech Legion movement. To entrust such a prominently Czech-orientated personality with the Home Office, of all things, was decidedly risky. The risk was accepted by Heydrich because after all, 'if it came to the worst', he still had a German police force at his disposal.[18]

To get the new government off to a good start and to make it look unexpectedly independent in the eyes of the Czech population, Heydrich made yet more concessions. On 19 January he dismantled all the remaining provisions of the state of emergency, and released from the concentration camp at Mauthausen a large number of Czech students arrested during the disturbances under von Neurath.

At 5 p.m. the next day Hácha received the new Cabinet and swore it in under an oath of allegiance to 'the Führer of the Greater German Reich Adolf Hitler as the Defender of the Protectorate of Bohemia and Moravia'. Hácha asserted that 'the government was to steer an entirely new course determined by positive and activist forces'.[19] 'Destiny', so Krejčí announced, had placed Bohemia and Moravia at the centre of the great Reich. Now the task was to 'see in the proper light the false developments of the past, to grasp the greatness of world events in all their revolutionary might'. Some very concrete threats were uttered, however, about 'taking severe defensive measures against all disruptive and destructive attack within the country or from outside'.

Among the Cabinet ministers present only one knew who had really composed the government's statement. Emanuel Moravec was the man in the know. Heydrich had passed on to him a draft written by himself, and the Minister of Information presented this to Krejčí as his own composition. Krejčí's own draft had meanwhile been rejected by Heydrich's sharp-eyed watch-dogs in the Office of the Reich Protector, so that as a way out of its difficulties the Cabinet adopted the draft written, as they thought, by Moravec.[20] No wonder the tone was familiar when Heydrich once again, in his own address to the new government, sketched the framework within which, and only within which, it was possible to conceive of the co-existence and collaboration expected by the German side in the partnership. For the first time he told the representative of the Czech government the plain unvarnished truth about what he thought of them and their state, in cutting language that frequently overstepped the bounds of provocation and insult. The independence of Czechoslovakia, which had, significantly, lasted a mere twenty years, he referred to once again as 'a historical aberration'. In Czechoslovakia, the 'darling of Western plutocracy and the latest offshoot of Moscow-directed Panslavism', *only* in Czechoslovakia was it possible for that proportionally far too numerous, selfish and ambitious intelligentsia to develop, which was responsible for the aberration of the Czech Republic. 'While these elements on the one hand were carrying out an unprecedented rearmament and whipping up popular feeling, on the other hand they were too cowardly to pursue the military implications of their own behaviour and to stand and fight in the autumn of 1939.' Only Hácha, 'with wise insight', had, in both a personal and a constitutional sense, understood the need to return to the Reich. However, the first government he had formed, under General Eliáš, had 'either through negligence or incapacity, or deliberately' played into the hands of the enemies of the Reich.

It had been 'reserved' for him, Heydrich, 'to make up by tough measures for what the Czech government had neglected to do in the last two and a half years'. Krejčí's new government was therefore faced with a particularly hard task. But the government statement which had just been read out showed that the problems had now been grasped 'in all their magnitude' and that there was a willingness 'to do the spadework'. The 'days of parliamentary-style Cabinet decisions were now past for good and all', for they would 'only hamper the practical and active work of leadership'.

Only a confident collaboration with him, Heydrich, could 'get the best out of' the Czech people.[21] All the signs were that Heydrich regarded the re-formation of the government as anything but a 'conventional re-shuffle', and that he saw behind it the conception of 'a historically significant change of direction'.[22] This change of direction could only mean the reversal of geopolitical alignment, this time from West to East.

Up until September it had been generally thought, not only among Czechs, 'here comes the dreaded Heydrich to open a reign of blood and terror'.[23] But Heydrich knew full well the truth of the lines from Edmund Burke, to which one of the leading German intellectuals of the Protectorate had drawn his attention, that 'force may subdue for a moment; but it does not remove the necessity of subduing again; and a nation is not governed, which is perpetually to be conquered'.[24]

So he did indeed employ blood and terror to gain his ends, to a degree previously unknown in the Protectorate, but that was not the end of the story. Above all he was not dependent on these tactics. The politically neutralizing impact of his social policies was far more effective in bringing about a 'historical change of direction'. And now, finally, Hácha, Krejčí and the whole of this second Cabinet of the Protectorate provided the keystone to be built into his short-term plan.

But at no time did he ever lose sight of the long-term aims enshrined in the traditional German policy towards the Protectorate. These long-term aims were not his alone to define. Their outlines had been established in the memoranda of Karl-Hermann Frank, and in the firm intention of the Czechophobe Hitler, to incorporate the area of Bohemia and Moravia 'for all time' into the Reich. Even the moderate professional diplomat von Neurath had represented this line with conviction. Whatever the difference of opinion on questions of tactics there was unanimity about the need for Bohemia to be 'Germanized'. This had to be Heydrich's guiding star as well. He was able to work all the more purposefully towards it since his sway was so much greater than his predecessor's had been. The concessions to the Czechs, which looked so generous in the context of the general policy for Czechoslovakia of the Third Reich, and for which Heydrich was clearly able to gain such ready acceptance in Berlin, would have been impossible for the politically 'lightweight' von Neurath. And in this way Heydrich naturally induced in the Czechs an increased willingness to collaborate, genuinely convinced as they were that expressions of loyalty could be traded for further concessions from the Reich. For example, on the occasion of the 'Führer's Birthday', in the spring of 1942, when Hácha handed over to Heydrich, as a present from the Protectorate, a fully-equipped hospital train, he exploited the opportunity to intercede for the numerous Czech concentration-camp inmates. And in fact Heydrich did grant the release from Mauthausen of many students and officials of the Czech Athletics Union.[25]

From the very beginning Heydrich knew how to conceal his final objective behind bloodshed on the one hand and the vague hopes he allowed the Czechs on the other. Only 'within four walls', with the executors of his policy, did he speak openly about this long-term objective. Just a few days after his arrival in Prague he let the cat out of the bag before a select audience in the Czernin Palace consisting of officials of the administration, agents, German regional governors and officers of the Security Service. 'This part of the Reich', he said of Bohemia and Moravia, 'is just that – a part of the Reich.' In the long term the Bohemian-Moravian region must 'not be allowed to retain a form which would make it possible for the Czech interests to claim it as their own'. The basis of his policy, therefore, was to make this region secure and stamp out every sign of Czech independence. 'For military and tactical reasons, however, "the pursuit of this aim" must at the moment avoid arousing the Czechs to fever-pitch over certain things.' He pointed out to the German hotheads 'that for the moment, for certain tactical reasons, we must be hard, but must not, all the same, act in such a way that we seem to leave the Czechs no alternative but to stage a desperate last-ditch revolt'. But the unspoken object remained the same: 'this region must become German and the Czechs relinquish all claim to it'.[26]

All shades of opinion about the German policy for Czechoslovakia were agreed on this issue. But the precise opposite was the case when it came to deciding how this aim of 'assimilation to the Reich' was to be achieved, and, particularly, what to do with the six to seven million Czechs. A number of National Socialist *Gauleiters*, for example, wished to annex a suitable portion of the Protectorate to round off their own territory. *Gauleiter* Fury in the adjoining *Reichs-gau* (administration district) of 'Lower Danube' (i.e. Lower Austria) had let it be known that he was still looking for a suitable capital for his district, and felt that Brno, in Moravia, would be the most suitable town.[27] The *Gauleiter* of Silesia had a long-standing claim to Ostrava. Similar ambitions were in evidence in Upper Danube and in the newly created *Gau* of Sudeten itself.[28]

State Secretary Frank had written a memorandum suggesting a division of the Protectorate, too. Heydrich himself, as head of the Security Police and the Security Service had raised the idea, in a note to Karl-Hermann Frank in the autumn of 1940, of 'a division of the Bohemian-Moravian area among the neighbouring *Gaus*'. It would clearly be advantageous if a 'uniform and centrally directed' course of action on the part of the Germans was confronted by only 'a dispersed and uncoordinated Czech opposition'. He would make a final decision only when the 'Reich Commissioner for the Consolidation of German Nationhood' had delivered his opinion on what was to happen to that remainder of the population consisting of a percentage of 'Czechs not suitable for Germanization'.[29] To leave these 'residual Czechs' in 'a Bohemian reservation' would run counter to the aim of 'making this a German area once and for all'. Heydrich retreated at the time into a 'for the moment hypothetical objective' of evacuating the remaining residual Czechs into a 'for the time being hypothetical *"Government general"*'.

Now, having become Reich Protector, Heydrich successfully opposed to this policy of fragmentation one of maintaining the integrity of the area; he thereby gained a victory for himself and the SS over the demands of the Party *Gauleiters*. As long as he was able to establish the case, as he did (and not only with propaganda), for Bohemia and Moravia being the genuine 'heartland of the Reich', and as long as it was possible, with Heydrich and Frank working in harness, to create what amounted to a separate 'SS-*Gau*', the outcome was not in doubt: the Protectorate would become the *Reichsgau* of Bohemia and Moravia. As ever, Heydrich took care of the outer signs and gestures. He had no trouble in getting Himmler to accept a re-designation of SS departments. This re-labelling took effect from 15 March 1942. The department of '*Waffen-SS* Commander in the Protectorate' now sailed under the flag of '*Waffen-SS* Commander in Bohemia and Moravia'.[30] The Führer's Wallenstein had begun to stake out his territory.

There was a quick answer, too, to the problem of what to do with the Czechs. The solution was a compromise between Habsburg and Hitler. The Germanizing policy of the Habsburgs, still surviving in 1941 in Sudeten-German and Austrian circles in the Party, had been content with linguistic assimilation. Nationalist, or in a narrower sense racial, consideration played no particular part. Hitler on the other hand, inspired precisely by anti-Czech feelings in reaction to the assimilation policy of the

Habsburg Empire, would have preferred to see 'the whole Czech rabble' entirely removed from the territory of the Reich.

First of all Heydrich declared to his leading officials, with repeated injunctions as to absolute secrecy, that he was not going to try to 'turn this Czech rabble into Germans by the old methods'. He pointed out, however, that a large number of Czechs 'were not racially inferior to the Germans'. He announced a 'national and racial stock-taking census' on which he would base all his decisions on any question concerning the Germanization of Czechs.

> I must have an overall picture of the nation, and then I can say the population is of this or that type. People fall into the following categories: some are of good racial stock and well-disposed. That's a simple matter; we can turn them into Germans. Then there are the others, the complete antithesis: bad racial stock and ill-disposed. Those are the people I have to get rid of. There's plenty of room to the East. There remains a group in the middle, who will have to be looked at very closely.[31]

In this middle group he envisaged 'those well-disposed but of bad stock' and 'those of sound stock but ill-disposed'. A 'good' disposition was shown by a willingness to collaborate, to get on with one's job untroubled by politics. The 'ill-disposed' section were the followers of Beneš and Masaryk, the 'fools of the resistance', the saboteurs, the economic pests. Of sound racial stock were all those who corresponded to the minimum standard established by research carried out among the Germanic race, 'a nordic-dinaric-Western mixture'; to be 'weeded out' as racially bad were 'pure Eastern types' and members of non-European races.

Heydrich viewed the 'racially good, ill-disposed' types as 'the most dangerous, for they form the racially superior leader-class'. For a part of this class there was only one thing to do: they would have to be settled in a pure Germanic environment and Germanized by a slow process of education. Or, if that did not work 'settle the matter by putting them up against a wall – I can't afford to exile them, because they would form a leadership-group over there in the East to turn upon us'.

This was the old Heydrich again; it was the language of Security Service reports being used here to describe policies. To be sure, he did say that this was for the time being 'a theoretical view'. But only fourteen days later it all began to look much more like practice than theory. Conference notes taken by Frank about 'planning for the future in the Protectorate' record Heydrich's instructions: a beginning was to be made with the selection and evacuation of 'poor racial types' and 'the Germanization of the racially sound residue, to be carried out methodically and in a manner psychologically appropriate to all walks of life'. The racial census was to comprehend and classify every person in the Protectorate. Access to some age-groups could be achieved via the Work Service Camps, others could be brought in under the pretext of a compulsory X-ray scan. A central racial filing system was to be established covering the whole population. The 'Territory Office', to be entrusted to an SS-officer, was to coordinate resettlement efforts. Heydrich's idea was to establish in the first place a 'German bridge' to span Moravia in a north-south direction and cut off the areas of Bohemia and Moravia, destined for Germanization, from Slovakia, continuing as a Slav area; the concept being to 'rupture the Slav link with Slovakia'.[32]

A further piece of territory soon to become a German settlement was also in preparation. At the same meeting, Heydrich announced *á propos* of the Jewish question in the Protectorate that a first transport of 5000 Jews was being evacuated to Lódź in Poland, with the immediate object of demonstrating 'how quickly Reich Germans got down to work'. In the meantime the other Jews from Bohemia and Moravia were to be assembled for evacuation. 'For this purpose Army Command . . . will clear all Army units from Terezín (Theresienstadt). Czechs will be told to move out.' The territory would be bought up by the Central Agency for Jewish Emigration, an office of the Reich, 'and so would become a German estate'. From Terezín, which could 'easily' accommodate 60,000 Jews, the latter would then be moved 'to the East'. Heydrich liked quick, accurate work. On the subject of Terezín he gave precise orders: 'After complete evacuation of all Jews, by immaculate planning, Terezín will be settled by Germans and thus become a focal point of German life. Its situation is ideal for the purpose.'[33]

After Heydrich had rendered the Protectorate 'free of Jews', he would go on to rid it of the remaining Czechs. For them too he had in mind, in February 1942 – about a fortnight after the Wannsee Conference – a suitable settlement area. In confidence he told his staff what would happen to the Jews. They were to open up the Arctic Ocean area ('where the concentration camps will later on provide a perfect homeland for the eleven million Jews of Europe'). That was also where he would have liked to send the residual Czechs at the end of the war, 'with a positive mission, a pro-German task'. He planned to use well-trained Czech craftsmen as foremen or overseers, 'with the opportunity of bringing their families out later'. He did not mean this at all cynically. He spoke at length about the prospects of this area. The Arctic territory was by no means as barren as people thought. Certainly it had a long winter, but also 'very good intensive agriculture and an excellent basis of raw materials'. From enquiries made by the Security Police in Russia it had been noted that the Arctic area had become practically self-sufficient agriculturally in the last few years and was no longer dependent on supplies from the Ukraine.

During these months Heydrich's attitude to the Czechs clearly evolved. In October he was still talking about the 'Czech rabble', and he had adopted the language decree from his Berlin discussions with Hitler. Three months later he bases his thinking about the destiny of the residual Czechs on the conviction that they should not be 'chased off to the East as enemies, but sent there with a mission useful to the Reich'. The evacuated Czechs, he says, should create 'European outposts'.[34] He believes that the Czech youth suitable for Germanization can 'have a positive effect' within the Protectorate itself in as little as one year to eighteen months. He successfully resists Bormann's intention of depriving all Czechs in the Sudetenland of Reich citizenship.

There was one row after another with Bormann at this time. The friction was caused by the question of which Czechs were to be Germanized and which not. The old controversy about 'suitability for Germanization' as against 'capability of Germanization', which bedevilled the whole of National Socialist racial policy, broke out anew. In the Sudetenland it had been enough simply to profess oneself German, and countless Czechs had in fact opted for Germany. But a Security Service report had remarked with indignation that among the Germanized there were in particular many 'workshy and criminal elements', and even gypsies![35] This must not be allowed to happen again on a large scale in the Protectorate. Racial affiliation was to be established objectively rather than left to personal choice. In this struggle for authority against Bormann, Heydrich won Hitler over to his side.

With particular malice he recorded the first results of the racial survey. There was every indication that at least sixty per cent of the Czechs achieved the same racial average coefficient as the Germans. From a study commissioned by him on a routine basis from the Race and Settlement Office it emerged that the 'racial portrait' of the Czech people, when judged by the National Socialist criteria of racial characteristics, was considerably more favourable than that of the Sudeten Germans. While Bohemia and Moravia returned a figure of forty-five per cent 'predominantly nordic, dinaric or Western types', the equivalent figure for the German Sudetenland was only twenty-five per cent. Among the Czechs, at the most fifteen per cent were registered as 'of alien race', whereas among the Sudeten Germans twenty per cent were in this category.[36] This was useful ammunition for Heydrich to use in the dispute with Bormann to back up the case of his 'objective' attribution of nationality. 'Heydrich and his Czechs,' Bormann is said to have grumbled after this defeat, 'he's still got one or two surprises coming to him.'[37]

'Heydrich's Czechs', however, remained unaware of the tug-of-war over their future. Their blissful ignorance was due to strict secrecy about long-term German aims, as much as to positive measures in the field of social policy, and finally to Heydrich's renunciation of large-scale resettlement measures and his moderate cultural policy. The ultimate object, to deprive the Czechs of their nationality, was concealed by concessions. Heydrich could after all afford a few gestures. In the spring of 1942, for instance, he advertised in the official circular a competition for Czech artists, with a prize to be awarded for the best settings for Dvořák's opera *Rusalka*. He arranged that the Ministry of Culture should buy eleven entries by Czech designers.[38]

But precisely in the harmless world of music, in which Heydrich had grown up, he was to demonstrate how much his mind was set on the future of *German* culture in Bohemia. It was at his bidding that the budget of the Protectorate included funds for the building of a specifically German home for the operetta in Prague. An opera-house was to follow. He was especially interested in the German Philharmonic Orchestra and performed music in general.[39] Even music could be used for political ends. In a state ceremony to mark the reopening of the Prague 'Rudolfinum' as a concert hall, Heydrich urged the artists that their duty was 'always to be German artists for the honour of the Reich'. To the politicians and officials his message was 'to smooth the paths of creative artists, to provide them with the intellectual and material preconditions for work, free of day-to-day concerns'.

The same event provides an example of his ability to represent unpopular

Reinhard Heydrich

cultural measures to the Czechs simply as rectification of the wrongs committed by the Czechs against the Germans in the days of the Republic. The Rudolfinum, he expounded, had been founded in 1872 by the Bohemian Savings Bank ('at that time a completely German institution') and opened in 1875; for thirty-three years it had been able to fulfil its original purpose: 'The staging of German concert performances'. Such men as Karl Muck and the opera-composer Nikolaus von Reznicek had begun their careers there. 'The installation of the organ in the great concert hall was the achievement of the greatest composer of his day, Anton Bruckner.' Then he described how philistine had been the treatment of German culture by those in power in the Republic. As early as October 1918 the 'Society for the Advancement of Music' had been forced to disband; the Prague *conservatoire* became a Czech institution. The 'Society of Patriotic Art-Lovers', too, had had to quit the hall, together with its collections, and in 1921 the Czech state had acquired the building by compulsory purchase order. With disgust in his voice Heydrich exclaimed, 'The great concert hall was converted into a Chamber of Deputies! . . . The organ-console, at which Anton Bruckner had once sat, had been smashed with the axe to make way for a bust of Masaryk!'[40] 'Look at the contrast – see what a patron of the arts Reich Protector Heydrich is'; this was the propaganda message of the occasion for the Czechs. On the following day, in the Castle, he awarded to three German artists the newly created Culture Prize of the Reich Protector. His policy towards the universities maintained the same tendency. Heydrich did not even consider the suggestion of reopening, at least in modified form, the Czech University of Prague, which had been closed down by his predecessor. He could see no reason, he said, why mathematics and medicine should be studied exclusively in Czech.

The German University became the particular darling of the Protector. He was certainly not going to miss the chance of playing upon the theme of the oldest German university in the Reich as a further proof of Bohemia's centuries-long adherence to the Reich. Numerous new Chairs were created during his term of office, and a 'Reich Foundation for Research in National and Intellectual History' was associated with the University.

The vision of an enlarged, German Prague, a city to rival Berlin and Vienna, emerged very early on from the mists of the various plans and sketches for the future of Bohemia. Heydrich saw Prague taking its place, as a special symbol of the unity of the Reich, among the series of cities

234

symbolically important to 'the movement', such as Munich, Nuremberg and Linz. German history, the Reich-myth, and the demonstration of National Socialist power were to merge here and be associated with his name. He had been deeply impressed by the unique beauties of Prague's architecture,[41] and succeeded in interesting Reich Minister Albert Speer in his plans for the future of the city. Speer and his colleague, the architect and town planner Niemeyer, travelled to Prague in 1942 to have discussions with Heydrich about the outline of a new construction plan for the Bohemian capital. 'It was partly a matter', Speer reminisced later, 'of the usual expansion of the residential areas. But at the centre of the plan was a new prestige government complex in the hinterland of the Prague Castle, with the Castle itself as the dominating feature. There was to have been a fast ring-road around the city, linked to the *Autobahn*.'[42] Prague was for Heydrich, according to his widow, the most beautiful German city. 'He found it even more German than Nuremberg'.

At this point, in the spring of 1942, Reinhard Heydrich was at the height of his power. Despite his appointment as Protector he was still head of the Reich Security Service, and therefore master of the most powerful executive organization Europe has ever seen. As head of the Security Police and the SD, the Gestapo and the German Criminal Police, nothing could be hidden from him for long. In his capacity as organizer of the 'Final Solution of the Jewish Problem', there was effectively no check whatsoever on his authority. Whether in terms of police work, of executive powers and Intelligence activities, or in terms of morality, he seemed free from all restraint.

Bormann had intended to strike a blow against the growing power of Himmler and the SS when he had suggested to the Führer the appointment of the young, thrusting, careerist Heydrich as the successor of von Neurath. It seemed to Bormann that Heydrich would be out of his way in the Protectorate, in the provinces, and no longer able to threaten his own claims to power. And now the 'brown eminence' had to swallow the bitter pill of defeat, in such matters as racial policies for example. Heydrich no longer owed Bormann a debt of gratitude, but was beginning to eclipse Bormann as Hitler's favourite.

As for the tedious 'schoolmaster', Heinrich Himmler, there was no longer anything more than lip-service due to him from Heydrich. Whereas in earlier years Heydrich had been allowed to do no more than supply the frequently hesitant and impractical *Reichsführer* with arguments to present to Hitler, Heydrich could now address the Führer in his own right.

Heydrich had definitely arrived. Above him there was only Hitler himself. And, as Heydrich confided to his Foreign Affairs man Walter Schellenberg, in the middle of May, Hitler was satisfied. By the flickering open fire in the manor-house of Panenské Břežany the two security chiefs held long, intimate discussions, lasting into the small hours. To his subordinate, whose intelligence, ability and natural instinct for Secret Service work he valued highly, Heydrich confided his personal worries: the tension between himself and Himmler; Bormann's jealousy. Only Hitler was wholly pleased with what Heydrich had achieved in the Protectorate. He had shown his worth.[43]

Heydrich counted on being offered a higher office by Hitler. Look at his achievement, after all: with carrot and stick, with unprecedented severity, clever propaganda tactics and a rare instinct for the effective wielding of the administrative instrument, he had pacified the Protectorate, and set the course for the future development of Bohemia and Moravia as a province of the Reich. Now was the time to test his manifold talents, perfected upon the guinea-pig of Bohemia, in another sphere of action: things were coming to a head in France and Belgium, where trouble was being stirred up by the resistance movements nurtured and supplied by London. And, apart from strikes and other unrest, there had been a wave of sabotage following the opening of the front against Russia, which had goaded the communists into action for the first time. This problem, too, Heydrich wanted to solve in his own way. In May he was already at work on a new Occupation Statute for occupied France. He counted on his appointment as Head of the Civil Administration in Belgium and Northern France and as 'Protector' of Vichy France. On 27 May he was due to fly to Berlin to discuss the final details.[44]

It was not only in Berlin, however, that Heydrich had provided food for thought, whether welcome or unwelcome, but he had been discussed on the opposite side, too, in London and Moscow. Independently of each other, the Intelligence Services and the political leaders of the two wings of the Alliance had come to the conclusion that Heydrich was their most dangerous German opponent, and had arrived, independently, at the decision to eliminate him. A last parallel to Wallenstein was in the making.

In March 1942 officials of the Security Police, in the course of a routine check at Warsaw railway station, picked up a musician who was behaving conspicuously. His papers were in order and showed him to be a 'German musician' on his way to Prague. His instrument-case genuinely contained nothing but an instrument. But his brand-new, altogether *too* new suitcase aroused suspicions. In a secret compartment the Security Police found a special weapon, equipped with telescopic sights and silencer, which could be dismantled into conveniently small sections. After days of interrogation in the HQ of the Security Police and the Gestapo in Warsaw the man's story eventually broke down. He was a Russian sent by Moscow. His objective, he said, was to liquidate Heydrich en route from Panenské Břežany to Prague. Nobody believed this tale. He was questioned further, in order to discover his 'real' mission. Before the Gestapo interrogators had grasped the fact that there was nothing more to be found out than the man had already confessed, he was able to evade whatever fate may have awaited him, by commiting suicide in his cell.[45]

While the Security Police were still pondering the credibility of the Russian agent, the competition from London had almost reached its target.[46] In the woods around Panenské Břežany, behind hedges, in gateways, and from vantage points offered by the undulating landscape, a couple of young men were busy gathering information. They noted every detail of the route taken by Heydrich between his country house and the capital, his travelling habits, his speed. A really alert and suspicious German corps of bodyguards could not have missed spotting the two young men. After all, the incautious appearances of two loafers always and inseparably together, in broad daylight and during working hours, ought instantly to have aroused suspicions.

But the two NCO's of the former Czech Army, Jan Kubiš and Josef Gabčík, remained undetected. By mid-May they had ascertained the best spot for their assassination attempt on the Reich Protector. It was at a hairpin bend in the Holešovice quarter of Prague. Heydrich, or his driver, was obliged to change down to a lower gear at this point because of the sharp bend and the steep incline.

It was clear to Kubiš and Gabčík that this moment, before the car could start gathering speed again, was the perfect one for an ambush. Kubiš intended to dispatch Heydrich, unprotected in his open car, with a burst from his Sten-gun, after which Gabčík was to make absolutely sure of their victim by a second strike in the form of a special hand-grenade. His English-made Mills bomb had an extra powerful charge, a high explosive velocity, and detonated on impact.

The two other possible spots for the assassination had been quickly discounted: Heydrich's saloon carriage, attached to the scheduled Prague-Berlin express train, was too fast and too uncertain a target. And Panenské Břežany itself was rendered too dangerous by the SS-guard stationed there.

The two NCOs were well prepared for their mission. Jan Kubiš, twenty-seven years old, the son of a peasant from Moravia, had received his initiation in resistance activities against the Germans as early as the spring of 1939. He belonged to one of the small resistance groups which had sprung up spontaneously all over the place after the occupation of Czechoslovakia. The group was soon mopped up by the Gestapo and Kubiš was among those arrested. He escaped from custody, however, and fled, before the beginning of the Polish-German war, to Poland. In a refugee camp he met Josef Gabčík, a mechanic from Slovakia and, like Kubiš, an NCO in the former Czech Army.[47]

The French Foreign Legion had a recruiting station within the camp and was doing good business. Many of the penniless and homeless young men signed on with the Legion, Kubiš and Gabčík among them. They were sent into action in the Western Campaign, but after the fall of France were evacuated to England. There, in accordance with inter-Allied agreement, they were recruited to the Czech Legion, the military arm of Beneš' government-in-exile.

The British Special Operations Executive (SOE), the armed commando group of the British Intelligence Service, formed for operations in occupied Europe, was looking for Czechs to operate within the Protectorate, and, along with 160 others, the two NCOs volunteered. At a spy-school near Manchester they were instructed in the basics of undercover work, and in sabotage techniques, close-combat and killing at a sabotage training-centre at Cambusdarroch in West Invernesshire. It was not until they were undergoing special training at the Villa Pellasis near Dorking, and finally in Woldingham, that they learnt the precise nature of the mission for which they had been selected: to liquidate Heydrich.[48]

After a number of abortive attempts they made a successful parachute drop on the Protectorate from an RAF Halifax, between Christmas and New Year 1941/42. Their code-name was 'Anthropoid'. Two other groups jumped over the Protectorate that night into an uncertain future: 'Silver A' and 'Silver B'. Their job was to restore the contact between resistance and the government-in-exile, which had been disrupted by Heydrich's well-aimed strikes. By the end of May, and the attempt on Heydrich's life, sixteen other agents had been sent out from England to drop by parachute, but none achieved their objectives. Two were captured by the police, two placed themselves voluntarily at the Gestapo's disposal, some were shot or committed suicide before they could be caught. Others appear simply to have gone to earth among their families and forgotten about their missions.[49] Only the radio team 'Silver A' and the assassination team 'Anthropoid' enjoyed success. The success of Kubiš and Gabčík, however, was almost entirely accidental.

Their series of errors and failures started with the parachute drop. In England they had been told that they would land near Plzeň, 150 kilometres (93 miles) west of Prague. Their contact addresses, too, were all in Plzeň, where they were to establish links with resistance organizations. By mistake, and evidently also because the proper dropping-zone was too risky for the RAF pilot, they landed in the vicinity of the village of Nehvizdy: not in Plzeň, therefore, but 20 kilometres (12 miles) east of Prague. Their addresses were useless to them.

At the very moment that they set foot on Czech soil, the second mishap occurred, the worst thing that can happen to a parachutist: a bad landing. Gabčík sprained his ankle and could not move from the spot.

Then came the first dangerous mistake, by which they offended against all that they had been taught in the SOE training-camps. Instead of burning their parachutes immediately in order to cover their tracks, as instructed, they decided to hide them – 'as souvenirs for later'. This was especially dangerous as the Halifax had lost two much altitude making its run-in to the drop, and the noise of its engines had awoken half the village. At least two of the inhabitants had seen the parachutes descending. By all the rules of probability the Gestapo would sooner or later get on to their trail and capture them. The assassination project seemed to have failed.

And then came a stroke of luck. The first two people they stumbled across, in a deserted quarry where they had withdrawn to nurse Gabčík's injury, were friendly. They were a gamekeeper, and the miller of Nehvizdy. The lives of the two depended on these men's discretion. It was purely a coincidence that the miller turned out to be friendly towards the Beneš government. He was an ex-member of the old Czech gymnastics movement, 'Sokol'. Under the umbrella of this movement one of the largest Czech resistance movements, the OSVO, had been formed. Kubiš and Gabčík were directed to Prague and met there by the OSVO. With their help they survived the five months necessary for their preparations for the attack.[50]

This did not prevent them, however, from continuing the series of hair-raising mistakes which they had been told to avoid at all costs. One of them was swept off his feet by a love-affair, whose intensity broke all the rules of undercover work. By the careless use of apartments, bicycles, clothing and briefcases belonging to others, a number of persons and families which were connected with the resistance found themselves unnecessarily compromised.

But their luck held, while Heydrich's deserted him. When a resistance informant got wind of Heydrich's plans for France, and when Gabčík and Kubiš were told that their victim would be summoned to Berlin on 27 May and in all probability would not return to Prague, or return only for a brief visit, the date of the attack was fixed as well as the place. It had to be on 27 May.[51]

On this glorious spring day, Heydrich did not leave his country home until 10 a.m. He had spent much longer taking leave of his family than usual. He was expecting a fairly long stay in Berlin and then perhaps a trip immediately afterwards to Brussels and Paris. At the airport, his plane stood ready for take-off. He was going to fly it to Berlin himself.

While Heydrich was still playing with his sons and little Silke in the gardens of Paneńské Břežany and putting off the moment of departure, the tension was becoming unbearable for the two members of 'Anthropoid'. Since 9.30 a.m. Gabčík and Kubiš had been positioned at the hairpin bend in the Prague suburb of Holešovice. Observation had established that Heydrich's car passed this point every day at about this time. Further back from the bend the Czech SOE agent Valčík was posted. He too had been dropped in by parachute and had joined Kubiš and Gabčík a few weeks earlier. His job was to give warning of the approach of the green Mercedes, by means of a whistle or a flashing mirror signal. It was past 10 o'clock, Valčík had given no sign as yet, and the two agents were becoming uneasy. Had the Gestapo got wind of the plan? If the agents harboured such fears, they were unfounded. It was certainly known in the Prague Gestapo HQ in the Petschek Palace that enemy agents had landed by parachute. Most of them had, after all, been shot, were in Gestapo hands or had by now been 'converted' to Gestapo employment. But the spy-hunters knew nothing of 'Anthropoid', least of all its mission.

At 10.30 a.m. Valčík's mirror flashed and there was no more time for brooding. It was time for 'Anthropoid' to begin. Kubiš moved to the other side of the road. Heydrich's heavy 3½ litre limousine took the corner. The chauffeur, Klein, was at the wheel, Heydrich next to him. As Klein changed down once again, Gabčík's chance came. He threw off the rain-coat that concealed his weapon, jammed the butt of his Sten-gun into his shoulder, took aim at Heydrich and pulled the trigger. But nothing happened. In his excitement the agent had forgotten to release the safety-catch.

It was as though Heydrich had nine lives. Was he protected against death by a magic spell? Now he even turned the tables on his attackers. The would-be victim of 'Anthropoid' stood up in the passenger-seat, drew his pistol and began to fire at Gabčík. Klein stopped the Mercedes in order to join in the chase. That was the fatal mistake made by the two crack-shots in black uniforms, and also the last chance for 'Anthropoid'. Before Heydrich and Klein could jump out of the car and chase Gabčík, Kubiš threw his grenade. The stationary car was an easy target. The Mills bomb landed close to the right-hand rear wheel and exploded instantly. Heydrich was badly injured by flying shrapnel. Still he got out to empty his magazine at the second assassin. Then he collapsed across the bonnet of the car. Chauffeur Klein ran after the fleeing Kubiš, but he disappeared behind a tram that was just turning the corner.

Two Czech policemen barred his way, but Kubiš shot himself clear, severely wounding one of the gendarmes. A blonde Czech lady ran to Heydrich's aid. The passers-by emerged from the paralysis of their shock, and halted a baker's van to carry the injured Heydrich to hospital.

Chapter 15

THE MARTYR
OF PRAGUE

When time runs out, well then, it has run out.

Heinrich Himmler

When the grenade went off, the Prague Music Festival had just begun.[1] Despite the attack, performances were not cancelled. As the lorries of the military police and SS units were pouring out across the roads of Bohemia to form a large cordon around Prague; as the raiding parties of the Security Police stormed through the capital, and the Gestapo dragnet hauled in suspects from private houses, factories and offices, the German Philharmonic Orchestra was playing Bach and Mozart, Reger and Respighi in the Valdštejn Gardens, at the Palace and at the Rudolfinum . . .

At dawn the first shots of the execution squads rang out, while the mild summer evening was filled with the tones of violin and harpsichord. Columns of *Der Neue Tag* contained long lists of the condemned, next to the music magazine section of Dr Peter Seitenberg. 'An unforgettable moment', he wrote of the appearance of the Leipzig Thomaner-Choir. 'These lads in their smart Hitler Youth uniforms'.[2] The lads sang some of the finest motets of Johann Sebastian Bach: 'The spirit doth minister to our weakness', and the Fugue, 'All that draws breath, praise ye the Lord'. The sounds of death and of the highest musical perfection confront each other here with a dissonance which says a good deal about the dual aspect of the black-uniformed lords of Bohemia – and about Heydrich above all. On the evening before the ambush he and his wife had attended a chamber music *soirée* in the Banqueting Hall of the Valdštejn Palace, despite the fact that what he had really wanted to do was to continue his preparations for the flight to Berlin the next morning and the conversations with Hitler and Himmler.

But there was no way for him to evade this Chamber Music evening given by the German Music Society, for the Bohnhardt Quartet, from his home town of Halle, was to play. In honour of their guest the Quartet were going to perform a work by Reinhard Heydrich's father, Bruno Heydrich, who had died four years earlier. It was a piano quintet, a pleasant piece of Nature Romanticism, of which a critic said that it was characterized most of all by a 'fantastic and demonic element'.[3] Heydrich for Heydrich.

Two weeks earlier, during the preliminary stages of the Music Festival, which on Heydrich's orders had been opened by the music of the German Mozart and the Czech Dvořák, he had written in his angular hand in a preface:

Music is the creative language of those who are artistic and musical, the medium of their inner life . . . solemn admonition in great times of struggle . . . In this sense the Prague Music Festival is a contribution to the struggle to master the present and intended as a foundation for a healthy musical life in this region within the Reich for years to come.[4]

Since the attack another language was being spoken. The ambush had taken place at 10.30 a.m. Until shortly before 1 p.m. State Secretary Frank was present in the Bulovka Hospital, staying on there more out of a sense of impotence than because he could help the injured Heydrich in any way by his presence. In an instant the hospital had been turned into the HQ of the Reich Protector. A delegation from the Protectorate government waited patiently to convey their sympathy, police officers and adjutants came with reports and received their orders. The Führer's HQ had been informed by the police.

At 12.30 Frank was called to the telephone to receive an urgent call from Hitler. He commanded Frank to take over, 'until Heydrich recovers', the duties of Reich Protector, and to offer a reward of one million Reichsmarks for the capture of the assassin.[5] Hitler was beside himself with rage about the attack. He personally drew up two orders, showing the significance of the event for him. 'Any person who aids and abets the assassins or knows of their whereabouts and fails to report to the police, will be shot together with his entire family.' And 'As an act of atonement 10,000 Czech suspects, or those who have anything to answer for politically, are to be arrested or, if they are already in custody, to be shot immediately in the concentration camps.' Frank, in the spirit of Heydrich's system of 'graduated terror', was to say the least out of sympathy with this demand of Hitler's for blind, mass shootings, and tried to gain time by suggesting to Hitler that he would visit Hitler's HQ to discuss the reprisal measures. Hitler agreed.[6]

Now, for the first time since those September days of the previous year, Frank declared a state of emergency. Prague Radio announced it first for the Prague district in its German programmes continuously from 4.30 p.m. onwards, and in the Czech ones from 5.04 p.m. 'Anyone who harbours or aids the persons involved in the attack, or, with knowledge of them or their whereabouts, does not report them, will be shot together with his family.' Simultaneously a curfew was imposed from 9 p.m. until 6 a.m. and in accordance with Hitler's instructions a reward of ten million crowns was offered. There was also a tightening up of the duty to report to police stations, and at 9.32 p.m. the state of emergency was extended to cover the whole of the Protectorate.[7] All these orders and their amendments expressed one dominant theme, always ending with the words '. . . will be shot'. But even this was not enough for Hitler and Himmler. Although Frank wanted preliminary consultations with the Führer about the reprisal measures, in an urgent telegram at 9.05 p.m., Himmler pressed for the mass shootings. Among other things he demanded that 'among the 10,000 hostages ordered . . . the chief concern should be to make sure of the arrest of the entire intelligentsia for the opposition'. Of these the 'hundred most important' were to be shot that very night.[8]

In the course of the afternoon Heydrich's colleague-in-office Kurt Daluege, Chief of the Order Police (regular police) in the Reich, to whom Heydrich never referred in private except by his nickname, had rushed to Prague; while the Heads of Offices IV and V, Müller and Nebe of Gestapo and Criminal Police respectively, unaccountably remained in Berlin and sent two subordinate officials instead, Chief Inspectors Dr Wehner and Kopkow.[9] At some point during the evening Daluege was instructed to take over the Reich Protector's duties himself, instead of Frank.[10] All this confusion of appointments, questions of authority, order and counter-order, goes to show very clearly how difficult it was for the German leadership to fill Heydrich's shoes. These difficulties continued after Heydrich's death, and were intensified when it emerged that no successor could be found who could successfully take over all of Heydrich's many functions. Daluege, Dr Geschke the Gestapo Chief, and Dr Böhme, Commander of the Security Police, turned Prague into an ant-heap during the night following the attack. At the Gestapo HQ in the Palace it was decided by late afternoon that a massive search operation should be instituted, and as dusk fell, when the curfew had taken effect, this search was accordingly begun.

In the course of the afternoon, even before the radio had announced the state of emergency, before loudspeaker vans and extra editions of the German and Czech press had begun to hurl their continuous, cold and menacing 'will be shot' messages against the walls of the Bohemian metropolis, Frank had, as a first step, immobilized the railways, and soon afterwards he imposed a ban on all modes of public transport and closed off trunk routes to all traffic.[11] The evening was heavy and oppressive. Cinemas and theatres, restaurants and cafés were shut; there was no-one out walking, no lovers along the banks of the Vltava, no music. Even the performances of the Prague Music Festival were briefly interrupted on that evening. The city seemed to have given up the ghost.

Armed police and Army patrols, the occasional vehicle bearing messengers and couriers, were all that could be seen moving, with an eerie clatter, through the streets. Then, all at once, around 10 o'clock, the city was in uproar. Fanning out from fixed starting points, the greatest police search action of European history abruptly began. It was carried out by Gestapo units with the aid of large contingents from the Security Police, the *Waffen-SS*, the local police force, the Czech gendarmerie, the SA, the Nazi Motor Corps and three Wehrmacht battalions. German and Czech police were assigned to a few special command details.[12]

Right from the start the search was hopeless. How could anyone hope to find single, unknown persons in a city of a million inhabitants? Although hardly a tram, hardly a house was overlooked, the net was hauled in empty. Quite a number of people were picked up and arrested for being without their identity cards, and quite by chance the police pulled in a few criminals they had wanted for some time, but there was not a single pointer to the assassins.

In the reports to Berlin, the failure of the great raid was covered up by references to the operation as being 'mainly for political and demonstration purposes'.[13] The chief reason for the operation's lack of success was Daluege's completely mistaken assumption that the attempt on Heydrich's life had a base among the Czech population and that it might be the signal for a general insurrection. During the raid the procedure had been to divide the units engaged into two single files moving along each side of the street, in street-fighting style, so that they could keep their eyes and their weapons trained upon the house fronts opposite.[14] And when powerful units of the Security Police marched into the city next morning from neighbouring regions, Daluege turned this too into a demonstration of German power and his personal authority, in order to intimidate the Czech population. He was clearly convinced that 'Heydrich's Czechs' had rebelled, after all.[15]

Karl-Hermann Frank, who arrived at the Führer's HQ during the night after the attack, had the very difficult task of defending his quite opposite view, that the ambush had been a remote-controlled operation. It was only with great reluctance that Hitler had allowed Heydrich to persuade him, a year before, that the Czechs could play a very important and useful role in his plans for the future.[16] Now he was blinded by hatred, because his benevolence, as he called it, had been so ill repaid. The brutality of his intentions towards the Protectorate after the attack is shown by his first telephone conversation with Frank, when he demanded the price of 10,000 heads to atone for one. Before his audience with Hitler, Frank learned from a long discussion with Himmler that immediately after this telephone call Hitler had decided to entrust somebody other than Frank with the succession to the Reich Protector's Office, partly in order to maintain the tactically very useful team of State Security and Reich Protector, and partly, said Himmler, because 'the Führer wanted to appoint SS-General von dem Bach-Zelewski', Chief of German Anti-Partisan Forces, who had gained a certain reputation for himself in Russia fighting the resistance. Hitler 'saw in him evidence that he would act even more severely and brutally than Heydrich and have no scruples about wading through a sea of blood.' The Czechs would find out, he said, that 'when they shoot down one, then someone else much worse will follow'.[17]

This is a most interesting remark of Hitler's, both with respect to his verdict on Heydrich and to the assault on Heydrich's life, because it shows that Hitler still had someone up his sleeve who was 'more severe', 'more brutal' and 'worse' than Heydrich; and because it reveals that he too assumed that the attack was dreamed up by the Czechs. Frank attempted to undermine this view in his report to Hitler. He and all his colleagues were agreed 'that the assault was an isolated act instigated by the enemy and did not arise from a widespread popular Czech insurrectionist and resistance movement'. It was the shades of Heydrich which dominated this discussion, for Frank conjured up once again for the Führer's benefit the principles and the successes of Heydrich's policy. Its results had been that: 'the armaments industry was working at full swing'; 'the battle for productivity was raging'; 'acts of sabotage were diminishing'; and 'the government had the confidence of the Reich Protector and was actively collaborating'. 'If we were now to carry out mass arrests and mass executions on such a vast scale (as ordered by telephone), we would be departing from Heydrich's own line and endangering his achievements.' When Hitler hesitated, Frank threw in the argument that mass executions would only feed enemy propaganda, which was concerned to give the impression of a great 'insurgency movement supported by the Czech population'. Apart from that, '50,000 to 100,000 people related to those arrested would indeed be driven into the bitterest hostility towards us,' and finally 'we would forfeit of our own volition valuable political forces and neutralize and abandon their collaboration, although at present they are available for positive collaboration.' He named as the most important of these forces the government of the Protectorate itself, the trade unions, the Czech gendarmerie and large sections of the press.[18]

Without a doubt, the noted Sudeten-German Czech-hater Frank was very much influenced in these arguments by Heydrich's principle of graduated selective terror, and the policy, so successfully followed by Frank's political tutor, of divide and rule. It was in no small measure due to Frank's invocation of Heydrich himself, and the fact that it would have been unwise to abandon his principles just at this moment, when there was hope that he would soon recover from his injuries, that Frank succeeded in persuading Hitler to revoke his reprisal measures. The threat of shooting, it was now decided, would now apply only 'to any person suspected of the assault or of aiding the perpetrators or withholding information about them'. In addition to this, the 'activist' Czech elements, that is those hostile to Beneš, would be induced to mount a propaganda campaign against the government-in-exile.[19]

Heydrich himself remained completely ignorant of the tug-of-war about reprisals and the hunt for the assassins. In the Bulovka Hospital, events during these hours were far removed from politics. A Czech baker had delivered the all-powerful overlord to the hospital on the floor of his delivery van. A nurse called the doctor on duty in Surgery, Dr Vladimír Šnajdr.[20] 'Dr Šnajdr, come quickly, Heydrich's lying there.' At first the doctor thought it was a joke, but when he saw that the Sister was trembling all over and hardly able to speak for shock, he could see for himself: it *was* the Reich Protector.

Heydrich was alone in the waiting room, sitting on the edge of a table, doubled over. The doctor greeted him in Czech. Heydrich replied silently, raising his arm. Šnajdr reported later, 'I took a pair of tweezers and some swabs and examined the nature and extent of the wound in his back. Heydrich did not move, he never winced at all, though he must have been suffering severe pain.'

In the meantime another nurse had telephoned the German medical superintendent, Professor Dr Diek. He came immediately, drew himself up to attention out of sheer confusion, and then started his examination. At first he suspected an injury to the kidneys. No, Heydrich seemed to have been lucky. The spine was intact too. He was then taken by wheelchair for X-ray. 'Heydrich wanted to retain his dignity and got up unaided from his chair to go to the X-ray machine.'

Only now did it become apparent that an operation was needed instantly. One rib was smashed, the diaphragm was punctured, there was a splinter in the spleen. There had to be an operation straight away. But Heydrich refused. He wanted the best possible treatment: he was distrustful and demanded a surgeon from Berlin. Dr Diek insisted on immediate surgical intervention, and after a pause to consider, Heydrich agreed, but only on the condition that Professor Dr Hohlbaum of the Prague German Clinic was also called in.

It was a difficult operation. Together with the splinter, minute particles of leather and horse-hair from the upholstery of the car seats had penetrated the spleen. It was uncertain whether a sepsis could be avoided if the spleen were not removed entirely along with the foreign bodies. Heydrich was unconscious until the evening of 28 May.

Himmler immediately sent his personal physician, Professor Dr Karl Gebhardt, Consultant Surgeon of the *Waffen-SS*, by plane from Berlin to Prague. Later other German specialists were sent in. Gebhardt was on the telephone every hour or so, reporting to the *Reichsführer* the condition of 'our good Reinhard', as Himmler called him in a letter to the Professor.[21] Gebhardt clearly believed at first that Heydrich would recover from his severe wounds. He placed his trust in new medicines, forerunners of the later Sulfonamide, and above all in Heydrich's constitution. If willpower alone had been enough, he later opined, then Heydrich would have survived.

While Heydrich's doctors could do nothing but wait and watch over the Master of Terror, now at the receiving end himself, the whole Nazi world was shaken to the core, friends and foes of Heydrich alike. Hitler and Himmler, both at this time in their field HQ at Rastenburg, reacted almost with hysteria, as their first orders to Frank and Daluege indicate.

Although these last days of May 1942 were crammed with dramatic military events on various fronts, the chief talking-point everywhere was the attack on Heydrich. In the encircling battle south of Kharkov, the three armies of von Kleist, Paulus and Hoth had destroyed the Soviet 6th, 9th and 57th Armies. In this battle alone the Soviets lost 240,000 men as prisoners, 12,000 tanks and more than 2000 guns. Major-General Rommel had just begun his successful offensive in North Africa, which was to lead to the fall of Tobruk and take the Axis troops to Egypt itself. The Navy and the Luftwaffe were scoring their first big successes against the Allied convoys to Murmansk: but none of these military victories could prevent the assassination of Heydrich being experienced as the rumbling of an earthquake, as the omen of a catastrophe which, at its height, might engulf the whole world of the Third Reich. Even the normally so cynical Dr Josef Goebbels noted in a diary entry for this date, 'Alarming news from Prague. There has been a bomb attack on Heydrich in a Prague suburb.' On 31 May he asserts 'the loss of Heydrich at this juncture would be irreparable'. And on the day Heydrich died, 4 June, he repeated, 'the loss of Heydrich *is* irreparable. He was the most radical and successful fighter of the enemies of the state.' And 'It will be hard to find the right man to succeed him.'[22] Adolf Eichmann, Heydrich's subordinate, and the man to whom he had passed on the routine work involved in the Final Solution, heard the news in Bratislava, at the bowling-alley, and stood there 'as though transfixed'.[23] On the other side, in the camp of the conservative opposition to Hitler, it was difficult to feel overjoyed by the fate of the hated Heydrich. There too, the Prague attack was seen as a sign that German power was on the wane. While Frank was still negotiating with Hitler over the number of hostages to be taken, Bonhoeffer and Schoenfeld as representatives of the German resistance were earning themselves a rebuff, after discussions with the Bishop of Chichester about a separate peace, when their efforts foundered in an abrupt rejection by the British government.

'The struggle over the Church, the air-raids and the attack on Heydrich are further causes for anxiety', wrote the Intelligence officer, Grosscurth, one of the leading conspirators of the anti-Hitler opposition, from the Eastern Front to his mentor, Major-General Beck.[24] Immediately there arose the wildest speculations about the perpetrators of the assault, their support-organization and their motives. Walter Schellenberg, who received the news by teleprinter during an SD meeting in the Hague, immediately suspected Bormann or Himmler, for whom Heydrich had become too big for his boots. 'I was privately convinced that Heydrich had fallen victim to a secret sentence of death passed by the innermost circle of the leadership [Hitler, Bormann, Himmler].'[25] It is certainly true that the tensions between Bormann and Heydrich in the months before the latter's death had become unbearable; it may be true that Heydrich felt more and more convinced about a suspicion he had harboured for years, that the head of the SS was an agent of Stalin; it may be correct that Bormann was about to be unmasked by Heydrich.[26] In the last few months, too, the relationship between the former inseparables, Heydrich and Himmler, had become distinctly cool. Admittedly it is also very strange that in Himmler's desk diary, which was for years kept up carefully and without a gap, only one leaf is missing. It was torn hastily and incompletely from the book; perhaps because it contained an entry that posterity was not supposed to know about? It is the page for 27 May 1942, the day of the assassination attempt.[27] However, Schellenberg's conclusion, however understandable and plausible in his day in the light of the no-holds-barred feuding by rivals at Hitler's court, was, as we now know, incorrect.

Others, like Hitler and Himmler himself, had instantly assumed that Czech resistance fighters were responsible; Frank, however, had immediately thought of an assassination squad directed from London. But when the assassins could not be traced in the days that followed the attack, despite the fact that the Gestapo concentrated all available resources on this one case; despite the fact that in the special team formed by Wehner, Kopkow and Pannwitz the best criminal investigators in the German Reich were engaged on the case;[28] and the fact that Daluege and Frank daily announced the shooting of hostages, until Heydrich's death;[29] in the light of all this, it was suspected on the German side that the Czechs in the Protectorate were in league with the Czechs in London. 'In the hour of crisis', so ran the clearest comment in the German press, it was 'the inexorable law that warfare demanded decisions, not only decisions about the outcome, about victory or defeat, but decisions as to loyalties, as to friend or foe'.[30] It had been thought in various quarters in the Protectorate 'that this decision could be artfully avoided. This apparent artfulness had been very detrimental to the Czech people and had led to the result that the English-Bolshevik sniper strategy had believed it possible to build upon it as a quality useful to the enemy.' The search for the culprits would now force a decision. Other newspapers in the German-dominated areas accused British radio propaganda of being responsible for the assassination by 'ceaselessly whipping-up the population to criminal attacks'.[31]

Abroad, particularly in England, Heydrich all at once received a great deal of press interest, albeit unfavourable. Whereas *The Times,* for example, had mentioned Heydrich all of nine times in the years from 1936 to the day of the attack, there were now Heydrich items every day – his victims, his deeds, his origins, his career – for months at a stretch. In the process it became clear that the general public in the country from which the attack had been launched were at least as much in the dark about its originators and their motives as the German investigators in Czecho-slovakia. In *The Times,* for example, the bomb goes off just at the moment when Heydrich is 'travelling with high German officials through a suburb of the city'.[32] The paper obviously does not trust the various official versions of the story, as it emerged later that, if the assassination attempt really was 'the work of Czechs, it shows patriotism seeking a desperate outlet. But in the unnatural conditions of life in the Nazi Reich it is not surprising that other explanations of the attack should be afoot.' And there are dark hints that 'Heydrich would not be the first victim of vendetta within the Nazi camp.'[33] In contrast to reports in many newspapers an article in the *Manchester Guardian* of 29 May contains a premonition of the significance of Heydrich's death for Czechs and Jews, and cuts through the public elation with the grave statement that the attack is 'bad news, for it provides another occasion for savage reprisals'.[34]

Beneš, and with him the Allied war propaganda, attempted to pass the assassination off as a 'spontaneous act' of the repressed 'Czech people', and indeed, if this attack had actually emanated from the Czech resistance, it would have been their most spectacular blow against one of the most sensitive spots of the German security and terror apparatus. After a special session of the Czech Cabinet-in-exile in London on 29 May, which ended by making a proclamation 'against German bestiality', the acting Foreign Minister of the exile-Cabinet, Dr Ripka, declared on the radio that the government-in-exile had received the news of the attack 'in the knowledge that a tried but unbroken people is replying with ever-increasing persistence to the fury of the German oppressors'.[35]

Even the House of Commons, a few days after the event, took an interest in Heydrich – and nothing could do more to indicate the British inability to interpret the assassination than a Parliamentary question put by the Labout MP Dr Morgan, who asked the Prime Minister to tell him whether it had yet been suggested to the Czech government-in-exile 'to mark as an historic site for future commemoration the scene of the shooting of Heydrich'![36]

In Prague, in Brno, in the whole of Bohemia the problems were now quite different ones. Almost daily the press and the radio carried new lists with the names of hostages who had been shot. By the date of Heydrich's death the number had already reached 157.[37]

Because the Czech resistance, in comparison with the Dutch, Russian and French, had in Allied opinion so far put up only 'a poor show',[38] it was natural for the Czech exiles to claim the assassination as a spontaneous act by Czechs in the Protectorate. 'The freedom-loving peoples of the Czechoslovakian Republic are in the vanguard of the fight,' it was claimed; the two assassins were celebrated as 'the two heroes of liberty', who 'in the certain expectation that they were sacrificing themselves',[39] had shown the world that the working population of the Protectorate had not been deceived by 'the cunning monster Heydrich'.

Dr Hácha and the government of the Protectorate, of course, took precisely the opposite view. Their overriding concern was to shift the blame for the assassination from the Protectorate. While Daluege could think of no other way to deal with the Protectorate government than to frighten it by crude threats that 'he had frequently carried out to the letter the Führer's special orders',[40] Frank tried to continue the Heydrich line of cooperation between Czechs and Germans. He directed Hácha and Moravec to take active steps to cooperate. Consequently Hácha and the government declared in the press and on the radio[41] that the deed had been carried out by Beneš' agents, and they condemned Beneš as 'Enemy No. 1 of the Czech nation'. 'In our country', ran their statement, 'a model calm prevailed and does prevail.' The Greater German Reich had valued this highly, and through Heydrich it had been persuaded of the loyalty of the

Czechs to the Reich. In consequence, the autonomous government of the Czechs had been extended just 'one day before the vile deed', and those strict measures had been dismantled which the Reich 'had had to impose on Czechs who had been suborned by the enemy. Many Czechs had been saved, sentences reduced, trials deferred. What the exiles had destroyed for us, we would attempt to reconstruct. At that very moment a heinous crime was jeopardizing all that had been achieved so far.'

From 31 May onwards, Propaganda-Minister Moravec spoke at countless mass-meetings, in factories, on the radio. There was a number of compulsory mass demonstrations, one on the Old Town Square in Prague, the other in the Vegetable Market at Brno. Moravec described them both as 'Demonstrations against England and Beneš'. He went on:

> We're not going to tell ourselves any fairy-tales: the truth is much too black and horrible for that. There's just one thing to be said: while the perpetrators of the attack on the Reich Protector remain at large, the Czech people can swear a hundred thousand oaths of loyalty to the Reich, make millions of promises to submit humbly and countless millions of genuflections to the agencies of the Reich, but none of that will help them. It is deeds, not words, that are wanted now.[42]

In accordance with the 'indignation of the Czech people' alleged by Moravec, Beneš was even deprived of his Czech nationality by the Czech National Council.[43] The real opinions of the people emerged, however, from the confidential and usually very frank 'reports from the Reich' of Heydrich's own SD. According to them, 'the failure to take the expected savage measures' had 'led to a certain disappointment' among the German population of Bohemia and Moravia; while the majority of Czechs, after their first reaction of malicious satisfaction, 'condemned the attack out of fear of the serious consequences they anticipated', but by common consent refused to betray the assassins. Condemnation of the attack was supposed to be particularly widespread among ordinary people, workers and peasants.[44] It was these people who took part in the mass meetings, but in whose faces, according to the Prague correspondent of the Swiss newspaper *Weltwoche* (World-week), 'there was no message to be read'.[45] Thus the attack on 'the best man in the SS',[46] as he was later called, clearly revealed once more the constellation of forces in Bohemia and at the Führer's court, the aims of the various cliques and groupings, the situation

253

of the whole exile government and the state of internal security in the Reich: all this emerging from the subterranean shifts and rumblings of recent years, demonstrated again, in the process, Heydrich's former status among the tangle of political relationships.

The real political thinking behind the momentous decision in London to launch the attack is recorded neither by Beneš' nor by Churchill's memoirs. The relevant British documentation has not yet been released. According to information received, access to the SOE records 'would by their very nature not be granted'.[47] The only answer the Historical Branch of the British Ministry of Defence was prepared to make can be reduced to the bare statement that it can be assumed 'that as head of the Czech government-in-exile in London, Beneš conceived the idea, and that the role of the SOE was limited to the training and transport of the agents'.[48] In his memoirs the head of the Czech Secret Service, František Moravec, states that Beneš decided on the action both as a manifestation of resistance to improve Czechoslovakia's international standing and as a spark which would activate the mass of the people against the Germans. Speculations of varying value have been offered from many different quarters.[49] In an 'expert' report, the historian Michael Freund implied that it was 'probable' that the attackers primarily intended to destroy, not so much the Reich Protector and enemy of the Czechs, but the engineer of the Final Solution of the 'Jewish problem'. 'The Jewish horror was common knowledge abroad.' The action did not primarily serve short-term war strategy, but was entirely in keeping with the overall political war-aim of the British. This war-aim of course was the destruction of Nazi despotism. No direct military purpose could be achieved by the murder of Heydrich. But 'it was dramatically in keeping with the Allied warning, given voice by Roosevelt, Churchill and Stalin, that atrocities committed in occupied areas would be ruthlessly repaid in kind'.[50] This view failed to convince the court to which it was submitted, and it is indeed an unconvincing piece of guesswork. It cannot even be supported by any fragmentary documentation or eye-witness accounts, and it predicates the assumption that the destruction which was beginning to overtake European Jewry was nothing more than a whim of Heydrich's which would not survive its originator.

Somewhat more credible at first sight, however, is another collection of theories which interpret the assassination as a move imperative for Allied Intelligence. The assumption here is that it was, in the final analysis the British Secret Service which lay behind the plot, obliged as it was to protect its double agents inside the German Counter-Intelligence Service, and ultimately even Canaris himself among them, from destruction by Heydrich. It was his armour-plated filing-cabinet alone which contained all the various bits of the jigsaw-puzzle which, completed, could expose members of German Counter-Intelligence as Allied agents. Walter Schellenberg, who can be granted a certain amount of experience in this area, maintained that the dismissal, even the liquidation of Canaris would have become inevitable in the course of 1942 if Heydrich had not been stopped by the assassin's grenade.[51] One of the semi-official explanations of the attack accepted throughout the Eastern Bloc discusses at length the question 'whether Heydrich was not liquidated to prevent the liquidation of Canaris, and whether the assassination of Heydrich was not after all really carried out in order to rescue a valuable informer'.[52]

It is well known that colleagues of the head of Counter-Intelligence were Allied informers, and that Canaris was at least prepared from time to time to cover for such activities. According to a communication from Sir Kenneth Strong, former head of Allied Secret Services, 'one of these individuals was Admiral Canaris himself'.[53] And yet, although Strong's statement must carry a great deal of weight (for he was in a good position to know the truth), convincing evidence is lacking.

More credence attaches to the Czech version of this theory, which has it that it was Paul Thümmel, a key agent of the Czech Secret Service, called 'A54', who was to be rescued from Heydrich's grasp.[54] A54 had entered the Service even before the war. After 20 June 1940 the transmitter known as Sparta I, operated by the resistance organization ÚVOD, had kept open the communications between the Czech exiles and Thümmel. Thümmel, as the best-informed member of the Prague Counter-Intelligence office, as holder of the Golden Badge of the Nazi Party, and as a personal acquaintance of Himmler, was in a position to supply the Allied Command with exceptionally useful information, for example a detailed list of the deployment of the German Armies, Army Corps and divisions right across Europe.[55] The Intelligence Service run by Colonel František Moravec was certainly the most successful of all the forms taken by resistance to the Germans and was held in very high esteem by Beneš: indeed, it was really only due to the valuable information with which he was able to supply the Allies that he owed his position in Allied counsels. And he could only supply this information because of Thümmel. In a radio message he had transmitted to the ÚVOD station, he told them, 'The British appreciate your work all the more because of the continual contrast to the efforts of the Poles, Dutch and others, whose results have not been at all comparable. The same applies to the French. Your work is thus a constant service to the good name of the nation.'[56] Beyond a doubt, the preservation of such an important agent was, in Allied eyes, worth the loss of hundreds or even thousands of people in the reprisals expected from the Germans.

A last point: the British Halifax bomber which undertook the risky flight to Bohemia in late December had three different groups on board to be dropped over Czech territory. Apart from 'Anthropoid', i.e. Gabčík and Kubiš, these included the groups Silver A and Silver B. And their explicit mission was above all to re-establish contact with A54, with 'René', 'Franta', 'Eva', 'Dr Holm' or 'Dr Steinberg', as Thümmel variously styled himself or was code-named by others. What could be more natural than the surmise that 'Anthropoid's' mission too was in some way connected with the presentation of this line of communication so vital to Beneš? Since December 1939 the Gestapo had been repeatedly coming across documents which pointed to Beneš' Intelligence Service having a very well informed source, whose code-name was 'Franta' or 'René'. Heydrich lost no time in setting up a special investigation squad from the Prague Gestapo under Police Inspector Willi Abendschön. He took up the hunt with zeal and expertise, but seemed to be hunting a phantom. It was not until the summer of 1941 that Abendschön for the first time included Thümmel in his list of suspects.

The efforts of the Prague Gestapo were at the same time being concentrated on the Czech Staff-Officer Václav Morávek, who had, near Prague, his own wireless transmitter for communication with London, and was Thümmel's executive officer. On 19 September 1941 Prague received from London a long shopping list of Intelligence items, mainly to do with the situation on the Eastern Front, which was going extremely badly for the Allies. Thümmel must have answered all these questions, via Morávek, to London's satisfaction 'by return of post', for on 22 September a message of thanks was transmitted: 'René's last reports were very good.'[57] This praise was accompanied by new questions. That was why Morávek had another meeting with Thümmel on the 26th, but the link with London had been broken, for on the 27th Heydrich had arrived in Prague. The declaration of the state of emergency which followed his arrival, the first summary court sentences, the intensification of Gestapo activity in Prague at the prompting of its own Head: all this led to the temporary paralysis of

Morávek's organization. When Heydrich began to dismantle the Czech resistance bit by bit after his arrival in Prague, Gestapo interrogations uncovered the existence of a secret transmitter somewhere in the area south-west of Prague, but at first they could not find it, because its transmissions stopped as a result of the suspension of the activities of Morávek's group. Heydrich became impatient and Dr Geschke spent some sleepless nights.

But during the night of 2 October radio detectors picked up the transmitter once more and were able to locate it in the course of the next few hours. The site was surrounded and the Gestapo found the transmitter in a second-floor flat. One of the radio operators committed suicide, the other was arrested along with other Czechs. After hours of unbroken and merciless interrogation it came out that Staff-Officer Morávek, who was still on the run, 'was in touch with an exceptionally well-informed German, who was probably on the staff at Wehrmacht HQ'.[58] The information found at the transmitter site was so highly confidential that only three German officials were in a position to know it, apart from Heydrich himself: Frank, Geschke and Dr Holm, or in other words Thümmel. Frank and Geschke were above suspicion. That left only Thümmel, whom Abendschön already had cause to suspect. On 13 October Thümmel was arrested in his Counter-Intelligence Service office. This step had powerful political implications, for it was obvious that Canaris was not simply going to stand by and see one of his most important colleagues arrested. Since from now on everything would be taking place 'at the highest level', it was Heydrich himself who gave the order for Thümmel's arrest. He was embittered about this degree of treachery, and it confirmed his old view that Admiral Canaris' Counter-Intelligence contained a whole collection of 'shady Barons'[59] as he called them.

Thümmel was interrogated for six long weeks. He denied his guilt and protested vociferously against his arrest. At his own request he was allowed to contact high-ranking echelons of the Party in Berlin. Protests and declarations of his reliability now began to flow in from Berlin, and Heydrich had to assert the last ounce of his influence just to keep Thümmel under arrest until completion of the interrogation. On 25 November Thümmel had to be released, and the Gestapo had no choice but to apologize to him for its 'mistake'.

At this point we find the link between the hunt for Allied agent A54 and the possible motives for the assassination attempt. An agent as well protected as Thümmel, veteran Nazi, close acquaintance of Himmler and intimate colleague of Admiral Canaris, even someone like Dr Geschke was likely to get his fingers burnt in such an affair. No, a man like this, against whom not a single shred of evidence had yet been established, could only be denounced, in the teeth of powerful Berlin establishment protection, by Heydrich himself. For Beneš' Secret Service, Abendschön's suspicions were, of course, no threat: as far as London was concerned Thümmel was still the most important agent at the heart of German Counter-Intelligence. And if Heydrich alone could lay him low, then the logical thing to do was to eliminate Heydrich as quickly as possible and regardless of loss of life. And in actual fact the conjectured date of the decision to launch the attack does coincide with the first great crisis of the agent Thümmel, that is to say October and November 1941. The fact that it took the assassins five full months after the air-drop to deliver their blow, must in this context be regarded simply as a regrettable delay in an extremely urgent piece of business.

Here then lies a very plausible motive for *sending out* the assassins. But the same is not true of the *execution* of the attack on 27 May. For Thümmel had already been arrested for a second time in February. Abendschön had been searching tirelessly for some concrete evidence of Thümmel's treason and by the end of January he had found what he wanted, in the records of the interrogation of two British Secret Service officers, Stevens and Best, whom the Security Service had abducted from Venlo in Holland. Over two years later, then, this operation bore fruit. Abendschön personally cross-questioned the two Britons once more. It emerged that 'a high-ranking German Intelligence officer' had met up in 1939 in the Hague with the Czech Secret Service man Frank, and – so much was proven – this officer was Thümmel.[60] After a renewed protest from Canaris, Thümmel was once more released, but this time only for appearance's sake. He was expected to put the Gestapo bloodhounds on the trail of the still elusive Staff-Officer Morávek, Thümmel's Czech executive officer. In mid-March Morávek was cornered and killed in a shoot-out. On 20 March Thümmel was arrested once more, and for the last time. The motive for carrying out the attack on Heydrich, if it was to protect Thümmel, had thus been removed. Even if the intention in dispatching the assassins from London was the protection of the informer, there must have been other, even more powerful reasons for the final execution of the attack.

Some communist authors assert that Beneš' plan was to provoke a wave of terror which was to lead to the wiping-out of the Czech Communist Party, relatively active in the spring of 1942.[61] This view implies that Beneš, at that time comparatively uninfluential in London, could have succeeded in directing savage German measures towards the communists exclusively and not towards the nationalist resistance: it even presupposes a certain amount of complicity between the nationalist resistance and the German security organizations. Absurd as this theory may be, it does bring in a further putative motive for the attack: an attempt to promote artificially a wave of terror.

What benefit could Beneš hope for from the inevitable reprisals that would follow the assassination? Let us cast our minds back to the spring of 1942. The Soviet winter counter-offensive has ground to a halt everywhere, and the German summer offensive is to roll forward into the Caucasus and up to the frontiers of Iran. It opens on 8 May with operation *'Trappenjagd'* (Bustard-hunt), carried out by the German 11th Army, and by the middle of May has achieved the collapse of the Soviet Crimean front. The Soviet Army in this one battle loses several hundreds of thousands of men. Shortly before, the Americans and British had discussed their contingency plan, 'Sledge-Hammer', for immediate action in the case of a Soviet collapse, which, in the Allies' view, was not to be ruled out.

Edvard Beneš' Czech government in London has still not been recognized by the British, and the ever more unambiguous reports of the Reich Protector's success in pacifying the Czechs disturb the Allies and frighten Beneš, for 'the more passive the attitude of the population of Bohemia and Moravia towards their German masters, the more untenable became the position of the government-in-exile in its dealings with the Allies'.[62] It is today beyond dispute that the resistance in Bohemia steered by Beneš at this point had already foundered in coming up against Heydrich, and that it was practically vanquished. But from March 1942 onwards, the groups centring on the Czech Communist Party had begun to step up dramatically their underground activities and their propaganda, stressing continuously in their message to the population that the Western-aligned organizations were 'sluggish and effectively useless'[63] and that the strategically much-needed active resistance could now only be set up and executed by the communists. Beneš was therefore afraid of losing all credibility with the Allies. Captain Bartoš, a Secret Service member of group 'Silver' sent a personal radio message to Beneš to the effect that 'the intensive, almost open activity of the communists is persuading the masses that they are the only ones not afraid of struggle and sacrifice. They are impressing the people and gaining their support.'[64] The two possibilities open to Beneš to restore his standing in Allied eyes and persuade them to have a proper regard for the interests of the government-in-exile, were either to produce convincing results in the field of Intelligence-gathering, or for an active resistance movement to strike some really effective blows at the German war-machine, now stretched to full capacity. But real resistance was impossible as long as Heydrich was able to neutralize Czech interest in the resistance movement steered from London, by means of his own unique and subtle blend of intimidation and paternalism.

Even after the removal of the Thümmel question, Beneš was left with the sober conclusion that Heydrich must be eliminated. Only a massive provocation to the Germans, so it was thought, could evoke the degree of brutality that was necessary to give the Czech resistance a sense of purpose and a broad popular base. The greatest conceivable provocation, undoubtedly, was an attempt on Heydrich's life – the despoiling of the temple erected to the great god Security.

Beneš received repeated predictions from the leaders of the organized resistance about the way the Germans would react to the assassination. So, for example, when Professor Vaněk, leader of the secret OSVO (originating in the old Czech 'Sokol' movement), upon which 'Anthropoid' depended for assistance, discovered that the target of his protégés Gabčík and Kubiš was Heydrich himself, he transmitted his personal misgivings to London on May 4, using the radio facilities of 'Silver A'.

> This assassination would not be productive for the Allies in any way, and for our own people it would have far-reaching consequences. It would not only endanger the lives of prisoners and hostages, it would also cost thousands of other lives, plunge the nation into unprecedented subjugation, and at the same time sweep away the last vestiges of any organization among us. That would ensure that nothing useful could ever again be achieved here to help the Allies.[65]

Here we have a man who was in touch with day-to-day life in the Protectorate telling the exiled leader in London that Heydrich's assassination would have precisely the opposite effect from that of stimulating resistance. Vaněk ended his dispatch by imploring, 'Please give us orders via Silver to stop the assassination.'[66] The leader of 'Silver' group, radio-operator Bartoš, added another sentence on his own account, endorsing Vaněk's views. A similar radio-message went out to London on 12 May from the former Czech Ambassador Arnošt Heidrich on behalf of the remnants of the ÚVOD organization, the 'Central Committee for Resistance in the Homeland'.[67]

Beneš clearly turned a deaf ear to these pleas; at any rate, he made no move to call off Gabčík and Kubiš, now consumed with impatience for action after their five months of preparation. In a very full message on 15 May Beneš gave, however, a very interesting final insight into the motives for the assassination, in the shape of a pessimistic evaluation of the Czech exiles' position: the context is his expectation that the Germans would throw absolutely everything at their disposal into the forthcoming summer offensive.

> If they made tremendous advances, perhaps right into the Caucasus, the situation would be grave and would above all mean a considerable lengthening of the war. If that happened I would not be surprised if the Germans were to suggest a peace treaty without a final victory. That would create a severe crisis and shake the resolve of some of the Allies, too.[68]

Clearly, Beneš feared that if such a peace were achieved, through a German initiative, the Protectorate of Bohemia and Moravia might be left in the hands of the German Reich, especially if the smooth relationship between Heydrich and the government of the Protectorate under Hácha and Moravec, and Heydrich's success in practically dissolving the resistance, had created the impression abroad that the Czechs were well off and contented with their Protectorate status. Beneš wrote: 'In such a dangerous situation the present conditions in the Protectorate, that is to say the collaboration of Hácha as President, Moravec and the rest of the government with the Germans is a great handicap for us, not to say a great danger, let there be no mistake about it.' That being so:

> . . . any acts of violence, revolts, direct action of any kind would be desirable, indeed essential. From an international standpoint, if there were peace negotiations, such action would be a redeeming feature, possibly our salvation, even if it were achieved only at the cost of great sacrifice.[69]

261

These words of Beneš make it clear that the intention was to impress on the outside world that there really *was* resistance in the Protectorate and that the long arm of Edvard Beneš reached out from London to Bohemia itself. For this purpose, be it said, an attack on a lesser luminary might have sufficed. Along this line of thought ran 'Silver A's' objection that if, despite all misgivings, 'there had to be an assassination attempt for international reasons, then let it be aimed at a native Quisling, preferably E M (Propaganda-Minister Moravec)'.[70] This corresponded to the appreciation of the situation on the ground by well-informed German observers in Bohemia. After the war the long-serving chief editor of *Der Neue Tag* in Prague said of the assassination:

> If the Czechs had been asked who they would like to see killed, they would pretty certainly not have said Heydrich, but Frank, for if they detested anyone it was their Sudeten-German enemy Frank. To them he appeared to represent the epitome of their loss of national greatness, the epitome of the slave-master. From a Czech nationalist point of view Frank was the obvious target for assassination. From the standpoint of Allied strategic interests it had to be Heydrich.[71]

There were, then, a variety of reasons why Heydrich's fate was sealed: the protection of the key agent Thümmel; the desire of Beneš' exiles to gain prestige with the Allies as a result of their influence in the Protectorate, and to provoke a particularly brutal wave of German terror. The British Labour MP, Ronald T Paget, wrote after the war that among the tactics of the underground and partisan war was 'provocation of reprisals in order to stoke up hatred against the occupying force and attract more recruits into the Resistance! That was the reason why we flew a squad into Czechoslovakia to murder Heydrich.'[72]

Now the attack had happened, and the attacker had had an easy job of it. Heydrich, who had taken every care before the war to fit out his Berlin flat and his official cars, a Horch and an Adler Diplomat, with the most sophisticated security devices, and whose responsibility it was to draw up security rules for leading figures in state and Party[73], drove around in the Protectorate without the slightest protection. The very man who took personal care of the security of his 'Führer', spending days in preparations for Hitler's entry into Warsaw on 1 October 1939,[74] for example; a man who exercised all his talents to scotch in advance the most brilliant planning of potential assassins, who never forgot a detail and left nothing to chance – this same man, where his own safety was concerned, did not even take the precaution of a bodyguard, but was accompanied only by a driver. He drove a well-known dark green Mercedes with an open top. During his visit to Prague, Munitions Minister Albert Speer had remarked upon this amazing nonchalance. 'We drove for hours around Prague, without an escort. I felt very uneasy,' Speer recalled after the war. But Heydrich had shaken off all remonstrations with the sentiment 'But why should my Czechs shoot at me?'[75]

Hitler and Himmler were extremely critical of Heydrich in this respect. Himmler went so far as to exclaim in front of the assembled high-ranking SS and Police Chiefs after Heydrich's State Funeral: 'Stupidity is always punished, too.'[76] He took what he called Heydrich's provocative posture as the text for an emphatic sermon:

If, as was the case with *Obergruppenführer* Heydrich, you are in the habit of leaving your homes every day, at a particular time and taking a particular route, then you are a sitting target for the lunatic who is lying in wait for you. If you are expected at an official function or elsewhere, then it is essential to establish reasonable protection. Secondly, it is essential that, on journeys you *cannot* avoid, you are accompanied by an escort vehicle.

The attack on Heydrich would have been made far more difficult if these elementary precautions had been observed. For all that, said Himmler, 'as Sons of Germania who, though no fatalists, are believers in destiny, we must say: when time runs out, well then, it has run out. All the same we cannot leave everything to the good Lord and make him our personal security guard.'[77] A similar belief in destiny had dominated Heydrich's mind during those days, during which his fighting spirit desperately struggled with death. He had been in the habit of pronouncing that 'Destiny strikes whenever and wherever it will, and there is no defence against it'.[78] His mother, a keen horsewoman, had broken her leg, not attempting daring jumps, but in the larder, and how many pilots had been shot down a dozen times and taken off again with a shrug of the shoulders? He too as a pilot had survived a crash landing and had once had to parachute to safety.

In this kind of belief in predestination, surely, lay an important motive for his carelessness, in combination with his much-flaunted and reckless personal courage and, moreover, that special attitude to sport which has already been described. He thought it was 'unsportsmanlike', or 'bourgeois' 'to be guarded on all sides like one of the "Party grandpas" and to allow his precious life to be protected'.[79] Scorn for life and scorn for death: it was all the same to Heydrich, as his typical reference to 'precious life' makes clear. With the largesse characteristic of an SS-leader he doled out death to his victims by the thousands; but in contrast to so many of his comrades and other leading Nazis he accepted it just as unquestioningly for himself. He often used to repeat with total conviction a question that echoed one of the themes of his Führer's speeches: 'What will it matter later if at a certain time a certain Fräulein Meier ['Miss Smith'] was happy? It is not a question of our own happiness, but whether we reach our goal or not.'[80]

When Heinrich Himmler visited his 'First Lieutenant' (in the phrase used by *The Times*[81]) for the last time at 11 a.m. on 31 May,[82] it was an impressive moment for Heydrich himself and for all those present. Heydrich lectured Himmler on Fate. He quoted from his father's fourth opera, *Amen*, some lines which he had often called to mind:

Yes the world is just a barrel-organ
Played by God himself.
We must all dance to the tune
That just happens to be on the roll.[83]

Chapter 16

TO THE SHADES
OF HEYDRICH

You, Reinhard Heydrich, were truly a good SS-man.

Heinrich Himmler

At daybreak on 4 June the doctors announced Heydrich's death. Despite the previous day's bulletin to the effect that he was improving, that the fever had begun to abate and that he might be over the crisis, he had died of blood-poisoning at 4.30 a.m.[1] Only penicillin might have saved him, but at that time only the British had sufficient quantities of this antibiotic in their possession, and not all the combined might of Heydrich and Himmler could procure a supply.

In the antechamber of the sick-room Heydrich's wife Lina had waited since midnight, with Karl-Hermann Frank and Kurt Daluege. They were informed by Professor Gebhardt and two other doctors that, contrary to the previous day's report, there was no longer any room for hope. The doctors succeeded just once more in bringing him round from his morphine coma. Fully conscious, Heydrich took leave of his wife, who had gone in to his bedside.

How little Heydrich was a political animal at heart is indicated by the complete absence of any reference to his political ambitions in his last words to his wife. No mention of the Reich, of Germany, the Führer, his enemies, the assassins. His words were far removed from all that had made up his life, and they reveal a deep resignation that reduces this restless, ambitious, sharp and cruel spirit at the last to a mere family man. His last concern, his last directive was for his wife and family: 'Go back to Fehmarn.' So ran the last order that Reinhard Heydrich was ever to give.[2]

On the German side the response to Heydrich's death was near-paralysis. Daluege, perplexed and panic-stricken by the fear that the news of Heydrich's death could easily be the signal for a desperate uprising of the Czechs, hoping to pre-empt what seemed to them the inevitable resprisals to come, withheld the news until the evening. The corpse itself was not released until 5 June, but kept in a room in the hospital under constant armed guard.[3]

Heydrich was laid to rest like one of the great rulers of antiquity, like a quasi-divine being to whose fame a temple is erected – and bloody sacrifices offered. A battalion of *Waffen-SS,* together with all the officers of the Security Police and Security Service stationed in Prague and the cadets of Heydrich's own new 'Reich School for the Sipo and the SD' founded the previous year, kept a vigil on the evening of 5 June, with standards and flaming torches, in the courtyard of the hospital. The 'Martyr of Prague', as, with bitter irony, the exiled Germans employed by the BBC in London were soon calling him, was conveyed on a gun-carriage to Prague Castle.[4] The streets through which the ghostly procession was to pass were entirely cleared of civilians, Czechs and Germans alike. Thousands of SS-men lined the route. The 'Black Order' wanted this night to itself.[5]

On the morning of 7 June the body was laid in state in the courtyard of the Hradčany, beneath a gigantic wooden model of the Iron Cross, flanked by pylons bearing flaming bowls. High-ranking officers of the Wehrmacht and the SS provided the Guard of Honour. The black and white flags of the SS flew at half-mast.

From the early hours of morning until the funeral ceremony, tens of thousands of Prague Germans and tens of thousands of Czechs filed in endless columns past the bier; Czech peasants in traditional dress, the women carrying bouquets of flowers; workers, gendarmes.

In the presence of Hácha, the Protectorate government, the German dignitaries and Himmler, Daluege (of all people) gave the first funeral address of the many that were to follow in the next few days.[6] 'Between thought and feeling, with tear-filled eyes and burning hearts and clenched fists', said Daluege, 'in these last few days hundreds of questions and thoughts' about 'this good, proud comrade' had come flooding in. It was as a 'model German', as a 'National Socialist leader and *thinker*' that

Heydrich was being celebrated, as the man 'with the penetrating glance, the confidence of Germanic manhood, the commanding and yet obeisant voice', the man who, in a short time had gained 'the love of *simple* people in this land of Bohemia and Moravia'. 'You have entered the annals of the German Police for all time as a great and shining example. One day your name will stand hewn in stone in the proud Hall of Honour of the SS.'[7] The British press called the occasion 'a gangster funeral in the pompous Chicago-style'.[8]

On the afternoon of 7 June a special train carried the coffin of Reinhard Heydrich from Prague to Berlin, where he lay in state first of all in the Central Security Department of the Reich in the Prinz-Albrecht-Strasse, and from 9 June in the Mosaic Hall of the new Reich Chancellery.

On 9 June, at precisely 3 p.m., began the solemn and bombastic state ceremony in honour of 'the most loyal liegeman of the Führer'.[9] This was beyond a doubt the biggest and most impressive memorial ceremony of the Third Reich since Hindenburg's death. It was attended by all the leading men of the state, the Party and the Wehrmacht, the entire leadership of the SS and the Police, Dr Hácha and the government of the Protectorate. The Berlin Philharmonic Orchestra played the funeral march from Wagner's *Götterdämmerung* (Twilight of the Gods). In a speech of, for him, unusual clarity and openness,[10] Himmler outlined the role of Heydrich in the SD, in the Germanic Order of the SS, and in their personal friendship. 'Irreplaceable' were his 'unique abilities', 'combined with a character of rare purity and an intellect of penetrating logic and clarity'. Loyalty and tenacity were his innate virtues; 'feared by inferior racial types and sub-humans, hated and calumniated by Jews and criminals', he was also 'a man whom at one time many Germans had failed to understand'. 'A gentleman of breeding and bearing', 'a shining example', 'a model of modesty', 'one of the most industrious men in the Reich'. As the creator and founder of the SD and the Security Police, he would always be, for members of these forces 'an ideal always to be emulated, but perhaps never again to be achieved'.

'You, Reinhard Heydrich,' ended Himmler's address, 'were truly a good SS-man. For myself, however, I am privileged to thank you here for your unswerving loyalty and for your wonderful friendship, which was a bond between us in this life, and which death can never put asunder!' It was as though National Socialism were taking leave of its own dream of a human type, realized only in Heydrich, and never to be achieved again.

Perhaps Hitler felt this. 'Obviously moved, he could hardly speak,' recalls a participant at the state ceremony.[11] In contrast to Himmler's long and carefully composed speech, Hitler spoke in a subdued tone, and confined himself to nothing much more than a single sentence.[12] 'He was one of the best National Socialists, one of the strongest defenders of the Reich concept, and one of the greatest adversaries of the enemies of this Reich.' Then he stepped up to the ceremonial cushion held by officers and pinned to it the 'wounded on active service' badge in gold and 'the greatest honour which I can bestow', the highest class of the German Order. Before Heydrich, only Todt had received it, and no-one else was to do so subsequently. As Hitler was leaving the ceremony, he patted almost absent-mindedly the cheeks of the two Heydrich sons and took his leave of Himmler and his intimate circle with a murmured 'Heydrich, he was a man with a heart of iron.' Agitated, he withdrew with Bormann to discuss the consequences of Heydrich's death.[13]

Meanwhile the funeral procession was forming in the Wilhelmstrasse.[14] Orders rang out; at the head of the procession, a General of the *Waffen-SS* led the parade. To the tones of a Beethoven funeral march there advanced three companies of *Waffen-SS*, an Army Company, and a company of green-uniformed regular police. Perched on their vehicles there followed an anti-aircraft company and a Guard of Honour from the Luftwaffe. Then came the wreath-bearers, among them staff of foreign embassies in Berlin, then bearers of the velvet cushions with the insignia of Heydrich's honours.

Pulled by six black horses, the gun-carriage passed along slowly; a huge swastika-flag draped the coffin, upon it the steel helmet and the sword of the man whose martyr-myth had just sprung to life. The escort of honour was led by Himmler; behind him came the Field Marshals, Ministers, Reich Chiefs, State Secretaries, Reich Deputies, *Gauleiters*: among them, too, all those who were privately glad to be rid of the interloping upstart, the much-feared colleague. Bormann, Ribbentrop, Lammers, Frick, Goebbels, Rosenberg . . . In this funeral procession they were wedged in-between the once-feared Heydrich and the closely following formation of officers of the Security Police and SD. The band was now playing the *Marche Funèbre* from the *Eroica*. Among the colourful costumes of folk groups there followed the representatives from the Protectorate, then Wehrmacht Generals, and Admirals, who, a bare decade earlier, had ordered the dismissal from their service of Naval First Lieutenant

Heydrich for 'unworthy conduct'. The SS brought up the rear of the procession. The Veterans' Cemetery, its layout designed by Frederick the Great, was the destination. Heydrich was buried next to Tauentzien, near Scharnhorst, not far from Richthofen, Udet, Todt and Reichenau.

It was clear that the Nazis were presenting Heydrich to the public as one of the greatest of Germans, as a combination of 'Prussian' disciplinarian and National Socialist revolutionary. The Heydrich cult faithfully followed these lines right up to the last days of the Third Reich. 'One of the most powerful political figures of the Great German Reich' is his encomium from the pen of a writer seeking to create the official version of history; 'a man with a capacity and a vocation for great deeds', writes one historian from the Central Security Department of the Reich;[15] while the SS-poet, Wolff, sings his praise in a sonnet as 'wolf leader' among 'the keen wolf-pack'.[16]

He was celebrated as SS-man and pilot, as sportsman and National Socialist, as supreme police commander and as statesman, as 'child of music' and as soldier. He was to be the ideal for later generations to strive after.

On the day of his death Adolf Hitler bestowed on a regiment serving at the Eastern Front, the SS-Infantry-Standard No. 6, the name and the shoulder-badge 'Reinhard Heydrich'.[17] The *Germanische Leithefte* devoted a special number to him in German, Dutch-Flemish, and Danish editions, and found that the text of a rune-stone of the year 1202 commemorating the Norwegian King Sverrit was totally appropriate to Heydrich:

Here he lies who was the ornament of kings, the pillar of faith, courage and honour, example and paragon, invincible heroic spirit, defender of the Fatherland, guardian of the maternal heritage, the champion of boldness, the terror of his foes, his people's fame and glory.[18]

From now on, every recruit to the SS was to learn in his 'ideological training' that 'under the leadership of SS-*Obergruppenführer* Heydrich, killed by craven assassins while serving Europe and the Reich', the SD had become the 'infallible conscience of the National Socialist world-view'.[19]

In the Protectorate of Bohemia and Moravia itself a Special Issue postage stamp appeared bearing a reproduction of Heydrich's death-mask and carrying the highest surcharge in German postal history.[20] A foundation for the advancement of culture and folklore, a concept initiated by Heydrich some months before his death, was now given shape in his honour as the 'Reinhard-Heydrich-Foundation'.[21] The chairman of a group of German industrialists from Heydrich's close circle of acquaintances held up Heydrich, whom he called a man 'whom it was not always very easy to get on with in ordinary contact', as an ideal, for he had 'maintained the exhausting daily struggle against all kinds of enemies of the Reich'.[22] His often controversial procedures had been necessary in order to deflect dangers away from the German people. Behind all these words of praise there lay, of course, an unmistakable propagandist intention, and there was a degree of opportunism among the writers and speakers quoted; but the tenor remained basically consistent even among intimates. After the state ceremony, in a secret speech to SS-Lieutenant-Generals, Himmler said of the assassination: 'The seriousness of this blow is clear to all of you.'[23]

One of Himmler's favourite topics in the next few weeks was the form to be taken by the monument for Heydrich's grave. Already, at the site of the assassination, on that hairpin bend in Holešovice, a memorial had been placed bearing a bust of the Protector, guarded day and night by two SS-men; and Professor Franz Rotter had made the death-mask, a bronze casting of which hung in Himmler's office for a long time. In the course of June and July there was a lively exchange of letters and memoranda between Himmler, Wolff, Bormann and others to decide on the execution of a 'monument for all time'. The centrepiece of the memorial was to be a boulder from the shore at Fehmarn. Professor Wilhelm Kreis, 'Superintendent of military cemeteries' and creator of the plans for Hitler's intended 'citadels of the dead' in the East, was to design it, but the SS and not the Party was to be responsible for its upkeep.[24]

The memorial had been erected. What came now were the sacrifices. The beginning was a reception by Hitler at 6 p.m., immediately after the state memorial ceremony, for President Hácha and the government of the Protectorate, as well as its Berlin Ambassador Chvalkovský, and in the presence of Bormann, Lammers, Himmler, Sepp Dietrich, Daluege and Frank. Hácha once again condemned the assassination 'from the depths of his heart' and declared among other things that he 'would never have believed the British capable of stooping to such methods'.[25] The Germans at the reception bridled at the reference to the British, and soon Hitler began to speak, at first quietly and slowly, then becoming louder and more agitated. He was 'not going to accept further serious damage to the interests of the Reich in the Protectorate'. There was no attempt to disguise his threats as he went on to say that he had already re-settled several million Germans. He had already begun to move the Germans of the South Tyrol out of Italy, he had re-settled the Russian-German colonies, and he might yet have to bring the German populations out of Hungary and Rumania. 'Nothing could prevent me from evacuating a few million Czechs, if they did not care to coexist peacefully.' If the Czechs did not reform, if Heydrich's assassins were not found or handed over, then he would have to assume that the Czech people did not want to live in peace in their present homeland. Then he would have to assume that the Czech people were hostile to the Reich. 'In that case, gentlemen,' Hitler concluded, 'let it be absolutely clear to you that I shall resort to extreme measures. Every compromise solution will be ruled out.'[26]

According to Hitler's later comments, the Czechs were completely shattered by this announcement.[27] They requested permission to relay at least some of Hitler's pronouncements for the benefit of the Czech public. Hitler agreed to a 'public campaign of enlightenment' by the government. He made this concession because, he said, he regarded the Czechs as 'intelligent and industrious workers' and because the restoration of stability in the Bohemian and Moravian area, with its important German armaments industry, was vital to him. That Hitler was prepared to put his threats into effect was made clear to the gentlemen from the Protectorate at the end of the reception, during a walk in the garden, by Minister of State Meissner. In response to the Czechs' anxious questioning, he assured them that Hitler's 'references to the possible evacuation of the Czechs were, if he knew Hitler, the Führer's last words on the subject'.[28]

In a confidential report on morale in the Protectorate and on reactions to the reception of the Czech government by Hitler and its participation in the state memorial ceremony for Heydrich, the Prague SD stated that the population of the Protectorate had 'taken a lively interest in this fact and seen it as the concession of further political autonomy', while the Germans in Bohemia and Moravia were now hoping 'for the most savage measures at last'.[29]

That such measures were *expected* on all sides is beyond doubt. They were, after all, inherent in the conception of the assassination. Goebbels had noted in his diary on the day of the attack that such an assassination was likely to attract imitators 'if we did not employ the most brutal methods'.[30] Hitler's first reaction was the same. The extremely clumsy handling of the assassination in Allied public life seemed to vindicate this view. For example, Gerbrandy, Prime Minister of the Dutch government-in-exile in London, gave a speech on 5 June to a gathering of Czech exiles at the Conway Hall in London, in which he threatened 'Heydrich was the first, but he will not by any means be the last.'[31] Baldur von Schirach declared that he now intended to clear Vienna of Czechs as soon as he had cleared it of Jews, and he demanded 'a lightning surprise air attack on some historic site in England' and that this be explicitly announced as 'an act of vengeance for Heydrich'.[32] But when the first few days following the assassination had produced not a single clue for the Gestapo as to the identity of the killers, it was certainly suspected by the Czechs under German rule that they would themselves have to bear the full brunt of German ferocity in the end. After Heydrich's death, there was very little room for doubt on this score.

Some efforts were now made to appease the vengeful Hitler. It is reported that he took the opportunity to mock the bishops of Bohemia and Moravia, who, after the death of the Reich Protector, had sought permission to ring a peal of bells in mourning for Heydrich and to hold a requiem mass for him. He had indicated to these gentlemen, however, that it would have been better 'to have prayed at the right time for the preservation of the Reich Protector's life'.[33] On the other hand, Propaganda-Minister Moravec repeatedly painted in vivid colours on the radio the dangers confronting the Czechs. 'I don't know if you are aware of what happened recently in France when a ordinary German non-commissioned officer was murdered in a certain town and the murderer could not be traced.' Ten French civilians had been shot for the death of one German soldier. 'What can these criminals have been thinking of when they carried out the assassination of the highest representative of the Greater German Reich on Czech soil? Just calculate a little what the Czech people can expect if the killers are not found!'[34]

The German and Czech press in the Protectorate were unanimous in their comment that it must be clear to everyone that the Reich was powerful enough 'to suppress and destroy within a few days any pocket of resistance whatsoever in Central Europe'. It was now up to the Czech people themselves, so long as Heydrich's murderers were still at large, 'to save themselves from their fate, which might in the very near future become closely comparable to the fate of Poland'.[35] Comparisons from world history were pressed into service: the generous behaviour of Alexander the Great after his conquest of the Greeks was recalled, a generosity which had nonetheless turned to implacable harshness when the Thebans revolted during the campaign against the Persians. Alexander had ruthlessly razed Thebes to the ground, including the house of the poet Pindar, and had sold the entire population into slavery, 'whereupon the democratic wire-pullers had crept back into their holes or, like Demosthenes, committed suicide, so that peace reigned in Greece for many years'. The lesson for the present was spelled out: 'in war, peace in the hinterland is as important as discipline at the front'.[36]

Meanwhile, Hitler was preparing his own 'Theban solution'. His Thebes was Lidice, a small mining community in the district of Kladno. At 7.45 p.m., barely an hour after the reception of the Czech delegation, Frank instructed the Commander of the Security Police and the SD in Prague by telephone from Berlin that, following a decision made at the Führer-Conference, the village of Lidice was to be dealt with on that same day in the following manner:

1 All adult male inhabitants are to be shot;
2 All females are to be evacuated to a concentration camp;
3 The children are to be collected together; if capable of Germanization, they are to be delivered to SS-families in the Reich, and the rest are to undergo a different education;
4 The place is to be burnt down and razed to the ground.[37]

Böhme set off for Kladno with Geschke to direct the operation, together with the head of the Gestapo branch there, Wiesmann.[38] The Kladno regular police surrounded the village and allowed inhabitants returning from work to enter the place, but no-one to come out. During late evening, by which time an Army detachment had taken over the roadblocks, the police moved into the village. Women and children were taken away in lorries and assembled in the gymnasium of the Czech Technical High School in Kladno. 'After the evacuation of the women and children', said Böhme in his later official report, '170 adult males were shot by an execution-squad of one officer, two NCOs and twenty men.'[39] Eleven men returning late at night from their night-shift, and fifteen relatives of Czech legionnaires serving in England, already under arrest, were also shot, so that 199 persons were directly murdered. 184 women were deported to the concentration camp for females, Ravensbrück in Mecklenburg; seven women went to the police prison in Terezín, and four, who were pregnant, were taken to a Prague hospital. Of the deported women, only 143 returned after the war. Of the ninety-eight children of the village ninety were taken via Terezín and Łódź to the Gneisenau concentration camp; eight were found worthy of 'Germanizing' and adopted by German families. Only sixteen of the children could be traced after the war.

The village itself was set on fire the same night, and the ruins were blown up. The Reich National Labour Service was for months engaged in 'razing the last vestiges to the ground'. It is not known who was the originator of the plan of destruction. It is almost certain not to have been Karl-Hermann Frank, who had steadfastly rejected collective measures.[40] It must have been some other participant in the Führer-Conference, most likely of all Hitler, Bormann or Daluege. The answer to the question of why Lidice specifically was chosen as the scapegoat, also points to Daluege. The widespread assumption that any village would have been good enough for the German authorities in order to make an example is not satisfactory. For after Lidice, on 24 June, the hamlet of Ležáky was also destroyed and all adult inhabitants shot because the radio-operator Bartoš had been seized there, together with his radio equipment, and because two contact-points for Czech-exile agents dropping by parachute had been discovered.[41] Attention had not been directed at Lidice by pure chance. In a report to the Protectorate Ministry of the Interior the action was described as based on 'impeccable evidence' that 'the population of Lidice . . . had aided and abetted the elements in question'. Further evidence of action hostile to the Reich was adduced, namely 'finds of anti-state leaflets, caches of arms and weapons, an illegal transmitter, and hoarded goods in enormous quantities'.[42] In Daluege's official report to Berlin, apart from the two contact-points for parachuted agents in Ležáky and forty-one others, there is mention of six in Lidice.[43] It seems that interrogation by the Gestapo did indeed reveal that Pavelka, the first captured parachute-agent sent out from London, had been given addresses in Lidice for his first contacts in Bohemia. Two young men from the village, Stříbrný and Horák, were serving in the Czech brigade in England and could have supplied the Czech Secret Service with addresses which were known or suspected to be useful to Czech agents who were sent out. Whether these contacts were ever used is doubtful. In any case, following a tip-off from a Czech source, the

Gestapo had combed through the village for the first time on 4 June and arrested the two families concerned.[44]

Apart from the crime against international law and the senselessness of such collective penal measures, no final *proof* seems to have been found on the German side to support the widespread hypothesis that Heydrich's attackers had been sheltered in Lidice. This remained pure conjecture. Hitler wanted to offer up a bloody act of vengeance to the shades of Reinhard Heydrich, and from his knowledge of Gestapo investigations Daluege would have suggested the village of Lidice as eminently suitable for the purpose. Without waiting for the capture of the assassins, perhaps indeed in order to bring it about, the First National Socialist responded with an overkill-reaction which made not only the Czechs the losers, but Reinhard Heydrich himself. Although he had not batted an eyelid at the Führer's previous extermination commands, and although he had on his conscience infinitely more victims than those sacrificed at Lidice, yet in the case of Bohemia and Moravia he had decided on a course of graduated, selective intimidation, and had completely renounced the blind terror applied in Poland, in the Soviet Union and in the Balkans. Because this more subtle course was bringing him success, he was killed. At Lidice, posthumously, he lost his last battle. For while he had lulled the will of the Czech masses to resistance, Lidice and Ležáky revived it.

Because of the scale of the terror instigated by his successors, this will to resist did not immediately take an active form, any more than was previously the case, but it remained latent; it built up a head of emotion which in 1945, after the withdrawal of German oppression and the end of German power, was worked off explosively in a blood-bath among Bohemian Germans. Whereas Heydrich had been well on the way to making allies of the greater part of the Czech population, Lidice turned these potential allies into enemies who had to be suppressed time and again.

For the outside world, because of the obvious lack of connection between deed and reprisal, Lidice was seen as one of the cruellest atrocities committed by Germans during the Second World War. It is true that there were in Russia numerous and greater Lidices, whose names have not even been recorded. On the Allied side, however, the small mining community became synonymous with the height of German ferocity, perhaps also because the Allied architects of the assassination had taken into account, or even expected and hoped for, something like this act of destruction. 'A barbaric revenge for Heydrich', said *The Times* in London, incidentally giving the extermination operation a different quantitative, if not moral, dimension by transforming a village of 500 into a 'locality of 12,000 inhabitants'.[45]

But the dead of Lidice were for Hitler and Himmler not sufficient sacrifice to the name of Heydrich. In his honour a campaign of plunder was put in motion, called *Aktion Reinhard*,[46] with the aim of collecting jewellery and valuables, including wrenched-out gold teeth, from the property of deported Jews. In Ravensbrück concentration camp the circumstances of Heydrich's death gave the final impetus to a programme of so-called 'humane experiments' with Sulfonamides.[47] The deporting of Jews was accelerated everywhere, especially deportations from the so-called 'old-age ghetto' in Terezín to the extermination camps in the East; but also from the Reich itself, from Berlin in particular.[48] The background of the assassination was not yet clear, wrote Goebbels, but 'in any event we are holding the Jews to account. I am ordering the arrest of 500 Berlin Jews which I had been planning, and I am informing the Jewish community-leaders that for every Jewish assassination and for every attempt at revolt on the part of Jews, 100 or 150 Jews in our hands will be shot.' In the wake of the Heydrich assassination, a large number of convicted Jews were shot in Sachsenhausen. 'The more of this filth that is eliminated, the better for the security of the Reich.'[49]

In the Protectorate itself, in the aftermath of the persecution and the revenge measures of 28 May to 1 September, 3188 Czechs had been arrested and 1357 had been sentenced to death by summary courts in Prague and Brno. The charges included 'illegal possession of arms', 'failure to report evidence to the police', 'false denunciation', and, in 477 cases, 'approval of the assassination'.[50] Czechs previously sentenced to death and now held in concentration camps, whose execution had been postponed, sometimes even by Heydrich's own intercession, were now shot. Among them was former Prime Minister General Eliáš. The terror was to be extended and stepped up to gigantic proportions: even after the promulgation of the news about the massacre at Lidice, and despite the fact that, following denunciations, the Gestapo were prosecuting over 1000 individuals, on 15 June Hitler ordered Frank, via Himmler, to shoot 30,000 politically suspect Czechs.[51] But the order became redundant immediately, for the very next day, 16 June, the Czech Karel Čurda presented himself at noon at Police HQ in Prague and asked for access to 'a gentleman in authority'.[52] It was not until he had explained to the officer on duty that he wanted to make an official statement concerning the search for Heydrich's murderers, that he was allowed to pass. During the subsequent examination the following emerged: this former Corporal of the Czech Army had, like Gabčík and Kubiš, been sent out from England to make a parachute-drop over Bohemia. After the break-up of his group following the attack, he had sought refuge in his mother's house in a village in southern Bohemia. From hiding he had followed the reprisals of the Gestapo, he had heard and read about the reward, first of all of ten, then of twenty million crowns. He had heard of the destruction of Lidice, which was supposed to have given assistance to parachuted agents, and he knew that an amnesty was being offered until 18 June to all informants, including parachute agents. As he admitted after the war, he was overwhelmed by greed and fear, and he made his way to Prague. One of the two briefcases found at the scene of the crime and reproduced on all the 'wanted' posters and in all the newspapers, had confirmed that it was one of the comrades from his group who had thrown the grenade. It was Josef Gabčík. Since 'Anthropoid' had involved only two men, he was able to give the name of the other attacker as Jan Kubiš.

Even Čurda could not betray the whereabouts of the two killers. But in the course of questioning he remembered that in a Prague suburb a re-sistance worker called Adolf Moravec had kept agents in hiding after their landing. This name was already on Gestapo files. Moravec was arrested, with his son Ata and his wife. While the wife was able to commit suicide immediately after arrest, when an official let her visit the lavatory, the father and the son were cross-questioned under the most severe torture in the cellar of the Petschek Palace. The expert eye of the investigators soon realized that nothing was to be expected from the father, but that the son on the other hand was the weak link in the chain. He broke down that same night. His statements led to the hiding-place in the Orthodox Church of SS Cyril and Method in Ressel Street in Prague, in whose crypt and loft the assassins and five other agents were being hidden by the priests.[53]

On the morning of 18 June the church was surrounded. The SS em-ployed altogether a force of nineteen officers and 740 NCOs and men, in order to create a double cordon, to protect the plain clothes members of the SD and to launch the actual attack upon the church.[54] After a battle lasting two hours, towards 7 a.m. the three agents who had taken cover in the upper part of the nave were outgunned and captured, one dead, two of them alive but badly wounded. They died soon after their capture. A priest from the church, who had been looking after the agents during the previous fortnight, was forced, using a light-shaft to communicate with the crypt, to urge the four remaining defenders to give themselves up. The answer was 'No', accompanied by shots. Thereupon tear-gas was piped into the cellar, and the Prague Fire Brigade flooded it with water pumped up from the Moldau. Nonetheless, the SS did not succeed in taking even one of the Czech fugitives alive. All four either died fighting or had kept a last bullet for themselves. Čurda identified the bodies laid out in a row on the stone flags of the church. Among them were Gabčík and Kubiš.

Despite the fact that the case had now been cleared up the Gestapo did not rest for a moment until they were on the trail of the last 'accomplices'. Among them were the two priests, Petřek and Čikl, who had kept the assassins hidden, the churchwarden of the Czech Orthodox Church in Prague, Jan Sonnevend, and his Bishop, Gorazd.[55] An orgy of death and vengeance had accompanied Reinhard Heydrich's exit from the stage of world history.

Chapter 17

A LIFE SUMMED UP

Most of them see their ruin before their very eyes; but they carry on, nonetheless!

Reinhard Heydrich on the opponents of the regime, under observation by his Security Service

It is difficult to sum up this life. The superficial view of the literature of the post-war years, concerned with 'coming to terms with the past', uniformly saw Reinhard Tristan Eugen Heydrich as the hangman-figure of the Third Reich. Eugen Kogon could attribute to him the invention of the concentration camps. Eye-witnesses and casual observers picked out such highly readable details as this example from Jacob Burckhardt: 'pre-Raphaelite, lily-like hands, as though made for protracted strangling'. Echoing Allied propaganda – which called him 'Heydrich the Butcher' – he was credited with sadistic cruelty. More perceptive observers, however, noticed the contradiction between this crude impression and many historical details: the divergence from the cool, indeed cautious and, for long periods at a time – if we compare him to the ideological fanatics of the Nazi movement – even moderate traits which reveal a completely different Heydrich.

The writer Joachim Fest erected for himself a very narrow bridge via which he hoped to cross the chasm. For him Heydrich was a thoroughly divided personality, 'a prey to secret anxieties and constantly plagued by tensions, bitterness and self-hate'.[1] But even this little bridge could only hold up if one accepted the support for it provided by the legend of the divided hero's alleged Jewish ancestry. But these tales, nothing but gossip for the most part, have now been banished to the realm of fiction. The Master of all Security was not at all 'stained with an irredeemable blemish and in a condition of mortal sin'. He had no Jewish forbears to be hidden from his superiors, and therefore, he was not, on account of such a blot on his racial purity, either depressive or vulnerable to blackmail, as alleged by Felix Kersten, so often quoted by German contemporary historians, but so unreliable as a historian himself.[2]

The opposite view inescapably presents itself as the summing-up of his life: far from being afflicted by an 'irredeemable blemish', Heydrich became identical with the image that National Socialism liked to draw of itself. He had that impressive charismatic quality which was most admired by National Socialists. His external appearance helped greatly, for, had National Socialism looked into a mirror, Reinhard Heydrich would have been looking back out of it. At the centre of the historical vision of an enclosed racially pure homeland upon which the Nazi Utopia of the future was constructed was the quintessence of a human prototype whose ex-ternal features were best described by Hans F K Günther, the race theorist of the Third Reich, as blond and tall, with a long head and narrow features, 'with pronounced chin, thin nose with a high bridge, soft fair hair, light eyes set well back and a pink and white complexion'. The very small degree of correspondence between this ideal and the leading Nazis led to some curious twists in the media of the Third Reich. Popular wit quickly and accurately epitomized the state of affairs in the joke: 'As blond as Hitler, as tall as Goebbels, as slim as Göring and a good drinker like Ley.'

Heydrich was an exception. The SS-newspaper *Das Schwarze Korps* (The Black Order) celebrated him in an obituary of June 1942 as 'a man who was a perfect whole': 'Even in his outer appearance he corresponded to the popular conception of an SS-man.'[3] Heydrich was what the ideal prescribed: tall, fair-skinned and blond; exceptionally successful as an athlete, he combined high intelligence 'with that steely quality which was a sign of a special racial birthright'.[4] For all their criticism of certain prickly or repugnant traits in their superior, his former colleagues were unanimous in their verdict on the way he conducted his life. It corresponded in every way to the ideals of the National Socialist paragon. 'Whatever he de-manded from his men', summarized the historian of the SD, Spengler, 'by way of effort, toughness and stamina, untiring pursuit of perfection, cleanliness and simplicity in their private lives, Heydrich had not only demanded of himself but already put into effect as a perfect example.'[5]

The magical coincidence of the general and the individual, of which Burckhardt speaks, was expressed even more accurately in his inner qualities than in his appearance. Here was to be found what Ernst Nolte felt was missing from most of the fascist movements of the period: all the historical and structural elements of fascism found their counterpart in ex-Naval Lieutenant Heydrich. As early as 1922, a perceptive critic of Italian fascism, Giovanni Zibordi, in his study *Critica Socialista del fascismo*, established that fascism was primarily 'a violent revolution of *déclassé* soldiers'.[6] This hypothesis applied better to Heydrich than to any other leading Nazi. It was the loss of his officer's uniform and his military career alone which, after an initial refusal and long hesitation, in the end made Heydrich conceive of National Socialism and the SS as his salvation, the path to self-fulfilment for a demoted soldier.

It was not least Heydrich's frustrated love of soldiering, which he could indulge within National Socialism, that led to the high degree of militarization of Heydrich's gigantic police machine, beginning with the SD and ending with the wartime Central Security Department of the Reich. One is forcefully reminded of Mussolini's nostalgia for Army life, with its clear orders and its solid, hierarchical world. '*That* was a good life. I'll abdicate, I'll abdicate. Who will give me orders?'[7] It was no accident that Heydrich achieved the high point of his power not in peacetime, but in the middle of war. 'War was its proper climate,' said Otto-Ernst Schüddekopf of fascism, and the remark is just as appropriate to Heydrich.[8] The structure and domestic policy of all fascist states were comprehensively geared to the capacity to wage and survive a war. In this sense, fascism has been rightly called a permanent state of emergency. The condition of the nation was conceived of as that of permanent crisis. This had obvious results in domestic and policing policies. The concept of a preventive police force, able to nip in the bud all kinds of developments hostile to the state, whether criminal or political in nature, was developed by Heydrich to perfection and translated into action.

Out of the social breakdown of the German bourgeoisie after defeat in the Great War, Heydrich had slid into Himmler's Security Service. He gathered around him, as Heinz Höhne has put it, in his comprehensive monograph on the SS, 'the most intelligent men whose services National Socialism was ever able to recruit . . . They were the rearguard of a bourgeoisie in whose pre-war scheme of values they were no longer able to believe.'⁹ In the place of the Weimar Republic, which for them and for Heydrich quickly became synonymous with the decline of national greatness, of German power and theirs along with it, they wanted to substitute a system to make Germany once more the Fatherland of the future, by dint of personal renunciation, an overwhelming sense of national duty, personal commitment and exceptional effort.

The value-system of the *déclassé* bourgeois was abandoned in the process, and without too much regret. In Heydrich's case this attitude was reinforced by the conventionally negative approach to politics of the average officer, his formal abstention from politics being completely reconcilable with an anti-democratic mentality. In the early years of his SS career, Heydrich conformed closely to this pattern of the ostensibly a-political officer of General Seeckt's Army of the Weimar Republic. He created a unique amalgam out of the few, mostly romantic-historical, fragments of ideology he found ready-made in the SS, and the principle of efficiency which he followed both in his private and his official life and which was somewhat similar to the outlook of today's managerial technocracy, thinking of itself as devoid of values. In his attitude there is some anticipation of the spirit of our own time. It is precisely this which creates for our generation that mixture of historical unease and fascination which is associated with Heydrich today.

In a typically fascist manner Heydrich appropriated the left-wing revolutionary methods and the technology of the machine age for the purposes of revolution and the National Socialist Reich, that curious combination of revolution and reaction, as the Italian author G A Borgese wrote from his American exile in 1938.¹⁰ As so often in fascism, with Heydrich a right-wing mentality went hand-in-hand with the highest technical perfection, with modern know-how. This is part of the reason for the meteoric rise of Heydrich and with him of Himmler, in the Third Reich. After a tough initial phase, when he was fobbed off with junior positions, Heydrich's turning-point came, so to speak, with the unreserved embracing of modernity. During the years when the Nazi state was being consolidated, characterized by the events surrounding the 'Röhm Putsch', Heydrich steered his craft on to the right course. From then on it sailed by itself into harbour, for it was identical with the general direction of German fascism, implicit in the system, so to speak. In contrast to the stocky hothead Röhm, in contrast to the SA, which, as Heydrich mockingly objected, dissipated itself 'in senseless, undirected, individual acts of illegality', the team of Heydrich and Himmler quietly occupied the most vital nerve-centres of police and administration.[11] With his consistent technocratic-administrative line, Heydrich, quietly working away in the background, was a revolutionary in a much more modern sense than Röhm, who made a fetish of revolution. Heydrich understood that a revolution, in a highly developed Central European industrial state in the middle of the twentieth century, was solely a matter of occupying the structures. Anyone who could capture them would have power. It was the political opponents of National Socialism who first experienced the effects of Heydrich's policy, then Röhm and the SA, and finally other National Socialists like the Reich Minister of the Interior, Frick, whose position – though he was nominally Heydrich's superior – was reduced to little more than a thin façade, while the structures had long since been built into Heydrich's system of power.

However true it was, then, that this or that element of the Nazi world-view, within the framework of which Heydrich had to carry out his policies, stemmed from the nineteenth century, he himself was deeply wedded to the twentieth century and to the spirit of the technological age: indeed, he was its respresentative. He had no roots in the past. He embodied what Karl Kraus said of fascism in 1933, the 'coexistence of everything which already and no longer exists'. With cold logic he represented a Futurism of the past, and in this respect too he was permeated with the history-creating substance of fascism. There was no doubt: of all the leading National Socialists, Heydrich at least lived up to his ideological identity.

This raises the question of where Heydrich's roots were if they were not in the past. Clearly he was not at home with any of the various world-views produced by the Judeo-Christian world. Religious or divine revelation remained a closed book to him, despite, or perhaps because of, his bigoted upbringing in an atmosphere of inauthentic belief, commonly found in convert families. This upbringing and background ensured that during the 1920s, he felt no attraction to Marxism as a surrogate religion (although many of the aspects which people in the West today find repellent might otherwise have appealed to him). And when he came to know it better, in the Security Service after 1933, he rejected it on intellectual grounds. Like Mussolini after his election defeat in 1919, he openly despised all varieties of 'Christianities' and all creeds from Moses and Christ to Marx, pouring scorn upon all shades of political conviction, be they white, red or black, and soon having cause to frown over the 'brown' charlatans on his own side. He taught his SD-officers that encyclicals these days were issued from two Vaticans, the Roman one and the one in Moscow. 'We are the heretics of both these religions.' In later years he was not only anti-clerical, but anti-Christian. *Paganus erat:* he was a heathen.

With him and many other fascists, a human type had achieved power and political influence without ever knowing the conventional basic loyalties of the Western world, having consciously rejected, in its search for new tenets, those which the whole century had questioned: the classical humanity of antiquity, of the Judeo-Christian West and of the liberal democracy of the last few centuries. The poet Heimito von Doderer, too, pointed out after 1945 that it had not yet been clearly enough recognized that this rejection of previous European tradition, this denial of the happiness of the individual as the highest aim, demanded an outlook 'which had previously been applied only to the animal kingdom'. By this he meant the rise of the 'biological age', of 'heroic vitalism', to which the SS itself was such an eloquent signpost. The individual ceased to be the focus of interest and became instead subject to racial or national calculations which redefined the principle of *raison d'état*. Heydrich throughout his life was never 'pious', never seeking the unknown God who would give direction to his vitality. The chief driving forces of life, in D H Lawrence's sense, passion and the will to power, were Heydrich's law. The combination of a vital animal following its instincts with an ice-cold logic and an invincible will to power, were the strands which made up the driving force of Heydrich's not always consistent, often many-layered and rather fractured world-view. A certain racial arrogance, death-symbolism and reverence for war were native to him. Altogether his outlook contained the thoughts of modern life-philosophy from Bergson to Klages, of the poetic world-view of D H Lawrence and Friedrich Nietzsche.

This quality marked him out for certain success in the SS. Their catechism had merged biological-vitalistic thought, glorification of war and the sober doctrine of *raison d'état* in what was 'basically a dynamic force without doctrines, a technology of ruling', as Höhne said of the SS.[12] Heydrich's constant restlessness, his tendency to make the tempestuous thrust forward, the ambitious will to succeed which could tolerate no-one, no better man over him (whether in fencing, the decathlon, or the front-line fighter-plane sorties which no-one had asked him to fly), his wily manoeuvres in the Intelligence Service – all of this proves that it was not the

Nazi programme that was decisive for him, neither a hybrid nor a stringent doctrine, but the *élan vital* of modern vitalist philosophy, of activism, and finally the unreflecting use of violence.

At the same time, it is highly unlikely that Heydrich had ever in his life read the philosophers who represented this current of thought, neither Bergson nor Georges Sorel. But that was typical: his quality lay in action, not in reading. Allied to this was a carelessness bordering on negligence and unreflectingly cutting across the boundaries of good and evil, just like the ideal described by the Italian fascist Pilot Officer De Pinedo in 1928: 'a superior contempt for danger in one's heart'.[13] In the end it cost Heydrich his life, when he drove constantly without an escort in an open car as the Protector of Bohemia and Moravia. A single trait of character brought the Waterloo of the refined and idolized system of state security erected by Heydrich himself. The sensation of invincibility, says Otto-Ernst Schüddekopf, is an essential element of fascism.[14]

Another of his decisive driving-forces was in no way contradictory to this: the anxiety in the face of life, conjoined in Heydrich with a specific fear for the future. 'If we do not do it, who will? We *must* do it!' These fears, students of fascism suggest, are then transformed into violence and terror against all genuine or suspected opponents.[15] The repressed themselves become repressors, the tortured become the torturers. The myth of force became, then, the substitute for those values which were no longer believed in. Thus arose the glorification of main force, which appealed to atavistic impulses in the masses as well as in the romantic intellectuals of Heydrich's SD. For Heydrich, power in itself became the new ethical norm, became the obligatory pursuit of a new élite, who were to convert the dream of the Reich into a lasting reality. The healing notion of the future Reich could alone reliably overcome fears for life and the future. This aim demanded in Heydrich's view an 'unprecedented' harshness ('unprecedented' was his favourite word). Carl Jacob Burckhardt supplies evidence, after long conversations with Heydrich, that he himself did not always command the harshness he preached, and that, despite the 'steely' quality of which he liked to boast, his personality tended more to the sensitive than the stoic pole. 'Sharp, and yet also delicate and morbid' was the first impression Heydrich had made upon Burckhardt, who, as League of Nations Commissioner, had sought from Heydrich a permit to visit the German concentration camps, and had obtained it after some to-ing and fro-ing. He reports that during the discussion about political prisoners in the concentration camps Heydrich had planted himself in front of Burckhardt and, 'looking over my left shoulder' had said, 'in a choking voice': 'They think we're bloodhounds abroad, don't they?' And then: 'It's almost too hard for the individual, but we must be as hard as granite, otherwise the work of our Führer will fail. Much later we will be thanked for what we have taken upon ourselves.'[16]

This obligation to be hard was an essential element of that elite to which Heydrich belonged. In its view of itself it was an elite in two senses: an elite of birth by virtue of its racial selection, and an elite of function by virtue of its claims to achievement, ability and discipline. Heydrich himself had demanded of the true SS-man in *Die Wandlungen unseres Kampfes* (The Fortunes of our Struggle) that he be best in all spheres. The new order of the Third Reich, which Heydrich was prepared to consolidate and secure, was to reflect the spirit of this elitist principle in its internal construction and in its representatives. This led Heydrich to a low esteem for, and even a very negative attitude to, the Party itself, within which, once power had been achieved, primitive power-lust and time-serving proliferated. The 'gilded peacock' type above all became the object of his intense dislike, far more than all the political opponents of the new system. His hatred was reserved in particular for *Gauleiters* Wagner and Mutschmann; Bormann was likewise suspect. Only the peculiar construction of the Führer-state enforced, at least partially, a close cooperation between factions. All the greater then was the technocrat Heydrich's attraction towards those technical officials who had only a thin veneer of Nazi ideology, despite the key positions in the National Socialist state which their expertise commanded. This was particularly true of the State Secretary at the Ministry of Agriculture, Herbert Backe, whose cool rationalism moderated the extravaganzas of his boss, Walter Darré, and who secured the food supply to the Reich, even under the most difficult conditions, by the sheer excellence of his planning and administration. Heydrich was a friend of his, and on many occasions they exchanged complaints about the ideological fads of their respective superiors, Darré and Himmler.[17]

His respect was extended also to Hitler's Armaments Minister, Albert Speer, of whom Heydrich would often say, 'He's good, he knows what he's doing!' The compliment was returned. Speer recalled his first conversation with Heydrich, who had, for Speer, been preceded by a 'reputation for cruelty and unpredictability'. But Speer was pleasantly surprised. The odium connected with Heydrich's name had not in any way been borne out by the discussion. Heydrich had been 'very polite, not at all arrogant in his manner, and above all very self-assured and practical'. It was by the latter quality above all that Speer was impressed.

> There was no comparison with all those *Gauleiters* and other potentates I had had to deal with, who indulged in their hobby-horses, plans that were technically or architecturally impossible, perhaps an old dream from their youth or their wives' fantasies, which they obstinately stuck to . . . By contrast, Heydrich was uncomplicated, he had only a few objections to my suggestions, all of which showed his sensible approach to the problem. If his objections were impractical for technical reasons, he was prepared to be convinced of this instantly.[18]

Heydrich looked up to Speer's predecessor in office, too; the brilliant master-builder, organizer and Armaments Minister Dr Fritz Todt. Todt's ability and achievements were evoked as a model in many a conversation. 'This was the first time', confirmed Heydrich's widow, 'that I had known him give his total recognition to anyone, for their ability, restraint and modesty. For him Dr Fritz Todt was a perfect example of the National Socialist human type.'[19] Todt was killed in an air crash at the beginning of 1942. Posthumously he received from Hitler the German Order First Class, especially created for him. When, barely half a year later, Heydrich followed this highly respected technical administrator to his death, he was, uniquely, honoured with the same Order. Clearly Hitler rated them both on the same level.

It has been rightly stressed by the specialists in this field that trouble was in store for Hitler from the younger members of the SS, who were essentially of the same mind as Heydrich.[20] The gulf opening up between the sober, rational, technocratic coolness of Heydrich and his group of intellectuals in the SD on the one hand, and the everlastingly bragging and resentful Party bigwigs on the other; between the unideological but thoroughly professional policemen of the Security Police and the fanatical Teutonicizing prophets; between sheer intellect and sheer prejudice – this widening rift was bridged only by the outbreak and the course of the war, which was the only reason it never became a decisive historical factor.

The whole quality of Heydrich lay in the way he went about solving the Czech problem in the autumn of 1941, when this problem had become insoluble for everybody else. The kind of xenophobia or hatred of the Slavs, the contempt for the Czechs, that characterized many Sudeten-German nationalists and ethnic Germans of Bohemia and Moravia, was unknown and alien to him. Many an old Party die-hard must have had grave doubts about Heydrich's plans as announced in a secret speech at that first meeting as new Reich Protector with German officials in Prague, when he spoke without the restraint imposed by wider publicity. He was interested, he said, in nothing but pacifying the area and making it a useful part of the German war industry. He was prepared, therefore, to work with all Germans who would further this aim, but he would get rid of any who obstructed it. And then: 'This is the essential thing, that our severity should be aimed at those things which really are wrong here. Because there's no sense in my lashing out wildly at the Czechs and forcing them with all the effort and vigour of police measures to go to their work, when they aren't actually getting what they need.' The same pragmatism had been applied to the conception of the protective custody instrument, so long as Heydrich, as the head of the Bavarian Political Police, had been in a position to apply it in sufficient doses for the purposes of destroying internal political enemies.[21]

Admittedly, the 'Central European Elite' as Heydrich conceived it, a mixture of the figure of the engineer and the soldier, as described by Ernst Jünger's *In Stahlgewittern* (Storms of Steel) – intelligent and cunning, strong and decisive, unsparing of himself and others, making up a completely new race – was bound to be in limited supply. Sooner or later it was inevitable that Heydrich would run into difficulties with his conception, for there were simply not enough of these paragons to go round. He was often enough made aware of these limitations – one example is his remark that the quality of the British Secret Service could not be achieved by the German Security Service from a standing start. It had to be built up over a whole generation.[22]

And furthermore, in the icy latitudes to which Heydrich's rise had taken him and to which he was taken above all by the increasingly drastic conditions of the war, not all of his SD intellectuals could survive for long. The Gestapo justiciary Dr Werner Best was forced out of office after difficulties with Heydrich. Although a dedicated Nazi and SS-leader from the early days of the struggle, Best had clung to the conviction that even the demands of Reich security could not be allowed completely to override the autonomy of the law; that there was a limit which even Heydrich's soulless perfectionism and rigour must respect. Heydrich knew no such scruples of morality or legal philosophy. He was used to tackling his allotted tasks with any means that seemed to him appropriate. In the last analysis the only thing he cared about was which side of the trench one stood on. In this demand for totality, too, he was predisposed to fascism. In contrast to the more or less patriotic political parties he had known during the Weimar period, he had found in National Socialism a distinctive character very congenial to his own mentality. The interests of the Reich justified any methods. The question 'did the Movement create him, or was he the force behind the Movement?' is an idle one: Heydrich and National Socialism had sought and found each other.

Despite this conformity to the ideal type, which was not exactly common in the highest echelons of the Third Reich, Heydrich was and always remained a loner, in this respect very closely resembling Hitler. But whereas it was possible to see the other leaders as types – Alfred Rosenberg perhaps as the 'priest', Heinrich Himmler as 'schoolmaster', Hitler as 'prophet' – Heydrich is not so easy to place. His colleague Best, who had the chance of observing him at close quarters practically every day for five years, confirms simply that: 'Heydrich cannot be typecast.' 'He incorporated elemental qualities which made him more of a "natural occurrence" than a socio-political phenomenon.'[23]

If we apply the word 'demonic' in its original sense to indicate the unusual effects of elemental powers – and not, as it usually is, a catchword to wrap around mystical and opaque metaphysical notions, or personal inadequacy in handling concepts – then Heydrich may be called the most 'demonic' personality among the Nazi leadership. In Best's judgement, Heydrich was 'full of an impetuous vitality' which was always casting around for new activity and challenges towards which to channel its energies.[24] In this constant tempestuous forward momentum, everything he undertook and achieved was merely a means to achieve ever more remote goals. Every foothold gained was a preparation for another step up; otherwise it was interpreted as a failure. 'He could never do anything for its own sake, nothing made sense to him except as a means to achieve a purpose not yet fulfilled.'[25] A first indication of this inclination was given by his manner and appearance. According to the unanimous testimony of his colleagues and subordinates, the close-set blue eyes gazed 'usually coldly, searchingly and suspiciously, and were often irritatingly restless'.[26] His appearance and gaze alone very often made others – subordinates and superiors alike – uneasy. Together with a clipped, abrupt manner of speaking and imperious, aggressive gestures, he revealed from the beginning an unusually wilful subjectivism. Best had the impression that 'with sudden forcefulness he straightaway put forward his views and intentions and thereby left his interlocutor with no alternative but to give way or to launch a counterattack'.[27] In this way Heydrich imposed his own rules of action upon everyone with whom he had dealings and confronted them with the choice of friend or foe, thus bringing out yet another characteristic of fascism. This was true of the previously anti-Nazi officers, Huber and Müller, of the Bavarian Political Police which he took over in 1933, just as it was of his dealings later with Canaris, and most particularly of his treatment of the Czech government of the Protectorate of Bohemia and Moravia when he took up the duties of Reich Protector there.

He never left it in any doubt that a negative attitude to the affair in hand would always be interpreted as enmity towards himself. This violent despotism had the required effect even when Heydrich observed the outer forms of good manners, which was not invariably the case in his dealings with the punctilious bureaucratic types of the police administration. This created an immediate contrast between himself and the other officials, who thought usually in terms of civilized standards and not those of friends or foes within the service. In his choice of colleagues he relied more on his own instinct than on references from others. His instinct would always decide in favour of those qualities he valued and sought: soldierly bearing, dash, intelligence, to a lesser extent racial characteristics and perhaps also an inclination to sport. 'Candidates who created an impression by their self-willed personality appealed to Heydrich's own subjectivity and were accepted,' even if, we are told, their spirit of contradiction later made them somewhat 'uncomfortable' subordinates.[28] It was not least this paradox that had a powerful selective effect on the men surrounding Heydrich in the course of his meteoric career: the lawyer Best, who thought in terms of norms and regulations, left Heydrich's service, while the young, impressionable, 'subjective' Walter Schellenberg, in many ways similar to Heydrich himself, was discovered.

What this 'subjectively defined' Heydrich sought for himself was power, and ever more of it. But he did not seek it, like all the time-servers of every political system, for the sake of material gain and public prestige, but simply for the fulfilment and assertion of his own personality. This turbulent ambition was not only expressed in his political and police career: as a physical entity he craved success. Here is one of the motives for his passion for sport, for fencing, shooting and the decathlon. He pursued the same success in riding, but it eluded him, for his mount would never respond to the alternative of friend or foe. He remained always a loner. He was outstanding in individual sports and indifferent to team games; when he was obliged to take part in them, as during his time in the Navy, his performance was never more than mediocre.[29] The only branch of sport connected with the military that appealed to him was flying. A fighter pilot, too, was completely on his own.

Even in the academic sphere, he was anxious to catch up sufficiently to allow him at least the appearance of self-assertion. He arranged with a Professor of Law, whom he had met through the Security Service, to sign on privately for the necessary number of university terms to gain a degree, though in fact working independently with the aid of a coach towards a law doctorate. He seems to have realized in time, however, that success in his plan to study would make him, of all people, look rather ridiculous, and so he abandoned it.

An incident that took place on the margin of his daily official life perhaps best characterizes his psycho-physical urge to self-assertion. Best reports:

> During a journey we were talking about what we would do if for any reason we were suddenly forced to leave the public service. While I talked about studying the areas of knowledge I had not previously had time for, such as philosophy and history, Heydrich declared that he would devote himself entirely to sport, take part in championships in various branches and also undertake to improve the organization of sport.[30]

Parallel to his physical vitality, Heydrich's intelligence was equally suited to the development of his personality. It was the intelligence of the conqueror and the hunter. He would grasp situations and problems in an instant. While others were still pondering practical problems, Heydrich 'switched on' (it was his own expression) immediately, that is to say he reviewed the significance of the matter for his own purposes. This analysis of utility was so intimately bound up with a rapid grasp of the matter itself that he was almost always instantly one jump ahead of others.

Aware of his own dynamic force, Heydrich had very little need of other people. A colleague testifies 'People were for him either obstructions in his path or the means to his ends'.[31] All those who denied him his due success or recognition were obstacles: sections of the Party, the bureaucracy and the Wehrmacht came into this category. The means to an end were his superiors and his subordinates. The view of the Israeli historian, Aronson, that Heydrich was merely 'the loyal and devoted servant of his master' is not accurate, at least for the years after 1934. 'The blond giant was humbly grateful until the end of his life to the bespectacled Heinrich Himmler, whose appearance radiated so little of the Nordic or the Siegfried quality,' writes Aronson.[32] In reality Heydrich was loyal and obedient to his superior, Himmler, because he represented the way forward. That does not mean, however, that he did not have a keen eye for Himmler's weaknesses and the mistakes he made. On the contrary, the higher Heydrich climbed up the ladder of power in the Nazi state, the more critical he became of Himmler, and the more unbearable became his position subordinate to him, so that in the end he found his appointment as Protector in Prague, which released him from Himmler's immediate sphere of authority, a great relief.[33]

His personal hatred was directed towards those who threatened his rise, and hardly at all at the opponents of the state and the system, whom he fought with the weapons he was entrusted with and whom he largely succeeded in eliminating as political factors. Best himself believes that he took over the task of carrying out the Final Solution of the 'Jewish Problem' with hardly a hostile thought for the Jews, but concentrating on 'the extent of his task and the geographical area it spanned, and on the need to demonstrate his energy and skill in mastering it'.[34]

This brings us to the enigmatic aspects of the Nazi superman, on which the historical sources throw very little light. For after 1945 the looters of the Third Reich's grave joined forces with those who had served the Nazi state in prominent positions. Some were prompted by a continuation of Allied war propaganda or by a sheer lack of reliable information at the time; others, moved by the desire to find an alibi and whitewash themselves; all gave Heydrich blanket responsibility for the various stages of the Nazi reign of terror. The accused and the witnesses at the Nuremberg war trials had, for example, agreed 'to shift as much as possible on to Heydrich; after all, he's dead already'.[35] From the Blomberg-Fritsch crisis right up to the Final Solution, all the evil that was done in the Third Reich was attributed to the diabolical mind of Heydrich. Absurdly, Joachim Fest even makes him responsible for occurrences of which Heydrich had no knowledge until the event. 'He was behind the attack on Hitler in the Munich Bürgerbräukeller,' and he 'organized the so-called *Kristallnacht*'.[36] It is now historical common knowledge that Heydrich was not involved in either event.

The case was different with the Final Solution. It cannot be said to have sprung from Heydrich's own mind in the form it historically took; he was not its initiator, but he was its architect. Even a task like this fascinated him because of its sheer size, and he performed it with zeal and intelligence. His first thought in this connection was to achieve the Final Solution by emigration, driving the Jews out by systematically making their lives unbearable. Then, when the war made this impossible, there came deportation to different, constantly changing areas; alongside this from the beginning, and after 1942 carried out systematically, there was extermination. There is much to indicate that he undertook the latter phase of his task with very mixed feelings. The planning and execution were handed over to subordinates like Adolf Eichmann. Whereas he had always loved to be informed of all the details of Intelligence-work intrigues, he supervised the Final Solution only in the most general sense. The terminology, which had been designed to keep the business of extermination a secret, had originated with him.

It is true that he was dominated by a supreme indifference to the sanctity of human life – including his own. That was a characteristic typical of the revolutionary and the technocrat alike. Death by shooting in the back of the head seemed to him just as normal as death by an exploding bomb, and the latter no more unusual than death through pneumonia or cancer. But, as it has rightly been stated, 'Cunning suited him better than brutality, and to see his opponent walking into an artfully constructed trap gave him far more satisfaction than any crude act of violence.'[37]

This renders credible Himmler's remark concerning Heydrich's scruples about organized genocide, incorporated in the commemorative address given on the occasion of the state Memorial Ceremony for the 'God of Death':

From many discussions with Heydrich, I know what it cost this man to be outwardly so hard and severe despite the struggles and suffering of his heart; to make decisions and to act always according to the law of the SS, which binds us 'to spare neither our own nor others' blood, when the life of the nation demands it'.[38]

Heydrich was proud of his 'historic achievement', which he conceived entirely in positive terms. Through his own strenuous efforts, the Reich had been provided for the first time in history with a police force able to surmount the fragmented, particularist traditions of the various lands and regions of Germany: a force with an entirely new sense of purpose, unified throughout the Reich; and also a universal political Intelligence Service, both of them instruments ready for instant alert at any time, with an effective and far-reaching strike potential.

But time and again the tasks allocated to him, precisely because of this successful police reform, created in him a state of inner conflict. He had been made aware of the profound incompatibility of means and ends as early as the days of his participation in the elimination of Röhm, the only man in the Party to whom he had extended his friendship, the only one whom, against his own self-imposed iron rule, he addressed with the intimate '*du*' form, the godfather of one of his sons; and then, once again, by the murders committed by his task forces, and finally by his function as architect of the Final Solution. With bitter cynicism he complained that he was sometimes 'the Chief Garbage Collector of the Third Reich'.[39] 'The strange thing is', said his widow, 'that he was fully aware of his hangman role and knew how to justify it positively.'[40]

He saw in his activities something like a heroic act, involving personal burdens and sacrifices, which he believed it his duty to shoulder for the sake of the future of the Reich. 'I feel myself to be free of all guilt,' the doubt-torn Heydrich was wont to conclude. 'I can only make myself available, where others follow their own selfish ends.'[41] This attitude has often led to a comparison between Heydrich and the Revolutionary Tribune of 1789, Saint-Just. Of him it is said that he carried his head high like a consecrated host as he demanded life upon life to be sacrificed. In this respect, in the last analysis, Heydrich was a revolutionary. The combination of reason and the striving for technical perfection, of desire for a heroic, dangerous life *à la* Saint-Just 'between deadly dangers and immortality', and a knife-edge, spiritual balancing act, where falls were accepted as inevitable: that was Heydrich.

One of his most able colleagues has stated that illuminating parallels to this personality can only be found among the conquerors of earlier ages, who did not set forth out of doctrinaire motives or for material gain, but because the elemental instincts of their tremendous vitality could only find self-realization by extending themselves into the outside world and in progressive expansion of their power.

A constant type of such conqueror-figures cannot be established, because their essence and their strength lies in their subjective, one-sided individuality, which bears no comparison with others. The main authority on Heydrich, Dr Werner Best, contemplates this comparison in his memoirs:

> At most, one might quote Nietzsche's Blond Beast and recall, on the one hand, Vikings and Normans, who strode conquering from land to land, and on the other hand a blond youth who began his path in life among the degenerate Vikings of a modern Navy, and in the course of a decade became one of the most powerful men in one of the most powerful empires, only to die at thirty-eight by the hands of an enemy assassin.[42]

Nietzsche's friend and antithesis Richard Wagner romanticized this 'Blond Beast' in his music dramas, and Heydrich's father presented these Wagnerian heroes of myth and opera on the stage. It was reserved for Reinhard Tristan Eugen Heydrich, the son of the Wagner-singer, to attempt to bring these Wagnerian models down off the stage and to make Nietzsche's dream of the 'Blond Beast' into a reality in his own person.

NOTES

Abbreviations used in the Notes:
ADAP – Akten zur Deutschen Auswärtigen Politik (Files of German Policy);
BA – Bundesarchiv Koblenz; DC – Document Centre, Berlin; DNT – Der Neue
Tag, Prague; DW – *Die Welt*; FAZ – *Frankfurter Allgemeine Zeitung*; F.b.V. –
Photo or photo-copy in the author's possession; IMT – Files of the International
Military Tribunal, Nuremberg; VB – *Völkischer Beobachter*; VJZG –
Vierteljahrshefte für Zeitgeschichte; WL – Wiener Library, London.

Chapter I: The Enigma

1 Charles Wighton *Heydrich – Hitler's Most Evil Henchman* London 1962; and
    expert reports on Wighton in WL (F.b.V.)
2 In particular Michael Freund, Karl Dietrich Bracher, Joachim Fest and Hugh
    Trevor-Roper, cf. Chapter 6, pp. 60 ff.
3 Cf. Heinz Höhne *Der Orden unter dem Totenkopf* Gütersloh 1967; Edward
    Crankshaw *Gestapo* New York 1956, p. 112
4 Cf. *Reichsführer!* Ed. Helmut Heiber, Stuttgart 1968, pp. 7 ff.
5 Carl Haensel *Das Gericht vertagt sich* p. 61
6 Heiber, loc. cit.
7 Shlomo Aronson *Reinhard Heydrich und die Frühgeschichte von Gestapo und
    SD* (Dissertation), Stuttgart 1971

Chapter 2: A Child of Music

1 Biographical data: Archiv für publ. Arbeit, Deposit 7323, 13.8.42; DC, SS-
    Personnel Document on Heydrich, from Shlomo Aronson *Reinhard
    Heydrich und die Frühgeschichte von Gestapo und SD* (Dissertation), Stuttgart
    1971, Appendix, Document 12, p. 320; and information from Dr W. Sommer
2 Cf. Aronson, op. cit. pp. 11 ff.
3 Ibid.
4 *Riemanns Musik-Lexikon* Mainz ed., 1959, vol. I, p. 789
5 Aronson, op. cit., pp. 15 f.; author's interview with Lina Heydrich
6 Documents of Karl von Eberstein, pp. 23 f., (F.b.V.)

7 Aronson, op. cit. p. 15
8 Ibid. pp. 16, 18
9 Documents of Eberstein, p. 24 (F.b.V.)
10 Aronson, op. cit. pp. 16 and p. 258 footnotes 24, 25
11 Ibid.
12 Ibid. p. 258 footnote 24
13 Information from Dr W Sommer
14 Author's interview with Dr Dr Erich Schultze
15 This view of Aronson's is contradicted by author's interview with Schultze
16 Letter from Schultze of 28.1.72 and information from Sommer
17 Interview with Lina Heydrich
18 Aronson, op. cit. p. 21
19 Statistic in *Meyers Konversations Lexikon* vol. 8, 1895
20 Information from Sommer
21 Interview with Schultze
22 Ibid.
23 Aronson, loc. cit.
24 Documents of Eberstein, p. 26 (F.b.V.)
25 Cf. Aronson, op. cit. pp. 23 f.

Chapter 3: The Would-Be Admiral
1 Author's interview with Dr Dr Erich Schultze; information from fellow crew member, naval Captain H H Lebram, in Shlomo Aronson *Reinhard Heydrich und die Frühgeschichte von Gestapo und SD* (Dissertation), Stuttgart 1971, p. 27
2 Author's interview with Lina Heydrich
3 Information from Dr W Sommer
4 Aronson, op. cit. p. 23
5 Information from fellow crew-member, naval Captain Rehm, in Aronson, op. cit. p. 26
6 Interview with Lina Heydrich
7 Aronson, op. cit. p. 27 and footnote 72; also interview with Schultze
8 Interview with Lina Heydrich
9 Aronson, op. cit. p. 29
10 Dates of Heydrich's Navy career in Archiv für Publ. Arbeit v, 12.2.42; *Reinhard Heydrich*; and in Aronson, op. cit. pp. 25–33
11 Gert Buchheit *Der deutsche Geheimdienst* Munich 1960, pp. 59 f.
12 Interview with Lina Heydrich
13 Buchheit, op. cit. pp. 55 ff.
14 Information from Frau Lehmann-Jottkowitz, in Aronson, op. cit. p. 32
15 Information from Beucke, in Aronson, loc. cit.

16 Manuscript on Heydrich from Dr Werner Best, Copenhagen 1.9.49, p. 10 (F.b.V.)
17 Information from Beucke, in Aronson, loc. cit.
18 Information from Lebram, ibid. p. 31
19 Interview with Lina Heydrich
20 Information from Beucke, in Aronson, loc. cit.
21 Author's interview with naval Captain Herbert Zollenkopf, and written information of 1.4.77
22 DC, SS-Personnel Document on Heydrich
23 Archiv für Publ. Arbeit, loc. cit.
24 Information from Vice-Admiral G Kleikamp in letter to *Der Spiegel* No. 9, 2.3.50
25 Interview with Schultze

Chapter 4: Trapped
1 Author's interview with Lina Heydrich
2 Ibid.
3 Ibid.
4 Ibid.; David Irving's interview with retired Admiral of the Fleet Kurt Freiwald and Rear-Admiral J von Puttkamer, 13.11.72 and 20.11.72 (F.b.V.)
5 As in e.g. Joachim Fest
6 Information from Beucke, in Shlomo Aronson *Reinhard Heydrich und die Frühgeschichte von Gestapo und SD* (Dissertation), Stuttgart 1971, footnote I/88, p. 260
7 Interview with Freiwald and Puttkamer
8 Ibid.
9 Information from Vice-Admiral G Kleikamp in letter to *Der Spiegel* No. 9, 2.3.50
10 Aronson lays the blame for this exclusively on Heydrich's bearing at the Court hearing
11 Author's interview with Dr Dr Erich Schultze
12 Ibid. and information from Dr W Sommer
13 Interview with Lina Heydrich
14 Ibid.
15 *Der Spiegel* No. 6, 9.2.50, 'Das Spiel ist aus', p. 23; Aronson, op. cit. p. 37; and Charles Wighton *Heydrich – Hitler's Most Evil Henchman* London 1962, pp. 36 f.; based on information from Lina Heydrich
16 Interview with Lina Heydrich
17 DC, SS-Personnel Document on Heydrich
18 Aronson, op. cit. pp. 51 ff.
19 Hoover Collection, Himmler Files, roll 39

20 *Der Spiegel,* loc. cit.
21 Interview with Schultze
22 Memorial speech by Heinrich Himmler 9.6.42, in *Reinhard Heydrich, Ein Leben der Tat* Prague 1944, p. 62
23 Interview with Lina Heydrich
24 Ibid.
25 Ibid.
26 Author's interview with Bruno Streckenbach
27 Information from Kleikamp, loc. cit.

Chapter 5: In the Secret Intelligence Service
 1 Reinhard Heydrich, Speech on German Police Day 1941, partly reproduced in *Reinhard Heydrich RSHA* (Memorial publication), Berlin undated
 2 Author's interview with Dr Dr Erich Schultze
 3 Author's interview with Lina Heydrich
 4 Reinhard Heydrich, 'Der Anteil der Sicherheitspolizei und des SD an den Ordnungsmassnahmen im mitteleuropäischen Raum', in *Böhmen und Mähren,* No. 5, Prague 1941, pp. 176 f.
 5 Heinrich Brennecke *Hitler und die SA* Munich & Vienna 1962, pp. 174 f.; Shlomo Aronson *Reinhard Heydrich und die Frühgeschichte von Gestapo und SD* (Dissertation), Stuttgart 1971, p. 40
 6 Ibid.
 7 Ibid.
 8 *Münchener Post* 28–9.11.31, 4.4.32 and 7.4.32; Aronson, op. cit. p. 42
 9 *Münchener Post* 25.11.31; Aronson, op. cit. p. 45
10 Aronson, op. cit. p. 55
11 Ibid.
12 Ibid. p. 56
13 Lina Heydrich, interview and *Leben mit einem Kriegsverbrecher* Pfaffenhofen 1976, pp. 33 ff.
14 Ibid.
15 DC, SS-Personnel Document on Heydrich
16 Heydrich's papers (F.b.V.)
17 Interview with Lina Heydrich
18 Ibid.
19 Aronson, op. cit. p. 57
20 Höhne *Der Orden unter dem Totenkopf* Gütersloh 1967, p. 161
21 Reinhard Heydrich, 'Der Anteil der Sicherheitspolizei', loc. cit.; Aronson, op. cit. pp. 57 f.
22 Interview with Lina Heydrich
23 DC, SS-Personnel Document on Leffler, in Aronson, op. cit. p. 269 footnote

24 DC, SS-Personnel Document on Albert, quoted in Aronson, op. cit. p. 57
25 DC, SS-Personnel Document on Oberg, quoted in Aronson, op. cit. p. 141
26 Reinhard Heydrich, 'Der Anteil der Sicherheitspolizei', loc. cit.; interview with Lina Heydrich
27 Manuscript by Leffler, in the possession of Dr Werner Best, partly reproduced by Aronson, op. cit. pp. 60 f.
28 Interview with Lina Heydrich
29 Author's interview with Bruno Streckenbach
30 Interview with Lina Heydrich
31 Ibid.
32 Ibid.
33 Ibid.
34 Ibid.
35 Aronson, op. cit. p. 61
36 Manuscript from Dr Werner Best, Copenhagen 1.9.49, p. 10

Chapter 6: The Alleged Jew

1 Shlomo Aronson *Reinhard Heydrich und die Frühgeschichte von Gestapo und SD* (Dissertation), Stuttgart 1971, p. 61
2 DC, SS-Personnel Document on Heydrich
3 *Riemanns Musik-Lexikon, 1916*; post-war editions omit the reference to Süss; Mainz ed. 1959, vol. 1, p. 789
4 DC, SS-Personnel Document on Heydrich
5 Author's interview with Lina Heydrich
6 Expert report by Dr Gercke on the racial origins of retired naval Lieutenant Reinhard Heydrich 22.6.32; DC, SS-Personnel Document on Heydrich, in Aronson, op. cit. pp. 312 f.
7 Ibid.
8 *Der Spiegel* No. 6, 9.2.50, 'Das Spiel ist aus', p. 23, and No. 11, 16.3.50, K. J. Fischer
9 Among others, letters to *Aufbau*, 11.11.60, and *WamS*, 24.5.53
10 *Der Mittag* No. 296, 17.12.40
11 *Der Spiegel* No. 6, loc. cit.
12 Manuscript from Dr Werner Best, Copenhagen 1.9.49, p. 9 (F.b.V.)
13 Walter Hagen (Höttl) *Die geheime Front* Linz 1950, pp. 20 ff.
14 Robert MW Kempner *Eichmann und Komplizen* Zürich 1961, p. 37
15 Diary of Milch, entry for 29.3.46 (copy in the possession of David Irving, London)
16 Manuscript by Helmut Maurer and correspondence between Ulrich Popplow and Helmut Maurer of November 1963 (F.b.V.)
17 Letter from Popplow to Maurer 6.11.63 (F.b.V.)

18 Interview with Lina Heydrich
19 *Der Spiegel* loc. cit.
20 Felix Kersten *Totenkopf und Treue* Hamburg 1952, pp. 128 ff.; A Besgen *Der stille Befehl* Munich 1960, pp. 185 f.
21 Interview with Lina Heydrich
22 Kempner, loc. cit.
23 Expert report on Kempner's *Eichmann und Komplizen* in WL (F.b.V.)
24 Charles Wighton *Heydrich – Hitler's Most Evil Henchman* London 1962, pp. 125 ff.; and expert reports on Wighton in WL (F.b.V.)
25 Professor Hugh Trevor-Roper in *The Times* 3.6.62
26 Trevor-Roper in the Foreword to the English edition of Kersten's memoirs
27 Expert evidence from Michael Freund given to the Landessozialgericht Schleswig (copy in WL), partly reproduced in *Die Gegenwart* No. 322, pp. 626 ff.
28 Cf. Gert Buchheit *Der deutsche Geheimdienst* Munich 1960
29 Karl Dietrich Bracher *Die deutsche Diktatur* Cologne & Berlin 1969, pp. 60 f.
30 Joachim Fest *Das Gesicht des Dritten Reiches* Munich 1963, pp. 142 f.
31 Gerald Reitlinger *Die Endlösung* Berlin 1961, p. 15
32 Reitlinger *Die SS* Vienna & Munich 1957, p. 43
33 HG Adler *Theresienstadt* Tübingen 1955, p. 645
34 Friedrich Hacker *Aggression* Vienna & Munich 1971, pp. 34 f.
35 Cf. Heinz Höhne *Der Orden unter dem Totenkopf* Gütersloh 1967, p. 153
36 Expert evidence from Michael Freund, loc. cit.
37 Carl J Burckhardt *Meine Danziger Mission* Munich 1960, pp. 55 ff.
38 Ibid.
39 Kersten, loc. cit.
40 Höhne, loc. cit.
41 Interview with Dr Dr Erich Schultze

Chapter 7: 'O Sancta Securitas'

1 Shlomo Aronson *Reinhard Heydrich und die Frühgeschichte von Gestapo und SD* (Dissertation), Stuttgart 1971, p. 106
2 Ibid., p. 107
3 DC, SS-Personnel Document on Heydrich, in Aronson, op. cit., Appendix, Document 12, p. 320
4 Author's interview with Lina Heydrich
5 Erich Kordt *Nicht aus den Akten, Die Wilhelmstrasse in Frieden und Krieg 1928–1945* Stuttgart 1950, p. 53; Rudolf Nadolny *Mein Beitrag* 1955, pp. 129 ff.
6 Nadolny, loc. cit.

7 Ibid.

8 Interview with Lina Heydrich

9 Cf. K D Bracher *et al. Die nationalsozialistische Machtergreifung* Cologne 1962, pp. 57, 137 ff.; Aronson, op. cit. pp. 88 ff.

10 DC, SS-Personnel Document on Heydrich

11 DC, Schu 464, in Aronson, op. cit., Appendix, Document 15, p. 323

12 Aronson, op. cit. p. 99

13 Cf. Aronson, op. cit. pp. 107 ff.

14 Interview with Lina Heydrich

15 Ibid.

16 Aronson, op. cit. p. 111

17 Eugen Kogon, *Der SS-Staat, Das System der deutschen Konzentrationslager* Berlin 1947, p. 4

18 Aronson, op. cit. p. 104

19 Documents 17 and 17a in Aronson, op. cit. p. 325

20 Aronson, op. cit. p. 118

21 Cf. Aronson, op. cit. pp. 117–20

22 Ibid.

23 Aronson, op. cit. p. 123

24 Heinz Höhne *Der Orden unter dem Totenkopf* Gütersloh 1967, p. 165

25 Walter Hagen (Höttl) *Die Geheime Front* Linz 1950, p. 86

26 Interview with Lina Heydrich

27 Ibid.

28 As in 'The Jeckel Case', Aronson, op. cit. p. 165

29 Interview with Lina Heydrich

30 Ibid.

31 Höhne, op. cit. pp. 82 f.

32 Rudolf Diels *Luzifer ante portas* Stuttgart 1950, p. 328

33 Author's interview with Bruno Streckenbach

34 Höhne, op. cit. p. 88

35 Charles Wighton *Heydrich – Hitler's Most Evil Henchman* London 1962, pp. 63 f.

36 Cf. Hans Buchheim *SS und Polizei im NS-Staat* Bonn 1964, and by the same author 'Die SS – Das Herrschaftsinstrument' in *Anatomie des SS-Staates* vol 1, Olten 1965

37 Aronson, op. cit. pp. 225 f.

38 Ibid.

39 Manuscript from Dr Werner Best, Copenhagen 1.9.49 (F.b.V.)

40 Intervew with Streckenbach

41 Interview with Lina Heydrich

42 Alfred Schweder *Politische Polizei* (Dissertation), Berlin 1937, pp. 141 ff.

43 Höhne, op. cit. p. 172
44 Reinhard Heydrich *Wandlungen unseres Kampfes* Berlin 1936, p. 4
45 Aronson, op. cit. pp. 195 ff.
46 Hoover Collection, Himmler Files, roll 17, frame 307–30
47 Cf. Aronson, op cit. pp. 142 ff.
48 Aronson, op. cit. p. 162
49 Ibid.
50 Höhne, op. cit. p. 196
51 Buchheim *SS und Polizei* pp. 62 ff.
52 Ibid. pp. 48 ff.
53 Interview with Lina Heydrich
54 Buchheim, *SS und Polizei*, op. cit. p. 51
55 Gerd Rühle *Das Dritte Reich. Dokumentarische Darstellung des Aufbaues der Nation* vol. IV, Berlin 1936, pp. 270 ff.
56 Ibid.
57 Werner Best, 'Die geheime Staatspolizei' in *Deutsches Recht* 1936, pp. 125 ff.
58 Adolf Liepelt *Über den Umfang und die Bedeutung der Polizeigewalt im nationalsozialistischen Staat* (Dissertation) Würzburg 1938, pp. 21 ff.
59 Walter Hamel, 'Die Polizei im neuen Reich' in *Deutsches Recht* 1935, pp. 412 ff.
60 Reinhard Heydrich, 'Die Bekämpfung der Staatsfeinde' in *Die deutsche Rechtswissenschaft* vol. 1, No. 2, 1936, pp. 97 ff.
61 Werner Best, op. cit. p. 126
62 Reinhard Heydrich, 'Der Anteil der Sicherheitspolizei und des SD an den Ordnungsmassnahmen im mitteleuropäischen Raum' in *Böhmen und Mähren* No. 5, Prague 1941, p. 176
63 Höhn, op. cit. p. 184
64 Ibid.
65 Ibid.
66 Kogon, loc. cit.
67 Aronson, op. cit. p. 111
68 Höhne, op. cit. p. 190
69 Ibid.

Chapter 8: His Favourite Target: Rome

1 Reinhard Heydrich *Wandlungen unseres Kampfes* Berlin 1936, p. 7
2 Author's interview with Lina Heydrich
3 Reinhard Heydrich, loc. cit.
4 Ibid. p. 9
5 Ibid.
6 John S. Conway *Die nationalsozialistische Kirchenpolitik* Munich 1969,

Notes

pp. 177 f.

7 Ibid. p. 145

8 Gerd Rühle *Das Dritte Reich, Dokumentarische Darstellung des Aufbaues der Nation* vol. IV, Berlin 1936, p. 155 ff.

9 Reinhard Heydrich, 'Die Bekämpfung der Staatsfeinde' in *Die deutsche Rechtswissenschaft* vol. 1, No. 2, 1936, pp. 97 ff.

10 Reproduced in Shlomo Aronson *Reinhard Heydrich und die Frühgeschichte von Gestapo und SD* (Dissertation), Stuttgart 1971, pp. 242 f.

11 Ibid.

12 Walter Hagen (Höttl) *Die geheime Front* Linz 1950

13 Interview with Lina Heydrich

14 Ibid.; and author's interview with Dr Dr Erich Schultze

15 Interview with Lina Heydrich

16 Conway, op. cit. p. 179

17 Interview with Lina Heydrich

18 Cf. Friedrich Zipfel *Kirchenkampf in Deutschland 1933–1945* Berlin 1965, p. 7

19 Chief of Security HQ, Special Report No. 285, 'Zersetzung der nationalsozialistischen Grundwerte im deutschsprachigen Schrifttum seit 1933', Berlin 1936, typescript (F.b.V.). Subsequently referred to as 'Sonderbericht Zersetzung'

20 Ibid. p. 48

21 Ibid. p. 56

22 Ibid.

23 Ibid. p. 69

24 Ibid. p. 58

25 Ibid. p. 66

26 Ibid. p. 67

27 Reinhard Heydrich, 'Die Bekämpfung der Staatsfeinde', op. cit.

28 Chief of Security HQ, Situation Report No. 037, 'Katholische Bewegung', Berlin 1934, reprinted in Zipfel, op. cit. pp. 272–326

29 'Sonderbericht Zersetzung', p. 48

30 Ibid. p. 65

31 Ibid. p. 69

32 Reinhard Heydrich, 'Die Bekämpfung der Staatsfeinde', op. cit.

33 Interview with Lina Heydrich

34 Zipfel, op. cit. p. 67

35 On Klausener: Walter Adolph *Erich Klausener* Berlin 1955

36 Zipfel, op. cit. p. 63

37 Ibid. p. 64 footnote

38 Statement by Göring in Nuremberg, in Robert M. W. Kempner *SS im Kreuzverhör* Munich 1964, pp. 254 f.

39 Trial papers of Gildisch, in ibid. pp. 255 ff.
40 Zipfel, op. cit. p. 64 footnote
41 Conway, op. cit. p. 112
42 Ibid. pp. 250 ff.
43 Ibid. p. 251
44 Ibid. p. 254
45 Ibid. p. 274
46 Ibid. p. 301
47 Hagen (Höttl), op. cit. p. 35
48 Conway, op. cit. p. 301

Chapter 9: The Duty to Excel

1 Cf. J Kramer *The World's Police* London 1964, p. 442
2 From: 'SS-Gruppenführer Heydrich, Präsident der Internationalen Kriminalpolizeilichen Kommission' in *Bodensee-Rundschau* 1941
3 Ibid.
4 'Weltzentrale der Kriminalpolizei' in *Hamburger Fremdenblatt* No. 103, 14.4.42
5 Ibid.
6 E.g. in Reinhard Heydrich, 'Der Anteil der Sicherheitspolizei und des SD an den Ordnungsmassnahmen im mitteleuropäischen Raum', in *Böhmen und Mähren* No. 5, Prague 1941, pp. 176 f.
7 Author's interview with Bruno Streckenbach
8 Author's interview with Lina Heydrich
9 *Der Spiegel* No. 6, 9.2.50, 'Das Spiel ist aus', p. 26
10 Author's interview with a former officer from squadron 55, 1.9.73
11 Interview with Lina Heydrich
12 Heydrich's papers (F.b.V.)
13 Letter from Himmler to Heydrich 15.5.40, reproduced in Helmut Heiber (Ed.) *Reichsführer! Briefe an und von Himmler* Stuttgart 1968, p. 80
14 Memorial speech by Heinrich Himmler 9.6.42, in *Reinhard Heydrich, Ein Leben der Tat* Prague 1944, pp. 61 f.
15 Author's interview with Dr Paul Schmidt
16 Ulrich Popplow, 'Reinhard Heydrich oder die Aufordnung durch den Sport' in *Olympisches Feuer* Celle, August 1963, pp. 14 ff.
17 The following information is taken from: 'Procès verbal du compte rendu sténographique du XXVIIème Congrès tenu le 8 novembre 1946 à Bruxelles', Brussels undated
18 Cf. Jan Rijckoordt *De tragische dood van Joris van Severen* Bruges undated
19 Author's interview with Paul Anspach
20 'Neue Reichsfachamtsleiter' in *Der Mittag* No. 300, 21–22.10.40

21 Copy of a letter in the possession of Paul Anspach, Brussels
22 Letter from Anspach to Talman 16.2.41 (collection of P. Anspach, Brussels)
23 Letter from Heydrich to Anspach 25.6.41 (collection of P. Anspach, Brussels)
24 Letters from Anspach to Heydrich on 14.7.41 and 11.8.41 (copies in the collection of P. Anspach, Brussels)
25 H E von Daniels, 'Reinhard Heydrich als nationalsozialistischer Leibeserzieher' in *Leibesübungen und körperliche Erziehung* August 1942, pp. 114 ff.
26 Ibid.
27 Popplow, op. cit.: Popplow gives some interesting information about Heydrich as a fencer, though he unreservedly supports the notion of Heydrich's Jewish origins
28 'SS-Obergruppenführer Heydrich bester Einzelfechter' in *Hamburger Fremdenblatt* late ed. 15.12.41; Daniels loc. cit.
29 Heinz Höhne *Der Orden unter dem Totenkopf* Gütersloh 1967, p. 162
30 Author's interview with Dr Otto-Ernst Schüddekopf
31 Daniels, loc. cit.
32 Popplow, loc, cit.
33 Ibid.
34 Ibid.
35 Ibid.
36 Author's interview with Benno Wundshammer, who photographed Heydrich fencing
37 Interview with Streckenbach
38 Reinhard Heydrich *Wandlungen unseres Kampfes* Berlin 1936, p. 19
39 H E von Daniels, 'Der deutsche Sport trauert um Reinhard Heydrich' in DNT No. 155, Prague, 7.6.42
40 Ibid.
41 W Hoops, 'Heydrich' in *Deutsche Brüsseler Zeitung* 16.6.42
42 Reinhard Heydrich, 'Der Anteil der Sicherheitspolizei', loc. cit.
43 Hermann Rauschning *Gespräche mit Hitler* Zürich & New York 1940, p. 237
44 Interview with Lina Heydrich

Chapter 10: The Chief Suspicion-Monger
1 Author's interview with Lina Heydrich
2 Author's interview with Dr Robert M. W. Kempner
3 K R Grossmann, 'Berthold Jacobs Entführung' in *Ossietzky, Ein Deutscher Patriot* Munich 1963, p. 442
4 Ibid. p. 443
5 Ibid.
6 Ibid. p. 444

7 Ibid. pp. 444 f.
8 Ibid. p. 445
9 Interview with Kempner
10 Ibid.
11 Grossmann, op. cit. p. 447
12 Ibid.
13 André Brissaud *Die SD-Story* Zürich 1975, pp. 99 ff.; Heinz Höhne *Der Orden unter dem Totenkopf* Gütersloh 1967, pp. 211f.
14 Otto Strasser *Hitler und ich* Konstanz 1948
15 Höhne, loc. cit., names 'Müller' instead
16 Ibid.
17 Ibid. pp. 212 f.
18 Cf. Heinz Boberach *Meldungen aus dem Reich* Neuwied 1965
19 Höhne, op. cit. p. 212
20 Ibid.
21 Ibid. p. 213
22 André Brissaud *Canaris* Frankfurt 1976, pp. 38 f.
23 Ibid. p. 39
24 Ibid. p. 41
25 Ibid.
26 Interview with Lina Heydrich; Brissaud *Canaris,* pp. 42 f.
27 Brissaud *Canaris* p. 43
28 Ibid.
29 Information from Vice-Admiral G Kleikamp in *Der Spiegel* No. 9, 2.3.50
30 Ibid.
31 Lina Heydrich *Leben mit einem Kriegsverbrecher* Pfaffenhofen 1976, p. 63
32 Ibid.
33 Gert Buchheit *Der deutsche Geheimdienst* Munich 1960, pp. 169 f.
34 Höhne, op. cit. p. 213
35 Buchheit, loc. cit.
36 Klaus Benzing *Canaris* (unpublished manuscript 1972), p. 59
37 Buchheit, op. cit. p. 171
38 Walter Hagen (Höttl) *Die geheime Front* Linz 1950, pp. 57 ff.; contribution to Hagen's *Kristall* No. 31, 2.8.53
39 Brissaud *Canaris* p. 104
40 Robert Conquest *Am Anfang starb Genosse Kirow* Düsseldorf 1970, pp. 266 f.
41 Lew Nikulin, 'Die Affäre Tuchatschewski' in *Geköpfte Armee* Berlin 1965, p. 90
42 Conquest, op. cit. p. 266; Höhne op. cit. pp. 214 ff.
43 Conquest, op. cit. p. 267
44 Höhne, op. cit. p. 217

45 Cf. Höhne, op. cit. p. 224
46 Cf. ibid. pp. 221 ff.
47 Manuscript from Dr Werner Best, Copenhagen, 1.9.49, p. 11 (F.b.V.)
48 Ibid.
49 Ibid. p. 12
50 Interview with Lina Heydrich
51 Ibid.
52 Reinhard Vogelsang *Der Freundeskreis Himmler* Göttingen 1972, pp. 74 f.
53 Walter Schellenberg *Memoirs* pp. 36 f.
54 Quoted freely in Peter Norden *Salon Kitty* Munich 1973; Cf. *Der Spiegel* No. 14, 1976
55 Author's interview with Dr Paul Schmidt
56 Hans Buchheim, 'Die SS Das Herrschaftsinstrument' in *Anatomie des SS-Staates* vol. 1, Olten 1965, pp. 71 f.
57 Ibid.
58 Memorandum from Heydrich in VJZG 1963, No. 11, pp. 206 ff.
59 Reinhard Heydrich, 'Der Anteil der Sicherheitspolizei und des SD an den Ordungsmassnahmen im mitteleuropäischen Raum' in *Böhmen und Mähren* No 5, Prague 1941
60 VB 10.10.38
61 Cf. Jürgen Runzheimer, 'Der Überfall auf den Sender Gleiwitz im Jahr 1939' in VJZG 1962, pp. 408 ff.
62 Interview with Lina Heydrich
63 Brissaud *Die SD-Story* p. 240
64 Höhne, op. cit. pp. 262 ff.
65 Brissaud *Die SD-Story* pp. 233 f.
66 Reinhard Heydrich, Speech on German Police Day 1941 (F.b.V.)
67 Buchheim, op. cit. p. 71
68 Martin Broszat, *Nationalsozialistische Polenpolitik, 1939–1945* Frankfurt 1965
69 Helmut Krausnick (see Buchheim, H. *et al.*), 'Judenverfolgung' in *Anatomie des SS-Staates* vol. 2, Munich 1967, p. 288

Chapter 11: From Policy-maker to Executioner

1 Cf. especially Uwe Deitrich Adam, 'Judenpolitik im Dritten Reich' in *Tübinger Schriften zur Sozial-und Zeitgeschichte* vol. 1, Düsseldorf 1972, pp. 97 ff.
2 Reinhard Heydrich *Wandlungen unseres Kampfes* Berlin 1936, p. 5
3 Ibid. p. 10
4 Lina Heydrich *Leben mit einem Kriegsverbrecher* Pfaffenhofen 1976, p. 97
5 Cf. Carl Schmitt *Der Begriff des Politischen* Berlin 1963, p. 26

6 Cf. Adam, op. cit. p. 102 f.; Reinhard Höhn, 'Polizeirecht im Umbruch' in *Deutsches Recht* 1936, pp. 128 ff.; and Werner Best *Die deutsche Polizei* Darmstadt 1942, p. 26

7 Best, loc. cit.

8 Reinhard Heydrich, op. cit. p. 20

9 Adam, op. cit. p. 104

10 Shlomo Aronson *Reinhard Heydrich und die Frühgeschichte von Gestapo und SD* (Dissertation), Stuttgart 1971, pp. 221 f., p. 294

11 Helmut Krausnick (see Buchheim, H. *et al.*), 'Anatomie der Endlösung' in *Anatomie des SS-Staates* vol. 2, Munich 1967, p. 284

12 Heinz Höhne *Der Orden unter dem Totenkopf* Gütersloh 1967, p. 298

13 Ibid. p. 299

14 Charles Wighton *Heydrich – Hitler's Most Evil Henchman* London 1962, p. 162

15 Ibid. p. 169

16 Quoted from ibid. p. 162

17 Höhne, op. cit. p. 299

18 Karl Dietrich Bracher *Die deutsche Diktatur* Cologne & Berlin 1969, p. 399

19 Höhne, loc. cit.

20 Adam, op. cit. pp. 15 ff., 229, 355 ff.; cf. also Hellmuth Auerbach, 'Die Endlösung nicht perfekt geplant' in FAZ 12.6.74

21 Cf. Walter Petwaidic *Die autoritäre Anarchie* Hamburg 1946

22 Adam, op. cit. p. 229

23 Höhne, op. cit. p. 303

24 Ibid.; Adam, op. cit. pp. 114 f.

25 Cf. Hans Lamm *Über die innere und äussere Entwicklung des deutschen Judentums im Dritten Reich* (Dissertation), Erlangen 1951, pp. 47 f.

26 Quoted from Adam, op. cit. p. 115 footnote 5

27 Ibid. p. 115

28 Höhne, op. cit. p. 304

29 Adam, loc. cit.

30 Ibid.

31 Gerd Rühle *Das Dritte Reich, Dokumentarische Darstellung des Aufbaues der Nation* vol. III, Berlin 1935, pp. 109 f.

32 Höhne, loc. cit. p. 304; Adam, op. cit. pp. 118 ff.

33 Adam, op. cit. p. 118

34 Ibid. footnote 23

35 Ibid. p. 118

36 Ibid. p. 155

37 Rühle, op. cit. vol. IV, 1936, pp. 59 f.

38 Krausnick, op. cit. pp. 270 ff.; Adam, op. cit. pp. 153 f.
39 Rühle, op. cit. vol. VI, 1938, pp. 381 ff.
40 Aronson, op. cit. p. 205
41 Höhne, loc. cit.
42 Reinhard Heydrich, op. cit. p. 13
43 Ibid.
44 Aronson, loc. cit.
45 Ibid. Aronson's verdict
46 Reinhard Heydrich, op. cit. p. 6
47 Höhne, op. cit. p. 301
48 Ibid. p. 302
49 *Das Schwarze Korps* 5.6.35
50 Hans Lamm, op. cit. p. 161
51 Aronson, op. cit. p. 203
52 Höhne, loc. cit.
53 Aronson, loc. cit.
54 Adam, op. cit. p. 154
55 Quoted from ibid. p. 157
56 Quoted from Hans Mommsen, 'Der nationalsozialistische Polizeistaat und die Judenverfolgung vor 1938' in VJZG No. 12, 1962, pp. 68 ff.
57 Adam, op. cit. p. 154 footnote 53
58 Höhne, op. cit. p. 200
59 Adam, op. cit. p. 200
60 Author's interview with Lina Heydrich
61 Heydrich, op. cit. p. 11
62 Adam, loc. cit. footnote 333
63 Höhne, op. cit. p. 306
64 Adam, op. cit. p. 200; cf. also Rolf Vogel *Ein Stempel hat gefehlt* Munich 1977
65 Adolf Eichmann *Vernehmungsprotokolle vor der israelischen Polizei* vol 1, column 61 f.
66 Höhne, op. cit. pp. 309 f.
67 Eichmann, op. cit. column 90
68 Quoted in Höhne, op. cit. p. 310
69 Adam, op. cit. p. 201
70 Ibid. footnotes 335, 339, 340
71 Eichmann, op. cit. column 94 ff.; Bernd Nellessen *Der Prozess von Jerusalem* Düsseldorf 1964, pp. 189 f.
72 Cf. Höhne, op. cit. pp. 310 f.
73 Cf. Krausnick, op. cit. p. 282
74 Reproduced in Robert Kempner *Eichmann und Komplizen* Zürich 1961, p. 45
75 Ibid. p. 44; Höhne, op. cit. p. 311

76 Reproduced in Gerald Reitlinger *Die Endlösung* Berlin 1961, p. 8
77 Quoted in Höhne, op. cit. p. 311
78 Victor Reimann *Goebbels* Vienna 1971, p. 254; Helmut Heiber *Joseph Goebbels* Berlin 1962, pp. 286 f.
79 ADAP, vol. V, pp. 754 ff.
80 Ibid. p. 98 ff.; Höhne, op. cit. p. 312; Adam, op. cit. pp. 199 f.
81 Cf. Hermann Graml *Der 9 November 1938* Bonn 1958; L. Kochan, Pogrom – *10 November 1938* London 1957
82 VB 8.11.38
83 Kochan, op. cit. p. 51
84 Höhne, op. cit. p. 313
85 Adam, op. cit. p. 207
86 Krausnick, op. cit. p. 276
87 See Maser's commentary in Lina Heydrich, loc. cit.
88 Quoted in Höhne, op. cit. p. 314
89 Kochan, op. cit. p. 55; Höhne, op. cit. pp. 314 f.
90 IMT, XXXI, Doc. 3051 PS reproduced in full in Maser's commentary in Lina Heydrich, loc. cit.
91 Graml, op. cit. p. 15
92 Adam, op. cit. p. 208
93 Höhne, op. cit. p. 315
94 Interview with Schultze
95 Helmut Grosscurth *Tagebücher eines Abwehroffiziers 1938–1940* Stuttgart 1970, p. 162
96 Ibid.
97 Krausnick, op. cit. p. 277
98 Rühle, op. cit. vol. VI, 1938, p. 398
99 Kochan, op. cit. pp. 54 ff., 76 ff.
100 Adam, loc. cit.
101 Ibid.
102 Notes of discussion in IMT, XXVII, Doc. 1816 PS, pp. 499 ff.; partly reproduced in Kempner, op. cit. p. 44
103 Ibid.
104 Adam, op. cit. p. 210
105 ADAP, V, pp. 780 f.
106 IMT, XXVI, Doc. 710 PS pp. 266 f.; see also H G Adler *Der verwaltete Mensch* Tübingen 1974, pp. 15 ff.
107 Ibid. p. 16
108 Adam, op. cit. p. 229
109 ADAP, V, pp. 786 f.
110 Fully discussed in Adler, op. cit. pp. 17 ff.

111 Krausnick, op. cit. p. 284
112 Höhne, op. cit. p. 113
113 Adler, op. cit. p. 67
114 Höhne, op. cit. p. 318
115 David and Jon Kimche, *The Secret Roads. The Illegal Migration of a People, 1938–1948* London 1955
116 Adler, op. cit. p. 24
117 Höhne, op. cit. p. 320
118 Adler, op. cit. p. 27
119 Ibid. p. 29
120 Ibid.; and Krausnick, op. cit. p. 307
121 Raul Hilberg *The Destruction of the European Jews* Chicago & London 1961, p. 717
122 Adam, op. cit. p. 360
123 Cf. Martin Broszat *Nationalsozialistische Polenpolitik 1939–1945* Frankfurt 1965, p. 20
124 Ibid. pp. 36 ff.
125 Adam, op. cit. p. 249
126 Reproduced in Krausnick, op. cit. p. 289
127 Adam, loc. cit.
128 Ibid.
129 Archiv für Aussenpolitik und Länderkunde (contemporary section), Deposit for October 1939, p. 824
130 Eichmann, op. cit. column 124; Höhne, op. cit. pp. 321 ff.
131 Adam, op. cit. p. 254
132 Krausnick, op. cit. p. 291
133 *Faschismus-Getto-Massenmord* Berlin (East) 1961, Document 12, p. 50
134 Krausnick, loc. cit.
135 Ibid. p. 292
136 Adam, loc. cit.; Höhne, op. cit. p. 323; Reitlinger, op. cit. p. 51
137 ADAP, VIII, p. 716
138 Adler, op. cit. p. 69, is mistaken when he gives 1931
139 Egon van Winghene *Arische Rasse, christliche Kultur und das Judenproblem* Rotterdam 1927, quoted from 4th German ed., Erfurt 1934
140 Interview with Schultze
141 Winghene, op. cit. p. 72
142 Ibid. p. 70
143 Ibid. p. 71
144 Ibid. p. 74
145 ADAP, IV, p. 420
146 ADAP, X, p. 386; Cf. Adler, op. cit. pp. 69 ff., pp. 254 f.

147 Adler, op. cit. p. 71, wrongly gives 300,000
148 Eichmann trial document 464 (F.b.V.)
149 Krausnick, op. cit. p. 293
150 Adler, loc. cit.
151 Eichmann, op. cit. column 137
152 Höhne, op. cit. p. 323
153 Reproduced in Adler, op. cit. pp. 75 ff.
154 Adam, op. cit. p. 257
155 Ibid.
156 Adler, op. cit. p. 72
157 Reitlinger, op. cit. pp. 88 f.
158 Adam, op. cit. pp. 303 f.; Adler, op. cit. p. 82
159 Adam, op. cit. p. 304; Lina Heydrich op. cit. p. 54
160 Adam, op. cit. p. 258
161 Ibid.
162 Cf. Heinrich Uhlig, 'Der verbrecherische Befehl', supplement BXXVII in *Das Parlament* 17.7.57, pp. 431 f.
163 Walter Warlimont *Im Hauptquartier der Deutschen Wehrmacht 1939–1945* Frankfurt 1962, pp. 167 ff.; Cf. Krausnick, op. cit. p. 298; Höhne, op. cit. p. 324
164 Werner Hubatsch *Hitlers Weisungen für die Kriegsführung 1939–1945* Frankfurt 1962, pp. 88 ff.
165 Ibid.
166 Warlimont, op. cit. p. 173
167 Ibid. p. 174
168 Reproduced in Hans Buchheim, 'Die SS – Das Herrschaftsinstrument' in *Anatomie des SS-Staates* vol. 1, Olten 1965, pp. 73 f.
169 Ibid.
170 Franz Halder *Kriegstagebuch I–III* Stuttgart 1962–4 vol. II, pp. 335 f.
171 Cf. Adler, op. cit. pp. 82 f.
172 Quoted in Krausnick, op. cit. p. 300
173 Höhne, op. cit. p. 326
174 Interview between Streckenbach and Höhne, ibid. p. 327
175 Ibid.
176 Robert M W Kempner *SS im Kreuzverhör* Munich 1964, pp. 18 ff.; Krausnick, op. cit. p. 297; Höhne, op. cit. pp. 328 f.
177 Author's interview with Bruno Streckenbach
178 Krausnick, op. cit. p. 301
179 Quoted in Höhne, op. cit. pp. 329 f.
180 IMT, IV, pp. 348 ff.

181 All these accounts taken from Kempner, op. cit. pp. 21 ff.

182 Ibid. pp. 22 ff.

183 Ibid. p. 24

184 Ibid. p. 27

185 Krausnick, op. cit. p. 302

186 Hilberg, loc. cit.

187 Adam, op. cit. p. 305

188 Ibid.

189 Thus Krausnick, op. cit. p. 298; Bracher op. cit. p. 460; Höhne, op. cit. p. 344; Reitlinger, op. cit. p. 92

190 Adam, op. cit. p. 306

191 Krausnick, op. cit. p. 307; Adam, op. cit. p. 310

192 Krausnick, op. cit. pp. 305 f.

193 Reinhard Heydrich, 'Der Anteil der Sicherheitspolizei und des SD an den Ordnungsmassnahmen im mitteleuropäischen Raum' in *Böhmen und Mähren*, No. 5, Prague 1941, pp. 176 f.

194 Adam, op. cit. p. 306

195 Ibid. p. 307

196 Joseph Goebbels *Tagebücher aus den Jahren 1942–1943* Zurich 1948, p. 114, entry for 7.3.42

197 Adam, op. cit. p. 308

198 Speech in camera by Heydrich 4.2.42, in Fremund and Kral (Eds.) *Die Vergangenheit warnt* Prague 1960, p. 142, Document 22

199 Adam, loc. cit.

200 Krausnick, op. cit. pp. 306 f.

201 Adam, op. cit. p. 309 footnote 24

202 Ibid. pp. 308 f.

203 Ibid. p. 310

204 Krausnick, op. cit. p. 308

205 Adler, op. cit. p. 86; Adam, op. cit. p. 311

206 Ibid.

207 Adler, op. cit. pp. 88 f.; Krausnick, op. cit. p. 322

208 The text of the minutes is reproduced in Robert M W Kempner *Eichmann und Komplizen* Zürich 1961, pp. 133 ff.

209 Adam, op. cit. p. 314

210 Krausnick, op. cit. p. 324

211 Ibid.

212 Kempner *SS im Kreuzverhör* p. 17

213 Adler, op. cit. pp. 89 f.; Adam, op. cit. p. 313

214 Buchheim, op. cit. p. 125

215 Ibid. pp. 125 ff.

216 Memorial speech by Heinrich Himmler 9.6.42, in *Reinhard Heydrich, Ein Leben der Tat* Prague 1944, p. 65
217 Interview with Streckenbach
218 Wilhelm Spengler, 'Reinhard Heydrich – Werk und Wesen' in *Böhmen und Mähren* Nos. 5/6 Prague 1943
219 Interview with Schultze
220 Ibid.; and interview with Lina Heydrich
221 *The Times* 5.9.39, p. 3
222 HG Adler *Die verheimlichte Wahrheit – Theresienstädter Dokumente* Tübingen 1958, p. 321
223 Ibid.
224 Lina Heydrich, op. cit. p. 139

Chapter 12: A Fresh Start?
 1 *Czechoslovakia's Guilty Men. What the Czech Provisional Government Stands for* London 1941, Modern Books (Communist Party Press), p. 16
 2 Ibid.; and *Evening Standard* 15.8.40, p. 10
 3 Author's interview with Albert Speer
 4 Kurt Lachmann, 'The Hermann-Göring-Works' in *Social Research* vol. VIII, No. 1, New York, 1941, pp. 24 ff.
 5 *Sozialistische Nachrichten* No. 25, 15.10.41
 6 Detlef Brandes *Die Tschechen unter deutschen Protektorat* Part 1, Oldenburg 1969, p. 196
 7 'Report by the Chief of Sipo and SD', 13.8.41, in ibid.
 8 *Rudé Právo* 25.6.41, quoted in ibid.; Jiří Hronek *A Volcano under Hitler* London 1941, pp. 90 ff.
 9 Ibid.
10 Author's interview with Walter Wannenmacher
11 Ibid.; and *Sozialistische Nachrichten* No. 4, 18.12.40
12 Koeppen-Report, p. 39, entry for 1.10.41 (F.b.V.)
13 RHSA, Division IV *Reports of State Police Activities* No. 13, 29.9.41
14 Author's interview with Lina Heydrich. This was also corroborated by the Czechs. Cf. Memorandum of the Czechoslovak Government: 'Reign of Terror in Bohemia and Moravia' London 1942, pp. 14 f.
15 Quoted in Brandes, loc. cit.
16 Files of the personal staff of the *SS-Reichsführer* and Chief of German Police, microfilm in National Archives, Washington, Filmgroup T 77, roll 1050, frame 6216
17 Interview with Wannenmacher
18 Koeppen-Report, entries from 22–24.9.41, pp. 28–35 (F.b.V.); DNT, No. 159, 11.6.42

Notes

19 Henry Picker *Hitlers Tischgespräche im Führerhauptquartier 1941–1942* Stuttgart 1963, entry for 6.10.41
20 Interview with Wannenmacher
21 Statement by Karl-Hermann Frank before the Czech People's Court, 12.6.45, in Brandes, op. cit. p. 209
22 Walter Schellenberg *Memoiren* Cologne 1956, pp. 188 f.
23 Heinrich Heim *Diary 1941–1942* entry for 4.6.42, pp. 85 f. (F.b.V.); and author's interview with Heinrich Heim
24 Ibid.
25 Interview with Lina Heydrich

Chapter 13: With Carrot and Stick
1 Author's interview with Walter Wannenmacher; Detlef Brandes *Die Tschechen unter deutschem Protektorat* Part 1, Oldenburg 1969, p. 207
2 Author's interview with Lina Heydrich
3 Interview with Wannenmacher
4 DNT, local announcements section, No. 270, 29.9.41
5 Ibid. No. 270, 29.9.41
6 Interview with Wannenmacher
7 Ibid.
8 Leader by Wannenmacher in DNT, No. 270, 29.9.41
9 Military decree publication, No. 47, 30.9.41
10 Ibid.
11 Ibid. No. 48, 2.10.41
12 List of Court Martial verdicts in Memorandum of the Czechoslovak Government: 'Reign of Terror in Bohemia and Moravia', London 1942, pp. 97–101 (subsequently referred to as Memo)
13 Records of the Province of Bohemia and Moravia in *Sozialistische Nachrichten* No. 2, 15.11.41
14 Memo, op. cit. p. 22; and DNT
15 Ibid. pp. 29 f.; and DNT
16 Ibid.
17 Brandes, op. cit. pp. 244 f.
18 Speech in camera by Heydrich 4.2.42, in Fremund and Král (Eds) *Die Vergangenheit warnt* Prague 1960, pp. 145–8; Č Amort, *Heydrichiáda* p. 126–42
19 Expert evidence from Michael Freund given to the Landessozialgericht Schleswig. Verdict of 20.6.58, copy in WL
20 Brandes, op. cit. p. 249
21 Ibid. p. 213
22 Ibid. p. 293 footnotes 406–10

23 Ibid. p. 338 footnote 1638
24 Note on file, Reich Ministry of Justice (Schlegelberger) 30.9.41, BA, Deposit R22, 4070
25 Ibid.
26 Ibid. 1.10.41
27 Ibid.
28 *Der Spiegel* No. 6, 9.2.50, 'Das Spiel ist aus', p. 21
29 Brandes, op. cit. p. 215
30 Ibid.
31 Speech in camera by Heydrich, 4.2.42, loc. cit.
32 Karl-Hermann Frank in *Reinhard Heydrich* RSHA (Memorial publication), Berlin undated, p. 27
33 Brandes, op. cit. p. 216
34 DNT, No. 272, 1.10.41, p. 3
35 Memo, op. cit. p. 99
36 DNT, No. 281, 10.10.42
37 Koeppen-Report, entry for 2.10.41, p. 43 (Heydrich's report at dinner in the Führer's HQ) (F.b.V.)
38 Ibid.
39 Speech in camera by Heydrich, 2.10.41, in Fremund and Král (Eds), op. cit. pp. 122–33
40 *Sozialistische Nachrichten* 1.2.42 ('Hingerichtete Nazi')
41 Memo, op. cit. p. 100
42 Frank, op. cit. p. 26
43 Brandes, op. cit. p. 226
44 Frank, op. cit. p. 28
45 Memo, op. cit. p. 49; Jiří Hronek *Volcano under Hitler* London 1941, p. 90–92
46 Brandes, op. cit. p. 227
47 Ibid.
48 Interview with Lina Heydrich
49 Brandes, op. cit. p. 229
50 DNT, Nos. 296, 297, 25 and 26.10.41
51 Memo, op. cit. p. 65
52 Interview with Lina Heydrich
53 DNT, No. 303, 1.11.41, p. 5
54 Interview with Wannenmacher
55 Frank, op. cit. p. 30; Brandes, op. cit. p. 320
56 Frank, loc. cit.
57 *Two Years of German Oppression* London 1941, pp. 7 and 40 f.; Brandes, op. cit. p. 231
58 DNT, No. 120, 1.5.42

59 Brandes, op. cit. p. 342 footnote 1798
60 DNT, op. cit.
61 *Národní Práce* 1.5.42
62 *Národní Politika* 1.5.42
63 *České slovo* 1.5.42
64 Interview with Wannenmacher
65 DNT, No. 127, 9.5.42
66 *Der Spiegel,* loc. cit.
67 Memo, op. cit. p. 65
68 Brandes, op. cit. footnotes 1782, 1783
69 Henry Picker *Hitlers Tischgespräche in Führerhauptquartier 1941–1942* Stuttgart 1963, entry for 23.1.42, p. 234
70 Ibid., entry for 12.5.42, p. 333
71 Ibid., entry for 20.5.42, p. 363
72 Brandes, op. cit. p. 236
73 *Two Years of German Oppression,* op. cit. p. 40
74 *Der Spiegel* No. 1/2. 1975, 'Schuss von hinten', p. 69
75 Hans Bernd Gisevius *Bis zum bitteren Ende* Zürich 1946, p. 46
76 Letter from Fritz Tobias 21.7.73; *Die Zeit* 11.11.48
77 Letter from Tobias
78 Ibid.
79 Author's interview with Bruno Streckenbach; M. Reese in *La otra Alemania* Buenos Aires, 15.12.46
80 *Der Spiegel* No. 22, 31.5.47, 'Die Nase voll'
81 Letter from a survivor, from the Czech Secret Service Department of the USA (F.b.V.); *Der Spiegel* No 1/2, 1975, 'Schuss von hinten', p. 70
82 Author's interview with Dr Vilém Kahan

Chapter 14: The Führer's Wallenstein
1 Author's interview with Lina Heydrich
2 *Sozialistische Nachrichten* No. 6, 22.1.41
3 Interview with Lina Heydrich
4 Author's interview with Walter Wannenmacher; and information from Lina Heydrich
5 Interview with Lina Heydrich
6 Reinhard Heydrich, 'Der Anteil der Sicherheitspolizei und des SD an den Ordnungsmassnahmen im mitteleuropäischen Raum' in *Böhmen und Mähren* No. 5, Prague 1941, pp. 176 f.
7 Walter Wannenmacher, 'Sabotage am gesunden Menschenverstand' in *Böhmen und Mähren,* No. 11, Prague 1941, pp. 388 f.
8 Speech in camera by Reinhard Heydrich 2.10.41, reproduced in Fremund and

Král (Eds) *Die Vergangenheit warnt* Prague 1960, p. 127
9 Walter Wannenmacher, 'Reinhard Heydrich' in *Reinhard Heydrich, Ein Leben der Tat* Prague 1944, p. 55
10 DNT, No. 322, 20.11.41, p. 1
11 Memorandum of the Czechoslovak Government: 'Reign of Terror in Bohemia and Moravia', London 1942, p. 62
12 Speech by Reinhard Heydrich, 'Die Wenzelstradition' in *Reinhard Heydrich, Ein Leben der Tat,* op. cit. pp. 37–9; Memo, op. cit. pp. 57 ff.
13 Interview with Lina Heydrich
14 Memo, op. cit. p. 60
15 Detlef Brandes *Die Tschechen unter deutschem Protektorat* Part 1, Oldenburg 1969, p. 216
16 Official publication of the Protector of Bohemia and Moravia, January 1942, pp. 557–61
17 Brandes, op. cit. p. 218
18 Ibid.
19 Official publication, loc. cit.
20 Brandes, op. cit. p. 220
21 Reinhard Heydrich, 'Die Wenzelstradition', loc. cit.
22 Karl-Hermann Frank, 'Reinhard Heydrichs Werk für Böhmen und Mähren' in *Reinhard Heydrich, Ein Leben der Tat,* op. cit. p. 31
23 Memorial speech by Heinrich Himmler 9.6.42, in *Reinhard Heydrich, Ein Leben der Tat,* op. cit. p. 67
24 Interview with Wannenmacher
25 DNT, No. 110, 21.4.42, p. 2
26 Speech in camera by Reinhard Heydrich 2.10.41, op. cit. p. 129
27 Koeppen-Report, entry for 7.10.41, p. 53 (F.b.V.)
28 Memorandum from Frank to the Chief of the Reich Chancellery, Fremund and Kral (Eds), op. cit. pp. 60–73
29 Note from Heydrich to Frank 14.9.40, in ibid. pp. 74 f.
30 DNT, No. 81, 23.3.42, p. 4
31 Speech in camera by Reinhard Heydrich 2.10.41, op. cit. p. 132
32 Note from Heydrich to Frank 14.9.40, loc. cit.; note from Frank on a meeting chaired by Heydrich on 17.10.41, 1600 hours, ibid. pp. 134–40
33 Ibid.
34 Speech in camera by Reinhard Heydrich 4.2.42, ibid. pp. 145–8
35 Brandes, op. cit. p. 162
36 Written statement from Dr Walter König-Beyer (at Heydrich's request), RSHA, 23.10.40, in Fremund and Kral (Eds) op. cit. pp. 76 f.
37 Interview with Lina Heydrich
38 Official publication, op. cit. 26.2.42

39 K-H Frank, op. cit. pp. 45–8
40 Ibid.; and *Hamburger Fremdenblatt* No. 288, 17.10.41
41 K-H Frank, op. cit. p. 33
42 Author's interview with Albert Speer
43 Walter Schellenberg *Memoiren* Cologne 1956 pp. 225 ff.
44 Č Amort *Heydrichiáda* p. 37
45 Author's interview with Dr Ludwig Hahn, former Chief of Sipo and the SD
46 There follows the report of the assassination: RSHA, 'Summing up of the murder of SS-*Obergruppenführer* Heydrich' (F.b.V.); also Amort *Heydrichiáda*; information from Alan Burgess *Seven Men at Daybreak* London 1960; and Rudolf Ströbinger *Das Attentat von Prag* Landshut 1977
47 Archiv für Publ. Arbeit; Deposit for 6.8.42, 'Die Aufklärung des Attentats auf Reinhard Heydrich'
48 Charles Wighton *Heydrich – Hitler's Most Evil Henchman* London 1962, p. 268
49 RSHA, 'Summing up', op. cit. sheet 117 ff.; Brandes, op. cit. p. 248
50 Memorandum from Prof. Ladislav Vaněk, leader of the resistance movement OSVO, *Atentát na Heydricha* Prague 1962, in Brandes, footnotes 1962–4
51 Note from Heydrich to Dr Robert Gies, Frank office, 7.5.42, in Amort, op. cit. p. 37

Chapter 15: The Martyr of Prague

1 DNT, No. 136, 18.5.42 and No. 144, 27.5.42; *Die Weltwoche,* No. 449, 19.6.42
2 DNT, No. 136, 18.5.42
3 DNT, No. 146, 29.5.42
4 *Reinhard Heydrich* RSHA (Memorial publication), Berlin undated
5 Detlef Brandes *Die Tschechen unter deutschem Protektorat* Part 1, Oldenburg 1969, p. 254; Č Amort *Heydrichiáda* p. 38
6 Ibid.
7 Military decree publication No. 19, 28.5.42
8 Amort, op. cit. p. 169; J Doležal and J Křen *Czechoslovakia's Fight* Prague 1964, p. 70
9 *Der Spiegel* No. 6, 9.2.50, 'Das Spiel ist aus', p. 26
10 Brandes, op. cit. p. 254
11 DNT, No. 145, 28.5.42; *Der Spiegel,* loc. cit.
12 RSHA, 'Summing up of the murder of SS-*Obergruppenführer* Heydrich', Appendix 6, 30.5.42 (F.b.V.); Amort, op. cit. pp. 197 f.; eye-witness report in *Kristall* No. 7, 1953, pp. 216 ff.
13 Ibid.
14 *Der Spiegel,* op. cit. p. 27

15 Author's interview with Walter Wannenmacher
16 Cf. Chapter 14, 'The Führer's Wallenstein', pp. 244 ff.
17 Note from Karl-Hermann Frank in Václav Král (Ed.) *Die Deutschen in der Tschechoslowakei* Prague 1964, pp. 474 ff.
18 Ibid.; cf. Brandes, op. cit. pp. 256 f.
19 Ibid.
20 Note from Vladimír Šnajdr in M Ivanov *L'attentat contre Heydrich* Paris 1972, Chapter 7
21 Letter from Himmler to Gebhardt 9.10.42, in Helmut Heiber (Ed.) *Reichsführer! Briefe an und von Himmler* Stuttgart 1968, p. 157
22 Joseph Goebbels *Tagebücher aus den Jahren 1942–1943* Zürich 1948, entries for 27.5.42, 31.5.42 and 4.6.42
23 Robert M W Kempner in *Vorwärts* 8.6.72, p. 9
24 Letter from Grosscurth to Beck 25.6.42, in Helmut Grosscurth *Tagebücher eines Abwehroffiziers 1938–1940* Stuttgart 1970, p. 546
25 Walter Schellenberg *Memoiren* Cologne 1956, pp. 256 f.
26 Cf. Chapter 10, 'The Chief Suspicion-Monger', pp. 139 ff.
27 Hoover Collection, Himmler Files, roll 39
28 *Der Spiegel*, op. cit. pp. 26–8
29 Military decree publication 19.5.42 to 6.6.42; and DNT; and *The Times*
30 Walter Wannenmacher in DNT, No. 148, 31.5.42
31 *Gardista* 29.5.42
32 *The Times* 29.5.42, p. 4
33 Ibid.
34 *Manchester Guardian* 29.5.42
35 *The Times* 30.5.42, p. 4
36 Official Report, Fifth Series, Parl. Deb., Commons, vol. 380, p. 1266
37 See Note 29
38 Charles Wighton *Heydrich – Hitler's Most Evil Henchman* London 1962, p. 270
39 *Sozialistische Nachrichten*, No. 12/13, 15.6.42
40 Brandes, op. cit. p. 258
41 DNT, No. 149, 1.6.42
42 *Die Weltwoche* 1.6.42
43 RSHA 'Summing up', op. cit.
44 Amort, op. cit. pp. 194 ff.; SD reports from the Reich, No. 288, 1.6.42
45 *Die Weltwoche* 1.6.42
46 Memorial speech by Heinrich Himmler 9.6.42, in *Reinhard Heydrich, Ein Leben der Tat* Prague 1944, pp. 61 ff.
47 Report of Ministry of Defence, Historical Branch, 4.8.71
48 Ibid.

Notes

49 Brandes, op. cit. p. 251; Amort, op. cit. p. 27
50 Expert evidence from Michael Freund given to the Landessozialgericht Schleswig. Verdict of 20.6.58, copy in WL; partly reproduced in *Die Gegenwart* No. 322, pp. 626 ff. and *Die Zeit* No. 19, 10.5.56
51 Schellenberg, op. cit. p. 255; detailed account, though without source references, in Victor Alexandrov *051 – Services Secrets de Staline contre Hitler* Paris 1968, pp. 247 f.
52 D Hamsik and J Prazak *Eine Bombe für Heydrich* Berlin (East) 1964; Czech ed. 1963, also Polish ed. 1966 (quoted from Polish ed. pp. 246 ff.)
53 Kenneth Strong *Geheimdienstchef in Krieg und Frieden* Vienna & Hamburg 1969, p. 86
54 On Thümmel: C Amort and M A Jedlicka *The Canaris File* London & New York 1970, originally Czech *(Das Geheimnis des Agenten A 54)*; R Ströbinger *A 54 – Spion mit drei Gesichtern* Munich 1966
55 Brandes, op. cit. p. 190
56 Ströbinger, op. cit. p. 172
57 Amort and Jedlicka, op. cit. p. 127
58 Ibid. p. 129
59 Author's interview with Lina Heydrich
60 Amort and Jedlicka, op. cit. p. 141
61 See also, among others, R Kühnrich *Der Partisanenkrieg* Berlin (East) 1968; and Nedoresow *Die Befreiungsbewegung des tschechischen und slowakischen Volkes* given in expert evidence of Michael Freund (see Note 50)
62 Heinz Höhne *Der Orden unter dem Totenkopf* Gütersloh 1967, p. 458
63 Dolezal and Kren, op. cit. p. 68
64 Reproduced in ibid. p. 69
65 RSHA 'Summing up', op. cit. p. 38
66 Brandes, op. cit. p. 252
67 Amort *Heydrichiáda* p. 24
68 Brandes, op. cit. p. 253
69 Ibid.
70 RSHA 'Summing up', op. cit. pp. 37 f.
71 Interview with Wannenmacher
72 Reproduced in Wighton, op. cit. p. 270
73 *Der Spiegel,* op. cit. p. 27
74 Schellenberg, op. cit. pp. 75 f.
75 Author's interview with Albert Speer
76 Files of the personal staff of the SS-*Reichsführer* and Chief of German Police, microfilm in National Archives, Washington, Filmgroup T 175, roll 112, frames 7647–8, Himmler's speech 9.6.42 at 1940 hours
77 Ibid.

78 Interview with Lina Heydrich
79 Ibid.
80 Ibid.
81 *The Times* 29.5.42, p. 5
82 Hoover Collection, Himmler Files, roll 39
83 Interview with Lina Heydrich; *Der Spiegel*, op. cit. p. 28

Chapter 16: To The Shades of Heydrich
 1 Hoover Collection, Himmler Files, roll 39, *Diary*
 2 Author's interview with Lina Heydrich
 3 Charles Wighton *Heydrich – Hitler's Most Evil Henchman* London 1962, p. 276
 4 Commentary on the BBC monitoring of the Reich broadcasting service (Paris) 9.6.42, 2000 hours (WL)
 5 Author's interview with Walter Wannenmacher
 6 Reproduced in *Reinhard Heydrich* RSHA (Memorial publication), Berlin undated; also obituary by Martin Bormann
 7 This part in: BBC monitoring of the Reich broadcasting service (Paris), see Note 4
 8 *Daily Telegraph* 8.6.42, 'A Gunman's Burial'
 9 K Daluege, op. cit.
10 Reproduced in *Reinhard Heydrich, Ein Leben der Tat* Prague 1944, pp. 61 ff.
11 Interview with Wannenmacher
12 Reproduced in *Reinhard Heydrich, Ein Leben der Tat* op. cit. p. 16
13 Memorandum from Karl-Hermann Frank reproduced in C Amort *Heydrichiáda* pp. 208 f.
14 BBC monitoring of the Reich broadcasting service (Zeesen) 9.6.42, 1830 hours (WL)
15 Wilhelm Spengler, 'Reinhard Heydrich – Werk und Wesen' in *Böhmen und Mähren* 5/6, Prague 1943
16 In *Feldpostbrief für Sipo und SD* No. 1, Berlin, December 1942
17 Memorial speech by Heinrich Himmler 9.6.42, in *Reinhard Heydrich, Ein Leben der Tat* op. cit. pp. 61 ff.
18 *Germanische Leithefte* No. 6/II, Antwerp 1942, p. 2
19 'Syllabus for ideological training in the SS and the Police', Berlin undated, p. 16
20 DNT 25.5.43
21 Karl-Hermann Frank, 'Reinhard Heydrichs Werk für Böhmen und Mähren', in *Böhmen und Mähren* 5/6 Prague 1943
22 *Der Freundeskreis Himmler* pp. 85 f.
23 Files of the personal staff of the SS-*Reichsführer* and Chief of German Police, microfilm in National Archives, Washington, Film group T 175, roll 112,

frames 7647–8, Himmler's speech 9.6.42, at 1940 hours

24 Letter from Himmler to Wolff 22.6.42 in Helmut Heiber (Ed.) *Reichsführer!*
   Briefe an und von Himmler pp. 123 f.
25 Private notes of K-H Frank, op. cit.
26 Henry Picker *Hitlers Tischgespräche im Führerhauptquartier 1941–1942*
   Stuttgart 1963, pp. 176 f.
27 Ibid. p. 434
28 Private notes of K-H Frank, op. cit.
29 Daily report SD-command section, Prague 9.6.42, partly reproduced in
   Václav Král (Ed.) *Die Deutschen in der Tschechoslowakei* Prague
   1964, p. 474
30 Joseph Goebbels *Tagebucher aus den Jahren 1942–1943* Zürich 1948, entry for
   27.5.42
31 *The Times* 6.6.42, p. 5
32 Letter from B Schirach to M Bormann 28.5.42, ND PS 3877
33 Picker, op. cit. p. 396
34 D Hamšík and J Pražák *Eine Bombe für Heydrich* Berlin (East) 1964, pp. 287 f.
35 *Narodni Politika* 6.6.42
36 Ibid.; and DNT 7.6.42
37 Memorandum from Böhme to Frank and Daluege 12.6.42, in C Amort
   Heydrichiáda pp. 112 ff.
38 Detlef Brandes, *Die Tschechen unter deutschem Protektorat* Part I, Oldenburg
   1969, pp. 263 f.
39 Memorandum from Böhme, op. cit.; and Report of the State Police HQ,
   Prague 24.6.42: 'Reprisals against the village of Lidice' (F.b.V.)
40 Cf. Brandes, op. cit. pp. 262 f., 352; also this book Chapter 15, 'The Martyr of
   Prague', p. 242 ff.
41 Report of the State Police, Pardubitz section, to Prague HQ, 21.6.42, in
   Amort, op. cit. p. 233 f.
42 Letter from Böhme 10.6.42, ND NO 5413
43 RSHA 'Summing up of the murder of SS-Obergruppenführer Heydrich',
   Appendix D, pp. 21 f. (F.b.V.)
44 Brandes, op. cit. p. 263
45 *The Times* 11.6.42, p. 4; and following days
46 See among others, Robert M W Kempner, in *Vorwärts* 8.6.72, p. 9
47 A Mitscherlich and F Mielke *Medizin ohne Menschlichkeit* Frankfurt 1960, pp.
   132 f.
48 Kempner, 'Der Mord an 35000 Berliner Juden' in *Gegenwart im Rückblick*.
   Volume presented to the Jewish Community of Berlin, Heidelberg 1970
49 Goebbels, op. cit., entry for the end of May 1942
50 RSHA 'Summing up', op. cit. Appendix D

51 Ibid. p. 32; Brandes op. cit. p. 265
52 Ibid.
53 Report from State Police Central Office, Prague 25.6.42, 'Die Aufklärung des Attentats' (F.b.V.)
54 Report of the Commander of the Waffen-SS, from Treuenfeld to Daluege 23.6.42, 'Waffen-SS action', (F.b.V.)
55 Archiv für publ. Arbeit, No. 24455, 8.10.42. The verdict on the trial of the accessories to Heydrich's murder

Chapter 17: A Life Summed Up
1 Joachim Fest *Das Gesicht des Dritten Reiches* Munich 1963, p. 142
2 Felix Kersten *Totenkopf und Treue* Hamburg 1952, pp. 128 ff.
3 *Das Schwarze Korps* 11.6.42
4 Fest, loc. cit.
5 Wilhelm Spengler, 'Reinhard Heydrich – Werk und Wesen', p. 23 in *Reinhard Heydrich, Ein Leben der Tat* Prague 1944
6 Giovanni Zibordi *Critica socialista del Fascismo* Milan 1922
7 In Otto-Ernst Schüddekopf *Bis alles in Scherben fällt* Gütersloh 1973
8 Ibid.
9 Heinz Höhne *Der Orden unter dem Totenkopf* Gütersloh 1967, p. 196
10 In Schüddekopf, op. cit.
11 Reinhard Heydrich *Wandlungen unseres Kampfes* Berlin 1936, p. 4
12 Höhne, op. cit. p. 197
13 In Schüddekopf, op. cit.
14 Ibid.
15 Wilhelm Alff *Der Begriff Faschismus* Frankfurt 1971; Schüddekopf, op. cit.
16 Carl J Burckhardt *Meine Danziger Mission 1937–1939* Munich 1960
17 Author's interview with Lina Heydrich
18 Author's interview with Albert Speer
19 Lina Heydrich *Leben mit einem Kriegsverbrecher* Pfaffenhofen 1976, p. 84
20 Georg L Mosse, 'Fascism and the Intellectuals' in S J Woolf (Ed.) *The Nature of Fascism* London 1968, pp. 205 ff.; Schüddekopf, op. cit.
21 Speech in camera by Reinhard Heydrich 2.10.41, reproduced in Fremund and Král (Eds) *Die Vergangenheit warnt* Prague 1960, pp. 122–33
22 Interview with Lina Heydrich
23 Manuscript from Dr Werner Best, Copenhagen 1.9.49, p. 1 (F.b.V.)
24 Ibid. p. 11
25 Ibid.
26 Author's interview with Bruno Streckenbach; Best, op. cit. p. 2
27 Best, loc. cit.
28 Ibid. p. 5

29 Shlomo Aronson *Reinhard Heydrich und die Frühgeschichte von Gestapo und SD* (Dissertation), Stuttgart 1971, p. 30
30 Best, op. cit. p. 13
31 Ibid.
32 Aronson, op. cit. p. 254
33 Interview with Lina Heydrich; and Best, loc. cit.
34 Best, op. cit. pp. 13 f.
35 Interview with Lina Heydrich
36 Fest, op. cit. p. 149
37 Ibid. p. 150
38 Memorial speech by Heinrich Himmler 9.6.42, in *Reinhard Heydrich, Ein Leben der Tat* Prague 1944, p. 64
39 Lina Heydrich, op. cit. p. 43; Reinhard Heydrich 'Der Anteil der Sicherheitspolizei und des SD an den Ordnungsmassnahmen im mitteleuropäischen Raum', in *Böhmen und Mähren* No. 5, Prague 1941
40 Lina Heydrich, op. cit. p. 48
41 Ibid.
42 Best, op. cit. p. 14

SOURCES

Interviews and information received orally from:
Paul Anspach, Brussels 30.1.72
Dr Ludwig Hahn, Hamburg 5.7.71
Heinrich Heim, Munich 23.1.72
Lina Heydrich, Todendorf, Fehmarn 20–22.3.73
Dr Vilem Kahan, Amsterdam 3–4.5.73
Dr Robert M W Kempner, Frankfurt 17.10.74
Dr Paul Schmidt, Hamburg 1.6.73
Dr Otto-Ernst Schüddekopf, Braunschweig 1.9.73
Dr Dr Erich Schultze, Wiesbaden 15–16.9.72
Dr W Sommer, Kaiserslautern 28.9.77
Albert Speer, Berlin 19.1.72
Bruno Streckenbach, Hamburg 21.5.73
Dr Fritz Tobias, Hanover
Walter Wannenmacher, Darmstadt 3.3.72
Benno Wundshammer, Munich 21.3.71
Naval Captain Herbert Zollenkopf, Stade 29.3.77

Unpublished documents:
Files of the Central Archive, NSDAP, Microfilms in the Hoover Collection, Stanford
Files of the personal staff of the SS-*Reichsführer* and Chief of German Police. Microfilms in the National Archives, Washington, Filmgroup T 175
Files of the Reich Ministry of Justice, Bundesarchiv Koblenz, Deposit R 22, 4070

Unpublished notes and manuscripts:
BBC monitoring of Reich broadcasting service, 1941–2 — copies in the Wiener Library, London
Dr Werner Best, description of Heydrich 1.9.49, Copenhagen (F.b.V.)
Chief of Security HQ, Special report No. 285, 'Zersetzung der nationalsozialistischen Grundwerte im deutschsprachigen Schrifttum seit 1933', Berlin 1936, typescript (F.b.V.)

Reinhard Heydrich

Karl von Eberstein, description of Reinhard Heydrich (F.b.V.)
Michael Freund, expert evidence on Heydrich given to the Landessozialgericht
   Schleswig – copy in the Wiener Library, London
Heinrich Heim *Diary, 1941–1942* (F.b.V.)
Koeppen-Report 1941–2 (F.b.V.)
Ulrich Popplow, correspondence with Helmut Maurer (F.b.V.)
RSHA, Summing up of the murder of SS-*Obergruppenführer* Heydrich (F.b.V.)

Pre-1945 newspapers and journals frequently consulted:
Böhmen und Mähren, Prague 1941–2
Bodensee-Rundschau, Konstanz 1941
Daily Telegraph, London 1941–2
Das Schwarze Korps, Berlin 1935–42
Der Mittag, Düsseldorf 1940
Der Neue Tag, Prague 1940–44
Deutsche Brüsseler Zeitung 1942
Die Weltwoche, Zürich 1942
Evening Standard, London 1940
ardista, Pressburg 1942
Germanische Leithefte 1942–4
Hamburger Fremdenblatt 1941–2
Manchester Guardian 1942
Münchener Post 1931–2
Národní Politika, Prague 1942
Sozialistische Nachrichten, London 1942–2
The Times, London 1933–44
Völkischer Beobachter, Munich 1936–42

After 1945:
Aufbau, New York 1960
Der Spiegel, Hamburg 1947–76
Die Welt, Hamburg 1971
Die Zeit, Hamburg 1956
Frankfurter Allgemeine Zeitung 1974
Kristall, Hamburg 1953
The Times, London 1962
Vorwärts, Bonn 1972
Welt am Sonntag, Hamburg 1953

Books and articles:
Adam, Uwe Dietrich, 'Judenpolitik im Dritten Reich' in *Tübinger Schriften zur*

Sources

Sozial- und Zeitgeschichte vol. 1, Düsseldorf 1972

Adler, H G *Der verwaltete Mensche* Tübingen 1974

Die verheimlichte Wahrheit – Theresienstädter Dokumente Tübingen 1958

Theresienstadt Tübingen 1955

Adolph, Walter *Erich Klausener* Berlin 1955

'Akten zur Deutschen Auswärtigen Politik 1918–1945' from the Archiv des Deutschen Auswärtigen Amts. Series D. Bde. I–X

Alexandrov, Victor *051 – Services Secrets de Staline contre Hitler* Paris 1968

Alff, Wilhelm *Der Begriff Faschismus* Frankfurt 1971

Amort, Č and Jedlička, M *The Canaris File* London & New York 1970

Archiv für Aussenpolitik und Länderkunde, Deposits 1939

Archiv für publizistische Arbeit, Deposits 1941 and 1942

Aronson, Shlomo *Reinhard Heydrich und die Frühgeschichte von Gestapo und SD* (Dissertation), Stuttgart 1971

Auerbach, Hellmuth, 'Die Endlösung – nicht perfekt geplant' in *Frankfurter Allgemeine Zeitung* 12.6.74

Bennecke, Heinrich *Die Reichswehr und der Röhmputsch* Munich 1964

Hitler und die SA Munich & Vienna 1962

Besgen, A *Der stille Befehl* Munich 1960

Best, S Payne *The Venlo Incident* London 1950

Best, Werner *Die deutsche Polizei* Darmstadt 1942

'Die Geheime Staatspolizei' in *Deutsches Recht* Berlin 1936

Boberach, Heinz *Meldungen aus dem Reich* Neuwied 1965

Bracher, Karl Dietrich *Die deutsche Diktatur* Cologne & Berlin 1969

Bracher, K D *et al. Die nationalsozialistische Machtergreifung* Cologne 1962

Brandes, Detlef *Die Tschechen unter deutschem Protektorat* Part 1: *Besatzungspolitik, Kollaboration und Widerstand im Protektorat Böhmen und Mähren bis Heydrichs Tod, 1939–1942* Oldenburg 1969

Brissaud, André *Die SD-Story* Zürich 1975

Canaris Frankfurt 1976

Broszat, Martin *Nationalsozialistische Polenpolitik, 1939–1945* Frankfurt 1965

Buchheim, Hans *SS und Polizei im NS-Staat* Bonn 1964

Buchheim, H *et al. Anatomie des SS-Staates* 2 vols, Olten 1965 & Munich 1967

Buchheit, Gert *Der deutsche Geheimdienst* Munich 1960

Die anonyme Macht Frankfurt 1969

Burckhardt, Carl J *Meine Danziger Mission 1937–1939* Munich 1960

Burgess, Alan *Seven Men at Daybreak* London 1960

Conquest, Robert *Am Anfang starb Genosse Kirow* Düsseldorf 1970

Conway, John S *Die nationalsozialistische Kirchenpolitik* Munich 1969

Crankshaw, Edward *Gestapo* New York 1956

Czechoslovakia's Guilty Men. What the Czech Provisional Government Stands for

London 1940

Dallin, Alexander *Deutsche Herrschaft in Russland 1941–1945. Eine Studie über Besatzungspolitik* Düsseldorf 1958

Daniels, H E von, 'Reinhard Heydrich als nationalsozialistischer Leibeserzieher' in *Leibesübungen und körperliche Erziehung* Berlin August 1942
'Der deutsche Sport trauert um Reinhard Heydrich' in *Der Neue Tag* No. 155, Prague 7.6.42

Delarue, Jacques *Geschichte der Gestapo* Düsseldorf 1964

Diels, Rudolf *Luzifer ante portas* Stuttgart 1950

Doležal, J and Křen, J *Czechoslovakia's Fight* Prague 1964

Eichmann, Adolf *Vernehmungsprotokolle vor der israelischen Polizei* 6 vols

Faschismus – Getto – Massenmord Berlin (East) 1961

Feldpostbrief für Sipo und SD No. 1, Berlin 1942

Fest, Joachim *Das Gesicht des Dritten Reiches* Munich 1963
Hitler Frankfurt & Berlin 1973

Frank, Karl-Hermann, 'Reinhard Heydrichs Werk für Böhmen und Mähren' in *Reinhard Heydrich, Ein Leben der Tat* Prague 1944

Fremund and Král (Eds) *Die Vergangenheit warnt* Prague 1960

Gehlen, Reinhard *Jetzt rede ich* Mainz 1971

Gisevius, Hans Bernd *Bis zum bitteren Ende* Zürich 1946

Goebbels, Joseph *Tagebücher aus den Jahren 1942–1943* Zürich 1948

Graml, Hermann *Der 9 November 1938* Bonn 1958; supplement in *Das Parlament*

Grosscurth, Helmut *Tagebücher eines Abwehroffiziers 1938–1940* Stuttgart 1970

Grossmann, K R, 'Berthold Jacobs Entführung' in *Ossietzky, Ein deutscher Patriot* Munich 1963

Hacker, Friedrich *Aggression* Vienna & Munich 1971

Haensel, Carl *Das Gericht vertagt sich* Tübingen undated

Hagen (Höttl), Walter *Die geheime Front* Linz 1950

Halder, Franz *Kriegstagebuch I–III* Stuttgart 1962–4

Hamel, Walter, 'Die Polizei im neuen Reich' in *Deutsches Recht* 1935

Hamšík, D and Pražák, J *Eine Bombe für Heydrich* Berlin (East) 1964

Heiber, Helmut *Joseph Goebbels* Berlin 1962
(Ed.) *Reichsführer! Briefe an und von Himmler* Stuttgart 1968

Heydrich, Lina *Leben mit einem Kriegsverbrecher;* with a commentary by Werner Maser, Pfaffenhofen 1976

Heydrich, Reinhard, 'Der Anteil der Sicherheitspolizei und des SD an den Ordnungsmassnahmen im mitteleuropäischen Raum' in *Böhmen und Mähren* No. 5, Prague 1941
'Die Bekämpfung der Staatsfeinde' in *Die deutsche Rechtswissenschaft* vol. 1, No. 2, 1936 and *Völkischer Beobachter* 28.4.36
Ein Leben der Tat Prague 1944

Sources

RSHA (Memorial publication), Berlin undated

Memorandum in *Vierteljahrshefte für Zeitgeschichte* No. 11, 1963

Speech 'Die Wenzelstradition' in *Reinhard Heydrich, Ein Leben der Tat* Prague 1944

Speech on German Police Day 1941, in *Reinhard Heydrich* RSHA (Memorial publication), Berlin undated

Speeches of 2.10.41 and 4.2.42 in *Die Vergangenheit warnt* Prague 1960

Wandlungen unseres Kampfes Berlin 1936

Hilberg, Raul *The Destruction of the European Jews* Chicago & London 1961

Himmler, Heinrich Memorial speech on Heydrich's death 9.6.42, in *Reinhard Heydrich, Ein Leben der Tat* Prague 1944

Höhn, Reinhard, 'Polizeirecht im Umbruch' in *Deutsches Recht* 1936

Höhne, Heinz *Der Orden unter dem Totenkopf* Gütersloh 1967

Canaris – Patriot im Zwielicht Munich 1976

Hronek, Jiří *A Volcano under Hitler* London 1941

Hubatsch, Werner *Hitlers Weisungen für die Kriegführung 1939–1945* Frankfurt 1962

International Military Tribunal *The Trial of the War Criminals* 42 vols, Nuremberg 1947–9

Ivanov, M *L'attentat contre Heydrich* Paris 1972

Kempner, Robert M W *Der Mord an 35000 Berliner Juden* Heidelberg 1970

Eichmann und Komplizen Zürich 1961 – expert reports on this in the Wiener Library, London

SS im Kreuzverhör Munich 1964

Kersten, Felix *Totenkopf und Treue* Hamburg 1952

Kimche, David and Kimche, Jon *The Secret Roads. The Illegal Migration of a People, 1938–1940* London 1955

Kochan, Lionel *Pogrom – 10 November 1938* London 1957

Kogon, Eugen *Der SS-Staat. Das System der deutschen Konzentrationslager* Berlin 1947

Kordt, Erich *Nicht aus den Akten. Die Wilhelmstrasse in Frieden und Krieg 1928–1945* Stuttgart 1950

Král, Václav (Ed.) *Die Deutschen in der Tschechoslowakei* Prague 1964

Kramer, J *The World's Police* London 1964

Kühnrich, R *Der Partisanenkrieg* Berlin (East) 1968

Lachmann, Kurt, 'The Hermann-Göring-Works' in *Social Research* vol. VIII, No. 1, New York 1941

Lamm, Hans *Über die innere und äussere Entwicklung des deutschen Judentums im Dritten Reich* (Dissertation), Erlangen 1951

Liepelt, Adolf *Über den Umfang und die Bedeutung der Polizeigewalt im nationalsozialistischen Staat* (Dissertation), Würzburg 1938

Reinhard Heydrich

Reinhard Heydrich

Maser, Werner *Adolf Hitler, Legende – Mythos – Wirklichkeit* 6th ed., Munich 1974

see also Heydrich, Lina *Leben mit einem Kriegsverbrecher*

Memorandum of the Czechoslovak Government: 'Reign of Terror in Bohemia and Moravia', London 1942

Mitscherlich, A and Mielke, F *Medizin ohne Menschlichkeit* Frankfurt 1960

Mommsen, Hans, 'Der nationalsozialistische Polizeistaat und die Judenverfolgung vor 1938' in *Vierteljahrshefte für Zeitgeschichte* No. 12, 1962

Mosse, Georg L, 'Fascism and the Intellectuals' in S J Woolf (Ed.) *The Nature of Fascism* London 1968

Nadolny, Rudolf *Mein Beitrag* Wiesbaden 1955

Nellessen, Bernd *Der Prozess von Jerusalem* Düsseldorf 1964

Nikulin, Lew, 'Die Affäre Tuchatschewski' in *Geköpfte Armee* Berlin 1965

Nordon, Peter *Salon Kitty* Munich 1973

Petwaidie, Walter *Die autoritäre Anarchie* Hamburg 1946

Picker, Henry *Hitlers Tischgespräche im Führerhauptquartier 1941–1942* Stuttgart 1963

Poliakov, Léon and Wulf, Josef *Das Dritte Reich und die Juden* Berlin 1955

Popplow, Ulrich, 'Reinhard Heydrich oder die Aufordnung durch den Sport' in *Olympisches Feuer* Celle, August 1963

Rauschning, Hermann *Gespräche mit Hitler* Zürich & New York 1940

Reimann, Viktör *Goebbels* Vienna 1971

Reitlinger, Gerald *Die Endlösung* Berlin 1961

Die SS Vienna & Munich 1957

Riemanns Musik-Lexikon vol. 1, Mainz ed., 1959

Rijckoordt, Jan *De tragische dood van Joris van Severen* Bruges undated

Rühle, Gerd *Das Dritte Reich. Dokumentarische Darstellung des Aufbaues der Nation* 8 vols, Berlin 1935–9

Runzheimer, Jürgen, 'Der Überfall auf den Sender Gleiwitz im Jahr 1939' in *Vierteljahrshefte für Zeitgeschichte* 1962, pp. 408 ff.

Schellenberg, Walter *Memoiren* Cologne 1956

Schmidt, Paul *Statist auf diplomatischer Bühne 1923–1945* Bonn 1949

Schmitt, Carl *Der Begriff des Politischen* new ed., Berlin 1963

Schüddekopf, Otto-Ernst *Bis alles in Scherben fällt* Gütersloh 1973

Schweder, Alfred Politische Polizei (Dissertation), Berlin 1937

Spengler, Wilhelm, 'Reinhard Heydrich – Werk und Wesen' in *Böhmen und Mähren* 5/6, Prague 1943

Strasser, Otto *Hitler und ich* Konstanz 1948

Ströbinger, Rudolf *A 54 – Spion mit drei Gesichtern* Munich 1966

Das Attentat von Prag Landshut 1977

Strong, Kenneth *Geheimdienstchef in Krieg und Frieden* Vienna & Hamburg 1969

Sources

'Syllabus for ideological training in the SS and the Police', Berlin undated

Two Years of German Oppression London 1941

Uhlig, Heinrich, 'Der verbrecherische Befehl', supplement B XXVII in *Das Parlament* Bonn 1957

Verordnungsblatt des Protektorats Böhmen und Mähren 24 vols, 1941–2

Vogel, Rolf *Ein Stempel hat gefehlt* Munich 1977

Vogelsang, Reinhard *Der Freundeskreis Himmler* Göttingen 1972

Wannenmacher, Walter, 'Sabotage am gesunden Menschenverstand' in *Böhmen und Mähren* No. 11, Prague 1941

Warlimont, Walter *Im Hauptquartier der Deutschen Wehrmacht 1939–1945* Frankfurt 1962

Wighton, Charles *Heydrich – Hitler's Most Evil Henchman* London 1962 – expert reports on this in the Wiener Library, London

Winghene, Egon van *Arische Rasse, christliche Kultur und das Judenproblem* Rotterdam 1927 (4th German ed. Erfurt 1934)

Wulf, Josef *Martin Bormann* Gütersloh 1962

Zeiger, Henry A *The Case against Adolf Eichmann* New York 1960

Zibordi, Giovanni *Critica socialista del Fascismo* Milan 1922

Zipfel, Friedrich *Gestapo und Sicherheitsdienst* Berlin 1960

Kirchenkampf in Deutschland 1933–1945 Berlin 1965

INDEX

231, 235, 292-4; establishes and
directs the Reich Security Office,
183, 235; Protector in Bohemia and
Moravia, 7-8, 11, 29, 79, 109, 183,
187, 189-260, 287-8, 290, 292, *4, 7,*
receives Coronation Insignia from
Czech President Hácha in
Wenceslas Chapel of St Vitus'
Cathedral, Prague, 219-21;
assassination in Prague, 7-8, 10, 76,
237-256, 260-65, 270-72, 275-8,
285, 293; state funeral, 266-9, *9;*
state Memorial Ceremony, 270-71,
293; special postage stamp issued
showing his death mask, 269-70, *10*
Heydrich, Silke (RH's daughter),
216-17, 240
Hiemer, Ernst, 154
Hildebrandt, Richard, 45-6, 50
Himmler, Heinrich, 11-12, 106, 115,
134, 136-7, 200, 242-4, 246, 248-50,
255, 257-8, 265-6, 270, 276, 281-3,
286, 289; as SS-*Reichsführer,* 10, 22,
29, 38-9, 41-7, 49-50, 54, 56-8, 61,
63, 67, 69-71, 73-4, 81-3, 90-92,
95-6, 98, 102-3, 113-14, 123, 156,
181, 189-90, 217, 229, 235-6, 292, *1,*
creation with Heydrich of the
SS-state, 73-5, 80; compliance with
Heydrich and Hitler in the
extermination of Jews, 9, 64-7, 78,
141-2, 144, 147, 150, 156-8, 162-4,
175, 177-8, 180-1; gives address at
Heydrich's funeral, 263, 267-8, and
at the state Memorial Ceremony,
293
Hindenburg, President Paul von, 37,
73, 267
Hitler, Adolf, 7, 9, 11, 33-4, 39-40,
43, 47, 54, 61, 63-5, 69, 73, 77,
80-81, 87, 89-91, 94-6, 99-101, 103,

106-8, 113-14, 124, 128-9, 134-48,
151-2, 154-8, 163-6, 183-4, 187-94,
197-201, 204, 208, 212, 214, 219-21,
225, 227-31, 235-6, 242-4, 246-50,
252-3, 262-5, 270-72, 280, 286-7,
289, 293; orders Final Solution of
the 'Jewish Problem', 168-78,
181-2, 249; orders destruction of
the Czech village of Lidice as
reprisal measure for Heydrich's
assassination, 8, 273-7; at
Heydrich's state funeral, 267-9, *9;*
at Heydrich's state Memorial
Ceremony, 270-71; *see also*
'Leibstandarte Adolf Hitler'
Hitler Youth, 100, 242
Hohlbaum, Professor Dr, 248
Höhn, Professor Dr Reinhard, 89,
143
Höhne, Heinz, 67, 83, 96, 120, 130,
135, 144-5, 281-2, 284
Hölz, Max, 21
Holzhauser (SS-Second Lieutenant),
115
Hoops, Dr, 117
Horák (Czech from village of
Lidice), 274
Horninger (Police Captain), 40, 42
Höss, Rudolf, 180
Hoth, Hermann, 249
Höttl, Dr Wilhelm, 62, 80
Hrubý, Adolf, 224-5
Huber, Franz Josef, 75-6, 84-5, 290
Hus, Jan, 219

I

'Ic'-Service *see* SD
ICPO *see* International Criminal
Police Organization